Psychometric
TESTING

Psychometric TESTING

Dr R K Sahu

EXCEL BOOKS

ISBN: 978-81-7446-899-4

First Edition: New Delhi, 2010

EXCEL BOOKS
A-45, Naraina, Phase I,
New Delhi - 110 028

INDIA SALES OFFICES
2/8, Ansari Road, Darya Ganj, New Delhi-110002
21/65, Anand Nagar, Vakola, Santacruz (East), Mumbai-400055
106/2, 2nd floor, Ramnivas, 6th 'C' Cross, Gandhinagar, Bangalore-560009
2-2-1167/2H, Near Railway Bridge, Tilaknagar, Nallakunta, Hyderabad-500044
S-3/21-23, Shastri Market, Near "B" Block Circle, Indira Nagar, Lucknow-226016
1st Floor, ELCC 60/123, Aaranya, Karikkamuri Cross Road, Ernakulam, Kerala-682011

AFRICA SALES OFFICES
31 Field Street, Durban-4000, South Africa
71 Burg Street, Cape Town-8000, South Africa
211 Pietermaritz Street, Pietermaritzburg, South Africa
43 Biccard Street, Braamfontein, Johannesburg-2000, South Africa

Published by Anurag Jain for Excel Books, A-45, Naraina, Phase-I, New Delhi - 110 028
and printed by him at Excel Printers, C-205, Naraina, Phase-I, New Delhi - 110 028

Brief Contents

Detailed Contents

Preface

The most wonderful, complex and challenging phenomenon of the human mind is how to read it, unfold it, probe into it and quantify its traits or draw a picture of innate nature and characteristics of personality.

Psychometric testing is a method that has been used by the psychologists, psychotherapists and experts of behavioural sciences. Psychometric testing may consist of all those tests and instruments which decipher different aspects of human mind like intelligence, personality traits, aptitude, inclinations, abilities and competencies of a person.

This book is an endeavour to bring out this complex subject in a very structured and simple way, so that the people interested in understanding the concept and tools of psychometric testing are benefited and the subject becomes more popular and user-friendly.

Psychometric tests in recent years are being applied to various HR processes. Organisations are using it in recruitments, competency mapping, identifying development needs of employees, placement of employees in different assignments, assessment centres, etc.

The purpose of this book is to provide basic and simple descriptions of all the aspects of psychometric tests and their uses in organisations. The book is laid down in a stepwise manner, as though one were going to embark on developing and evaluating a test. Initial chapters begin by reminding the reader of the importance of tests and testing in our everyday lives. There is also a review of highlights in the testing field and some of the statistical procedures used in the latter parts of this book.

There is a dearth of resource material on psychometric testing including measures of psychological tests. This book fills this gap and makes available all the relevant inputs for psychometric testing. It will be a great help to all the psychologists, psychotherapists, psychiatrists, HR consultants and trainers, HR professionals, management teachers, MBA students and all individuals interested to know 'what', 'why', 'when', 'who' and 'how' of psychometric testing. At the end of this experience of reading about testing and assessment techniques, learners should be able to do two things—to effectively appraise any test they come across in terms of why and how it was developed and come to a decision about whether or not it meets the standards of testing and their needs and to effectively design and evaluate tests.

DR R K SAHU

About the Author

Dr R K Sahu is the founder Director of Human Resource Development Centre, New Delhi. Dr Sahu has held senior managerial positions with HMT and as HR Chief of Usha Beltron. He has trained over 15,000 management professionals in leadership, team-building and other areas of management over the last 14 years.

Dr Sahu has undertaken training and management consultancy assignments for over 360 companies including 24 factories of Hindustan Unilever, Nepal Lever, Tata Motors, Indian Oil, NHPC, Pepsi, Whirlpool, Coca Cola, Cadbury, Godrej, Electrolux, Becton Dickinson, Eureka Forbes, Parle Products, Polyplex, ICI, Ranbaxy, Jyoti CNC, PPAP, Hero Honda, KRIBHCO, Eicher Motors, HINDALCO, BALCO, NALCO, Hindustan Zinc, Hindustan Latex, Oil India, GRASIM, Lafarge, Rico Auto, SMC, MICO, Gujarat Gas, Delphi, Moser Baer, Mitsubishi, Thomson Press, Torrent Pharma, and UB Group, to name a few. Besides training, he has provided consultancy services to his clients for implementation of 5S, Kaizen, Zero Defect, Competency Mapping, Balanced Scorecard, Performance Management System, Psychometric Testing and other HR systems.

Dr Sahu has designed training modules for over 50 subjects like Psychometric Testing, TQM, Productivity, Leadership, Quality, Wastage Control and Cost Reduction, various Managerial, Attitudinal and Motivational subjects like time management, creative problem-solving and decision-making, training for trainers, competency mapping, emotional intelligence, balanced scorecard, man- management skills, etc.

He has published his research papers in various papers and journals like *The Times of India, Economic Times, Personnel Today, India Journal for Training and Development*, etc. and authored some best selling books namely *Training for Development, Performance Management System, Competency Mapping, Strategic Leadership, Group Dynamics & Team Building* and *Disciplinary Actions.*

CHAPTER 1

Psychometric Testing: Concept and Need

LEARNING OBJECTIVES

- To explain the importance of Psychometric Testing.
- To discuss what are Psychometric Tests.

THE IMPORTANCE OF PSYCHOMETRIC TESTING

In this chapter, we aim to establish why psychometric testing is important. That it is increasingly seen as important is evidenced in the substantial growth of the use of psychometric tests in recent times.

To do this, we will consider:

1. The human relations approach to management
2. The development of human-resource practices, and
3. People, the greatest asset.

❖ The Human-Relations Approach to Management

Since the 1930s and the experiment of Elton Mayo at the Hawthorne Lighting factor, we have seen the development of the human-relations approach to management. We have developed an understanding that the motivation of workers is a key factor in their productivity at work. The importance of human relations as regards the success and productivity of organizations has now been well established, accordingly the human relations movement has developed and matured. We now take it for granted that investment in people is as important as investment in other aspects of business or organizational life.

What is interesting is that although psychometric testing has been around for much of this century and has been widely available in many forms since the Second World War, it is only in the last few years that the growth has begun to accelerate.

Many of us, particularly in management positions, are likely to have encountered psychometric testing in some form or the other. Despite this, there are still many misconceptions about what psychometric tests are and what their potentials is in many areas of organizational and personal development.

❖ Environmental Influences

What are the influences that have stimulated the growth in testing? The broader influences on the organizations include:

1. Managing change
2. Competitiveness
3. Downsizing

4. A focus on productivity, and therefore on performance measurement
5. A focus on creativity/team-building, and thus on personal behaviour and skills.

As we move through what we have called the human-relation phase into the new millennium, priorities are changing. This is the information age, and along with it is developing the knowledge economy. This will surely see an increase in the importance of the skills, capabilities and knowledge that people hold. In fact, the meaning of the knowledge economy is precisely that the knowledge and skills of individuals and organizations will be tradable; and for many organizations, these factors will be the most important or their only asset.

Any organization in such a position will want to defend its knowledge and skills. But before it can do that, it will need to know what it has got. This will involve an assessment and measurement of things that we have not traditionally been good at assessing and measuring. However, this is where psychometric testing can play a part.

❖ The Growth of Testing

More specifically, some changes that have had a direct impact on the need for testing include the following:

1. Testing itself has become more sophisticated, with many more tests and suppliers of test in the market.
2. Increased mobility in the job market, allied to a greater understanding of the cost of making the wrong appointment, has led to a search for more 'intelligent' tools to assess people for recruitment purposes.
3. A substantially greater priority has been given to learning and development in many organisations. This includes a greater need to assess people in terms of strengths, weaknesses and development needs, and psychometric tests have proved useful in doing this.
4. There has been a movement towards assessment as part of performance management.
5. The professionalization of the human-resource function has occurred.
6. An understanding of the importance of personal skills, and of the influence of personal behaviour preferences on these, has also developed.
7. There have been changes in the 'contract' between organization and employee that encompass much more than just the exchange of labour for money.

WHAT ARE PSYCHOMETRIC TESTS?

This is an important question because there is much confusion as to what exactly makes a test psychometric. One particular misconception is that only tests that give us information about personality are in fact psychometric. This is not true, for the term can be applied to a much wider class of tests.

Similarly, this begs the question as to what are the defining characteristics of such a test. Or, to put it another way: what does a test have to be to be called psychometric?

To answer these and other questions we will consider:

1. The history of psychometric testing
2. What puts the 'psycho' in psychometric
3. What puts the 'metric' in psychometric
4. Interpreting test results.

The History of Psychometric Testing

It is fairly natural and human to make judgements about the behaviour or potential of other people. This has been done throughout history, and as individuals we probably carry on this tradition ourselves. Just think of those people who may have made judgements about you over the years. Your list might include:

1. Parents and relatives
2. Friends
3. Teachers
4. Workmates
5. Managers and potential employers.

However, on the whole, these judgements will most likely have been either subjective or based on flawed or incomplete information.

The first person to take a more systematic or 'scientific' approach to measuring some aspect of human behaviour or capabilities was a French psychologist named **Binet.** Binet was interested in the differences between children who achieved through education and those who did not, and he sought to be able to identify and measure those differences.

The focus of his interest was on those skills, including judgement, comprehension and ability to reason, which he felt distinguished achievers from non-achievers. He invented the term 'Intelligence Quotient' (IQ) to describe these characteristics, and he went on to develop a test to measure them objectively. Over the years, and for various reasons, the notion of IQ has been somewhat discredited, but today we are able to measure, by testing, a number of similar or related concepts.

The first major users of such tests were the military in the US, but since the Second World War psychometric testing has moved both to education and to organizational life in general. The main difference today is that we can now measure a much broader range of characteristics using a comprehensive range of sophisticated instruments.

What Puts the "Psycho" in Psychometric?

Although there are many definitions, the British Psychological Society describes a psychometric test as: 'an instrument designed to produce a quantitative assessment of some psychological attribute or attributed'. 'Some psychological attribute' is a good description, but it doesn't tell us too much!

An alternative definition talks about: '.........a capacity, propensity or liability to act, react, and experience or to structure or order thought or behaviour in particular ways'.

In general, psychometric tests tend to relate to distinct (but overlapping) kinds of performance:

1. ***Maximum Performance:*** Tests here relate to our capacity or capability to do certain things. They include tests of intelligence, aptitude or ability. It is worth nothing that they typically:

   (i) Have right and wrong answers.

   (ii) Measure the ability of achievement under strict conditions.

   (iii) Involve a certain level of difficulty so that performance can be compared from person to person.

2. ***Habitual Performance:*** This is also sometimes called 'typical performance', and tests here involve attempts to measure characteristic ways of behaving. They can also involve a consideration of how we perceive the world, and of attitudes, values and interests. These tests:

   (i) Are self-descriptive,

   (ii) Indicate the most typical behaviour or preferences, and

   (iii) Don't involve right or wrong answers.

   They are sometimes also refereed to as 'psychological tests' or 'personality tests'. Interestingly, it is a common mistake for people to assume that it is just these (rather than the ability tests also) that are 'psychometric'.

What Puts "Metric" in Psychometric?

Clearly, as the name implies, this has something to do with measurement. It is primarily the fact that we are measuring and quantifying attributes that distinguishes psychometric testing from subjective judgement. However, developing a test is a whole process, and one, which involves a number of components.

So, there are a number of criteria that enable us to classify a test as psychometric. These include the following:

1. It is constructed according to psychometric principles.
2. It is administered in a standardized way.
3. It is scored in a standardized way.
4. It is interpreted in a standardized way.

❖ How Tests are Developed?

Most tests are of the pencil-and-paper type and consist of questions – or items, as they are called – the basic process of constructing a test involves:

1. Generating a large number of items;
2. The piloting and selection of items. This is done on the basis of a number of statistical tests which are described above;
3. Standardizing the scores. This enables raw scores to be translated into comprehensive scores;
4. Writing the technical manual.

This process should be available to users of all robust tests, and should contain information both about the relevant statistics and about the appropriate administration, scoring and interpreting of the test.

❖ Items for Tests

For *ability* tests, like tests of intelligence, items can take various forms. Here are some examples:

1. ***Analogy:***

   Sparrow is to bird as minnow is to....

   (a) animal (b) ant (c) fish (d) bird (e) reptile

2. ***Odd one out:***

   24 63 10 48 35

3. ***Sequences:***

   8 11 14 17 ......

For most purposes, items are multi-choice, with only one right answer. However, there are variations, such as matching items.

For *personality* tests, there are a number of possibilities:

1. ***Dual response:*** Like 'yes/no' or 'true/false'. A variation on this is where a third, interim category is added, e.g., 'yes/not sure/no'; 'mostly/sometimes/never'; 'agree/uncertain/false'.

2. *Rating scales:* Where words are on a continuum and each associated with a number, e.g.:

   Always.........often..........sometimes..........never

   1 2 3 4

3. *Forced choice:* Sometimes called ipsative. Here, subjects are forced to choose, usually from a pair of words, which one most applies to them.

Selecting and Testing Items

There are a number of statistical tests that the items and the tests as a whole should pass, and we will provide here a brief (and not too technical) overview which should give you an idea of the important considerations and questions to ask.

The two basic concepts that are involved are:

❖ Validity

A test is valid if it measures what it says it measures. This is a simple starting point, but validity can be a complex topic. There are a number of facets to it, and thus a number of different ways of describing, measuring and demonstrating validity. The most important are:

1. *Face validity:* This is the extent to which the test appears to the user to test the attribute in question. Its main value is in gaining co-operation from test takers.

2. *Construct validity:* The question here is whether the test fully describes the variable being measured.

3. *Content validity:* This answers the question 'Does this test measure all aspects of the variable in question?'

4. *Criterion-related validity:* This establishes the predictive value of the test: whether it can predict some measured, real-world criterion. In general, this is quite difficult to achieve to a high degree. However, where it can be justified, it is obviously very powerful.

❖ Reliability

Reliability has two distinct meanings. A test is reliable if it is self-consistent, that is, its various parts are measuring the same thing. A good test should also give the same score for each subject (as long as their ability has not changed) when they are re-tested. This is called *test-retest reliability*.

Reliability is also important in influencing the validity factor; valid tests are also *consistent* ones.

Whenever you are faced with choices about using tests, you should ask searching questions about the reliability and validity of a test. As a user, you need to be assured by its robustness and effectiveness.

Administering Tests

The result of a test is meaningful and reliable only if everyone takes it in the same conditions. This can be illustrated by a very simple example. Suppose you want to test a group of people using a numerical-ability test. You could just hand the test out and ask the subject to return it in the next few days. However, there would be a few disadvantages to this:

1. They might 'crib' the answers.
2. They would be doing the tests in different conditions and environments.
3. They would take different amounts of time to do the test.

If any or all of these were the case, then we would not be comparing apples with apples.

In the case of an ability test, the time to answer might be an important part of the variable being measured, which is why many ability tests are timed.

To get over these problems, test suppliers should supply a user manual, which describes the test administration in some details.

For the reason outlined above, it is important that these instructions to be kept to precisely.

Interpreting Test Results

If a subject scores 20 out of 25 on a verbal-reasoning test, what does this mean? A first response might be to say that because they have scored more than half that must be a good result. But, on the other hand, doesn't it depend on how 'difficult' the test is?

It is for this reason that raw scores on a test are always converted into a 'profile score' which compares the score for this subject with the scores of some knows group of people. This process is called **standardizing the scores**. It works as follows:

As with most variables that occur in the natural world, measurements for a population are distributed in a characteristic way. For instance, if we measured the heights of a large and representative sample of the population and put these on a *frequency diagram,* they would look as shown in Figure 1.1. The shape of this line occurs so often that it has been given a name – the **'normal distribution'**. It is bell-shaped and symmetrical, and the average (or mean) is the highest point on the curve.

Another statistic, which is very relevant in this distribution, is called the **'Standard Deviation'** (SD). This is the square root of the average distance of the scores from the mean, and it measures the spread of the distribution. Its main advantage is that we can workout the proportion of people who scored above or below any particular standard-deviation score. For instance, we know that 68% of people will score between plus and minus 1 SD score (the area shown in the figure). When raw scores are converted into standardized scores, each score in placed in relation to the test of the population. There are two popular ways of doing this:

1. ***Sten (standard ten) scores:*** These 'carve' the distribution up into 10 units, with the middle being at 5.5 (see the figure 1.1).
2. ***Percentiles:*** These carve the distribution up into 100 units, with the middle being at 50.

A question worth asking with the standardized scores used for any test is — what is the group or population against which I'm being compared? A percentile score, on an ability test, of 60 (which means a score higher than 60% of the population) is one thing if you are being compared with the population *as a whole*. However, if you are being compared to just a graduate or a senior-management population, then the interpretation will be slightly different.

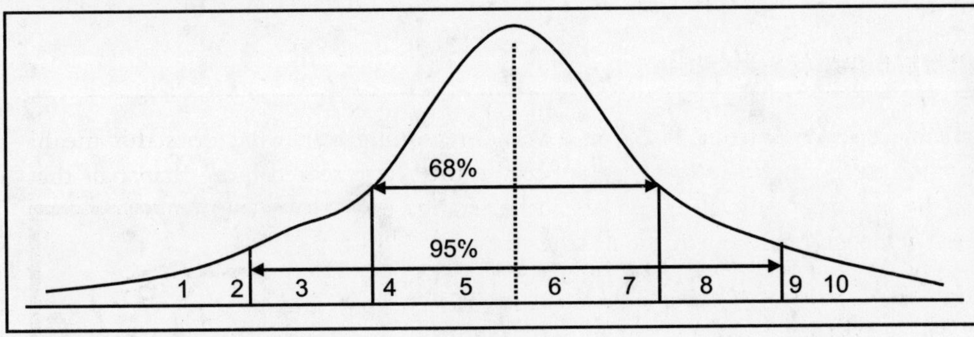

FIGURE 1.1

CHAPTER 2

Test of Ability and Aptitude

LEARNING OBJECTIVES

- ❖ To discuss concept of intelligence and types of tests.
- ❖ To explain the guidelines for selecting and using tests.

INTRODUCTION

We made the distinction between tests of maximum performance and tests of habitual or typical performance. It is the former that are the tests of ability and aptitude, and these we shall focus on in more detail.

Specifically, we shall look at:

1. The concept of intelligence
2. Types of test
3. Guidelines for selecting and using tests.

CONCEPT OF INTELLIGENCE

We need to consider this topic because, as we have explained, it is at the heart of the development of psychometric testing. Many of the reasons that made it of interest at the turn of the last century are just as valid today. Although the language and the degree of sophistication of the testing process have changed, it is still just important.

Binet's approach to intelligence, as already mentioned, was expressed in terms of the Intelligence Quotient (IQ). This expressed the ratio of the mental age to the chronological age, and was based around an average of 100, because it related intelligence to development, and its primary focus was on children, the measure was not appropriate when applied to adults. However, the concept was nonetheless considered to be important. Having said that, we also need to understand that it has been remarkably difficult to define the concept without colliding with different cultural definitions as to what constitutes intelligence.

What we do know is that the ability to perform certain types of task successfully means that it is more likely that we can also perform other, similar types of task successfully. Thus, psychologists have postulated such a thing as 'General Intelligence'. Intelligence has been described by Spearman as the quality that allows people to do well on most tasks. This is seen as the 'driving force' behind many of the more specific abilities that we recognize and which we can measure. This description does suggest some types of continuum:

Generalized intelligence/ability ←——→ Specific skills

Potential to act ←——→ Real action/behaviour

Far from job ←——→ Near to job

This demonstrates that either we can seek to look at the underlying capability or we can focus on specific skills that are known to be of interest. It is the particular contexts that will dictate which of these (or both) is of most interest.

TYPES OF TESTS

We have already described that the early history of testing was focused on the generalized notion of intelligence. However, it soon grew from there. The recognition of the complex nature of ability, and of the continuum which moves from the very general to a highly specific, widened out the scope of interest. Any ability that humans can use or express, and any behaviour that they undertake, can in principle be tested for. This means that there is an astonishing range of possible candidates for testing. As a general guide, it is worth following the dictum that anything that can be tested almost certainly has been. In this section, we shall describe and illustrate some of the major categories of tests.

Before we look in detail at different types of tests, we should note that ability tests do have some characteristics that set them apart from the personality tests that we shall discuss later. These include:

1. They are not self-assessed
2. They involve right-wrong answers (with certain exceptions)
3. They are administered in rigorous circumstances, particularly in selection and recruitment procedures
4. They are often timed.

In general, there are three classes of tests:

1. *Objective Ability Tests:* Which test generally intellectual functions, or more specific abilities.
2. *Achievement Tests:* Like reading, clerical coding and basic operator skills.
3. *Performance tests:* Like standardized work sample tests.

❖ General Ability Tests

These are the tests underlying cognitive ability and mental functioning. Typical of these are tests of verbal and numerical reasoning. Many test suppliers supply tests with both these components, and sometimes a third component, abstract reasoning, is also added. Such collections are called 'batteries' of tests. A battery of test is a collection of tests that together give a rounded picture of the psychological attributes sought by the tester.

A typical battery is the GRT series by Psytech, which provides verbal, numerical and abstract tests. Typical (but not actual) items look like this:

1. *Verbal:* Designed to test an understanding of words and of relationship between words.

   Dark means the opposite of?

1	2	3	4	5	6
gloomy	happy	red	heavy	light	day

2. *Numeric:* Designed to assess the ability to work with numbers.

   4 is to 12 as 8 is to?

1	2	3	4	5	6
16	24	20	64	32	36

3. *Abstract:* Designed to assess relationships between shapes and figures.

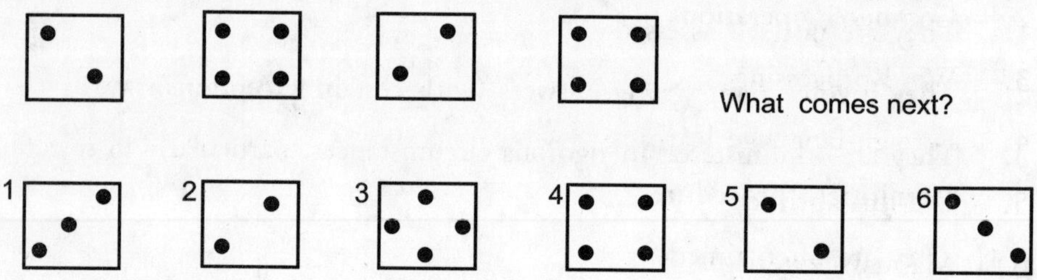

❖ Other Ability Tests

Some tests involve knowledge or achievement as well as ability. Examples might include tests of:

1. Mechanical reasoning or mechanical comprehension
2. Critical thinking ability.

This tests for a range of critical reasoning abilities like:

1. The ability to draw inferences
2. The recognition of assumptions
3. Deduction

4. Interpretation
5. The evaluation of agreements.

For example:

Statement: Some holidays are rainy. All rainy days are boring.

Therefore, Proposed conclusions (Yes/No)

1. No clear days are boring
2. Some holidays are boring
3. Some holidays are not boring.

❖ Occupational Ability Tests

Even more specific in their analysis of abilities, these tests have been developed for particular jobs or quite specific applications. Examples include tests for:

1. Programming
2. Computer operations
3. Word processing
4. Foreign-language learning
5. Clerical aptitude
6. Manual dexterity
7. Hand-eye coordination.

GUIDELINES FOR SELECTING AND USING TESTS

In this section, we shall gather some thoughts about how to use ability tests in practice.

1. ***Start with the job:*** As always with assessment exercises, it is necessary to have a detailed description of the required skills. The abilities, aptitudes, skills and knowledge required for the application should be well defined and based on a sound knowledge of the job under discussion. Test data will not provide you with good information if you do not know the standards you are seeking.

2. ***Use batteries of tests:*** In most real situations, a single test may not give wide or comprehensive data across all of the target abilities. Thus, you need to use a number of tests that provide this range of data.

3. ***Evaluate the proposed tests:*** Look at the supplier's data on reliability and validity. Check if the test/battery is levelled appropriately for your target audience.
4. ***Get expert help:*** You might use consultants at any or all points in the process:
   (i) To advice on test choice
   (ii) To be a licensed purchaser
   (iii) To add objectivity to the process
   (iv) To administer and interpret professionally.
5. ***Use results in conjunction with other data:*** This is a general rule, which makes a lot of sense.

CHAPTER 3

Personality Identification

LEARNING OBJECTIVES

- To understand what is personality and personality traits.
- To discuss the development of modern personality theory.

WHAT IS PERSONALITY?

We have examined the purpose of psychometric tests and the way they are designed and validated, as well as reviewed some of the main types. Today, we are going to examine one of the most important and perhaps controversial uses of these tests – to gain insight into the personalities of test-takers. Before we review the applications available to organizations and managers, we shall spend some time studying the nature of personality.

By the time you have finished this section, you should have a clear idea of what personality tests can or cannot do, and be ready to examine the various applications for psychometric tests in organizations.

❖ What do you mean by Personality?

Ask 20 psychologists to define personality and you will get 20 different answers. What they generally mention, however, is an individual's characteristic patterns of thinking, feeling and acting across a wide range of situations. What are the consistent features of the way they behave? What makes them unique? Already here we have the concepts of consistency and repetition, implying that aspects of personality can be measured.

THE DEVELOPMENT OF MODERN PERSONALITY THEORY

Interest in measuring an individual's psychology can be traced back to the Second World War when the need to recruit large number of men into the armed forces led to the development of mental aptitude tests in the US and Britain. Personality testing really did not get off the ground until after the war, although Allport developed the theory behind these tests in the 1930s.

Research into the nature of personality has mainly focused on 'personality traits' and on 'typologies'.

Personality Traits

Modern theories of personality can still be traced back to the early work of Galton from 1869 onwards. Galton was interested in the nature of genius, and began his work by reviewing all the words we use to describe personality (the lexicon approach). He then attempted to group these descriptions into a classification scheme. Allport continued this work in the 1930s, but it was only after the Second World War that the scientific measurement of personality really came into being with the work of Cattell.

Cattell began by asking individuals to rate each other using the description of personality used in everyday language. His review of the data suggested that there were no more than about 50 underlying dimensions. Further, work with larger samples and the advanced statistical techniques pioneered by Spearman led to his conclusion that there were no more than 12 Life (L) factors involved. Cattell then began to devise questionnaire items to measure these 12 factors and subsequently identified a further 4 factors (Q) from an analysis of the questionnaire returns.

The 16 primary factors identified by Cattell and now contained in the 16 PF test are as follows:

A	Warmth	L	Vigilance
B	Reasoning	M	Abstractness
C	Emotional stability	N	Private ness
E	Dominance	O	Apprehension
F	Liveliness	Q1	Openness to change
G	Rule-consciousness	Q2	Self-reliance
H	Social boldness	Q3	Perfectionism
I	Sensitive	Q4	Tension

Each factor is mentioned on a spectrum expressed as word pairs, e.g., *Warmth* is measured on a scale of *Reserved-Warm*.

❖ Factor Analysis

One of the key tools in this research was 'Factor analysis', which at its time was a revolutionary technique. Now it is a standard tool used by psychology students all over the world. Fortunately, we do not need to worry about the mathematics involved.

In simple terms, factor analysis studies the correlations between the variables in complex data sets containing many variables (multivariate analysis) and patterns of variation (variance) in the data. Computer programs attempt to distinguish between independent variation in each variable and the variation that can be explained by common unidentified factors linking the different variables. The final output is a list of equations for a series of common factors linked to a figure for the amount of variation in the data set that can be explained by the existence of each factor. Psychologists can then study the nature of these patterns and formulate models for the factors explaining human behaviour.

Cattell used factor analysis to identify the primary factors in his questionnaire.

❖ How Personality Tests are Designed?

A personality test is simply a series of questions that assess an individuals thinking, feeling and acting in different situations. Typically, these questions will ask you how much you agree or disagree with a statement on a five-point scale, e.g.,

I think personality tests are a load of nonsense

Strongly agree	Agree	Not sure	Disagree	Strongly disagree
O	O	O	O	O

Or, they ask the test taker to choose between options, e.g.:

When relaxing, I would prefer to:

1. Listen to some classical music
2. Go and play a game of squash

[Select option 1 or 2]

A key feature of these tests is that they measure your stated preferences (often referred to as 'self reports') and are not trying to uncover some hidden part of your nature you would rather cover over. In this respect, they are quite different from the use of handwriting tests, where a single interpreter seeks to identify 'hidden' aspects of your personality from a sample of hand writing.

Jungian Typology

The theory of psychological types was developed by Carl Jung (1875 – 1961) to explain some of the apparently random differences in people's behaviour. His theory of personality types recognized the existence of distinct patterns and provided an explanation for how these types develop.

According to Jung, differences in behaviour are caused by differences in the way people like to use their minds. The central idea is that when your mind is active, you are involved in one of two key mental activities:

1. Taking information in, i.e., *Perceiving*, or
2. Organizing that information internally and coming to conclusions, i.e., *judging.*

In turn, Jung observed that there were two opposite ways of *Perceiving*, which is called *Sensing* and *Intuition,* and two opposite ways of *Judging,* which he called *Thinking* and *Feeling*. Everyone uses these essential processes on a daily basis, both towards the external world of people, things and events (*Extraversion*) and towards the inner world of ideas, thought and reflection (*Introversion*). These four basic processes provide you with eight different ways of using your mind.

Jung believed that everyone has a natural preference for using one kind of Perceiving and one kind of Judging, and external or internal world. This idea was later expanded by Katherine Cook Briggs and her daughter, Isabel Briggs Myers, and used to develop the Myers-Briggs Type Indicator (MBTI) instrument.

Today the Myers-Briggs Type Indicator (MBTI) is one of the most widely used personality tests, and has been translated into a number of languages. It can provide considerable insight into the way an individual relates to others, and into their preferred team role and work environment.

The MBTI is based on Jung's typology, and reports your preference on four scales, each consisting of two opposite poles:

1. ***Extraversion or Introversion (E-I)***: Where you prefer to focus your attention;
2. ***Sensing or Intuition (S-N):*** The way you prefer to take in information;
3. ***Thinking or Feeling (T-F)***: The way you prefer to make decisions;
4. ***Judging or Perceiving (J-P)***: The way you orient yourself to the outside world.

Combinations of these four scales give us 16 different types as shown below. Each type can be referred to by a four-letter code.

	ST: Sensing – Thinking	SF: Sensing – Feeling
IJ – Introvert-Judging	ISTJ	ISFJ
IP – Introvert-Perceiving	ISTP	ISFP
EP – Extravert -Perceiving	ESTP	ESFP
EJ – Extravert-Judging	ESTJ	ESFJ

Contd...

	NF: Intuitive – Feeling	NT: Intuitive – Thinking
IJ – Introvert-Judging	INFJ	INTJ
IP – Introvert-Perceiving	INFP	INTP
EP – Extravert -Perceiving	ENFP	ENTP
EJ – Extravert-Judging	ENFJ	ENTJ

Many managers fall into the ESTJ type. Here is an abbreviated description of this type:

> *Practical, realistic and matter-of-fact with a natural ability for practical subjects like business or mechanics. They are not interested in abstract theories and expect their learning to have immediate and practical application. They love to organize and run activities. They are decisive, acting quickly to implement decisions and can be relied upon to pay attention to practical, routine issues.*

This seems to be a pretty good description of a typical manager. Of course, this does not mean that the other types who make poor managers and a quick review of the others will highlight those types who make great leaders (e.g., ENTJ) or entrepreneurs (e.g., INTJ).

Typologies have one great advantage: they are easy to understand and to relate to. They are often a great tool for developing individuals and for increasing their awareness of some of their main patterns of behaviour and how others see them. This approach also stresses a key principle about the usage of personality scales, namely that there is no right or wrong preference. On the other hand, typologies are generally less suited to selection because they are too simplistic and do not allow us to discriminate clearly between individuals.

The "Big Five"

Sooner or later, if you talk to anyone about personality tests, you will hear them mention 'the Big Five'. These arose from the work of Costa and McCrae in 1985 that studied the result of a range of personality questionnaires using factor analysis and who identified five *big factors* that could explain most of the personality space covered by all these different measures. On the basis of this research, they designed the NEO-Personality Inventory, which measures differences between individuals on these five dimensions as described below.

1. ***Neuroticism:*** High scores here are generally more sensitive, emotional and prone to feelings that are upsetting such as guilt or sadness. Low scorers are emotionally secure, resistant and relaxed individuals even under very stressful conditions.

2. *Extraversion:* High scorers here are extraverted, outgoing, active and high-spirited. They prefer to be around people most of the time. Low scorers are introverted, reserved and serious. They prefer to be alone or with a few close friends.

3. *Openness to experience:* High scorers here are open to new experiences, with broad interests and a strong imagination. Low scorers are down-to-earth, practical, traditional and pretty much set in their ways.

4. *Agreeableness:* High scorers here are compassionate, good-natured and generally eager to co-operate and avoid conflict. Low scorers are hardheaded, skeptical, and competitive. They tend to express their anger directly and forcefully.

5. *Conscientiousness:* High scorers here are conscientious and well organized. They have high standards and always strive to achieve their goals. Low scorers are easygoing, not very well organized and sometimes rather careless. They prefer not to make plans if they can help it.

In fact, these five factors can be related to the global factors found in multifactor tests like the 16 PFV5 and 15 FQ. They also link to the dimensions in the Jungian typology.

Sometimes the computer printouts from personality tests provide values for dimensions contained in other tests such as the Belbin Roles, Leadership and Subordinate Styles, and Jungian types. These are estimates provided by the test designers and should be treated with caution.

Since the publication of Costa and McCrae's work, the issue of the Big Five has attracted a lot of controversy, mainly on the grounds that they cannot cover all aspects of personality. However, a number of studies across a wide range of occupational groups have in fact shown correlations between ratings on these dimensions and job performance criteria.

Other well-known instruments include the California Personality Inventory (CPI), the Gordon Personal Profile Inventory, the Guilford-Zimmerman Survey and OPP.

Details of some of the main suppliers are provided at the end of this book.

❖ The Complex Nature of Personality

Little or no evidence of criterion validity (i.e. relevance to the job) has been found for many personality tests and scales. The fact that the questions themselves often have no relevance to the workplace does not help. In some well-documented cases, their value in selecting people from unusual backgrounds or different cultures has been questioned because test design is heavily influenced by culture.

This does not mean, however, that personality tests do not have an important role to play in organizations. But they must be used intelligently, and users need to recognize their limitations. Even as a perfect test (if it existed!) can be misused, and most of the examples used to criticize the use of personality test are due to the *misuse of the test* and not to the *test design* itself. Administering the test is the easy part, but the minute a test user receives the results they enter a danger zone with many traps for the unwary. This is because the two most important of stages use – *interpretation* and *using the result to make decisions* – are profoundly influenced by the situation and also may be left in the hands of those with insufficient expertise.

❖ Misinterpretation of Tests

Personality tests are very open to misinterpretation. Your stated preference is just that: it does not mean you always behave that way, and it does need to be placed in the context of your experience, acquired skills and environment. For example, if you are a strong introvert, this does not mean that you are automatically shy, retiring and unable to perform well in social situations. In reality, we all acquire skills that enable us to perform well in areas that that may be our natural preference. We know many consultants who are seen as extreme extraverts though they are actually the opposite, but whose lifestyle and job has taught them to behave as extraverts.

Inappropriate use of personality tests also lead people to arrive at the wrong conclusions and to take bad decisions. In selection, for example, you can only use the result of tests successfully if you have shown key features of personality to be critical to the job and have correctly interpreted the results for individuals. Ultimately, the test-taker is probably the best judge of the accuracy of the report, which is why detailed feedback is usually advised.

❖ Does Your Personality Profile Change?

Generally, the profiles of most individuals stable at least over several years. However, they can be affected by periods of change or stress, and this does need to be taken into account. Over longer periods of time, there is no doubt that individuals may 'drift' on individual scales, usually because they have learnt new skills and ways of thinking. People working in highly disciplined professions like the law or science may develop profiles matching the job requirements more closely. There seems to be some evidence that some effective managers can develop more balanced profiles as they increase their repertoire of behavioural skills (notably in Introversion – Extroversion).

CHAPTER 4

Selecting Psychometric Tests

LEARNING OBJECTIVES

- ❖ To explain selection process.
- ❖ To review the assessment methods available to select the right tests.

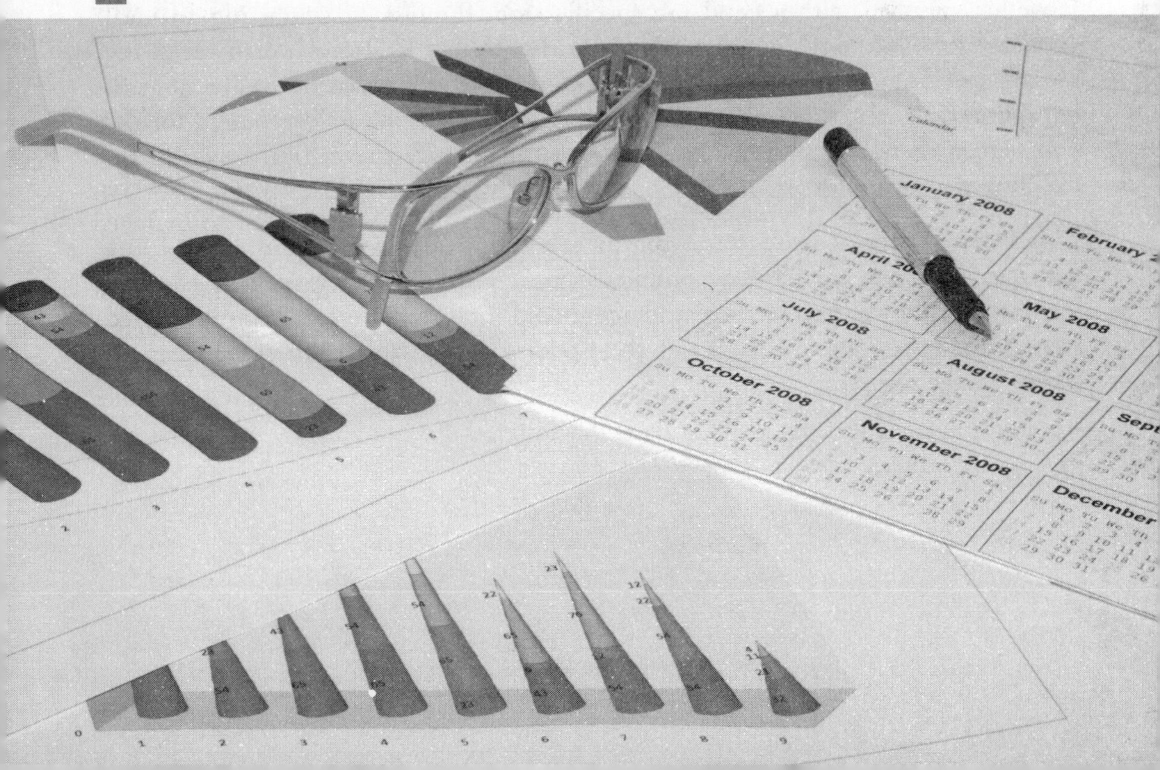

Today, we look in more detail at what is involved in selecting and using tests within a recruitment and selection context.

THE SELECTION PROCESS

Even if we know a psychometric test is reliable and valid, we can only exploit its full potential with an effective selection process. Most people can recall examples where candidates for a job have been exposed to a pretty gruelling procedure only to have all that effort wasted by one interviewer's prejudices. Before we can use a test, therefore, we must consider all aspects of the selection process.

❖ Identifying Job Requirements

In most selection situations, it is useful to regard the selection process as a process that brings together all the information we gain about an applicant, in the form of an 'applicant profile'. This profile will not just contain information about their personality but will also include information on their abilities and aptitudes, their qualifications and training, and their experience, as well as any other general information relevant to the job in question. This applicant profile clearly relates to the concept of an ideal job profile or 'person specification', which typically consists of a list of criteria matching our idealized impression of the jobholder. Of course, this ideal rarely matches reality, so we are forced to discriminate between the *essential* and *desirable,* and then to compare individual applicant profile against this final profile.

If we are supplied with a good job specification, the task of producing an ideal applicant profile should be relatively easy. However, it is always worth reviewing the job specification in a wider context to ensure that it is based on reality, not just on optimistic goals, and is expressed in terms of the specific tasks required for the post. From these, we should be able to clearly identify the critical qualities for fulfilling the requirements of the job.

This is the theory at least, but typically job specifications are produced by line managers and may not be that accurate. It is important to recognize that effective recruitment and selection of the workforce should form just one part of an integrated strategy for improving the quality of the workforce with several key components as shown in the diagram.

Human Resource Quality Improvement Model

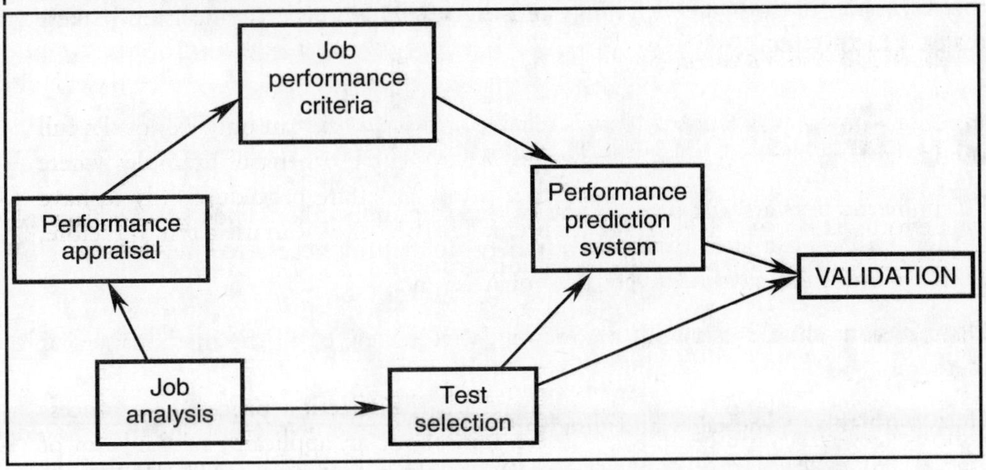

FIGURE 4.1: KEY COMPONENTS OF AN INTEGRATED SELECTION STRATEGY

1. **Job analysis** is the starting point, and can be achieved using several different techniques. Job analysis interviews and questionnaires can identify the elements that are most relevant to different jobs. A more specialised approach is the use of Repertory Grid Analysis (GRA) or Critical Incident Analysis (CIA) to clarify the characteristics of successful jobholders.
2. **Performance appraisal system** should of course, reflect the key element of a job identified by detailed job analysis. Staff needs to be trained to implement the system in a consistent and reliable manner.
3. **Job performance criteria** needs to be identified that will allow the organization to link assessment criteria (and therefore chosen tests) to job performance.
4. **Performance prediction system** will ultimately enable us to fine-tune human resource planning and assessment techniques.
5. **Validation** is of course, the key to the system, and should seek to determine whether individuals selected under the new system really do perform well than through previous procedures. One approach is to compare the performance of samples of employees selected under different systems.

❖ Prioritizing Requirements

No recruitment and selection process can cover all aspects of human behaviour, nor is any one individual likely to fulfill all requirements. The importance of prioritizing these requirements cannot be overemphasized. It is common for organizations to use a weighing scheme in the selection process (i.e. different dimensions are given different levels of importance), and although this may seem somewhat bureaucratic, the discussion of both the weighings and the results amongst the decision-makers is really what matters.

REVIEWING THE ASSESSMENT METHODS AVAILABLE

Psychometric tests are just one method of assessing individuals. Their great advantage is their ease of use and low cost, but they do require access to the right sort of expertise and may have relatively low job relevance.

Organizations should carry out a comprehensive review of all the methods available to them.

Here, with their advantages and disadvantages, are some of the options that should be considered when looking to balance psychometric data with other types of data:

1. *Application forms:* This is a method of collecting at the early stages of the selection of the selection process. It is standardized in structure, but provides minimal data.

2. *Curriculum vitae:* This is a method of evaluating career history and achievements. It can build up a good picture of a candidate, but it is not standardized and needs verifying.

3. *References and testimonials:* This is third party data about an individual. At best it can give a picture of a person's strengths through the eyes of a stakeholder. However, it is not standardized, and is likely to be subjective.

4. *Bio-data:* This is biographical data based on forced choice questions. It can be very effective when standardized, objective and verified. However, it has to be custom designed and evaluated.

5. *Biographical interview:* This is a structured interview covering education, achievements, interests, career and relationships. A more recent development is the competence-based interview, which focuses on individual style and achievement in relation to a specific competence framework. The biographical interview produces high-quality data if structured appropriately. However, it needs a great deal of skill to construct and to conduct. It also needs an appropriate competence framework to underwrite it.

6. *Records of qualification and achievement:* These are what as the name implies. They are objective and easily obtainable, but they are limited in scope.

7. *Performance Appraisal:* This comprises information about performance in the job; such appraisal adds some objective data from a range of stakeholders. A performance appraisal provides good data if conducted reliably; and the 360 degree process can be particularly powerful. However, it is difficult to obtain or verify as a third party. It is also time-consuming.

8. *Assessment centre:* This involves candidates in a variety of activities and exercises, each of which is designed to provide data on different aspects of aptitude, skill and knowledge in terms of real behaviour in realistic situations. However, it is also expensive and time consuming.

9. *Interview:* Already discussed, this provides first hand data and impressions of the persons involved. However, and again as mentioned above, it is not very accurate, objective and reliable.

Here are some simple rules to guide your decisions as to different assessment methods:

1. *Rule One:* Always remember that many of the traditional methods used in selection are notoriously unreliable.

2. *Rule Two:* If you are worried about the cost of applying a more rigorous approach to selection, try calculating the costs of wrong decisions.

3. *Rule Three:* The attention paid to the assessment of individual dimensions should be in direct proportion to the importance of the dimension.

4. *Rule Four:* The reliability and accuracy of the assessment increases rapidly when there are multiple assessments.

5. *Rule Five:* Always consider each job separately. You should not continue to use particular tests because the company 'has always done it that way'.

SELECTING THE RIGHT TESTS

Every manager considering the optimum mix of tests to use within current constraints of time and resources is faced with a dilemma:

1. Should they select or even design a specific test that gives a precise and highly reliable measurement of a limited but critical aspect of a job, or

2. Should they use a variety of tests that are less precise and predictive, but which provide a broader and more comprehensive range of competencies?

Given the pace of change in the modern work environment, there is probably a tendency to use broader-based tools.

In the final analysis, test users should be committed to using only those tests, which can be shown to meet the purpose for which they are to be used, and that are appropriate for the intended test-takers. This means test user should:

1. Define the purpose of the testing, and identify the target population.
2. Select a test that matches the purpose and population, based on a thorough review of all available information, including, where possible, independent test reviews.
3. Read all the support materials provided by test developers, and avoid using tests where the information in these materials is unclear or incomplete.
4. Ensure they become familiar with the background to the test's development, and that they understand the technical research data underpinning the test.
5. Examine specimen materials, including questionnaires, test instructions, answer sheets, manuals, scored results and computer feedback reports, before selecting a test.

This is clearly a rather rigorous process and a little off-putting. Small wonder that some organizations are inclined to cut corners and leave the decision to an expert. If you are tempted to do this, remind yourself that careless selection of tests has landed some large organizations in an industrial tribunal. At the very least, your selection process will be flawed and you can expect poorer results.

❖ Checklist for Selecting a Test

Let's imagine that you have followed the process through and are about to make a final decision on the use of one or more tests. Before you fix on your choice, it will probably be useful to double-check your findings against the following checklist:

1. Do you have enough evidence that the test measures a key requirement for the job concerned? Has a proper job analysis or validation study been carried out?
2. Does the test come with a manual that provides technical information and instructions for test administration?
3. Is there an alternative form of the test in case you need to administer it a second time or one of them is compromised?
4. Is there an objective scoring key?
5. Is each of the scales measured statistically reliable?
6. Is there evidence of validity for the targeted job and population?
7. Do you have someone trained to administer, score and interpret the score?

CHECKING THE STANDARDIZATION, EXPECTED RELIABILITY AND VALIDITY OF TESTS

These issues are especially relevant to the use of personality tests for two reasons:

1. **Personality tests are normative,** i.e. individual results are always scored by comparing them to the rest of the population. Quoting a score without referencing it to the general population or to some specific sector such as professionals or managers is meaningless.
2. **Personality tests are not infallible.** Unless we have some measure of their accuracy and their relevance to the issues we wish to explore, then once again we will be on shaky ground and in danger of misinterpreting the results. Even as a test user, we need to check out the three issues of norms, reliability and validity.

❖ Norms

Employers using personality tests must be confident that the test is not subject to bias, or, where there is bias (e.g., sex differences), that any discrimination that does arise is real and justified in terms of the job itself.

Here are some guidelines on what you are looking for:

1. *Size of sample:* This should be at least 1000, evenly distributed between males and females.
2. *Norm populations:* The overall sample for the general population should be taken from a wide range of organizations. Check the range of organizations used, a sample of three companies probably does not represent a balanced sample.
3. *Specialized norm groups:* Norm tables for groups closely related to your intended target should be provided.

❖ Reliability

Most modern tests are very reliable in terms of the design of items, given the free availability of computer software for item analysis. However, you do need to pay attention to test–retest reliability, which is a measure of the accuracy of the test. Obviously, it is not sensible to use a test whose results can vary considerably.

❖ Validity

The fact that a test has high reliability, i.e. that it produces consistent results, is no guarantee that it is actually measuring what the publisher claims it does (construct validity) or, more importantly, that it will provide useful information to the decision maker (criterion-based validity). Ask yourself whether what you are seeing really matches what you are seeking in your organization.

Here are four important rules for the use of personality tests that all test-users should follow:

1. ***Rule One:*** The results of personality tests must be interpreted by a qualified and experienced expert.
2. ***Rule Two:*** The results should normally be confirmed by a feedback interview with the respondent or through supporting evidence (e.g., peer reviews, assessment centre).
3. ***Rule Three:*** If the results cannot be confirmed by other means, their significance should be reduced and treated with caution.
4. ***Rule Four:*** Only draw conclusions for those factors or qualities that have been shown to be important predictors of performance.

When interpreting results, we often find people suffer from misconceptions as to what the tests show. Here are some simple principles that are often ignored:

1. There is no such thing as a right or wrong personal profile. Scoring high or low on one dimension is a measure not of how good you are but of how unusual you are.
2. Extreme personalities are interesting to us, but so are typical or average scores on personality dimensions. Someone who shows an average level of assertiveness will generally seek to gain a balance between being preoccupied with getting the job done to achieve results (whatever the cost!) and adapting to changes, circumstances and quickly finding new solutions.
3. We can only talk about the degree of match between your profile and the job or circumstances you find yourself in.
4. When there is a mismatch, people can experience discomfort or learn to adapt. An individual's natural preference is not the same as their observed behaviour.
5. The words used to describe personality traits are often emotive in common language and need professional interpretation.
6. Everything is relative, including our own reaction to the results. The use of the label 'sensitive' or 'sentimental' simply means you will probably appreciate music, arts, a film or book with a creative or emotive theme more than a practical hobby, an action-packed film, a detective novel or a biography.

CHAPTER 5

The Uses of Psychometric Tests

LEARNING OBJECTIVES

- To explain the methods of personality development.
- To discuss the guidelines for using tests in organizations.

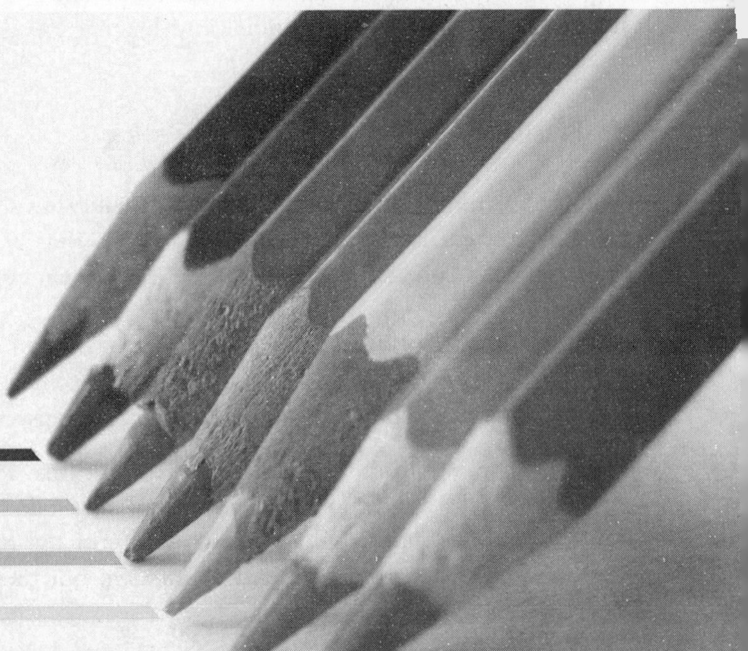

THE RANGE OF USES FOR TESTS

Psychological tests can serve a variety of uses in an organization like:

❖ Screening and Short-listing

By selecting this option, the management team is also deciding that for the job in question it would prefer to employ people with more developed skills in a particular area. The managers concerned need to be committed to the importance of the abilities in question, and candidates, on their part, will expect to be given a fair opportunity to demonstrate their potential.

❖ In Combination with other Methods of Assessment

Tests are probably best viewed as an integral part of the complete assessment of an individual, rather like examining the pieces that make up a complete jigsaw. They might be used, for example, to identify some key issues that can be explored in greater depth in a subsequent interview. Alternatively, they may provide complementary evidence, confirming aspects of behaviour or competencies identified by other means (e.g., 360-degree surveys or assessment centres).

The challenge for anyone interpreting results is to tease out the possible explanations for any inconsistencies in performance and to arrive at a reasoned and valid judgment about a candidate's true ability or personal disposition. Weighing up and evaluating psychometric results effectively requires experience and judgment, but in the right hands it leads to a more rounded and balanced evaluation of an individual's true strength and weaknesses.

❖ Placement

A detailed study of individuals using personality tests and questionnaires can play a valuable role in matching individuals to jobs that best suit them, thereby helping management to make optimum use of the human resources available to them.

❖ Other Applications

Creative managers can in fact identify many uses for psychometric tests in the workplace.

1. A newly appointed chief executive could use tests to handle sensitive issues relating to the senior manager group in a takeover or merger. Not only can they provide an insight into the nature of the team, especially if performance records/feedbacks are limited or missing, but they can also provide a source of

information to support future decisions on deployment, promotion, development and outplacements.

2. Tests can support initiatives to improve the quality of work performance.

3. In a company with sensitive industrial relations, the use of tests to identify the potential for retraining and job changes can significantly reduce the potential for conflict in the workplace.

PERSONAL DEVELOPMENT

One of the most exciting trends has been the growing use of tests to enrich individuals' insight into their own capability, potential and development needs. Providing individuals with professional feedback on test results in a career counseling session allows them to gain a better understanding of their personal qualities and to take ownership of their own development process.

For the use of personality tests to be effective, a number of conditions need to apply:

1. Subjects need to be volunteers not conscripts.
2. The test instrument must have a good level of face validity.
3. Written reports are not as powerful as a feedback discussion with someone qualified and experienced.
4. Such discussions need to be developmental – i.e. what can I do now I know this?

❖ The Ethical use of Tests

Most people tend to view uncertainty and change with unease and distrust, especially if it affects their job opportunities and careers. The user of tests has an important responsibility to recognize and deal with these natural fears, as well as to administer tests properly. The introduction of 'scientific' tests may well be met with negative responses from the workforce. Those who have not studied recently may find daunting and with no obvious relationship to the day-to-day realities of workplace. Test users must take their responsibilities to the test-takers just as seriously as they do those towards the organization.

❖ Communication

Any user of tests must take special steps to provide adequate information to clarify and clear up possible misunderstandings. Without this buy-in, you cannot expect potential test-takers to participate willingly or sit the tests without the potential for unreliable results. The purpose of the tests, the way in which they are developed and applied, and treatment of data must be explained to gain acceptance from the test-takers.

❖ Candidate Care

Before embarking on tests, provide the test-taker with adequate information regarding the use of the test, the procedure involved, the likely duration of the test and the likely outcome of the assessment process. Offer guidance and support only in a way that is consistent with the test administration instructions and does not invalidate the process.

❖ Equal Opportunities and Culture Fairness

There are some very simple steps managers can take to promote equal opportunities:

1. ***Evaluate the tests:*** Check out the procedures used by the test developers to avoid insensitive content or language and to identify potential bias.

2. ***Review the performance of test-takers:*** Compare the performance of test-takers of different gender and ethnic origin when samples of sufficient size are available.

3. ***Modify the test administration if necessary:*** Where necessary and feasible, use modified forms or altered administration procedures for test takers. Where bias in test has been demonstrated, identify the cause with the help of expert advice or consider scrapping the use of the test.

❖ Test Administration and Scoring

The facilities used for testing are critical. Candidates must be provided with a quiet, well-illuminated and ventilated room, complete with properly spaced tables and chairs. The tests must be carried out under the control of a properly trained administrator and be free from any interruptions, otherwise the test results are invalid.

❖ Test Feedback

As a general rule, you should take steps to ensure that test-takers are provided with adequate feedback from a qualified expert. Certainly, where tests are used in selection, you must ensure that all candidates are treated equally. Avoid the temptation to treat internal candidates differently from external applicants.

There will also be situations where it may be ill advised to provide detailed feedback. Providing too much insight into the assessment methodology might allow individuals to deliberately practice their skills in key areas and so lead to corruption of the process.

❖ Disposal

Most important, when the purpose for which the tests were used has been achieved, the user must ensure that steps are taken to dispose of any paperwork properly.

GUIDELINES FOR USING TESTS IN ORGANIZATIONS

Even the best test can deliver flawed information when it forms part of a poorly designed process. It is therefore good practice to establish a comprehensive policy on testing and to issue clear guidance to all those involved in the use of tests. Such a policy should identify:

1. On what basis tests will be used.
2. Who will take decisions on the use of tests.
3. Who will have access to results.
4. How the result will be used and incorporated within decision-making processes.
5. The policy for confidentiality and providing feedback.

CHAPTER 6

Personality Tests

LEARNING OBJECTIVES

- To know how to measure personality.
- To discuss about personality tests.

PERSONALITY TESTS

In reality, personality is best thought of as moderating your behaviour, or as guiding it in particular directions. This allows you to react in a number of ways that are natural to you, depending on the circumstances. So, if you are looking for a definition, personality is the characteristic way in which someone responds to situations or, if you like, their preferred way of behaving towards particular circumstances and other people.

To summarize, the important features of personality are that:

1. It stems from you as an individual.
2. It predicts your behaviour over a range of situations.
3. It doesn't alter dramatically over time.
4. It distinguishes you in meaningful ways from other people.

However, to complicate matters further, personality is also influenced by your beliefs, which you hold to be true despite the fact that there may be no evidence for them and by your values, which are really the set of beliefs against which you judge your own and other people's behaviour. You could also add motivation, or the aspect of your character that drives your behaviour: why you do what you do. This is usually expressed in terms of needs, such as the need to be successful or to be secure. Clearly, all these factors also have a part to play in explaining personality.

WHERE DOES PERSONALITY COME FROM?

There are at least three answers to this question. Some psychologists maintain that personality is matter of genetics, while others argue that it is a question of how you were brought up and of your life experience. Many believe that it is a combination of both factors. Whatever the answer, as a well-known wit said, make sure you choose your parents with care!

If we examine these ideas more closely, there are aspects of our behaviour that do appear to be automatic. This leads us to describe certain actions as being 'due to human nature', the implication being that some behavioral patterns are automatic functions of our brains. However, unlike the reactions of many other animals, this instinctual behaviour is not very strong. For example, while many women have maternal instinct, it is not true of all women. If it were, we would be able to predict exactly a whole range of female behaviour. We cannot because the same stimulus does not produce the same reaction in everyone. This means that people are very unlikely by nature to be inherently maternal, outgoing, criminal, or whatever.

What follows is an exercise that will start you on the process of finding out what you are like and what other people think you are like.

THE SELF-DISCOVERY EXERCISE

1. Find a blank piece of paper and write down ten adjectives that you feel describe your personality. Make sure they are about your personality and are not words describing your appearance. Try to complete the exercise in ten minutes. If you get stuck, there is a list of trait adjectives at the end.

2. Now find someone who knows you well and get them to write down ten words that also describe your personality. Do not show them your list first.

3. After about ten minutes, stop your friend or partner and compare the two lists. How have you described yourself? Was it difficult to find ten words? What has your friend written down? Do you agree with each other? What are the differences?

If you have completed the exercise, you will probably find that the way in which you see yourself is not identical to how other people see you. Furthermore, the two people involved knew quite a lot about you! What would an employer do?

ADJECTIVES DESCRIBING PERSONALITY TRAITS

Absent-minded	Enthusiastic	Private
Abstract	Expedient	Proactive
Accommodating	Experimenting	Prompt
Achieving	Explicit	Pushy
Affable	Expressive	Quarrelsome
Affectionate	Extroverted	Radical
Affiliative	Fearful	Rash
Aggravating	Flexible	Rational
Altruistic	Forceful	Reactive
Ambitious	Formal	Realistic
Amicable	Forthright	Rebellious
Analytical	Genial	Reflective
Animated	Gentle	Relaxed
Antagonistic	Genuine	Reliable
Anxious	Gregarious	Repressed
Apprehensive	Guarded	Reserved
Argumentative	Hasty	Restless
Artistic	Hesitant	Restrained
Assertive	Hostile	Retiring
Attentive	Humble	Rigid
Aware	Hurried	Ruthless

Contd...

Benevolent	Hypothetical	Satisfied
Blithe	Imaginative	Selfless
Blunt	Impetuous	Sensing
Bold	Impulsive	Sensitive
Calm	Incisive	Sensuous
Candid	Inconsistent	Shrewd
Capricious	Independent	Shy
Caring	Informal	Sober
Cautious	Inhibited Innovative	Stable
Changeable	Inquiring	Steady
Charitable	Inquisitive	Strategic
Competitive	Inspired	Stressed
Compliant	Intense	Striving
Composed	Introspective	Structured
Conceptual	Introverted	Stubborn
Confident	Intuitive	Subjective
Conscientious	Involved	Submissive
Consoling	Irrational	Suspicious
Contesting	Irresponsible	Systematic
Controlled	Jolly	Temperamental
Controlling	Lethargic	Tenacious
Conventional	Listless	Tender
Co-operative	Literal	Tense
Creative	Lively	Tidy
Critical	Loyal	Timid
Cynical	Modest	Tolerant
Decisive	Neat	Tough
Defensive	Neurotic	Trusting
Deferential	Obedient	Uncompromising
Democratic	Optimistic	Undisciplined
Determined	Organized	Unexacting
Diplomatic	Original	Unorthodox
Direct	Ostentatious	Unrestrained
Disciplined	Outgoing	Unselfish
Discreet	Outspoken	Unsentimental
Disorganized	Perceptive	Unworried
Distant	Perfectionist	Venturesome
Docile	Persuasive	Vigilant
Dominant	Perturbable	Vital
Domineering	Pessimistic	Vulnerable

Contd...

Doubting	Phlegmatic	Warm
Driven	Planful	Wary
Dutiful	Playful	Willful
Efficient	Practical	Willing
Emotional	Pragmatic	Yielding
Empathic	Precise	Zealous
Enterprising	Predictable	

Note: All the adjectives in the above list are used in real personality questionnaires.

MEASURING PERSONALITY

The history of personality measurement stretches back thousands of years. In fact, one of the earliest examples is provided by Gideon who saved the people of Israel from the Midianites. His army recruitment officers short-listed soldiers by the simple device of asking if anyone was afraid to return home. Those who were left were then asked to drink from a stream. The soldiers, who cupped the water in their hands, enabling them to notice an attacking force, were selected for their quality of alertness, unlike those who bent down and drank directly from the stream. Interestingly, this quality of 'awareness' is still important today and is a feature of some psychological testing systems designed for military selection.

In the next section is given a complete practice personality questionnaire – the Mind Style Questionnaire (MSQ). The MSQ is a self-report, 'Big Five" measure, constructed using the latest research on personality measurement. It is relatively short in that it contains only 88 questions. However, this is still longer than the two most popular quick questionnaires available in the UK.

This is not the place to explain the scoring system in detail, the MSQ contains a number of features that help to make your answers more positive and to make the results more accurate. For example, each question measures only one aspect of your personality, so saying 'No', or in fact 'False', does not mean that you score at the opposite end of a dimension – e.g., disagreeing with an 'extroverted' question does not automatically make you 'introverted'.

The other point to bear in mind when you work out your results is that most people are not at the extremes of each dimension, but towards the middle. Statistically, you would expect to find about 40 percent in the 'average' range, with the remaining 60 percent split between the two ends of a dimension – e.g., 20 percent highly, and 10 percent very highly extroverted; and 20 percent highly, and 10 percent very highly introverted. Furthermore, personality is neither 'good' nor 'bad'. It does not work in such a simple way. Each personality characteristic is a mixture of features that may or may not be useful, but this is only apparent when you actually apply your personality to work, to relationships, to education, or whatever.

MSQ: A Tool for Personality Test

The **Mind Style Questionnaire** is designed to find out what you are like as a person. It asks you about the way in which you react in different situations and how you deal with other people.

As with any personality questionnaire, there is no 'right' or 'wrong' answers; the idea is that you just say what most like you is. This can be difficult at times, but the more honest you are, the more accurate and useful the results will be.

You fill in your answers by putting a tick in the appropriate box.

		True	False
A.	I like to work by myself.	☐	✓
B.	I enjoy games of skill.	☐	✓
C.	People trust my judgement.	✓	☐

When you answer the questions, bear the following points in mind:

1. Don't spend too long thinking about each question; just give the first answer that comes into your head.
2. Make sure that you answer all the questions, if you change your mind about an answer, cross it out clearly and put a tick in the other box.
3. Even if a question does not seem entirely relevant, give the answer you consider would be most like you.
4. There is no time limit, but try to complete the questionnaire as quickly as you can.
5. Don't look at the scoring key until you have done the questionnaire.

Start when you are ready

		True	False
1.	I can easily talk to people about how I feel.	☐	☐
2.	If something goes wrong it preys on my mind.	☐	☐
3.	I like things to be neat and tidy.	☐	☐

4. I am good at listening to other people's problems. ☐ ☐
5. I tend to use tried and tested methods. ☐ ☐
6. I like to have plenty of time to myself. ☐ ☐
7. If people are rude to me I just shrug it off. ☐ ☐
8. I can work even when things are disorganized. ☐ ☐
9. I'm a competitive person. ☐ ☐
10. I like to have lots of variety in what I do. ☐ ☐
11. I enjoy talking to people at social gatherings. ☐ ☐
12. I always feel hurt if someone criticizes me. ☐ ☐
13. I have a systematic way of doing most things. ☐ ☐
14. I tend to trust other people. ☐ ☐
15. I am a practical-minded sort of person. ☐ ☐
16. I never tell 'white' lies. ☐ ☐
17. I'm more of a listener than a talker. ☐ ☐
18. I seldom suffer from feelings of stress. ☐ ☐
19. It's better to get a job done than aim for perfection. ☐ ☐
20. I like to be in charge of other people. ☐ ☐
21. I like coming up with new ideas. ☐ ☐
22. I am happy to make speeches in public. ☐ ☐
23. Sometimes little things really upset me. ☐ ☐
24. I always tell people exactly what I think. ☐ ☐
25. I like to have a daily routine. ☐ ☐
26. People often thank me for my support. ☐ ☐
27. I like to work within the rules. ☐ ☐
28. I feel uneasy if I'm the centre of attention. ☐ ☐

29. I am cool-headed when under pressure.
30. I never worry about a bit of untidiness.
31. I often lose my patience with other people.
32. None of my close friends has ever upset me.
33. I like to know how things work.
34. I enjoy socializing with large groups of people.
35. After a hard day I find it difficult to unwind.
36. If say I will do something, I always do it.
37. I worry when people are unhappy.
38. People describe me as having good common sense.
39. I prefer to talk to people on a one-to-one basis.
40. I can't remember ever being late for an appointment.
41. I keep going whatever happens.
42. Sometimes you have to break 'the rules'.
43. I'm good at getting people to do things.
44. My ideas are not always practical.
45. I like it when people call in unannounced.
46. I always get keyed up before important events.
47. I don't leave jobs unfinished.
48. I always keep other people's secrets.
49. I find it easy to put myself in someone else's position.
50. I'm a down-to-earth sort of person.
51. I'm happy sitting at home reading a book.
52. I take a relaxed view about most things.
53. I like to react to things on the spur of the moment.

54. I always get what I want from people. ☐ ☐
55. I like to think of new ways of doing things. ☐ ☐
56. I'm happy to see people, whatever the circumstances. ☐ ☐
57. I like playing noisy competitive games. ☐ ☐
58. I don't like unexpected responsibilities. ☐ ☐
59. I often find myself clearing up other people's mess. ☐ ☐
60. I'm good at detecting 'uncomfortable' atmospheres. ☐ ☐
61. I tend to 'live and let live'. ☐ ☐
62. If I'm doing something I don't like to be interrupted. ☐ ☐
63. I don't let things get on top of me. ☐ ☐
64. I never worry if I make a mistake. ☐ ☐
65. I often lose track of time. ☐ ☐
66. I'm a 'bad loser' at games. ☐ ☐
67. People sometimes say that my 'head is in the clouds'. ☐ ☐
68. I often act on impulse. ☐ ☐
69. I tend to be a cautious person. ☐ ☐
70. I never leave things to the last minute. ☐ ☐
71. People often comment on how patient I am. ☐ ☐
72. I've never been deliberately rude to anyone. ☐ ☐
73. I don't usually have extreme views on things. ☐ ☐
74. I need quiet atmosphere to work effectively. ☐ ☐
75. I am good at dealing with difficult people. ☐ ☐
76. I take each day as it comes. ☐ ☐
77. I like to challenge people and make them think. ☐ ☐
78. I am curious about most things. ☐ ☐

79. I often say things without thinking about them. ☐ ☐

80. Sometimes I feel guilty even if I haven't done anything. ☐ ☐

81. I can be something of a perfectionist. ☐ ☐

82. I tend to avoid confrontations. ☐ ☐

83. I like to deal with factual information. ☐ ☐

84. I have a small number of really good friends. ☐ ☐

85. I respond well in any sort of crisis. ☐ ☐

86. I often lose things. ☐ ☐

87. I don't back down in an argument. ☐ ☐

88. People see me as an 'ideas' person. ☐ ☐

End of questionnaire

✓ Check that you have ticked a box for each question.

Scoring the Questionnaire

To score the questionnaire you need to calculate the total scores for the five personality dimensions. Each scale has two ends, so there are ten simple calculations to complete. For example, the first dimension indicates whether you are predominantly extroverted or introverted, or a combination of both.

When you start the scoring, you will see that all the extroverted questions have negative (-) scores, and all the introverted questions have positive scores (+). (The fact that some things are negative and other things are positive does not mean that certain answers are better than others; it is just a way of calculating the balance of extroversion against introversion).

To make the calculation, you simply add up all the negative extroverted scores, add up all the positive introverted scores, and then add the two numbers together. For example,

Extroverted total = -10 Introverted total = +6

Overall total = -4 (i.e., -10 plus + 6)

Or

Extroverted total = -5 Introverted total = +12

Overall total = +7 (i.e., -5 plus + 12)

The calculations for the other four dimensions are done in exactly the same way. The tables that follow will help you to work out your five overall totals.

❖ Step 1

In each of the tables, put a tick by the question numbers to which you answered 'True". Ignore all those questions to which you answered 'False'. When you have ticked all the questions to which you answered True for both aspects of a dimension, add up the appropriate numbers in the two score columns, noting that some questions score more than others. Finally, add the two totals together, negative to positive, to get your overall score for the dimension. (It is possible to score 0, which indicates that you are in the middle of a dimension.)

Dimension 1

Extroverted

Question	✓	Score
1		-1
11		-2
22		-2
34		-2
45		-1
57		-1
68		-1
79		-2
	Total=	

Introverted

Question	✓	Score
6		+2
17		+2
28		+2
39		+1
51		+1
62		+1
74		+1
84		+2
	Total=	

Overall total = Extroverted + Introverted

Overall total = ______________________

Dimension 2

Tough-minded

Question	√	Score
9		-1
20		-2
31		-1
43		-1
54		-2
66		-2
77		-1
87		-2
	Total=	

Tender-minded

Question	√	Score
4		+2
14		+1
26		+1
37		+2
49		+2
60		+1
71		+2
82		+1
	Total=	

Overall total = Tough-minded + Tender-minded

Overall total = ____________________

Dimension 3

Conforming

Question	√	Score
5		-2
15		-1
27		-2
38		-2
50		-1
61		-1
73		-2
83		-1
	Total=	

Creative

Question	√	Score
10		+1
21		+2
33		+1
44		+1
55		+2
67		+2
78		+1
88		+2
	Total=	

Overall total = Confronting + Creative

Overall total = ____________________

Dimension 4

High Structure

Question	√	Score
3		-2
13		-2
25		-1
36		-1
47		-1
59		-2
70		-1
81		-2
	Total=	

Low Structure

Question	√	Score
8		+2
19		+1
30		+2
42		+1
53		+2
65		+1
76		+1
86		+2
	Total=	

Overall total = High Structure + Low Structure

Overall total = ____________________

Dimension 5

Confident

Question	√	Score
7		-2
18		-2
29		-1
41		-1
52		-1
63		-2
75		-2
85		-1
	Total=	

Emotional

Question	√	Score
2		+2
12		+1
23		+2
35		+1
46		+2
58		+1
69		+1
80		+2
	Total=	

Overall total = Confident + Emotional

Overall total = ____________________

❖ Step 2

Complete the table below to work out your impression control score:

Question	√	Score
16		+2
24		+2
32		+1
40		+1
48		+2
56		+1
64		+2
72		+1
	Total=	

Overall total = Impression control

Overall total = ____________________

❖ Step 3

You should now have six overall totals, five for the personality dimensions and one for impression control.

Scaling Table

A Score of:	Becomes:	A Score of:	Becomes:
-12	-6	+12	+6
-11	-6	+11	+6
-10	-5	+10	+5
-9	-5	+9	+5
-8	-4	+8	+4
-7	-4	+7	+4
-6	-3	+6	+3
-5	-3	+5	+3
-4	-2	+4	+2
-3	-2	+3	+2
-2	-1	+2	+1
-1	-1	+1	+1

❖ Step 4

Plot your results on the MSQ Summary Chart. You do this by filing in the little square that represents your overall (scaled) total for each dimension and for Impression Control. If you like, you can also fill in one square before and one square after each of your scores. This illustrates the variability of your scores as there is always a small amount of 'error' when you measure anything, including personality.

MSQ Summary Chart

- Scores	6	5	4	3	2	1	0	1	2	3	4	5	6	+ scores
Extroverted														Introverted
Tough minded														Tender-minded
Conforming														Creative
High structure														Low structure
Confident														Emotional
Impression control														

❖ Step 5

Determine whether each of your scores is 'average', high' or 'very high'.

1. *Average:* If you score between –2 and +2 (inclusive), you will show characteristics from each end of the dimension, e.g., extroverted and introverted, depending on the circumstances in which you find yourself.
2. *High:* If you score between –3 and –5 (inclusive) or between +3 and +5 (inclusive), you will have a definite tendency to show the characteristics described for the appropriate end of the dimension, e.g., extroverted or introverted a good deal of the time.
3. *Very High:* If your score is –6 or + 6, you will show the extremes of the appropriate dimension, e.g., you will be *predominantly* extroverted or introverted.

If you want to be very precise about your scores, you should take into account the 'error' mentioned earlier. In reality, this means that your score on each dimension could be one unit bigger or smaller. For example, if your score on the first dimension is +3, it actually ranges from +2 to +4. This could make a difference to the interpretation as you may fall between two of the above categories, for example, you may actually be average to high, or high to very high on a particular dimension.

It is important to realize that your scores relate to you as an individual. On the basis of this questionnaire, you may be more extroverted than you are introverted, but no attempt has been made to compare you precisely with the rest of the population. This would happen if you were being selected for a job. In fact, you might well be compared with a representative sample of people who already do the job, who in turn might be more extroverted than the general population. So, for example an, employer might actually be looking for 'high' or 'very high' scores. It depends on the requirements for a particular job.

❖ Step 6

Interpreting your Results

Look at the descriptions that follow to find out about your personality profile:

Dimension 1: Extroverted ←——————→ Introverted

1. **Extroverted** people are open, talkative, expressive and lively. They enjoy other people's attention and like social gatherings. They are good at meeting people and dealing with strangers, and are generally energetic, active and enjoy taking risks. However, they can act on impulse and may not always think through the consequences of their actions. This can mean that they rush in where angels fear to tread'. Sometimes, such unplanned actions can be seen as irresponsible.

   In a work context, extroverts prefer to work with people, usually in teams or groups. They do not like doing jobs by themselves, and prefer to seek out other people's views and to collaborate jointly on projects. Highly extroverted people may appear to be very outspoken and will actively (and sometimes very assertively) put their point of view across. This can be an advantage in situations where persuasive skills are required, e.g., in selling situations.

2. **Introverted** people are quiet and reserved. They like to keep themselves to themselves, and are content with their own thoughts and feelings. They do not need the company of other people (as an extrovert would), and are unlikely to seek out actively and attend social gatherings. They do not usually act in an impulsive way, and are more likely to think to things through carefully before they do them. The theme is generally one of stability and considered decision-making.

At work, introverted people may be seen as shy, restrained and rather distant, and this can mean that they are sometimes overlooked. However, they are usually good at working by themselves, or in small groups, and this is an important factor in many jobs. In those situations where an introverted person has a good command of the relevant information or the appropriate experience, he can appear to be just as confident as the extrovert.

Dimension 2: Tough-minded ←→ Tender-minded

1. **Tough-minded** people are assertive and achievement-oriented. They tend to focus on the task at hand and can appear at times to be insensitive. Their view is that people are responsible for their own actions. Thus, the very tough-minded person is likely to be irritated if he has to deal with other people's problems, and may well appear rather intolerant.

   In the work context, the mentality is one of winning, even if this is at the expense of someone else. This is a sign of a strong competitive streak and of a determined and single-minded approach to the job. The same single-mindedness is also mirrored in social and leisure activities: tough-minded people like to win and are very poor losers. Whatever they do, they like to be 'in charge' and to seek to influence and control others. They tend to put their point of view over confidently and enjoy being the centre of attention.

2. **Tender-minded** people are warm, caring and considerate. They are concerned for those around them and how they feel. Other people see them as friendly and helpful, and as respecting different points of view. This empathy with other people is generally coupled with a sharing, cooperative approach to life. However, the problem with such a 'benevolent' personality is that other people may take advantage of it. This is reinforced by the fact that tender-minded people are not overtly ambitious, do not seek social prominence, and tend to keep out of the spotlight: it is an easygoing, 'take life as it comes' attitude.

   At work, tender-minded people are viewed as being sensitive and approachable. As such, they tend to take on other people's problems, sometimes at the expense of their own well-being. They also dislike conflict and are uncomfortable giving orders to other people. This means that they are not usually natural leaders, but may do well in supportive and socially sensitive roles.

Dimension 3: Conforming ←→ Creative

1. **Conforming** people are conservative, down to earth and moderate. They like to deal with what they know, and to solve problems using tried and tested methods. This is a pragmatic, low-risk approach to life, frequently characterized by a high degree of self-discipline. As such, conforming people would not

describe themselves as being particularly creative. However, they are usually skilled at adapting existing methods. This is not to be dismissed lightly, as those who build on ideas in a practical way usually reap the benefits.

At work, conforming people tend to defend the established way of doing things. They value integrity and like to provide a good example for others to follow. However, this protection of the status quo is often seen as a resistance to new ideas and to change. In extreme circumstances, this may also be viewed as a rejection of the need to debate alternative ways of working. Thus, the conforming person strives to avoid risk and favours stability. In consequence, work environments that do not change, have well-established rules and an understood routine, will tend to be the most attractive. This generally means larger rather than smaller organizations.

2. **Creative** people are open-minded individuals who like to experiment with unconventional ways of doing things. They are always on the lookout for a new method or a way of getting round the rules. They like to come up with numerous ideas and they enjoy change. This can mean that they are resistant to tradition and will tend to fight against what may be perfectly good way of solving problems. As the creative solution is not always very practical, creative people will sometimes be described as having their 'heads stuck in the clouds'.

   At work, creative people tend to embrace new opportunities and promote innovative methods. Other people will see them as enthusiasts, but at times as not very reliable or consistent. This desire to be different can lead to other sorts of problems, and highly creative people are unlikely to be placed in charge of teams. The reason for the latter is that they are better at generating ideas for other people to work on, rather than being able to take command of operations. Indeed, left to their own device, creative people would probably take risks that would lead to real business problems or, in the worst case, failure.

Dimension 4: High Structure ←——→ Low Structure

1. **High structure** people take a precise, controlled and formal approach to their life and work. They are sensitive to detail and like things to be done on time. This is frequently a sign of great self-control and restraint and also of a marked intolerance to clutter and mess. At times, others can see the control the high-structure person brings to tasks as obsessive. This perfectionist approach can also cause problems if tasks have to be completed within very tight time deadlines.

   At work, high-structure people will appear organized and in control. Indeed, those who are less tidy and find organizing their work a chore may even admire them. However, they may also be quite difficult to deal with, as they demand very high standards from other people.

High-structure people in the workplace usually have an extremely tidy desk, with their papers in precise heaps and their writing instruments gathered together in a container. They always clear their papers away at the end of the day.

2. **Low-structure** people are not detail conscious and can be quite casual about the way in which they do things. They are tolerant of other people's methods and take an informal approach to daily life. They are not concerned by clutter and disorganization, and can happily work in chaotic surroundings (which a high-structure person would find extremely uncomfortable). A low-structure approach is also characterized by an enthusiasm for starting things off, but with a rapid loss of interest if a project takes longer than expected. In addition, there is a tendency to become bored easily and to suffer a degree of absent-mindedness, e.g., losing things and being late for appointments.

   At work, low-structure people are good at getting things started but need to be complemented by more organized colleagues if jobs are to be done precisely. For example, they are unlikely to get things done on time without copious reminders. However, in contrast to the high-structure person, they do not suffer from an overly perfectionist style, which can also be a real brake to progress.

Dimension 5: Confident ←——————→ Emotional

1. **Confident** people are relaxed, assertive individuals. They know their own minds and are comfortable with themselves. Their approach is usually characterized by an optimistic and positive view of the world. They can take criticism and do not spend time worrying about what other people think about them. The highly confident person is unlikely to suffer from stress or to be troubled by most things. As a result, other people may well describe them as being 'thick-skinned'. This supreme lack of concern can make the very confident person appear to be somewhat blasé.

   At work, confident people stand their ground and defend their view of how things should be done. Others will see them as 'cool headed', even when they are severely provoked. However, while these can be desirable qualities, confident people can often be difficult to motivate as they tend not to react to criticism or censure. Yet practically, they are unlikely to 'go to pieces' in stressful situations and can cope well with pressure.

2. **Emotional** people are frequently rather tense and anxious. They worry about what other people think and find it difficult to ignore what is going on around

them. In many situations, an emotional person will fret, even over small problems. This worry can become acute, especially before important events. At times, matters are made even worse by the fact that emotional people often find it difficult to relax or to 'switch off'.

At work, emotional people will be sensitive to criticism and will try very hard therefore, not to make mistakes. They tend to plan things to reduce the chance of problems occurring. As such, they can act as useful counterweights to their overly confident work colleagues. However, unlike the confident person, if things go really wrong, the emotional person may well panic. Sometimes the sense that things are out of control can bring the emotional person close to tears.

❖ Impression Control

The impression control scale is designed to find out whether you have a tendency to present yourself in an overly positive manner. The questions asked about facts that the vast majority of people, if they are honest with themselves, are rated as being 'True', For example, we have all told 'white lies' at one time or another; very few people always say exactly what they think; your close friends are bound to have upset or annoyed you at some time; we have all been late for an appointment; told someone's secret to another; pretended to be out when we didn't want to see someone; worried over a mistake; and have been driven (even mildly) to rudeness on occasions.

If you have a total score of over four, you are probably not being completely honest with yourself. In this case, the best thing to do is to complete the questionnaire again. This time, ignore what you feel are the most 'socially desirable' answers and reflect on what you are really like.

Some Things to Remember

The Mind Style Questionnaire may have confirmed what you know about yourself or contained a number of surprises. If you were surprised or discovered something with which you disagree, just bear in mind that it gives a very broad view of your personality. Each of the dimensions could quite easily be broken down into many smaller categories. If this had been, some of the finer points of your personality would have emerged. Also, remember that you did the questionnaire by yourself and that it was not administered or controlled by a psychologist. This would most definitely be the case if you completed a questionnaire as part of the selection process for a job. The results would also have been compared with a representative sample of other people, i.e., an appropriate normative group.

Strictly speaking, if you want a really accurate view of your personality, you need to complete a number of questionnaires under carefully controlled conditions. This can be arranged and if you are interested, you could contact a professional psychologist (look in yellow pages) or a local careers organization. They will be able to give you a detailed assessment of your personality, which is invaluable in the search for a suitable career or when applying for a job. After all, it is useful to know what an employer is likely to discover about you. It is also the case that if you realize what you are like; you can try to change certain aspects of your personality if you wish. Although you cannot change your basic personality, you can develop appropriate coping mechanisms.

For example, you can train yourself to be more adaptable or to be more organized and structured. Some of these techniques are described in the next chapter.

Finally, you might like to consider the observation made by the German psychologist, Angleitner. He likened the results of personality questionnaires to classifying living things as animals or plants. Although it is an interesting analogy, to be more accurate it is more like classifying animals as mammals, birds, fish, insect, amphibians or reptiles. The point is that these classifications contain creatures with very different characteristics. For example, both humans and whales are mammals, but there is something of a difference between us! So while personality questionnaires do help to classify our behaviour, even those of us who have 'identical' profiles will still show all sorts of individual differences.

❖ Key Points

1. The Mind Style Questionnaire describes your personality using five dimensions.
2. The interpretations describe how you are likely to behave in a variety of situations.
3. Some aspects of your personality cannot be measured by this questionnaire.
4. To obtain a really accurate picture of your personality, you need to complete a number of questionnaires.

CHAPTER 7

The Personality Tool Kit

LEARNING OBJECTIVES

- To know the reasons how people change.
- To discuss about the ten ways to change and verbal reasoning.

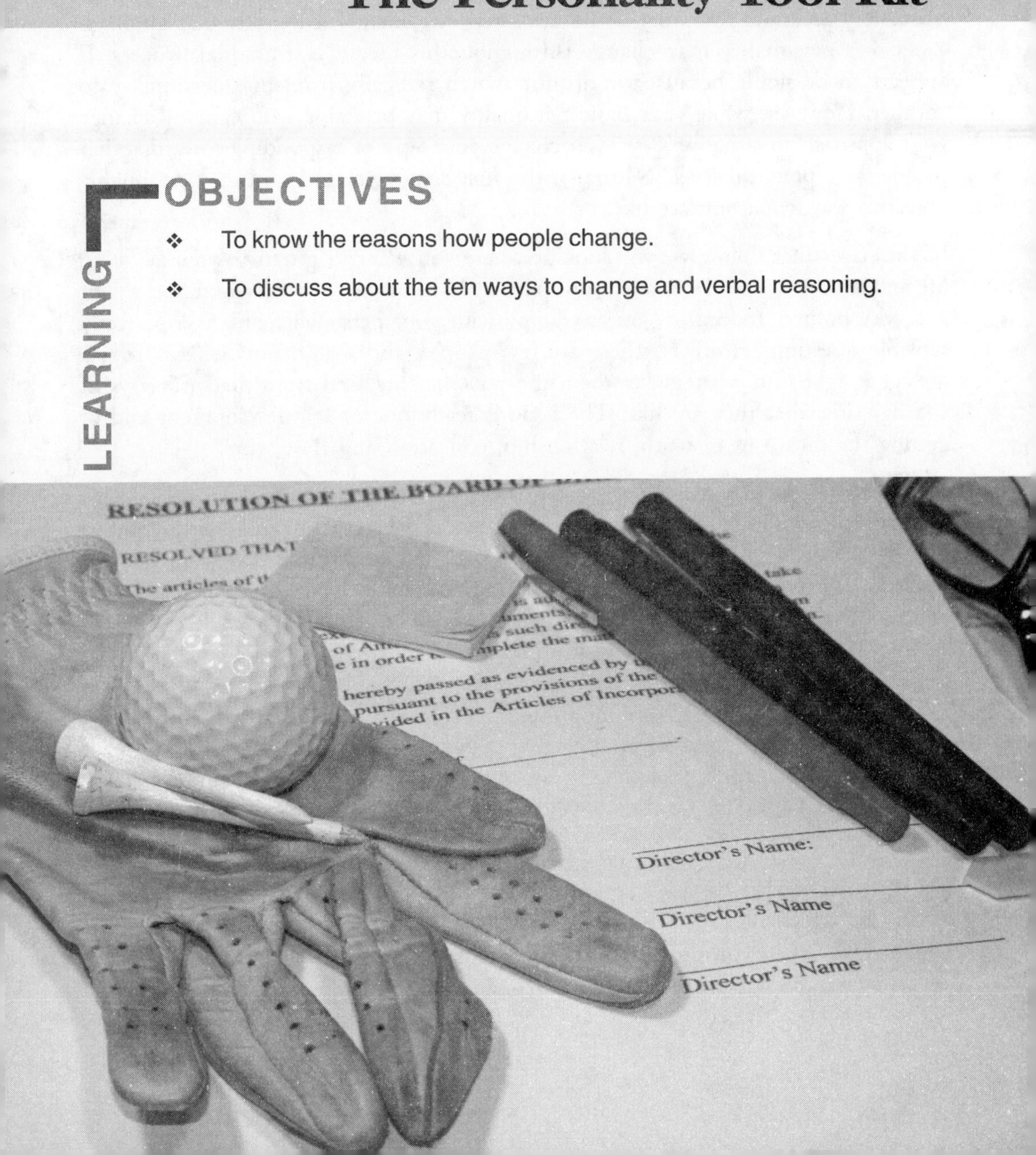

INTRODUCTION

These days, most people are too busy getting on with the everyday business of living to stop and assess what they really want. However, it is important to reflect occasionally on what we want to achieve and how we are going to get there. Part of this process involves looking at our thoughts and feelings, values and attitudes, and critically, at what motivates us to do things.

If you have completed the Mind Style Questionnaire you would have discovered a few things about your personality. Hopefully, you will feel that the results are reasonably accurate. But what is the next step? We mentioned earlier that although a person's personality may change throughout his life, it is a gradual process. It appears to be stable because we do not switch radically from one personality to another. However, while your basic personality may be stable, you can still change your approach to situations, or even change your way of responding towards other people, at a practical level. Naturally, the first step is to find out, in a reasonably objective way, what you are like.

In the pages that follow we will look at where you want to get to in your working life and what you can do to alter your pattern of behaviour. At this point you might ask, why bother? Indeed, if you are happy with your personality, this is a perfectly sensible question. However, there are few people who would not benefit from a greater insight into what makes them the way they are, and from practical ways of coping with what they are like. The issue is really one of self-development and of getting the most out of work, relationship, education and the future.

Some people feel that playing about with their personality is frightening. However, the issue is not one of changing someone's basic personality, but of helping them to modify the behaviour that springs from a particular personality. Far from being a dubious activity, this is a natural thing to do, as studies have shown that between adulthood and middle-age, 69 percent of people actually change their ratings of their own personality. To look at it another way, during this period of about 20 years, the majority of people develop new ways of using their personality. This does not mean that people are running around acting out what they would like to be, rather that there are ways of comfortably changing their behaviour, and hence of other people's perceptions of them – an important factor when it comes to being selected for a job or for forming any sort of satisfying relationship.

HOW PEOPLE CHANGE?

The way in which you present yourself is something over which you have control, yet some people will have more control than others. However, irrespective of the sort of person you are, you can choose to change yourself and to adapt to the situation in which you find yourself. The effect of change depends upon how much you want to change and the speed at which you want to do it. You should bear in mind that for most people rapid change is quite stressful and that while we can all 'act' a part for a short time, it requires a great deal of energy to do it for a long period. Thus, the secret is to incorporate changes in your behaviour that complement or boost the changes you could make naturally, with a little effort. In a work context, this can mean adopting a style that is different from your 'off-duty' personality. Those who think this sounds artificial should consider the various activities we do everyday. Is there a single 'social' situation when we are not trying to present ourselves in a particular, usually favourable, light?

We all are consciously, or unconsciously, trying to influence other people. It may be on special occasions, like an interview or a business meeting, or more generally when we are trying to present ourselves to our friends, partners or acquaintances. So whether you like it or not, you do it all the time, and in many instances without even having to think about it. Furthermore, most people use the same four techniques, regardless of their personality, for impressing other people. These techniques are:

1. ***Behaviour matching:*** This is when we mirror another person's behaviour. For example, if someone tells us something personal, we tend to respond with some personal information of our own.
2. ***Conformity:*** We adopt the correct behaviour for the situation. For example, there are differences between the way in which you would act at a party and at an employment interview.
3. ***Appreciation:*** A little flattery can go a long way, and we try to be actively interested in what someone has achieved or in the information he discloses about himself.
4. ***Consistency:*** We act in a predictable way. For example, if we want to be taken seriously we do not support a person one moment and attack him the next. That is because we all know that inconsistency is usually taken as a sign of weakness.

Clearly, these are not the only behavioural techniques you can use to influence other people, but before we look at more we need to give our search a focus. This could be, for example, on developing personal relationships.

The first step in the process of self-development is to identify those features of work that you consider to be important. Once you have done this, you can decide on the aspects of your behaviour on which you would like to focus, remembering that there is much research to show that personal growth and development is directly related to job satisfaction. The following exercise is a good way of focusing on the important factors.

The Ideal Job Exercise

In this exercise you write a description of your ideal job. This should include all those aspects that you feel are personally important or that you would like to develop. To help you begin, you might like to consider the work values that are important to you. For example,

1. Do you like a structured working environment? Do you value a well-defined job, conformity, security, predictability, and regular ways of doing things?
2. Do you want independence? Is it important that you do not have someone 'breathing down your neck'? That you have freedom and flexibility in what you do? That you do not have to work regular 9 to 5 hours?
3. Do you want to achieve? Do you like to be recognized and rewarded for what you do, and to feel a personal sense of achievement?
4. Do you want power? Many people value power, but do you actually want to control other people and dictate what they do?
5. Do you want to be creative? Is it important that you can use your imagination, or express yourself in a creative way? That you have many new tasks to do?
6. Do you want to help other people? Are you driven by the need to put something back into society? To use your skills actively to help those who may not be able to help themselves?
7. Do you like to see a tangible end product? It may be that you do not want to be one cog in a very large machine, but like to see a job through from beginning to end. If this is true, purely administrative jobs are probably not for you.
8. Do you want money? Is it the thought of earning a large salary that motivates and drives you? Perhaps you don't mind what you do, as long as you get well rewarded.
9. Do you want to work with other people? Some of us want to work alone or in one-to-one situation; others are only happy in large offices where they can talk to lots of other people.

This is not an exhaustive list, but it should give you some ideas. You also need to consider the structure of your ideal organization. What sort of goals does it have? Is it small or large? Does it have a complicated hierarchy or no hierarchy at all? What opportunities are there? Can you travel? Can you work in different countries?

Finally, what sorts of relationships do you want at work? How would the boss manage you? What would your work colleagues be like? What sorts of customers or clients would you like to deal with?

1. Now write your ideal description on a piece of paper. (If you want an example, part of a description is given at the end of this exercise.)

2. Look at your description and answer these four questions:

   (i) Would you really be happy in this job?

   (ii) If not, what would you change about the job?

   (iii) Does your ideal job fit your personality, or MSQ results?

   (iv) If not, how would you change yourself?

   The critical factor is the connection between how you are now and what the job demands. Where does your personality fit in? For example, are you really a shy person, but would like more responsibility? Do you tend to worry about things, but actually feel you want to take a few risks?

3. Summarize, on your paper, the four aspects of your behaviour on which you would like to work. A technique that might help you is to complete the following sentences:

   (i) My greatest wish is...........

   (ii) I also want to................

   (iii) My greatest problem is..............

   (iv) I also have problems with...........

❖ Example of an Ideal Job

I would like to work in a relaxed environment where I am not always being told what to do. I am quite capable of working by myself and of setting my own targets. In fact, there are a number of parts of my job that I could do from home. It would be useful to be able to plan my week so that I could work at home, say, for two days and come into work for the other three. Having flexible hours is more important because it means that you can fit work in to your life and vice-versa.

The organization would be small and friendly, and interested in everyone making the most of his potential. There would be an emphasis on training and keeping up-to-date with the latest technologies and techniques. Most of the work would be done in teams and they would be made up of the best people to do a particular job. My job in the team would be to provide the ideas and to get other people to think creatively. I would not be interested in being 'in charge' as I think that stifles innovation. Of course, we would have to work-to-time deadlines, but somebody else would do that.

I am an ambitious person and would like to be recognized as an expert in my field. I am not sure whether I would like to be a straightforward manager as that makes me think of great heaps of paperwork.

The person who wrote the above description actually worked in a large, somewhat bureaucratic organization. The points he focused on concerned flexibility, team membership, creativity and control. However, he realized that there was something of a conflict between his ambitions and there was something of a conflict between his ambition and the sort of job he wanted. To fulfill his wish in real life it would be necessary to assume a higher profile. In reality, he was introverted and rather disorganized as an administrator. He also needed to take more responsibility for his own actions.

TEN WAYS TO CHANGE

If you have completed the ideal job exercise, you should have identified some aspects of your behaviour that you want to explore. However, depending on how formal you want to be, there are six aspects of each 'problem' to examine. For example,

1. What is the problem? Being confident with new people and being able to talk to them in an open manner.
2. What does it affect? My work and social activities.
3. Where does it happen? At work with customers and at social events like parties.
4. When does it happen? Most of the time. Although I do find it easy to talk to some people.
5. Why does it happen? I am a shy person. I get embarrassed easily.
6. What can I do about it? Learn ways of appearing and of being more extrovert.

The example given is not at all unusual. So what can be done about it? The clue lies in the word 'extroverted', because what this person would like to be is less self-conscious and introspective, and more outgoing and sociable. What follows are guidelines on some of the ways of promoting this, and of other patterns of behaviour. The advice is centered on the five main personality dimensions used throughout this book.

❖ I Would like to be more Assertive and Socially Skilled

If you feel yourself to be more introverted than you would like you can address the 'problem' by concentrating on being more assertive and persuasive, and by developing your social skills. The question is really one of having more personal impact and of being comfortable interacting with other people.

Interestingly, when it comes to assertiveness, most people operate in one of three ways, or sometimes they switch at random between all three. So in those situations where you want to make a mark you either act submissively (a typically introverted approach), aggressively (which happens with some extroverts), or assertively. There is a difference between these responses in that assertive behaviour is about putting your point of view across in a positive way without 'steam-rolling' the other person; aggressive behaviour means standing up for your rights regardless of anyone else, and submissive behaviour means accepting what comes your way.

Most submissive people are self-effacing and tend to express what they think in an apologetic sort of manner. They use lots of qualifying phrases such as, 'If you have the time… Could you possibly…' – 'I'm sorry to bother you.' In addition, they tend to work around or avoid problems, rather than confront them. Thus, if you tend to be submissive and want to make a greater impact, consider using the following strategies:

1. Use more statements beginning with 'I' – e.g., 'I think …', 'I want …', 'I feel…'
2. Try not to use qualifying statement, e.g., 'Can you…?' Rather than 'I wonder if…?'
3. Actively ask other people what they think about things, e.g., 'What do you think?'
4. Suggest ways of fixing problems, e.g., 'We could do…'

These are also ways of being more persuasive. In addition, you will find that if you are more positive with other people, they will be more positive and interested in you. This will, in turn, make you feel more confident. Furthermore, in situations such as meetings or indeed just social gatherings, introverted people tend to be 'themselves' regardless of the social setting. This is actually a bad habit, because to fit into a social situation you actually have to behave in the appropriate way. We talked about this earlier when we highlighted the four main ways in which we tend to impress other people. It is also what distinguishes introverted people from extroverted people. Extroverts are always on the lookout for cues from other people as to how they should behave. In this way, they are also quicker to respond to different situations and are more likely to start conversations. The trick for the introvert is to read the situations more like an extrovert and to make the effort to match the mood of the situation. In a curious way, this actually means not letting your feelings dictate your behaviour. Thus, if you do not constantly worry about how you feel and whether or not you are enjoying a situation, you will actually feel more comfortable.

❖ I Would like to be More Self-aware

If you are, highly extroverted person you may need to become more self-aware and to consider your actions more thoroughly before you launch yourself into situations. This involves taking particular notice of your own behaviour, because it is only this sort of feedback that will help you to change. In particular, concentrate on the following sources:

1. *Criticism:* This may sound like a strange thing on which to concentrate, but it is a useful source of direct personal feedback. So the next time that someone comments on your behaviour, hold on to the information and consider what it means. The chances are that if it is constructive feedback, they will have pinpointed an aspect of your behaviour that you can at least modify, e.g., talking over people when they are talking or generally being insensitive to another person's feelings.
2. *Successful situation:* This is about realizing how you affect other people. Be aware of the reasons why you were successful and what this tells you about yourself. Was it at the emotional or psychological expense of another person? How could you have achieved the same result in a more sensitive way?
3. *Extreme reactions:* If people seem to react to you in extreme ways, the problem is that you probably strike them as being extreme. Always assume that it is something that you are doing that is producing reactions in other people. If you do this, you will get nearer to understanding your own behaviour.

In summary, the best advice to someone who wants to 'tone down' his behaviour is to be more aware of the cues about himself that other people give him. Also, he should use this information to adapt the way in which he deals with other people.

❖ I Would like to be More Open

The issue with tough-minded people is that they may lack the ability to project themselves as being genuinely concerned, and they may find it difficult to establish an easy rapport with other people. They can also be very impatient with those who are not performing jobs or doing things in the way in which they would like.

The practical side to being seen as more genuine is to accept that other people, including yourself, are fallible. Also, you should take care to share your thoughts and feelings with those you are dealing with and to make a point of finding out how they feel. These are key aspects of achieving a working rapport with people. In fact, psychologists have extensively examined the whole business of establishing rapport. They have found that there are a number of important behaviours:

1. *Use of small talk:* This is something the tough-minded person can find irritating (because it appears to waste time), but it is the basis for starting and establishing a relationship. The best approach is to discover some mutually safe topic and to use it to prime the conversation, e.g., sports or the news.

2. *Being empathetic:* Again, the tough-minded person may find that he has little time for other people's problems. But it is an established fact that being able to 'see' problems or situations from another person's perspective is a good way of maintaining rapport. In particular, it is important to demonstrate that you know how it feels and to give other people the space to express their feelings.

3. *Use of humour:* This is arguably another behaviour that gets in the way of business, but it is an important tool for putting people at their ease. Telling a joke at your own expense also makes you appear more genuine and human.

Tough-minded people need to accept that there are behaviours that will make them appear more tender-minded and thus, more approachable. Also, they need to realize that they do not have to be 'tough' with people to achieve results.

❖ I Would like to be Less Sensitive

The 'problem' with being tender-minded is that you are usually too sensitive to other people and you sometimes feel hurt as a result of what they say or do in their relationship with you. Classic causes of hurt are:

1. The feeling that you are being taken for granted.
2. A direct criticism of your behaviour.
3. An unexpected sarcastic or personal remark.
4. Being put down in front of other people.
5. Being ignored by someone who knows you well.
6. Having your feelings overlooked.

This behaviour can provoke unhappiness, make you feel angry or encourage you to take revenge. It is also the case that these reactions on your part are counterproductive.

They do not make you feel better, apart from may be the revenge option. However, if you really are tender-minded, it is unlikely that you will ever put a revenge plan into operation. A better way of dealing with your feelings is to indulge in what psychologists call constructive 'self-talk'. For example,

1. 'You really can't please everyone. Some people will always get upset with me.'
2. 'Why should I always want people to approve of me? I should be confident in myself.'
3. 'This reaction is only revealing a flaw in them. They are obviously rather insecure.'

   And, the classic psychiatric mantra:

4. 'I decide whether to be hurt or not. It's up to me if I want to be upset'.

As with the tough-minded individual, the other way of changing your behaviour is to adopt an empathic, rather than a sympathetic, style of responding to other people. Empathy concerns 'being with' another person and not losing track of the fact that this is a separate person with his own thoughts and feelings. It is impossible and unrealistic to take on the burden of caring about every single thing that happens to the people you meet. You must realize that it is quite acceptable to put your own emotional welfare first.

❖ I Would like to be More Creative

Those who operate in a conforming way, and so tend to favour rules and regulations, can sometimes benefit from taking a 'looser' view of life. In fact, highly conforming people can learn something from those who are more creative.

Creativity is not necessarily a flash of inspiration; rather it is a process of generating new or improved ideas. It is a reaction against the generating new or improved ideas. It is a reaction against the mindset that states 'that's the way I've always done it', which stands in the way of improving and capitalizing on new ideas and techniques.

If you are unfamiliar with creative techniques, they are just ways of 'viewing' a problem from a different angle. An expression that is sometimes used is 'unfreezing' – an appropriate term because it encapsulates the process of moving *away* from fixed and established ways of doing things. The process of unfreezing can also act as the stimulus for what are recognized as the four main creative skills:

1. ***Fluency:*** This is having numerous ideas. The way to do this is to think of every solution you can to a problem. A technique used here is 'brainstorming',

which has only two rules: the more ideas, however (apparently) bizarre, the better; and judgement is always left until after all the ideas have been generated.

2. *Originality:* This is the production of unusual ideas. One method you can use is to avoid logic (lateral thinking). For example, you can simply reverse situations. Imagine that fuel is free at petrol stations; what effect would this have? What would happen if the shop-floor workers decided how much the Managing Director should earn?

3. *Flexibility:* This is the production of a range of solutions to a problem. Obviously, you are more likely to hit on a successful solution if you have more than one thing to choose from. A method that is used here goes under the grand title of 'morphological analysis'. Basically, this involves detailing all the possible combination of an item. For example, if you were designing a paint container, you could alter the volume, shape and material. In this way, you could suggest a one-litre rectangular, paper container. Well, if it works for milk, why not for paint?

4. *Elaboration:* This is the ability to build on existing ideas – an ability that should not be underestimated as many successful products and services are extensions of old ideas. For example, many products or services are based on very old ideas, such as aspects of nature or biological systems.

If you would like to try to use creative techniques, there are many books on the subject. A large bookshop or library will be able to provide you with plenty of choice. However, you should bear in mind that creative techniques, by their very nature, involve an element of risk. So you have to be able to cope with potential failure. However, a quotation by the management guru, Tom Peters, may be useful, 'the way to accelerate your success rate is to double your failure rate'!

❖ I Would like to Plan Things Better

The highly creative person tends to suffer from a degree of disorganization. One solution to this problem is to address the question of planning. Paradoxically, while this is viewed by most people as being important, very few actually plan in a logical way. Indeed, the creative person in particular may believe that things are best left to work themselves out and that formal planning stifles their spontaneity. However, in the modern business world it is seldom a good idea to leave things to chance in this way.

Planning is the process of defining a goal and of deciding how you are going to get there. To be effective, the goal must be started in specific terms and ideally should be measurable, attainable, realistic and time-bounded. This means that you must know that when you have achieved it, it is a realistic target to which you can commit yourself, and that it is underpinned by some sort of timetable. This process, which can be summarized by the mnemonic SMART (Specific, Measurable. Attainable, Realistic, Time bound), forms the basis of informed goal setting.

In addition to goal setting, the creative person needs to realize that many business activities, by their very nature, have to be performed in a predictable and methodical way, and that the smallest part of the processes have to be organized and controlled. Thus, while it is valuable to be able to think of new ways of performing tasks, these ideas need to be properly thought out and supported with appropriate evidence. In consequence, if you are in the position of presenting new ideas you should:

1. Choose the right time.
2. Prepare for likely objections.
3. Explain the idea fully and effectively.
4. Involve others and (ideally) and appeal to their self-interest.
5. Generate interest, i.e., what are the benefits?
6. Justify the use of resources.
7. Be enthusiastic.

These are ways of giving your arguments structure and of making them more convincing. In addition, while as the owner of a new idea you may be rightly proud of and want acceptance, you should always, bear in mind that there is frequently a reaction against anything that upsets the status quo. In the light of this, your best approach is to use your creative drive in a planned and disciplined manner.

❖ I Would like to be Less of a Perfectionist

If you are a very high-structure person, you may want to control your desire to organize and control your environment. You may find that you may wish always to finish jobs to your high personal standards actually hinders your progress, because it is difficult to perform perfectly within specific time deadlines, and that it is almost impossible to live up to your own standards. The reason that you must complete tasks yourself is that you have no external reference point, other than the fact that nobody seems to do anything as well as you. This can cause real problems if you have a job that involves organizing or managing other people. In this situation, your perfectionist attitude will make you a very critical person, but more importantly, it will make it difficult for you to delegate tasks. Yours will be a 'if you want it to be done properly, then you've got to do it yourself' approach. Naturally, this will only make matters worse because if you do jobs for people or 'tidy-up' after the, they will never improve. The whole situation can rapidly become completely circular.

The only solution is to step outside your feelings and to accept that not everyone believes that precision is important; that people have different ways of doing things, which may not be the way you would do it, but which can be just as effective. Thus, the crucial thing to explore is how you affect other people. Your ability to plan and to be systematic is no doubt inspirational, but perhaps because of your skills in this area you make other people feel inadequate. You should also consider whether your perfectionism is more of a 'problem' in some situations than in others. Perhaps it would be possible to make a deal with yourself and to give yourself permission to be a perfectionist in some areas if you are the sort of person who is very tidy, and then try to confine your tidiness to a particular aspect of your life rather than all of it. This could manifest itself in keeping your own office or special room at home tidy and attempting to live with the untidiness in the rest of your world. In fact, while this may sound like a difficult thing to do, it is the only way to start the process of desensitizing yourself to other people's culture. It boils down to altering the way in which you perceive disorder.

❖ I Would like to be More Organized

If you are a low-structure person, you probably have completely the reverse problem of the perfectionist just described. Stereotypically, you are someone who suffers from low personal organization, who goes through life in a casual and spontaneous way. This can show itself in being absent-minded and, practically in losing things and being late for appointments.

The answer is to start to plan formally what you need to do. In particular, pay attention to the points made in the previous 'I would like to plan things better' section. Also, because low-structure people frequently have little concept of time – hence they are late for appointments – you could try to manage your time more effectively.

The simplest way to manage your time is to keep a diary. However, there is no point in doing this unless you record the appropriate details and consult it each day. But if you are a low-structure person, this probably strikes you as being complete anathema, because you don't like conforming to structured ways of behaving. To complicate matters further, you may also be the sort of person who likes to disregard rules and regulations. So perhaps the only way to square this particular circle is to say that to organize yourself, because it makes you more effective, does not necessarily mean that you have to accept all the restraints that society tries to impose on you.

At a programmatic level, you will need to:

1. Plan ahead.
2. Keep proper up-to-date files.

3. Delegate to others.
4. Cut time 'social grazing' (spending long periods socializing).
5. Control and prioritize paperwork.
6. Control procrastination.

You can also use the 'salami' method, which involves breaking jobs down into manageable chunks and deciding what needs to be done first. In particular, you may need to recognize the difference between tasks that are 'important and urgent', 'important and not urgent', 'not important and urgent' and 'not important and not urgent', because while the first sort of task tends to get done, the last two get in the way of the second. It is part of the human condition that unless we discipline ourselves, we spend most of our time dealing with the easiest things, in the latter case the 'not important and not urgent'. In contrast, what you should always do are important things before urgent things.

Overall, the best approach is to get the worst over with first (it will make you feel better), and if you tend to be a procrastinator, to tell other people what you are going to do. It is a fact that if you 'go public' you are more likely to get it done. It is also important to realize that you should do difficult tasks during your prime time, i.e., the time of day when you work best, which is usually not the first hour, nor the hour before you are ready to go home.

If you embrace some of these ideas you will start to become better organized and to manage your time more effectively.

❖ I Would like to be able to Motivate Myself

One of the 'problems' of being a highly confident person is that you can be too placid and easygoing. This may make it difficult for you to motivate yourself and to achieve your full potential. In addition, you may find that you do not react to stressful or difficult situations in the same way as other people. Indeed, you may be what is termed a low-reactive person, and give the impression of being 'thick-skinned' and unresponsive. Sometimes, this can work to your disadvantage as you may project, unwittingly, an uncaring or even a smug image.

The solution is to become more aware of other people and to develop a more empathic approach. You also need to consider what would actually move you, and those aspects of work that you find exciting, and stimulating. Perhaps the problem is that your confidence is reinforced by a job or a lifestyle that is too easy for you, and which is not providing enough challenge. It may be necessary to re-examine the work or life values that are important to you, and to seek to incorporate more of them in what you do. Some example values were given in the ideal job exercise (achievement, independence, creativity, money, altruism), but it was by no means a complete list, and you could also include the following:

1. Excitement – Doing new and stimulating work.
2. Status – Having a powerful position.
3. Role modeling – Being an inspiration to other people.
4. Risk – Gambling for the prospect of money or status.
5. Intellectual challenge – Stretching your mind.
6. Responsibility – Being in charge of other people.
7. Expertise – Being the 'best' in your field.

Some of these may hold the clue to your motivation. If it is a question of wanting to be the best, then further study or a professional course may be the answer. If you desire responsibility, then taking on a more managerial role could be the way ahead. Indeed, being put in charge of other people is a good way to be forced to develop a more open style, and a good arena in which to practice a more consultative and empathic approach. You should also remember that all of these values can be stimulated outside work, e.g., by helping in the community or by doing voluntary work. The really important issue is that your rewards are 'self-administered' and that you identify how to motivate yourself. Thus, the ideal situation is to isolate attainable rewards that require considerable effort and a combination of factors to achieve.

❖ I Would like to Feel Less Anxious

There are many people who would like to be less anxious or emotional, but the first point to realize is that we could not live without anxiety. It is an extremely useful aspect of our personality and behavioural repertoire because it alerts us to 'dangers' and can actually make our minds more agile. However, it is possible to be too emotional and this can be a cause of disorganized thinking, unwanted emotion and even panic. It is also closely related to stress, as being very emotional can cause us to feel stressed.

Like anxiety, stress can either be helpful or make us feel depressed and miserable because there is 'good' stress, or stimulation, and 'bad' stress, or strain. For example, most sales people thrive on the 'kick' (stimulation) they get from selling products to new people every day. Other professionals, such as business executives, suffer strain from being overloaded with too many appointments and having to meet many different people.

The first step to take in controlling feelings of anxiety or stress is to acknowledge those situations in which it is a 'problem'. For example, at work the following are all potential cause of stress:

1. *Change:* Any change to your working environment.
2. *Selling*: Selling products or services, or yourself.
3. *Time:* Having do so things with insufficient time.
4. *Bureaucracy:* Having to fight through many rules and regulations.
5. *Conflict:* Dealing with 'difficult' customers or colleagues.
6. *Isolation:* Having to work by yourself.
7. *Status:* Having no authority or power.
8. *Promotion:* Having poor or badly defined promotion prospects.
9. *Routine:* Having to do boring or undemanding work.
10. *Support:* Having little or no support for what you say or do.

More generally, you may also become anxious in a whole range of non-work situations that involve making decisions or dealing with other people. You may also react in an emotional way to how other people feel. For example, you may become affected by other people's pain or even by the injustice you see in the world.

Whatever the cause, you need to develop ways of coping with those situations that you know make you feel anxious. For instance, you could use strategies such as confrontation or distancing. The first involves getting other people to change their behaviour and so reduce your anxiety; the second is to detach yourself from the situation and forget it. Other important approaches include:

1. Goal-setting and time management
2. Being more assertive
3. Relaxation training

The last suggestion is one of the most important to explore because it provides you with a 'portable' way of reducing anxiety. The important techniques to learn about are muscle relaxation, meditation and visualization. What is more, you can easily teach yourself about any of these by acquiring one of the many books on the subject. Thus, a visit to a good book-shop or your local library will equip you with a number of extremely practical 'How to ...' publications.

PRACTICING NEW BEHAVIOURS

Before we look at the best situations in which you can practice new behaviours, it is worth examining some of the barriers that prevent you from achieving what you want. These barriers are common beliefs that can block change; the two most common are:

1. If I have problems I must be inadequate. Nobody goes through life without encountering problems and without changing the way in which they respond to situations. The process of overcoming obstacles is part of living and has little to do with being inadequate.

2. It is better to keep your problems to yourself. Sometimes this is true, but if you want to alter your behaviour successfully, you will need, by definition, to involve other people. The word 'feedback' has been mentioned a number of times in this chapter, and importantly it centres on observing how other people react towards you, and at times actually asking them what they think.

The point is that in order to change your behaviour, you need to accept that you can improve and that it is a perfectly normal wish to want to project yourself in the best possible light. Indeed, the belief you have in yourself, and the attitudes you have towards people and situations, are some of the few behaviour patterns that are totally within your control.

Some situations are better than others for practicing new behaviours. The following guidelines are based on actual research to help people to change their behaviour:

1. If you are going to try out something new, start with situations in which your chances of success are high. For example, if you have a job, do not decide immediately to practice on the boss, but pick a safe situation where you will be able to see immediate benefits from your new behaviour.

2. Choose situations where the person will not be too surprised. Remember that we expect other people's behaviour to be consistent and are suspicious when somebody suddenly starts to act out of character. Indeed, a common reaction is to think that the person must be guilty of something. Obviously, this attitude is to be avoided at all costs, so make sure that you practice either where others don't know what to expect of you, or in situations where people know you are trying something new. The latter suggests that you try out new behaviours with friends, colleagues or partners.

3. All successful change depends on feedback. This implies that you should practice in situations where you know quickly what the effect has been. In reality, this usually means in safe one-to-one situations or when you are dealing with new contracts or acquaintances.

We have discussed earlier MSQ; A tool for Personality Test. We give hereunder another tool for Personality Test along with Personality and Career Profiles.

PERSONALITY TEST

Look at each statement in turn. You have to assess yourself in relation to each statement on a scale of 1 to 10

If you gave yourself a score of 1, this would mean that the statement was not true of you at all. A score of 10 would mean that the statement described you perfectly. A score of 5 or 6 would mean that the statement is sometimes true for you, and sometimes untrue. Therefore, the larger the score you give yourself, the more you think the statement describes you.

You have to respond to each statement.

You are not being tested, so you cannot be right or wrong.

Your answers will give a picture of how you usually are and the way you generally think and feel.

Tick the number in each scale that is true for you. For the time being, pay no attention to the letter at the end of each row. The letter is to assist you in scoring your results and how to do this will be explained later when you have completed the test.

1. **I prefer to be left alone to get with my work.**

1	2	3	4	5	6	7	8	9	10		SO

2. **I make myself known to everybody.**

1	2	3	4	5	6	7	8	9	10		A

3. **I always make sure I get my facts correct.**

1	2	3	4	5	6	7	8	9	10		F

4. **I can often speak or act without enough thought.**

1	2	3	4	5	6	7	8	9	10		SP

5. **I cannot get difficulties out of my mind.**

1	2	3	4	5	6	7	8	9	10		I

6. **I take proper time to prepare for things that might be difficult.**

1	2	3	4	5	6	7	8	9	10		D

7. **Nobody stops me from speaking if I have something to say.**

1	2	3	4	5	6	7	8	9	10		A

8. **I like it best when someone else takes the lead.**

1	2	3	4	5	6	7	8	9	10		P

9. **I do not like to do anything too different from my friends.**

1	2	3	4	5	6	7	8	9	10		G

10. **I am affected by how people feel.**

1	2	3	4	5	6	7	8	9	10		I

11. **I make sure that what I do is done as well as it possibly can be.**

1	2	3	4	5	6	7	8	9	10		D

12. **I am quick to sense people's difficulties.**

1	2	3	4	5	6	7	8	9	10		I

13. **I like to avoid dealing with feelings if at all possible.**

1	2	3	4	5	6	7	8	9	10		F

14. **I do not react hastily.**

1	2	3	4	5	6	7	8	9	10		D

15. **I am at my best when working alongside others.**

1	2	3	4	5	6	7	8	9	10		G

16. **I do not like going out very much.**

1	2	3	4	5	6	7	8	9	10		P

17. **To have fun and entertainment in my leisure time is important to me.**

1	2	3	4	5	6	7	8	9	10		SO

18. **I pay no attention to the way others are feeling.**

1	2	3	4	5	6	7	8	9	10		F

19. **I get bored easily.**

1	2	3	4	5	6	7	8	9	10		SP

20. **I am less sensitive than other people.**

1	2	3	4	5	6	7	8	9	10		F

21. **It takes a lot to dent my confidence.**

1	2	3	4	5	6	7	8	9	10		F

22. **Always doing something new and different appeals to me.**

1	2	3	4	5	6	7	8	9	10		SP

23. **A favourite activity of mine is entertaining friends.**

1	2	3	4	5	6	7	8	9	10		G

24. **I control any feelings of annoyance.**

1	2	3	4	5	6	7	8	9	10		P

25. **I always speak my mind.**

1	2	3	4	5	6	7	8	9	10		A

26. **I can lose sleep because I dwell upon past events.**

1	2	3	4	5	6	7	8	9	10		I

27. **I do not look for people to be with.**

1	2	3	4	5	6	7	8	9	10		SO

28. **I am a contented person.**

1	2	3	4	5	6	7	8	9	10		D

29. **I can easily make decisions by myself.**

1	2	3	4	5	6	7	8	9	10		SO

30. **I do not like to persuade people to change their minds.**

1	2	3	4	5	6	7	8	9	10		P

31. **I do not find it difficult to stick at one thing.**

1	2	3	4	5	6	7	8	9	10		D

32. **I can change my mind at a moment's notice.**

1	2	3	4	5	6	7	8	9	10		SP

33. **I am often the one who gets people involved when they get together.**

1	2	3	4	5	6	7	8	9	10		A

34. **I see no harm in passing on confidences to my friends.**

1	2	3	4	5	6	7	8	9	10		G

35. **People would consider me insightful.**

1	2	3	4	5	6	7	8	9	10		I

36. **I generally agree if someone feels very strongly about something.**

1	2	3	4	5	6	7	8	9	10		P

37. **I generally win arguments.**

1	2	3	4	5	6	7	8	9	10		A

38. **Having friends is not particularly important to me.**

1	2	3	4	5	6	7	8	9	10		SO

39. **I do not like people to intrude on my space.**

1	2	3	4	5	6	7	8	9	10		SO

40. **I like people to call me anytime.**

1	2	3	4	5	6	7	8	9	10		G

PERSONALITY CHART

You can place your scores in the chart of personality. You mark your score with a cross (x) at the appropriate place. Scoring is from the centre of the graph. Enter your own score on the left or the right of the graph according to your dominant letter. The example below shows you how.

Example:

SO	Solitary	50 45 40 35 30 25 20 **X** 10	10 15 20 25 30 35 40 45 50	G	Gregarious
A	Assertive	50 45 40 35 30 25 20 15 10	10 15 **X** 25 30 35 40 45 50	P	Passive
I	Imaginative	50 45 40 35 30 25 20 15 10	10 15 20 25 30 **X** 40 45 50	F	Factual
SP	Spontaneous	50 45 40 35 30 25 **X** 15 10	10 15 20 25 30 35 40 45 50	D	Deliberate

The personality characteristics drawn from the example chart are SO, P, F and SP, because these are the dominant letters shown by the score differences.

❖ If your Score is Borderline

The higher you score for any of the dominant letters, the more noticeably you behaviour will correspond to the description. If your score is borderline, your behaviour may change along that dimension, but may rarely become extremely noticeable. However, you will probably consider that your behaviour is generally more towards one side than the other. Therefore, choose the letter or letters that usually describe your behaviour.

Personality Chart

SO	Solitary	50 45 40 35 30 25 20 15 10	10 15 20 25 30 35 40 45 50	G	Gregarious
A	Assertive	50 45 40 35 30 25 20 15 10	10 15 20 25 30 35 40 45 50	P	Passive
I	Imaginative	50 45 40 35 30 25 20 15 10	10 15 20 25 30 35 40 45 50	F	Factual
SP	Spontaneous	50 45 40 35 30 25 20 15 10	10 15 20 25 30 35 40 45 50	D	Deliberate

Write in your dominant letters here.

Understanding Your Personality Further

Ask your partner, a friend or colleague to complete the questionnaire for how they perceive you. If the results differ from your own, it could lead to an interesting discussion. It is not that they, or you, are necessarily right or wrong.

In the end, it is up to you which of the results you decide to adopt as the truer representation of yourself. However, where there are differences, it always enlightening to ask: (1) how different perceptions of you might arise; and also (2) how important these differences might be in career terms.

Although, you behave in different ways, depending upon the circumstances you are in or the people you are with, you nevertheless have a personality that remains identifiable. If this were not true, people would not be able to anticipate your reactions; the very fact that there are aspects of you that are predictable testifies to your personality.

This is not to say that your personality will never change. It may well do so, especially if you make efforts to become aware of your potential and give yourself experiences that develop you. However, it seems practical to take your personality, as it is now in order to see how it may relate more successfully to one career rather than another.

Different careers do, by and large, require different characteristics. If you work at something that 'suits you' then you will avoid frustration, while your continuing satisfaction and enjoyment are more likely to be assured. It is also true that people with widely varying characteristics can do most careers equally enjoyably. It is bound to be so, since no two people are ever completely alike. However, in very broad terms, it makes sense to ask, 'In this career, how would my personality fit?' and, 'would I enjoy and be successful in this career for the very reason that my personality might be unusual?'

Personality is a complex subject. The aim here is to assist you to assess yourself in relation to some dimensions of personality that are useful in planning your career — what it is about the way you feel and behave that might make you more suited to one career rather than another. To do this, it is best to be honest with yourself as to how you see yourself. There are no rights or wrongs to a test of personality. What is wanted is a description of the real 'you'? Now, just in case you 'undersell' or 'oversell' yourself, you could ask other people who are close to you and know you well to complete the test for the way they see you. If that means you have to photocopy the test, it is all right for you to do so for this purpose. Then compare your own responses with that of others.

The most accurate description of 'you' is likely to be the person you are now, the way you behave and the person other people know and recognize. It is possible to answer the test on the basis of assuming how you think you want to be are day, but as you have not got there yet, you will need to think carefully what you have to do to change.

Another factor to consider is whether you might be using only some parts of your personality now, but wants to use other parts later on as you develop in your career. For example, if you are factual you might enjoy studying for a scientific career, but later on, if you find yourself working at a laboratory bench, you may find it has too little scope for you if your personality is also gregarious.

INTERPRETATION OF YOUR SCORES

People Dimensions

The personality test has two dimensions that describe the way you relate to people: (1) whether you tend to be solitary or gregarious; and (2) whether you tend to be assertive or passive:

SO – SOLITARY	**G – GREGARIOUS**
Self-reliant. Takes initiative on his own. Shows initiative. May be seen as either quiet or arrogant. Works in own way. Can socialize but sometimes shy. Not at ease socially. Detached and purposeful. Makes up own mind. Resourceful.	Seeks company. Hates to be alone. Loyal and provides support. May be persuaded by the group out of need to be accepted. Changes behaviour to fit in. Resolves differences between others. Participative, enjoys making decisions with others.
A – ASSERTIVE	**P – PASSIVE**
Aggressive. May be dominant and stubborn. Seen as 'pushy'. May talk	Keeps matters to himself. Gives way rather than argue. Easy to get on with. Often

Contd...

loudly. Gets the point across. Determined, sometimes risk-taking, gets what he wants. May be seen as a 'show off', but also gains respect. May lose sight of how people are affected. Critical. Demanding. Takes responsibility.	good team member. Accommodating and not easily annoyed. May avoid saying what is on his mind. Avoids confrontation. Tries hard to please. Cooperative, respectful and helpful.

Task Dimensions

The questionnaire also has two factors that relate to the task: (1) whether you tend to be imaginative or factual; (2) whether you tend to be spontaneous or deliberate:

I – IMAGINATIVE	F– FACTUAL
Sensitive and aware of people's feelings. Emotional and often expressive. Makes decisions with heart rather than head. Easily affected, hurt by criticism. Spends too much time on small things. Often discouraged and frustrated, but also intuitive and creative. Responsive to feelings and/or ideas.	Sees things logically. Usually composed and has 'feet on the ground'. Likes orderly, structured behaviour. Not easily distracted, does things in a controlled way. Objective and analytical, sees the essential point. May miss subtle issues that bother others. Likes information and facts.
SP – SPONTANEOUS	**D – DELIBERATE**
Lively and impulsive. Likes change and situations which are fast moving and different. Often finds it difficult to stick to one thing or to finish what he has started. Amusing and enthusiastic, his excitement can infect others.	Calm, stable and dependable. Patient in waiting for things to take their time. Takes things as they come. The slow, deliberate approach allows people to depend upon him. Could appear dull or unresponsive. Predictable. Copes with pressure. Gets things done in an orderly way.

Your orientations towards the task and the manner in which you relate to people have implications for all careers. Not all of the descriptions will necessarily match you exactly, though the general description they give may be important in relation to different areas of work.

DESCRIPTION OF PERSONALITY TITLES

The personality test provides 16 combinations, based upon the eight descriptions that are formed from the four dimensions. For example, a researcher is solitary, passive, factual and deliberate.

From your own four sets of letters, you can locate yourself in the chart of individual personality titles.

Look first at the top line. Locate yourself to the left or the right of the chart, simply by saying, 'Am I factual or imaginative?' Then, looking at the bottom line of the chart, ask you, 'Am I deliberate or spontaneous?' This will locate you in one of the four columns.

You repeat the procedure by looking at the rows. Looking at the left-hand side of the chart, ask yourself, 'Am I gregarious or solitary?' Then from the right-hand side of the chart, 'Am I assertive or passive? You will now have located yourself in one of the 16 boxes.

Remember that you are more clearly in one area than another if your scores are more at the extreme end of each dimension. Where your scores are around the middle range, you may consider that, on balance, an adjacent area might be more like you. For example, in the chart below, number 13, a researcher, might be number 9, an arranger, if he or she is a little more assertive.

Chart of Individual Personality Titles

Task	Factual	Factual	Imaginative	Imaginative	People
Gregarious	1 Director	2 Opportunist	3 Coach	4 Crusader	Assertive
Gregarious	5 Completer	6 Associate	7 Confidant	8 Colleague	Passive
Solitary	9 Arranger	10 Adviser	11 Designer	12 Idealist	Assertive
Solitary	13 Researcher	14 Implementer	15 Specialist	16 Wanderer	Passive

My dominant letters, from the personality chart, were:

1. **FDAG - Director**
   Characteristics: Factual, Deliberate, Assertive and Gregarious

2. **FSpAG - Opportunist**
   Characteristics: Factual, Spontaneous, Assertive and Gregarious

3. **IDAG - Coach**
   Characteristics: Imaginative, Deliberate, Assertive and Gregarious

4. **ISpAG - Crusader**
   Characteristics: Independent, Spontaneous, Assertive and Gregarious

5. **FDPG - Completer**
   Characteristics: Factual, Deliberate, Passive and Gregarious

6. **FSpPG - Associate**
   Characteristics: Factual, Spontaneous, Passive and Gregarious

7. **IDPG - Confidant**
   Characteristics: Independent, Deliberate, Passive and Gregarious

8. **ISpPG - Colleague**
   Characteristics: Independent, Spontaneous, Passive and Gregarious

9. **FDASo - Arranger**
   Characteristics: Factual, Deliberate, Assertive and Solitary

10. **FSpASo - Adviser**
    Characteristics: Factual, Spontaneous, Assertive and Solitary

11. **IDASo - Designer**
    Characteristics: Imaginative, Deliberate, Assertive and Solitary

12. **ISpASo - Idealist**
    Characteristics: Independent, Spontaneous, Assertive and Solitary

13. **FDPSo - Researcher**
    Characteristics: Factual, Deliberate, Passive and Solitary

14. **FSpPSo - Implementer**
    Characteristics: Factual, Spontaneous, Passive and Solitary

15. **IDPSo - Specialist**
    Characteristics: Independent, Deliberate, Passive and Solitary

16. **ISpPSo - Wanderer**
    Characteristic: Independent, Spontaneous, Passive and Solitary

Personality and Career Profiles

Code

F Factual

I Imaginative

S Spontaneous

D Deliberate

A Assertive

P Passive

G Gregarious

S. No.	Career	F	I	S	D	A	P	G	SO
1.	Accountant	✓			✓	✓			
2.	Actor		✓	✓					
3.	Administrator	✓			✓				
4.	Advertising copywriter		✓						
5.	Advertising executive					✓		✓	
6.	Aerobics instructor			✓		✓		✓	
7.	Aeronautical engineer	✓			✓				
8.	Airhostess		✓	✓			✓	✓	
9.	Anthropologist								✓
10.	Architect		✓		✓	✓			✓
11.	Armed forces officer	✓				✓		✓	
12.	Artist		✓						✓
13.	Armed forces personnel	✓				✓		✓	
14.	Art therapist		✓				✓		✓
15.	Artist		✓						✓
16.	Astronaut	✓			✓		✓		
17.	Astronomer	✓			✓		✓		✓
18.	Audiologist technician	✓					✓		✓
19.	Auditor	✓			✓		✓		✓
20.	Author		✓						✓
21.	Automobile technician	✓					✓		✓
22.	Bank clerk	✓			✓		✓		
23.	Bank manager	✓			✓	✓		✓	
24.	Biologist	✓					✓		✓
25.	Broker	✓		✓		✓			
26.	Bus driver						✓		✓
27.	Business consultant	✓				✓			
28.	Careers adviser						✓		
29.	Cashier	✓			✓		✓		
30.	Chef		✓	✓		✓			✓
31.	Chemical technologist	✓			✓		✓		✓
32.	Chemist	✓			✓				✓
33.	Chief executive					✓			

Contd...

34.	Child care worker						✓	✓	
35.	Civil engineer	✓			✓				
36.	Civil servant		✓		✓				
37.	Clerk	✓			✓		✓		
38.	Clinical psychologist	✓					✓		
39.	Club manager		✓			✓		✓	
40.	Commercial account manager	✓				✓			
41.	Community social worker		✓				✓	✓	
42.	Company secretary	✓			✓		✓		✓
43.	Computer hardware designer	✓			✓				
44.	Copywriter		✓						✓
45.	Cost accountant	✓			✓		✓		
46.	Counsellor		✓	✓			✓	✓	
47.	Customs officer	✓			✓	✓			✓
48.	Dental technician	✓			✓		✓		✓
49.	Dentist	✓			✓	✓			
50.	Design engineer		✓		✓				
51.	Designer		✓	✓					✓
52.	Dietician	✓					✓		✓
53.	Director media		✓			✓		✓	
54.	Editor		✓		✓		✓		
55.	Electrical engineer	✓			✓				
56.	Electrician	✓			✓				✓
57.	Electronics engineer	✓			✓				✓
58.	Elementary school teacher		✓				✓		
59.	English language teacher		✓	✓			✓		
60.	Environmental health officer	✓			✓				✓
61.	Fashion designer		✓	✓			✓		
62.	Financial controller	✓			✓	✓			
63.	Fitter						✓		✓
64.	Flight attendant		✓		✓		✓	✓	

Contd...

65.	Food hygiene inspector	✓			✓		✓		
66.	Freelance writer		✓	✓			✓		✓
67.	Furniture maker		✓		✓		✓		✓
68.	Graphic designer		✓	✓			✓		✓
69.	Head teacher					✓		✓	
70.	Hotel manager					✓		✓	
71.	Human resources manager	✓	✓			✓		✓	
72.	Industrial designer		✓		✓				
73.	Industrial relations officer	✓	✓			✓		✓	
74.	Interior designer		✓	✓					
75.	Interviewer		✓			✓			
76.	Journalist		✓	✓		✓			
77.	Judge				✓	✓			✓
78.	Laboratory technician	✓			✓		✓		
79.	Language teacher		✓	✓			✓		
80.	Lawyer				✓	✓			
81.	Legal executive				✓		✓		
82.	Librarian		✓		✓		✓		✓
83.	Library assistant		✓		✓		✓		✓
84.	Machinist						✓		✓
85.	Management consultant	✓		✓		✓		✓	
86.	Managing director				✓	✓			
87.	Marketing manager		✓		✓	✓			
88.	Mechanic	✓			✓		✓		✓
89.	Mechanic engineer	✓			✓				
90.	Medical representative			✓		✓			✓
91.	Miner				✓		✓	✓	
92.	Model fashion		✓	✓					
93.	Music producer	✓		✓		✓			
94.	Musician		✓	✓					
95.	Office manager	✓			✓	✓			

Contd...

96.	Outplacement consultant		✓		✓	✓		✓	
97.	Personal trainer			✓		✓		✓	
98.	Pharmacist	✓			✓	✓			
99.	Philosopher		✓	✓					✓
100.	Photographer		✓	✓			✓		✓
101.	Physical education teacher	✓		✓		✓		✓	
102.	Physiotherapist		✓	✓			✓		✓
103.	Pilot airplane	✓			✓		✓		✓
104.	Plumber	✓							✓
105.	Poet		✓	✓			✓		✓
106.	Police officer				✓	✓			
107.	Politician			✓		✓	✓		
108.	Producer films		✓		✓	✓		✓	
109.	Production manager		✓	✓		✓		✓	
110.	Programmer	✓			✓		✓		✓
111.	Psychiatrist		✓		✓		✓		✓
112.	Purchasing manager	✓		✓		✓			
113.	Quality controller	✓			✓				
114.	Quality inspector	✓			✓	✓			✓
115.	Quantity surveyor	✓			✓		✓		✓
116.	Receptionist		✓	✓			✓	✓	
117.	Reporter		✓	✓		✓			✓
118.	Sales executive			✓		✓			
119.	Sales manager					✓		✓	
120.	Sales trainer		✓	✓		✓			
121.	Salesperson			✓		✓			
122.	Science teacher	✓		✓			✓		
123.	Scriptwriter		✓	✓					✓
124.	Sculptor		✓	✓		✓			✓
125.	Secretary/PA		✓		✓		✓		

Contd...

126.	Security officer	✓			✓		✓		✓
127.	Soldier	✓		✓			✓		
128.	Solicitor		✓		✓		✓		
129.	Space salesperson		✓	✓		✓			✓
130.	Speech therapist		✓	✓		✓	✓		✓
131.	Sports coach			✓		✓		✓	
132.	Statistician	✓			✓		✓		✓
133.	Stockbroker	✓		✓		✓			
134.	Tax inspector	✓			✓		✓		✓
135.	Teacher						✓	✓	
136.	Training officer		✓		✓		✓		✓
137.	Work study officer	✓			✓	✓			✓
138.	Writer		✓	✓					✓
139.	Zoologist	✓		✓			✓		✓

SAMPLE MENTAL ABILITY AND APTITUDE TESTS

How to use this Test

Mental Ability and Aptitude Test is founded on research. It is designed to enable you to make better decisions about what you should do in the future. But whether you regard it as such.

The tests and questionnaires will give you an idea of what people can naturally do best—their aptitude. The term aptitude means a natural talent for succeeding in one area. The test seeks to identify the natural talent and they do not allow learning and knowledge to effect the results. In measuring aptitude of the people you may discover some potential which you have not explored in them and which should be focused and developed.

The tests are numbered 1 to 5, and they test logical, verbal, numerical, abstract and technological aptitudes of people. They are based on the type of tests used in vocational guidance and industrial training, but they are not the same. These tests will take about two hours to complete in total. But do not try to do them all without at least one break.

Detailed instructions and examples are given before each test, and one should complete the examples before beginning the actual test. Each test gradually gets more difficult. Answer all the questions, but do not linger too long over any one question.

If possible, time the tests with a stopwatch. If someone else can time the tests for you it is better. Do not stop in the middle of a test, and work quickly, but accurately.

1. Logical Reasoning

❖ Instructions

Each question has a string of shapes. There are three different shapes and each shape can be one of two sizes and white, black or black and white. You can see all the possible answers at the top of the page. Each string of shapes follows a pattern and you try to find the next two shapes in the pattern.

❖ Sample Tests

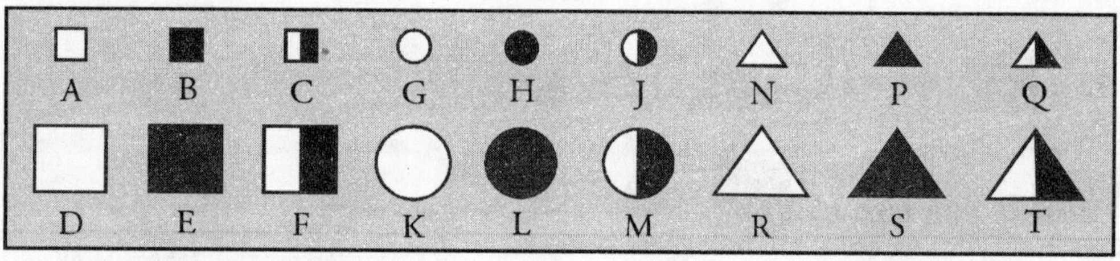

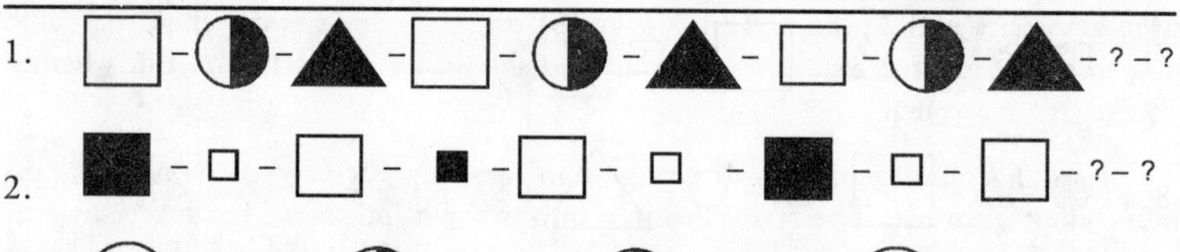

❖ Answer

1. DM 2. BD 3. KG

Check your answers. If you have made a mistake look at the question again and try to see where you went wrong. Now you can do the full test.

You have *20 minutes* to do as much as you can.

❖ Testing Logical Reasoning

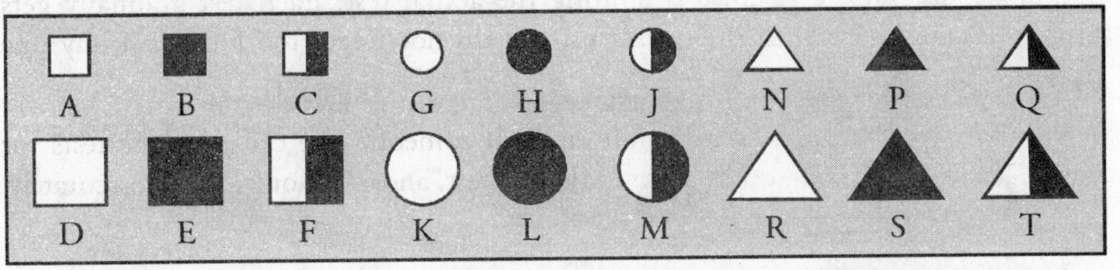

1. 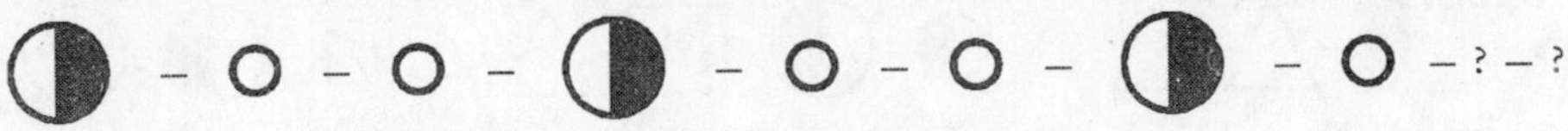

2. 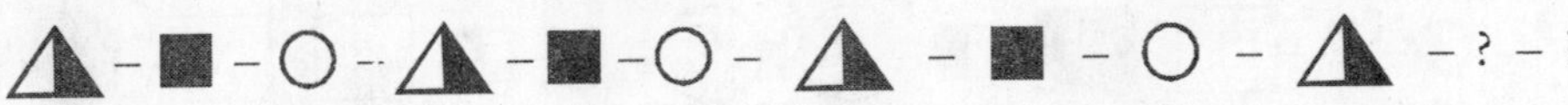

3. 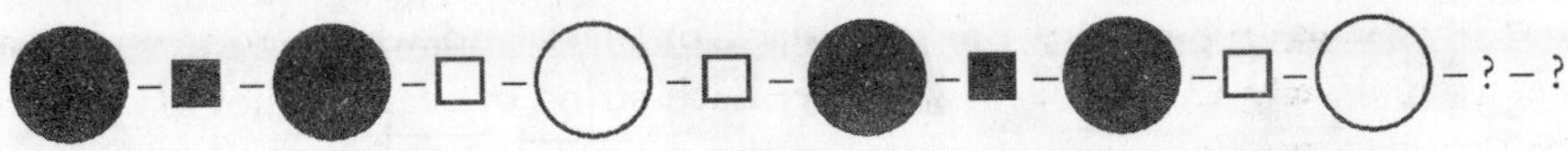

4. 

5. 

6. 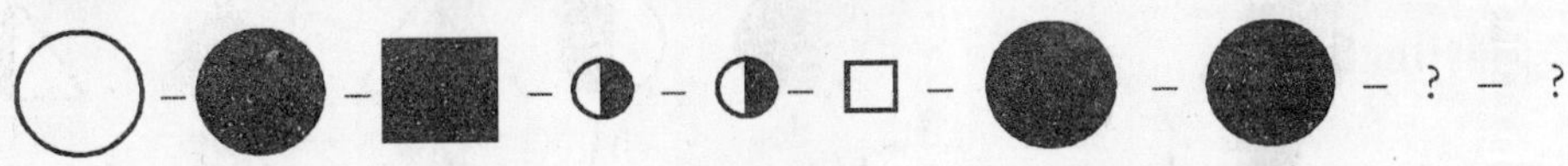

7. 

8. 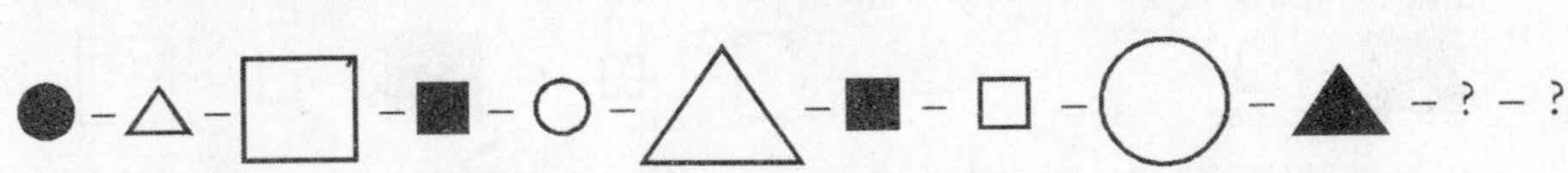

9. 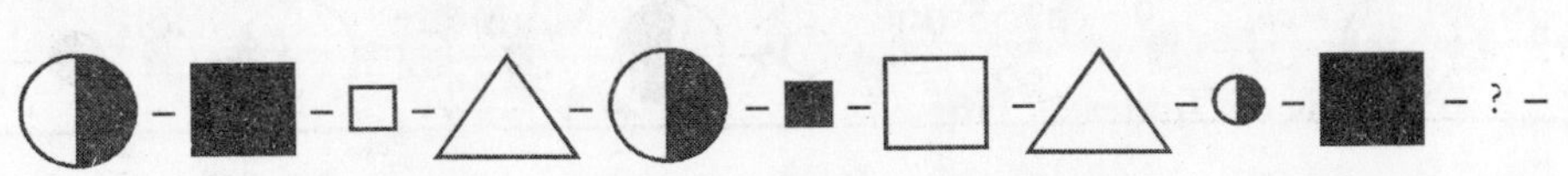

10. 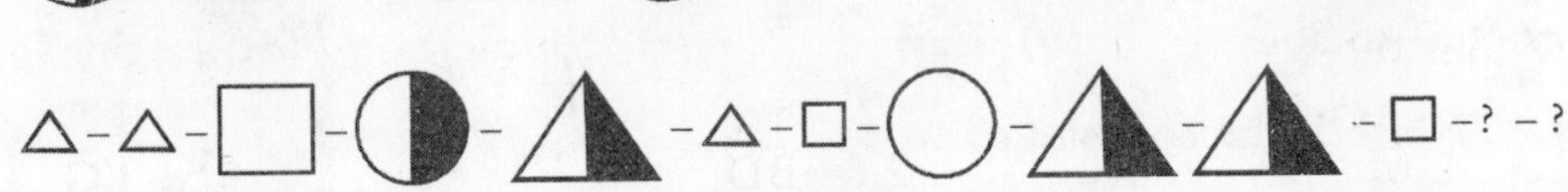

11. 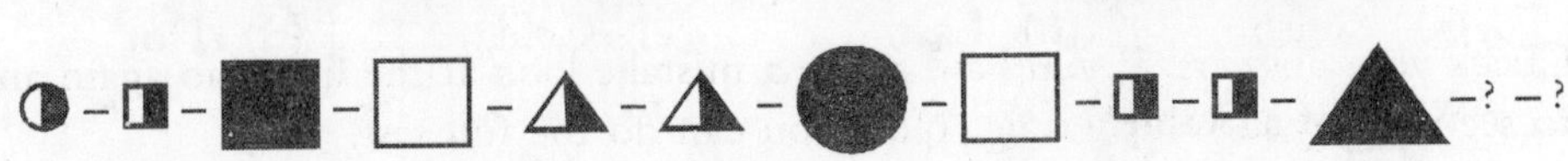

12. 

13. 

14. 

15. 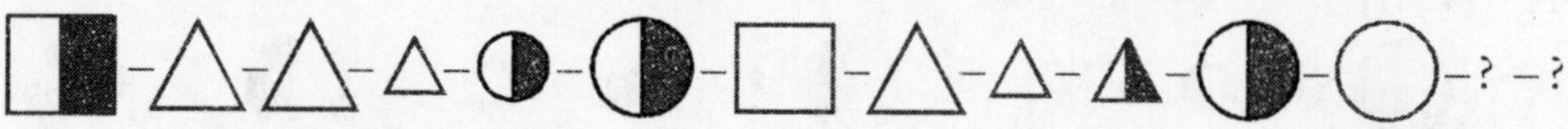

16. 

17. 

18. 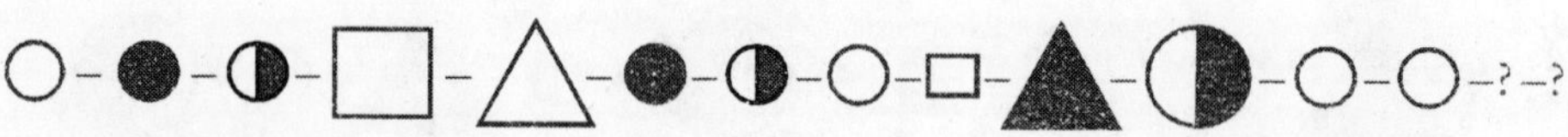

2. Words: Verbal Reasoning

❖ Instructions

For each question there are four alternative answers. Encircle the one which you think is correct. There are different types of questions but here are a few to try.

❖ Sample Tests

1. **Rock means:**

   (a) Water (b) Stone (c) Mountain (d) Roll

2. **Tractor is to Trailer as Horse is to:**

   (a) Stable (b) Cart (c) Saddle (d) Engine

3. **North is the opposite of:**

   (a) South (b) East (c) Cold (d) Hot

4. **What of a Stable?**

   (a) Pasture (b) Horse (c) Fountain (d) Building

❖ Answers

1. (b) 2. (b) 3. (a) 4. (d)

Now you can start the full test. You have 20 minutes to do as much as you can.

❖ Testing Verbal Reasoning

1. **Early is the opposite of:**

   (a) Evening (b) Late (c) Postpone (d) Breakfast

2. **Man is to Masculine as Woman is to:**

   (a) Intuitive (b) Madam (c) Girl (d) Feminine

3. **What does Frozen mean?**

   (a) Glued (b) Liquid (c) Solid (d) Water

4. **Circle is to Sphere as Square is to:**

   (a) Ball (b) Cube (c) Polygon (d) Triangle

5. **Cheap is the opposite of:**

   (a) Valueless (b) Trendy (c) Glitters (d) Expensive

6. **Who is third in alphabetical order?**

   (a) Rotring (b) Reynolds (c) Rodgers (d) Raymond

7. **Army is to land as Navy is to:**

   (a) Sea (b) Mountains (c) Ships (d) RAF

8. **What means the same as Portion?**

   (a) Whole (b) Part (c) Chip (d) None

9. **Poet is to Verse as Sculptor is to:**

   (a) Chisel (b) Statue (c) Stone (d) Artist

10. **What does Solitary mean?**

    (a) Crowd (b) Diamond (c) Partner (d) Alone

11. **Which is the odd one out?**

    (a) Feather (b) Egg (c) Fish (d) Beak

12. **Wise is to Foolish as Vain is to:**

(a) Modest (b) Pretty (c) Conceit (d) Proud

13. **Dynamic is the opposite of:**

(a) Electrical (b) Tardy (c) Static (d) Resistant

14. **Horse is to jockey as Car is to:**

(a) Vehicle (b) Butler (c) Cart (d) Chauffeur

15. **Acquiesce is the opposite of:**

(a) Clumsy (b) Obstacle (c) Quit (d) Protest

16. **What does Debate mean?**

(a) Comment (b) Talk (c) Argue (d) Create

17. **Which would be third in alphabetical order?**

(a) Sevene (b) Severn (c) Seveen (d) Seven

18. **Sentence is to paragraph as word is to:**

(a) Letter (b) Sentence (c) Paragraph (d) Phrase

19. **Wheels are to Car as Runners are to:**

(a) Lorry (b) Track (c) Tank (d) Sledge

20. **Permanent is the opposite of:**

(a) Stable (b) Temporary (c) Always (d) Part-time

21. **Which is the odd one out?**

(a) Seminal (b) Germane (c) Propagative (d) Derivative

22. **Which is the penultimate letter in the word REST?**

(a) R (b) E (c) S (d) T

23. **What is a Turbine?**

(a) Fish (b) Engine (c) Tower (d) String

24. **Capital is to Interest as labour is to:**

(a) Conservative (b) Wages (c) Authority (d) Machinery

25. **Never is to Seldom as Always is to:**

(a) Occasional (b) Usual (c) Sometimes (d) Everytime

26. **Certainty is the opposite of:**

(a) Correctness (b) Precision (c) Dubiety (d) Infinite

27. **Which is the odd one out?**

(a) Terse (b) Compact (c) Angry (d) Curt

28. **Bolt is to Nut as Hook is to:**

(a) Screw (b) Eye (c) Door (d) Grass

29. **Hereditary is to Environment as Nature is to:**

(a) Nurture (b) Ancestry (c) Health (d) Animal

30. **What is an Edifice?**

(a) Building (b) Illness (c) Boatyard (d) Executive

31. **Scabbard is to Sword as Quiver is to:**

(a) Tourniquet (b) Sheath (c) String (d) Arrow

32. **Irascible is the opposite of:**

(a) Striking (b) Flamboyant (c) Irritable (d) Phlegmatic

33. **Nurse is to Doctor as Secretary is to:**

(a) Dentist (b) Typewriter (c) Executive (d) Desk

34. **Which is the odd one out?**

(a) Marriage (b) Annul (c) Divorce (d) Separation

35. **Colour is to Bleach as Flushed is to:**

(a) Blush (b) Roseate (c) Watered (d) Wan

36. **Stint of the opposite of:**

(a) Surfeit (b) Prolix (c) Meticulous (d) Splint

37. **Which is the odd one out?**

(a) Foam (b) Mush (c) Bubbles (d) Surf

38. **Which is the odd one out?**

(a) Pretence (b) Subterfuge (c) Moonshine (d) Reluctance

39. **Direct is to Tortuous as Dilatory is to:**

(a) Expeditious (b) Straight (c) Curved (d) Circumlocutious

40. Which is the odd one out?

(a) Stand (b) Vegetate (c) Prevail (d) Subsist

3. Numerical Reasoning

❖ Instructions

There are two parts to this test. The first part has fairly simple questions using the four rules of numbers (+ - x ÷). The second part consists of numbers which go together in some way to form a series. You have to see how they go together and then choose the next number from the four answers. When you find the correct answer encircle it.

❖ Sample Tests

1. 12 10 8 6 4

(a) 3 (b) 2 (c) 1 (d) 0

2. 3 4 6 9 13

(a) 15 (b) 18 (c) 17 (d) 20

3. 1 1 2 3 5

(a) 7 (b) 10 (c) 8 (d) 9

4. 729 243 81 27 9

(a) 3 (b) 4 (c) 6 (d) -18

❖ Answers

1. (b) 2. (b) 3. (c) 4. (a)

Check your answers. If you have made a mistake look at the question again and try to see where you went wrong.

Now you can start the full test. You have 8 minutes to do as much of Part 1 as you can.

❖ Testing Numerical Reasoning – Part 1

1.
$$\begin{array}{r} 37 \\ 48 \\ +\ 35 \\ \hline \\ \hline \end{array}$$

2.
$$\begin{array}{r} 49 \\ \times\ 8 \\ \hline \\ \hline \end{array}$$

3.
$$\begin{array}{r} 28 \\ 364 \\ +\ 479 \\ \hline \\ \hline \end{array}$$

4.
$$\begin{array}{r} 47 \\ \times\ 5 \\ \hline \\ \hline \end{array}$$

5.
$$\begin{array}{r} 279 \\ 686 \\ +\ 755 \\ \hline \\ \hline \end{array}$$

6.
$$\begin{array}{r} 37 \\ \times\ 9 \\ \hline \\ \hline \end{array}$$

7.
$$\begin{array}{r} 249 \\ -\ 158 \\ \hline \\ \hline \end{array}$$

8.
$$7\overline{)364}$$

9.
$$\begin{array}{r} 924 \\ -\ 536 \\ \hline \\ \hline \end{array}$$

10.
$$8\overline{)584}$$

11.
$$\begin{array}{r} 612 \\ -\ 387 \\ \hline \\ \hline \end{array}$$

12.
$$12\overline{)1452}$$

13.
$$\begin{array}{r} 6016 \\ -\ 536 \\ \hline \\ \hline \end{array}$$

14.
$$12\overline{)14988}$$

15.
$$\begin{array}{r} 254 \\ +\ 612 \\ \hline \\ \hline \end{array}$$

16.
$$\begin{array}{r} 217 \\ -\ 138 \\ \hline \\ \hline \end{array}$$

17.
$$\begin{array}{r} 43 \\ \times\ 11 \\ \hline \\ \hline \end{array}$$

18.
$$6\overline{)3528}$$

19.
$$\begin{array}{r} 1051 \\ -\ 702 \\ \hline \\ \hline \end{array}$$

20.
$$\begin{array}{r} 543 \\ 311 \\ +\ 978 \\ \hline \\ \hline \end{array}$$

Go straight on to Part 2. You have 20 minutes to do as many as you can.

❖ Testing Numerical Reasoning – Part 2

1. **3 5 8 12 17**

(a) 25 (b) 26 (c) 22 (d) 23

2. **2 2 4 6 10**

(a) 14 (b) 10 (c) 20 (d) 16

3. **8 1 27 9 3 1**

(a) 1/2 (b) 1 (c) 1/3 (d) 1/6

4. **0.1 0.3 0.5 0.7 0.9**

(a) 1.1 (b) 0.11 (c) 11 (d) 0.011

5. **30 28 25 21 16**

(a) 9 (b) 10 (c) 11 (d) 12

6. **1 4 9 16 25**

(a) 32 (b) 36 (c) 48 (d) 49

7. **5 9 17 33 65**

(a) 101 (b) 108 (c) 143 (d) 129

8. **3 3 6 9 15**

(a) 24 (b) 30 (c) 18 (d) 36

9. **0 3 8 15 24**

(a) 36 (b) 30 (c) 35 (d) 31

10. **1 8 27 64 125**

(a) 250 (b) 216 (c) 185 (d) 196

11. **5** 7 **11 17 25**

(a) 35 (b) 27 (c) 31 (d) 39

12. **4 5 7 11 19**

(a) 33 (b) 27 (c) 37 (d) 35

13. 0 **3 2 5 4**

(a) 8 (b) 7 (c) 9 (d) 6

14. **0 8 8 16 24**

(a) 40 (b) 24 (c) 32 (d) 48

15. 2 5 11 23 47

(a) 80 (b) 95 (c) 92 (d) 101

16. 10 25 12 30 14

(a) 16 (b) 50 (c) 24 (d) 35

17. 3 9 6 15 9

(a) 18 (b) 15 (c) 12 (d) 21

18. 50 40 100 90 150

(a) 200 (b) 180 (c) 140 (d) 300

19. 2 4 4 16 16

(a) 32 (b) 64 (c) 24 (d) 256

20. 15 9 24 33 57

(a) 80 (b) 90 (c) 89 (d) 48

4. Abstract Reasoning

❖ Instructions

After each question there are four possible answers and, when you have found the correct one, encircle it. Here are some examples. The first one has been done for you.

❖ Sample Tests

1.

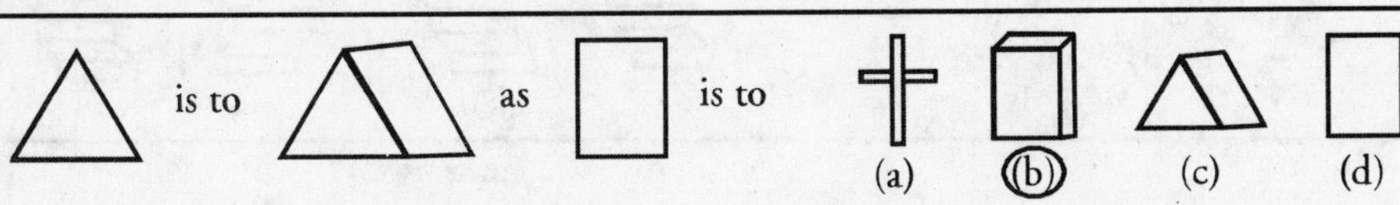

2.

3.

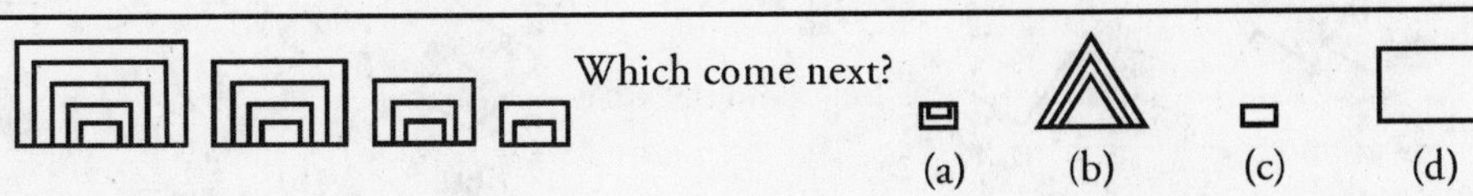

4.

5.

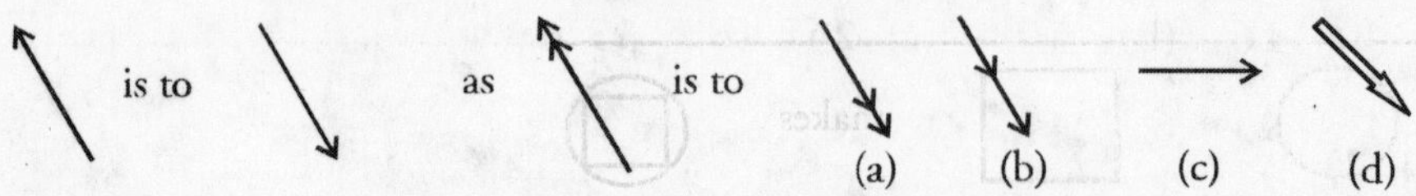

❖ Answers

1. (b) 2. (c) 3. (c) 4. (a) 5. (a)

Check your answers. If you have made a mistake, look at the questions gain and try to see where you went wrong. Now you can start the full test. You have 20 minutes to do as many as you can.

❖ Testing Abstract Reasoning

1.

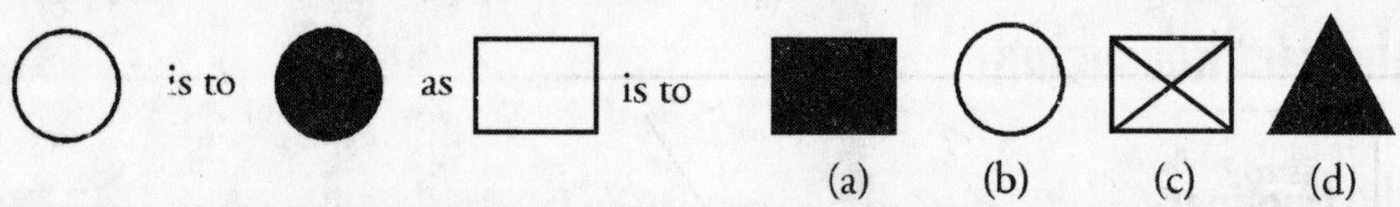

2.

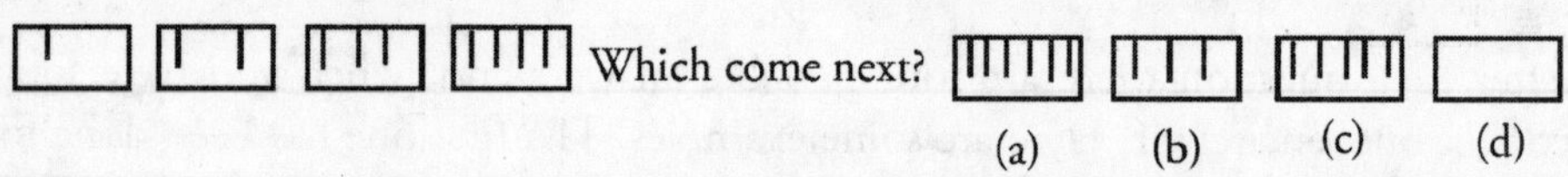

3.

Which is the odd one out?

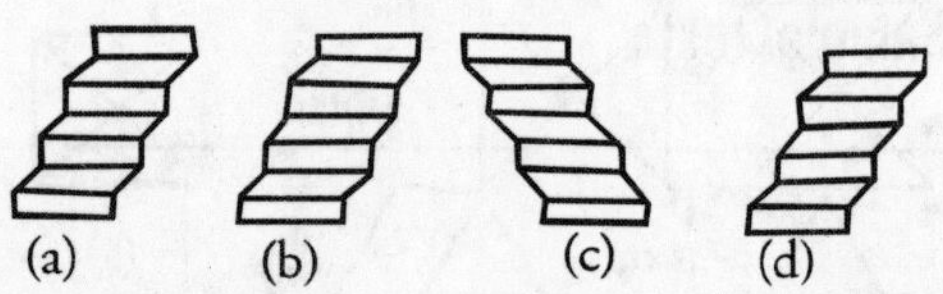

4.

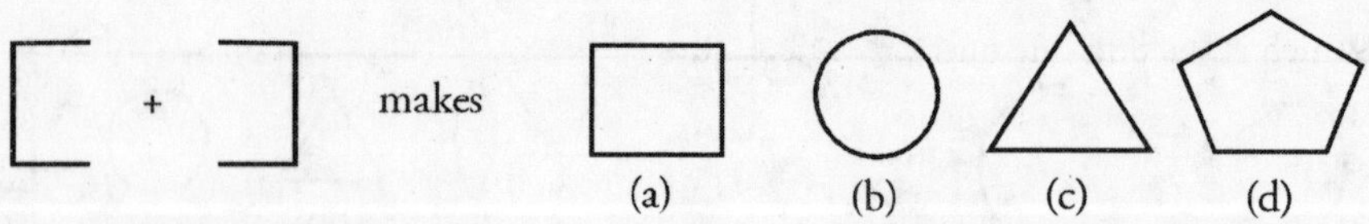

5.

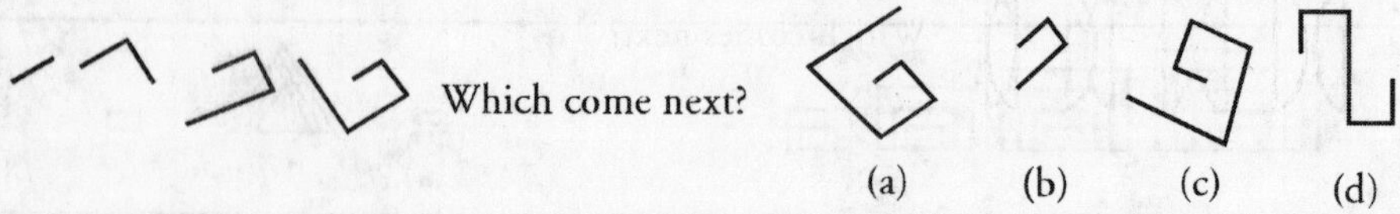

6.

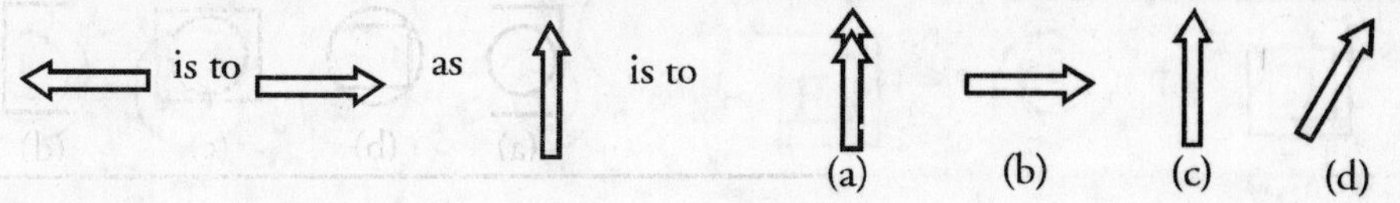

7.

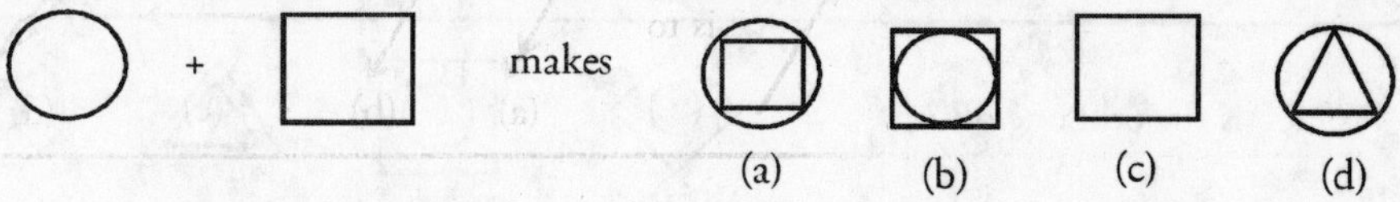

8.

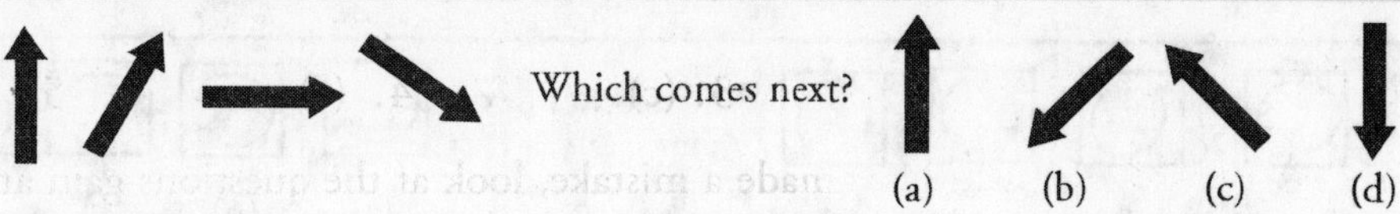

9.

Which is the odd one out?

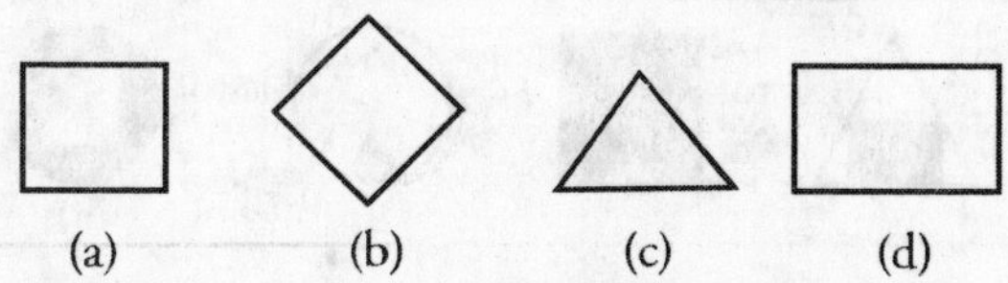

10.

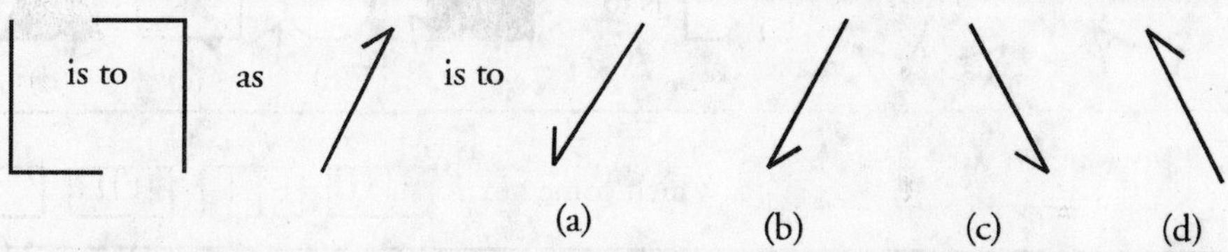

11.

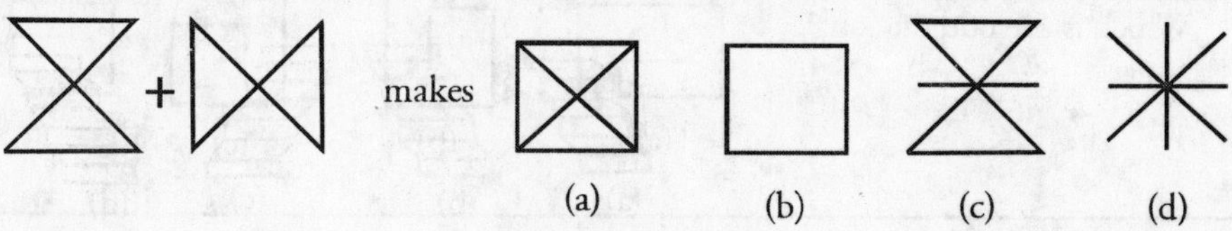

12.

Which is the odd one out?

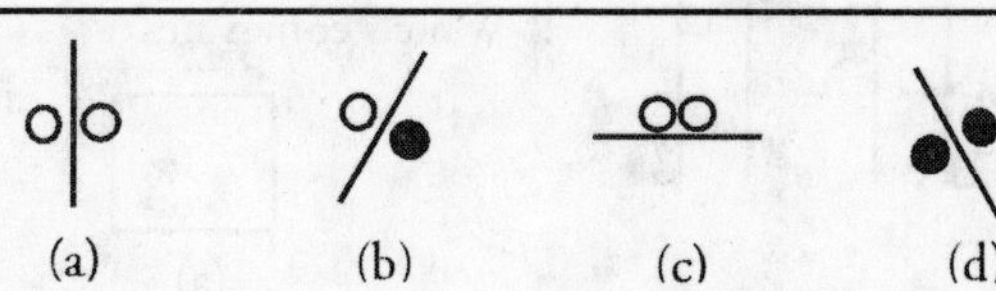

13.

14.

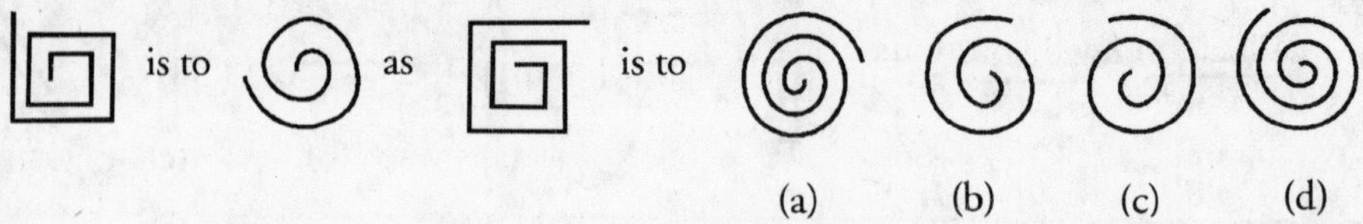

15. Which is the odd one out?

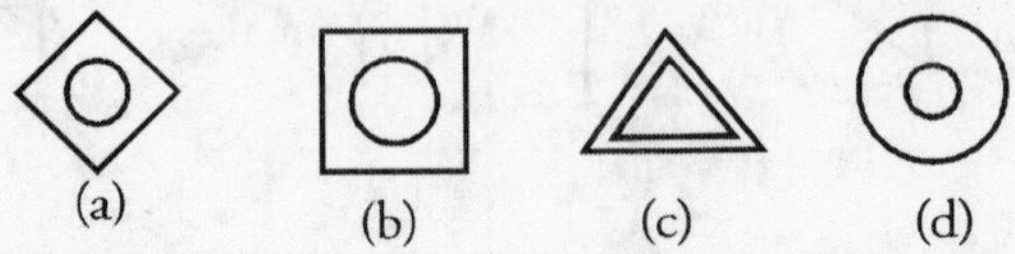

16.

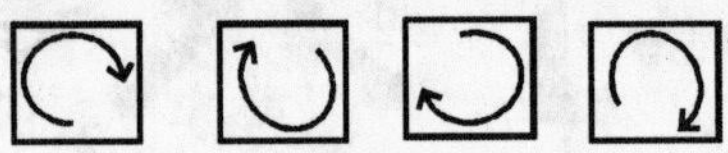

Which comes next?

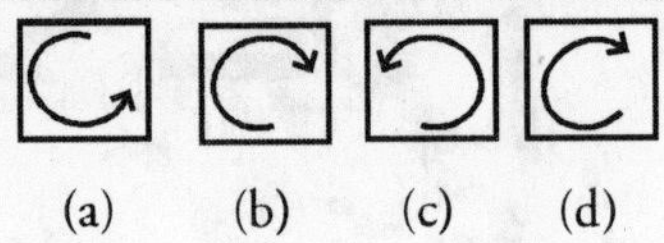

17.

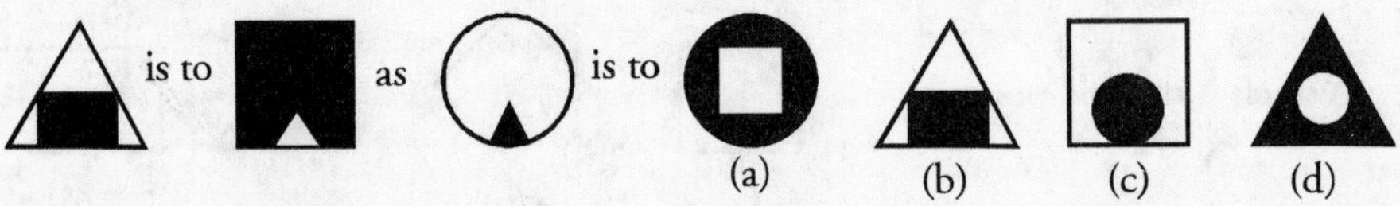

18.

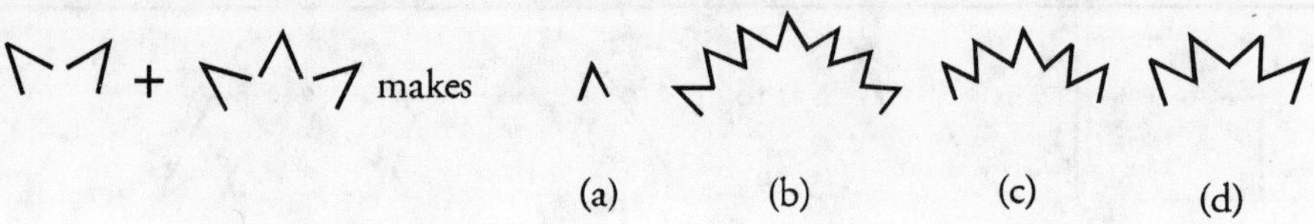

19. Which is the odd one out?

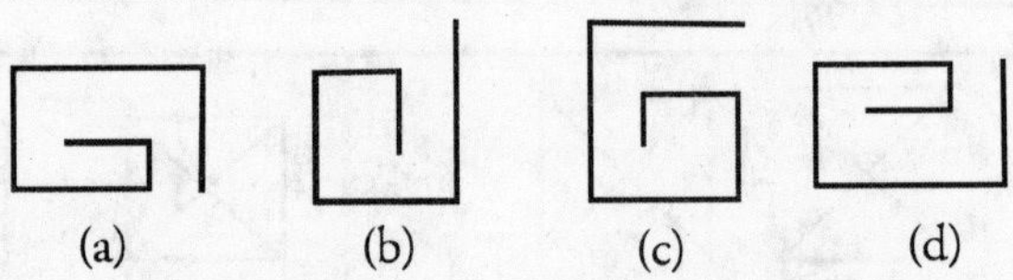

20.

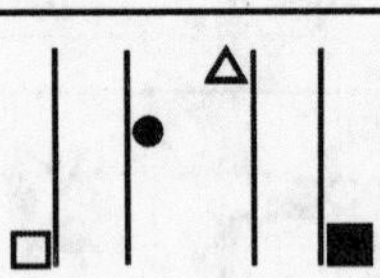

Which comes next?

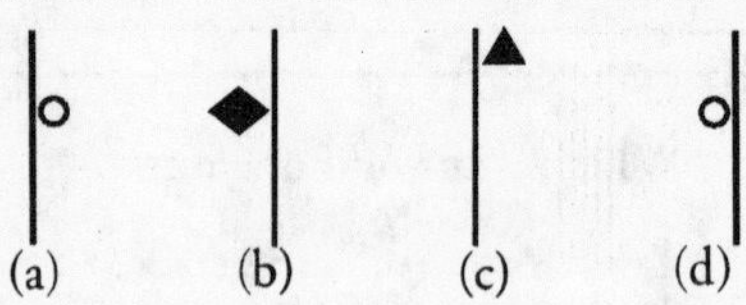

21.

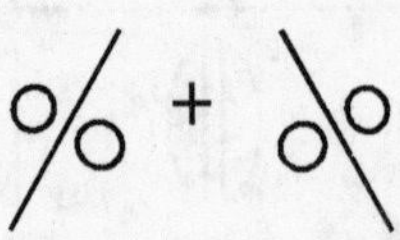

makes

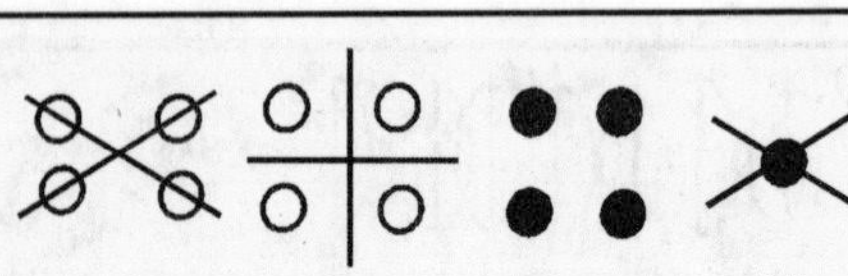

22. Which is the odd one out?

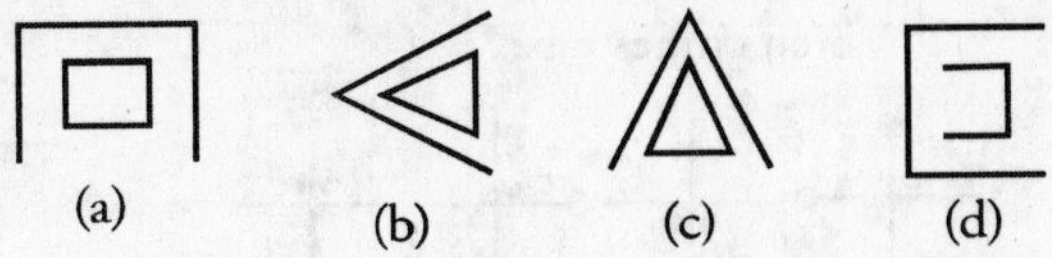

23. 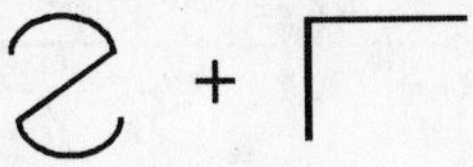 makes

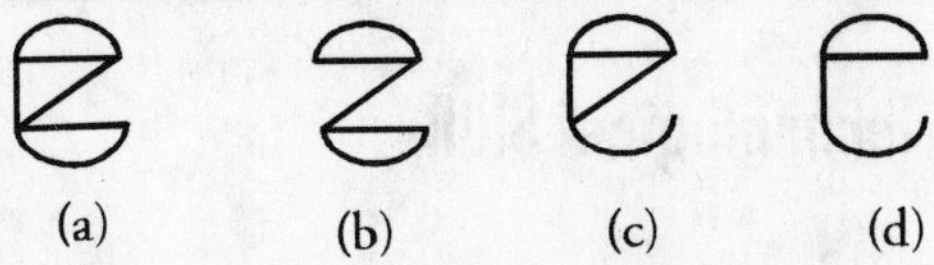

24. 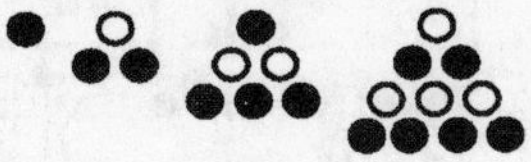 Which comes next?

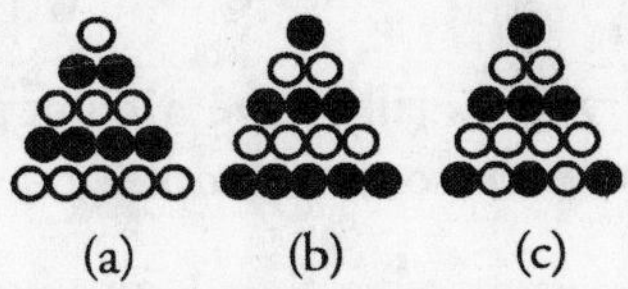

25. 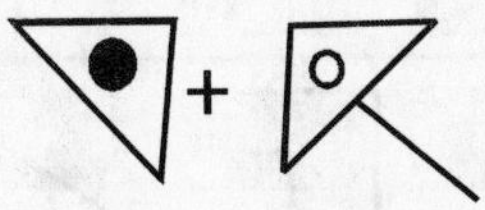 makes

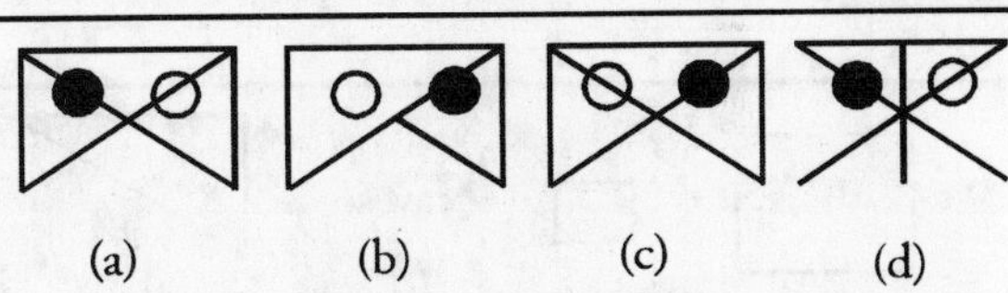

26. 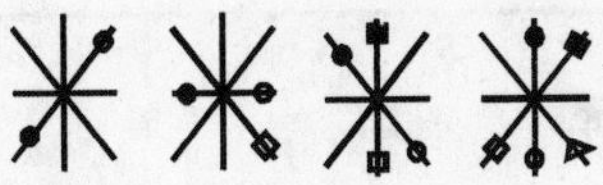 Which comes next?

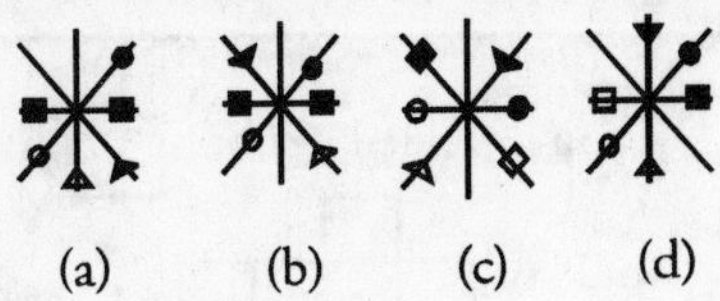

27. Which is the odd one out?

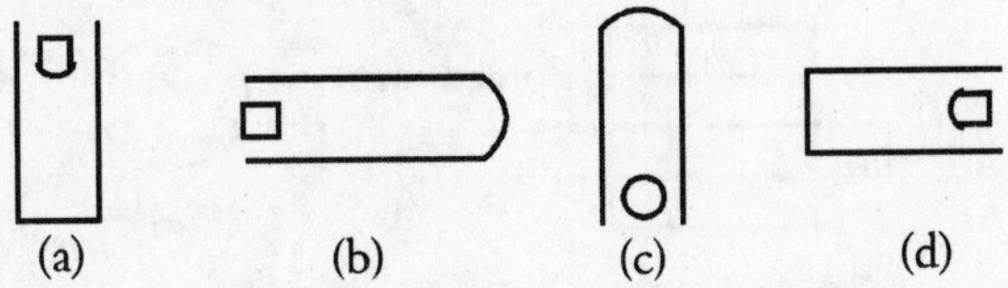

28. 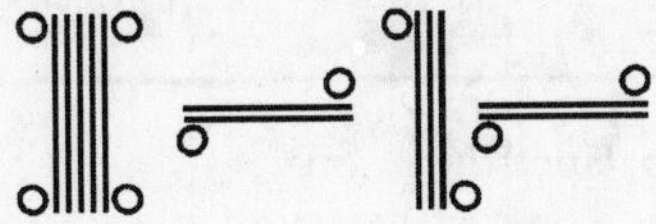 Which comes next?

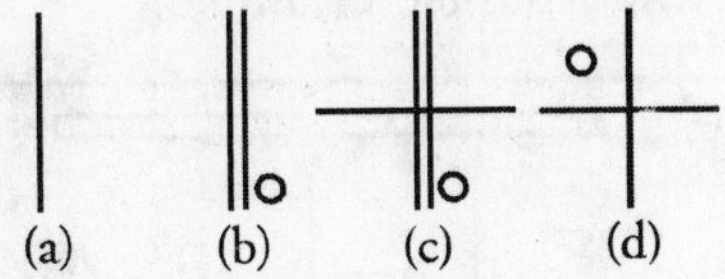

29. Which is the odd one out?

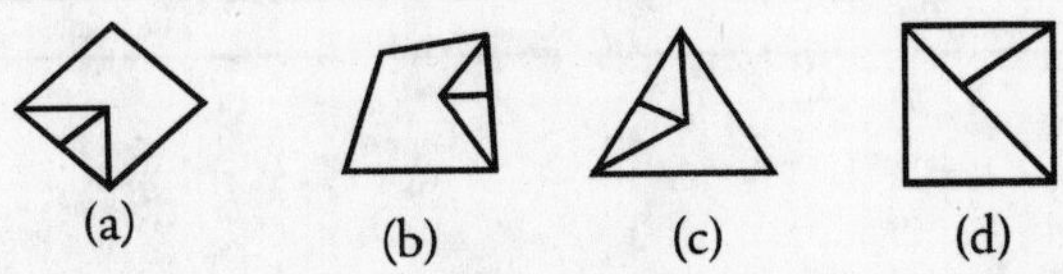

30. Which comes next?

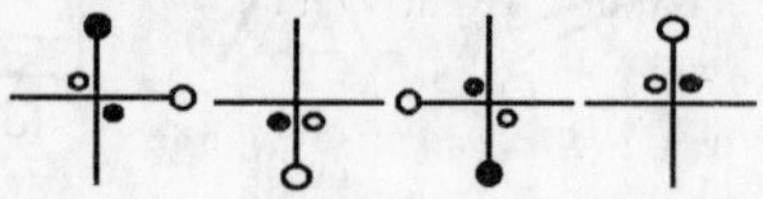

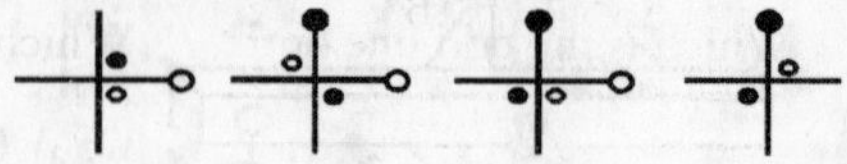

(a) (b) (c) (d)

5. Technological Skills

❖ Instructions

As before, you usually have a choice of four answers and you encircle the correct answer. Here are some examples.

❖ Sample Tests

1. 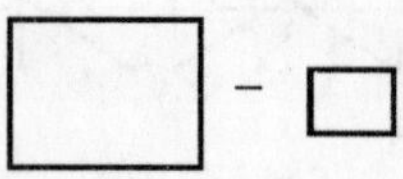 leaves 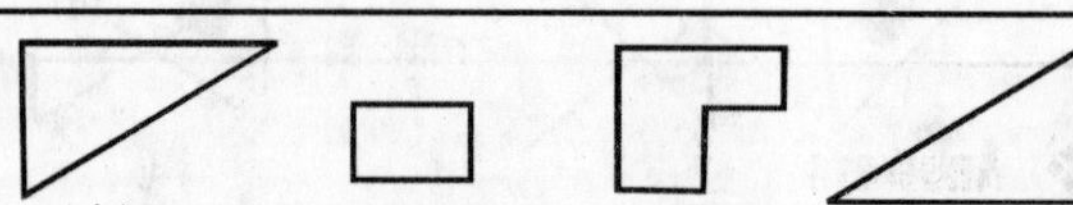

(a) (b) (c) (d)

2. If you unfolded a cube 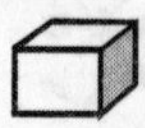 the shape you would get

would be 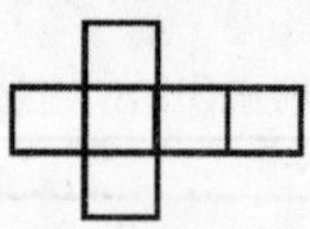

so 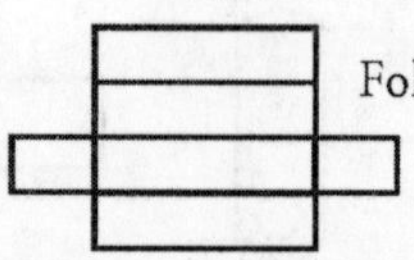 Folded makes 

(a) (b) (c) (d)

Now try these examples:

1. 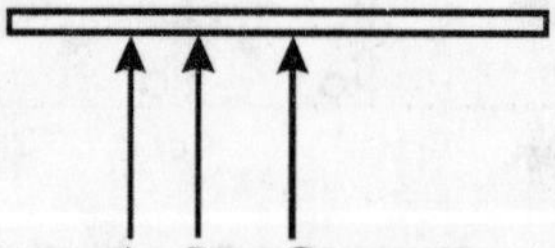

Which arrow would balance the beam?

A B C

(a) A (b) B (c) C (d) any

2.

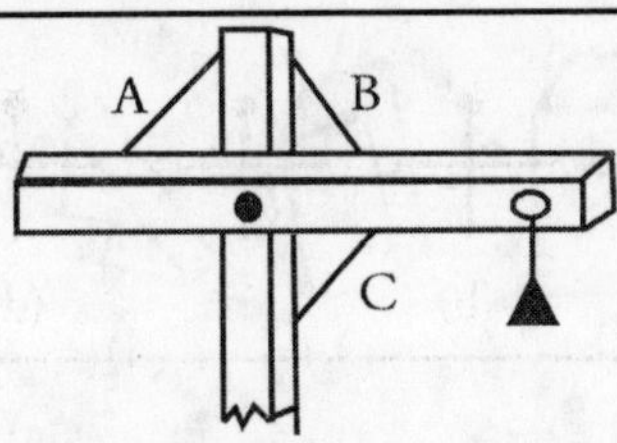

Which string is holding up the weight?

(a) A (b) B (c) C (d) none

3.

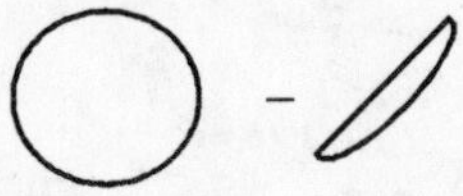

leaves

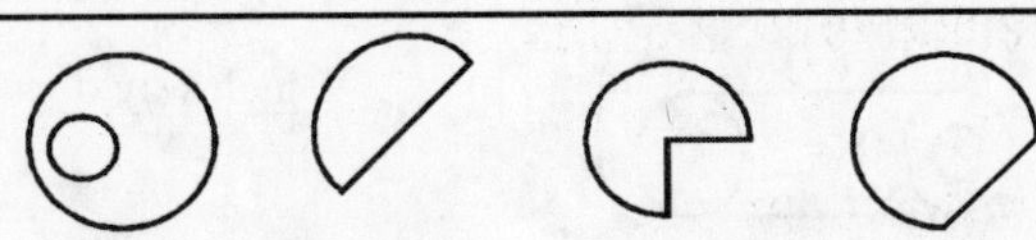

(a) (b) (c) (d)

4.

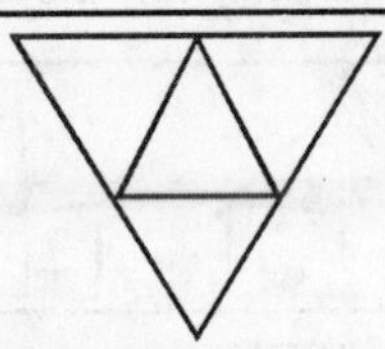

folded makes

(a) (b) (c) (d)

❖ Answers

1. (b) 2. (b) 3. (d) 4. (b)

Check your answers. If you have made a mistake check the question again and try to see where you went wrong.

Now you are ready to start the full test. You have 20 minutes to do as much as you can.

❖ Testing Technological Skills

1.

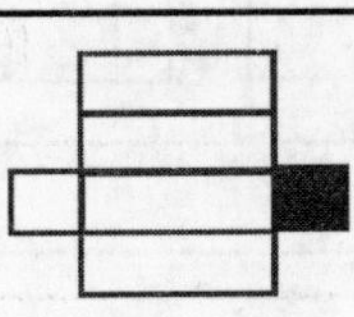

folded makes

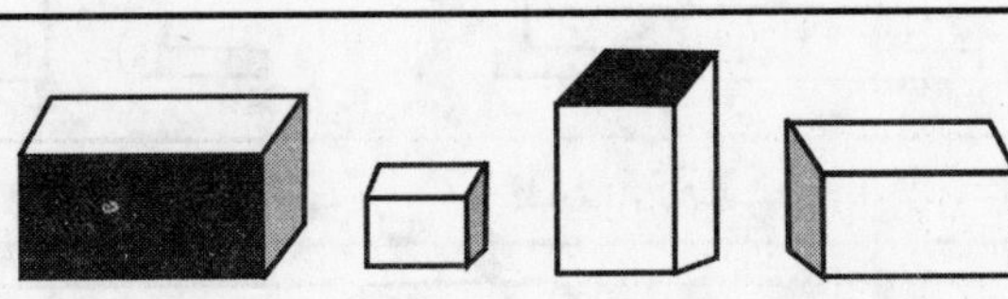

(a) (b) (c) (d)

2.

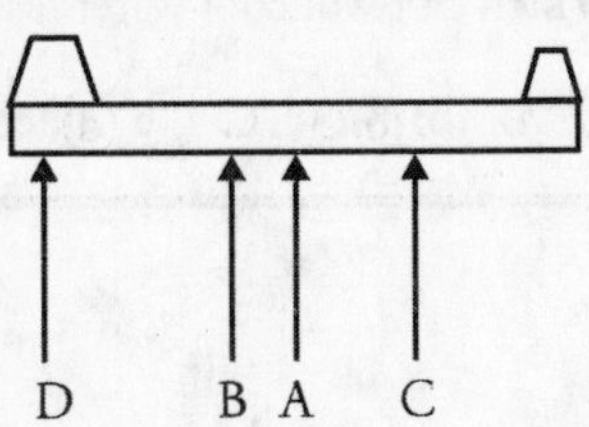

Which arrow will balance the beam?

(a) A (b) B (c) C (d) D

3.

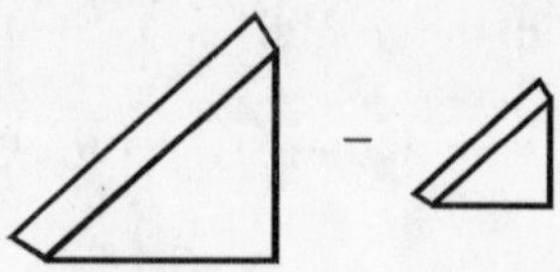

leaves

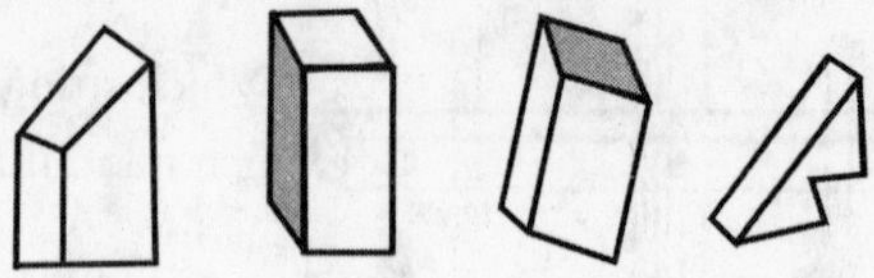

(a) (b) (c) (d)

4.

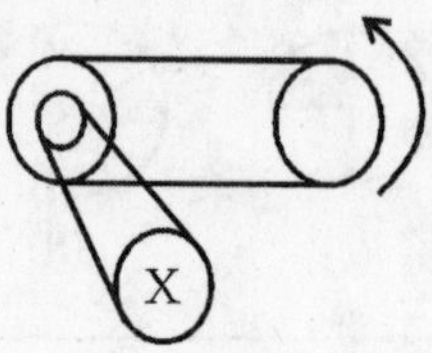

Which way does wheel X move?

(a) either (b) (c) (d) stays still

5.

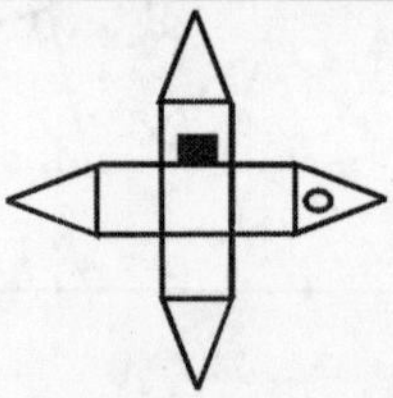

folded makes

(a) (b) (c) (d)

6.

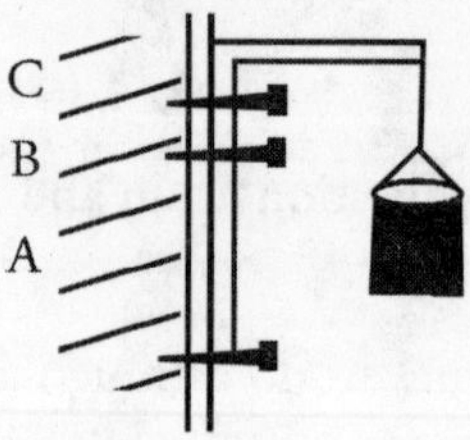

Which nail is most likely to pull out of the wall?

(a) A (b) B (c) C (d) all equal

7.

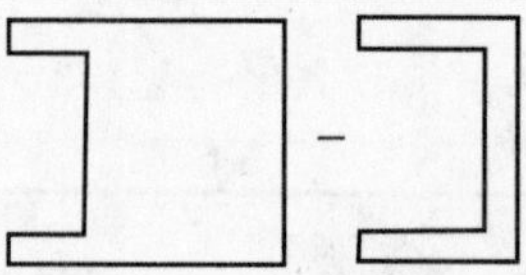

leaves

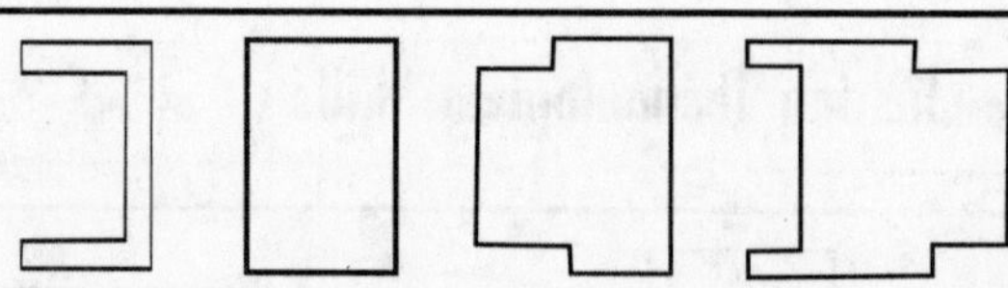

(a) (b) (c) (d)

8.

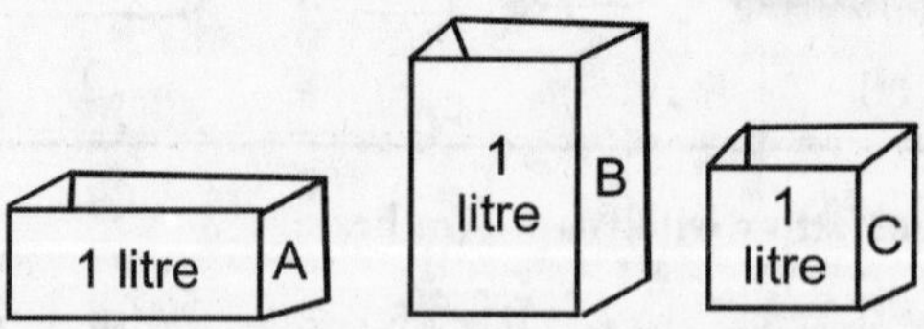

Which can will cool water fastest?

(a) A (b) B (c) C (d) all equal

9. 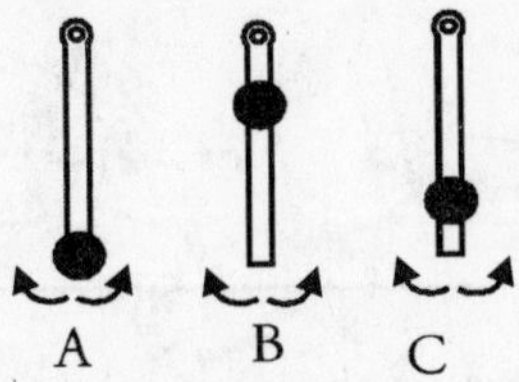

Which pendulum moves slowest?

(a) A (b) B (c) C (d) all equal

10. 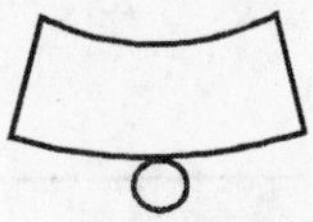 folded makes 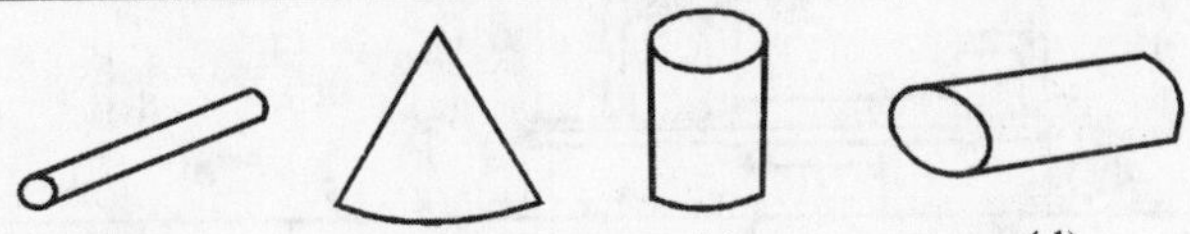

(a) (b) (c) (d)

11. 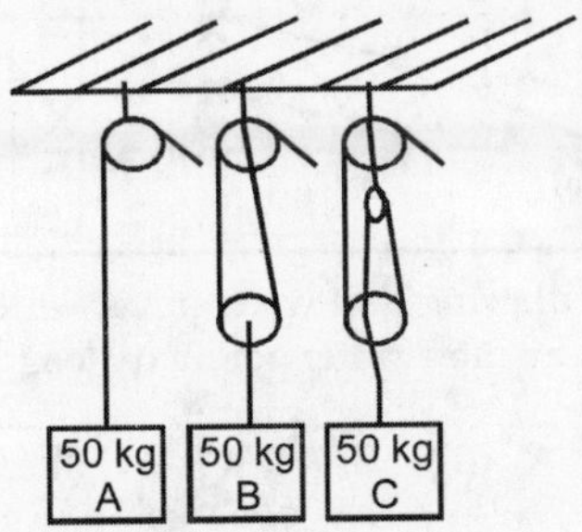

Which nail is most likely to pull out of the wall?

(a) A (b) B (c) C (d) all equal

12. 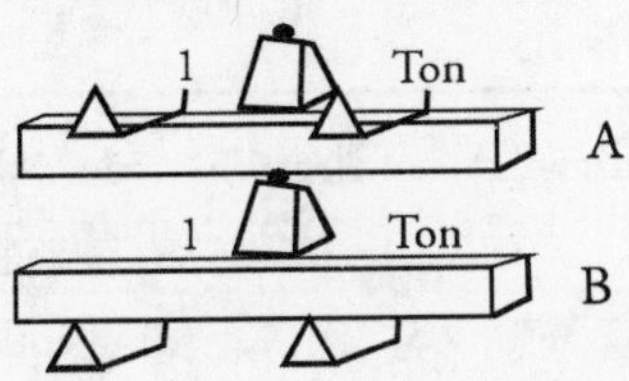

Which plank is most likely to break?

(a) A (b) B (c) either

13. Where is the cannonball most likely to land?

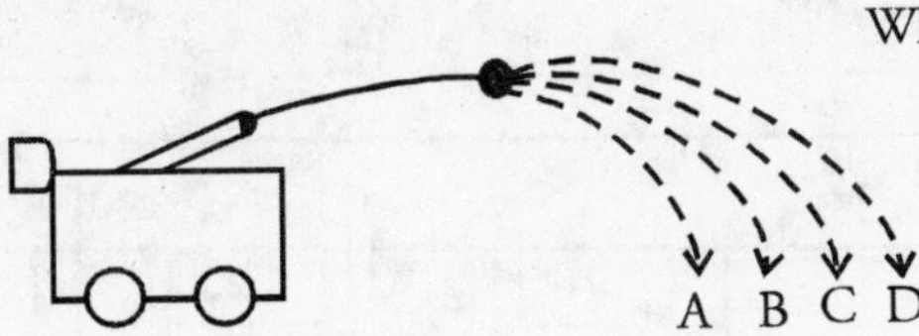

(a) A (b) B (c) C (d) D

14. 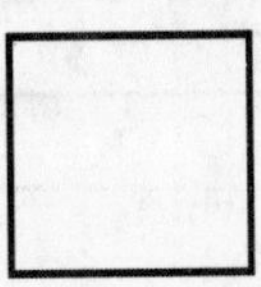 – 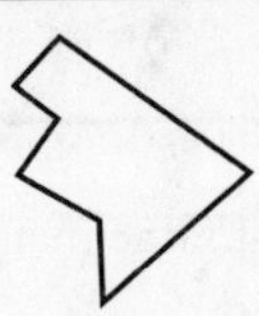 leaves 

(a) (b) (c) (d)

15. 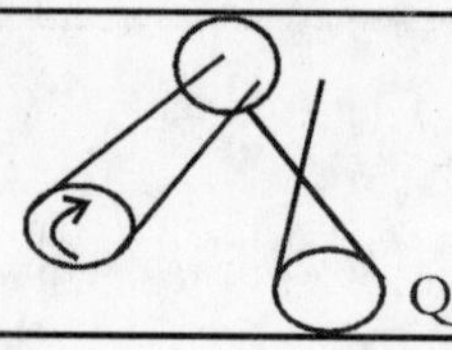

Which way will wheel Q turn?

(a)  (b)  (c) either

16. 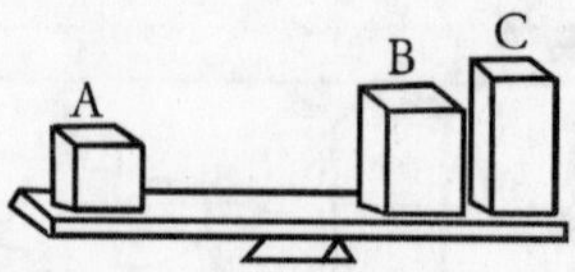

Which box is the heaviest?

(a) A (b) B (c) C (d) all equal

17. 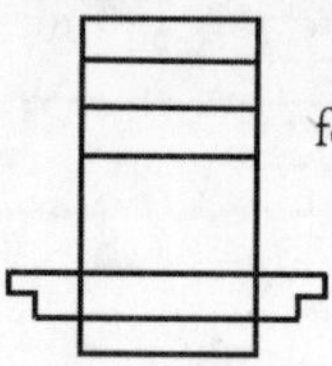 folded makes

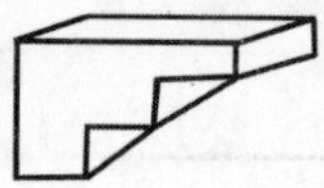
(a)

(b)

(c)

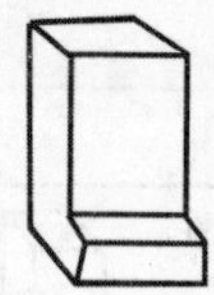
(d)

18. 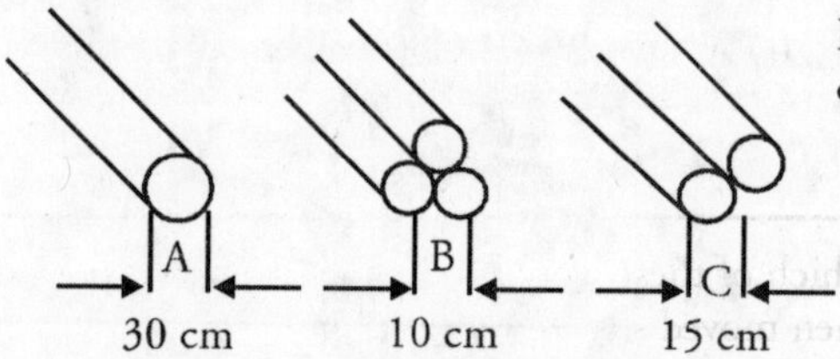

If the drawing is of water pipes, which carry the most water per metre length?

(a) A (b) B (c) C (d) all equal

19. 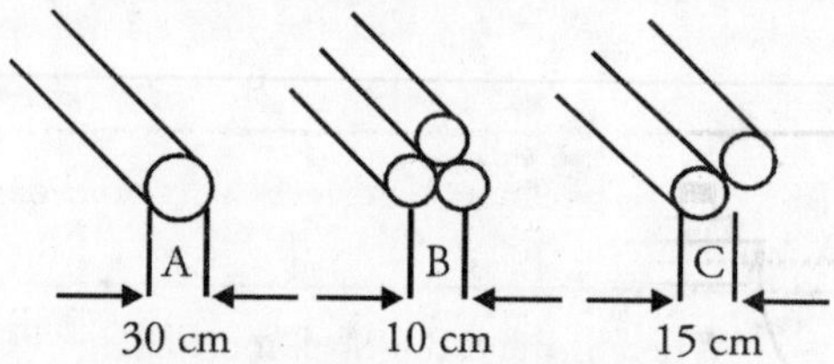

If the drawing is of electrical cables, which offers the most resistance per metre length?

(a) A (b) B (c) C (d) all equal

20. 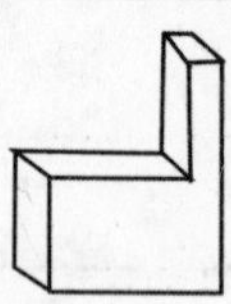 –  leaves

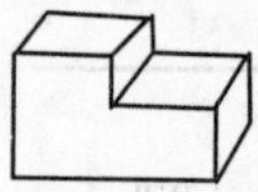
(a)

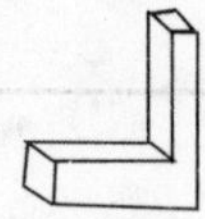
(b)

(c)

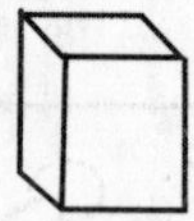
(d)

21. 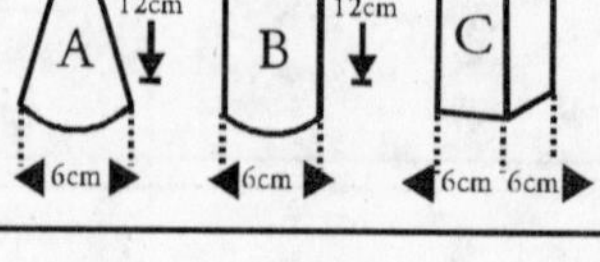

If the blocks are all of same material, which is the heaviest?

(a) A (b) B (c) C (d) all equal

22. 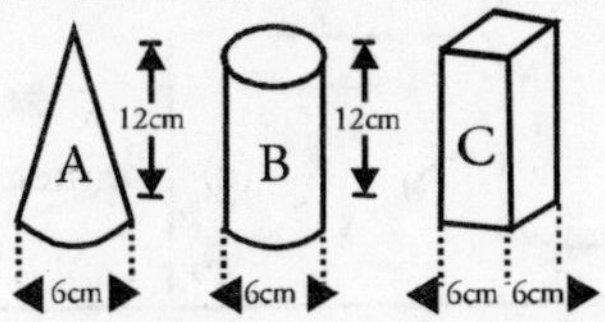

Which has the greatest density?

(a) A (b) B (c) C (d) all equal

23. 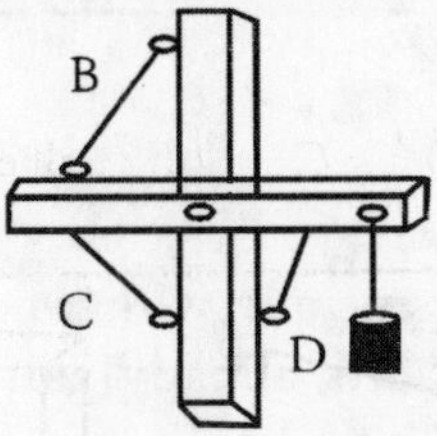

Which chain would support the weight by itself ?

(a) any equally (b) B (c) C (d) D

24. 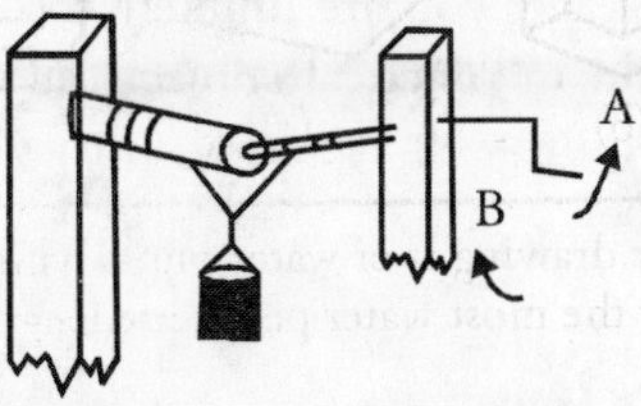

Which way will the handle have to turn to raise the bucket?

(a) A (b) B (c) either

25. 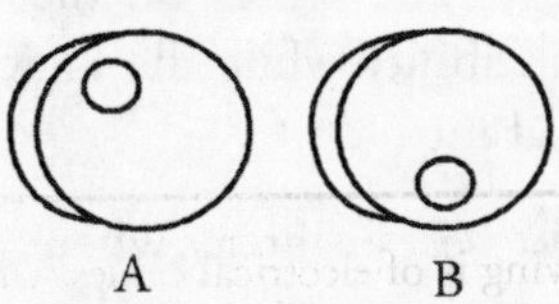

Which of these would return to its present position when moved slightly?

(a) neither (b) A (c) B (d) both

26. 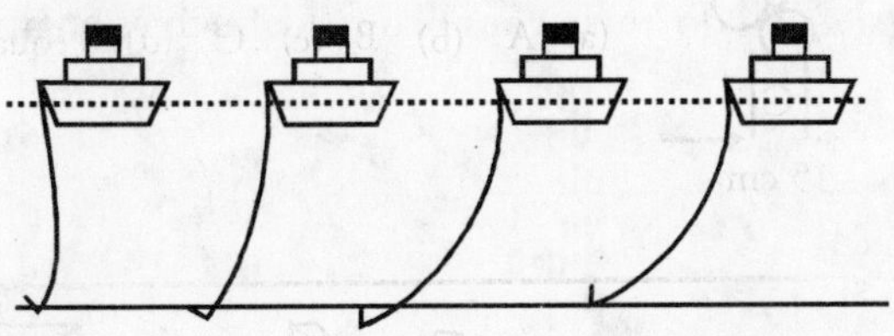

Which boat has the safest anchorage?

(a) A (b) B (c) C (d) D

27. 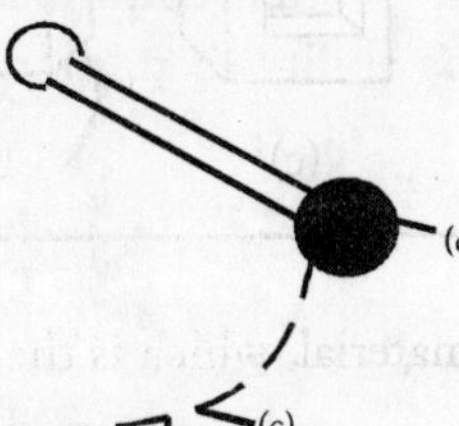

Where is the pendulum moving fastest?

28.

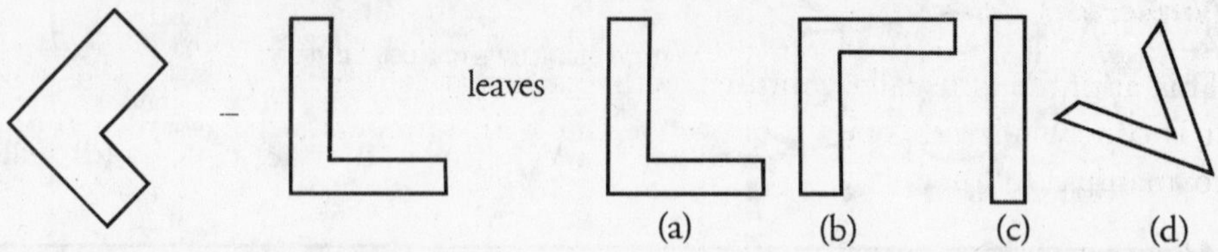

INTERPRETING THE RESULTS

Before you look in detail at the results, compare them generally with what you already know about yourself. How do they reflect results already gained in examination and other tests. Are the areas of strength and weakness same as you expected? If the test results are generally below average, you are unlikely to do well in examinations and were probably more successful in practical subjects at school. If the results are close to average you probably did quite well at school. If they are all above average, you can do well in most areas.

❖ Pattern of Results

It is possible to divide the tests into two general areas. The scores on the verbal, numerical and abstract tests indicate persons' academic ability while the logical and technological tests give an idea of his/her or applied ability.

If the academic group is higher, then she/he will do best in areas where she/he needs to work within a recognized structure, such as research or accountancy.

If the practical group is higher he/she will do best in applied fields such as engineering or business management.

❖ Individual Strengths

Logical Reasoning

This is the strength to reason in a factual, logical way. It is often combined with other strengths to indicate a way of thinking. It reflects the ability to think quickly, to solve problems and to deal with new ideas.

Verbal Reasoning

The ability to reason with words is usually concerned with language, but it also tests one's analytical strengths.

Numerical Reasoning

This aptitude is usually confused with mathematical ability. Although it is similar, it is concerned with one's capacity to 'think' in numbers rather than his/her ability to manipulate them.

Abstract Reasoning

To be able to reason with abstract ideas is the key to success in all science subjects. The concept-building stages of discovery and proving theory depend on the use of abstract reasoning. The 'purer' the science, the greater the abstract element.

Technological Reasoning

This test measures how well one can cope with applied ideas, such as understanding technical drawings. This also tests one's three dimensional thinking with scientific reasoning.

CHAPTER 8

Visual Reasoning Test

LEARNING OBJECTIVES

- To know the details of visual reasoning test.
- To analyse through interpretation.

VISUAL REASONING TEST

There are two types of problems in this test. In one type, you have to decide which of the objects you are shown is the "odd one out". This will be the one that in some way makes it different from the others in the set.

In the second type of problem you are shown a sequence of objects or shapes. Your task is to choose, from the alternatives you are given, the one that would come next in line where there is a large question mark. The examples will show you how to do this test.

Example 1

Which is the odd one out?

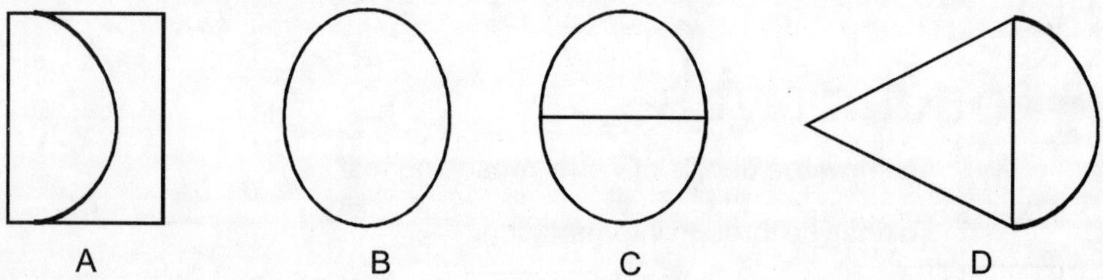

Example 2

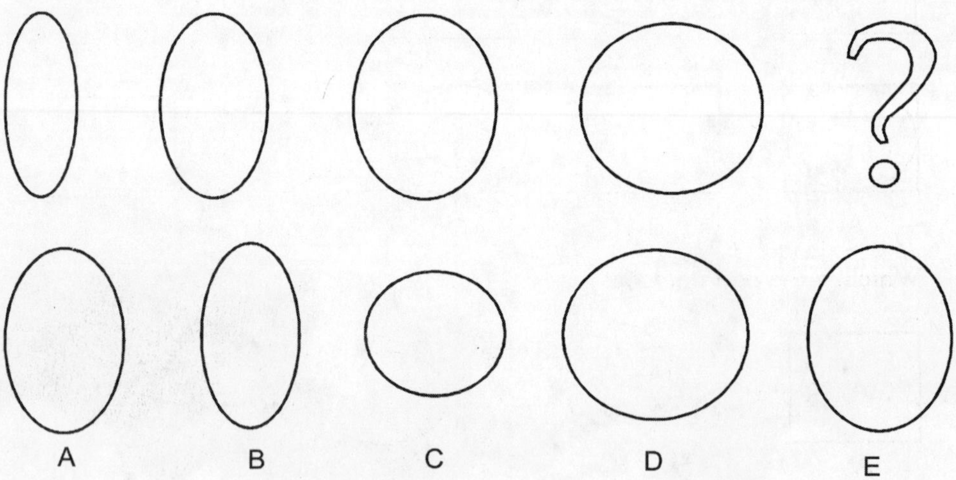

In Example 1, B is the correct answer. It is the only curved shape that does not have a straight line.

In Example 2, the figures are of a circle that is turning. The figures can also be seen as a shape that is expanding by equal amounts until it becomes a full circle. The next step would be for the circle to turn by the same amount as before or to decrease by the same amount as before. E is the correct answer. Although A is the correct shape, there is no reason why it should be shaded. D is not quite the correct size because it has not turned enough. B is not correct because it has turned too much. C is the wrong size and has not turned at all.

You have 10 minutes to do as many as you can. Begin as soon as you are ready.

1. Which is the odd one out?

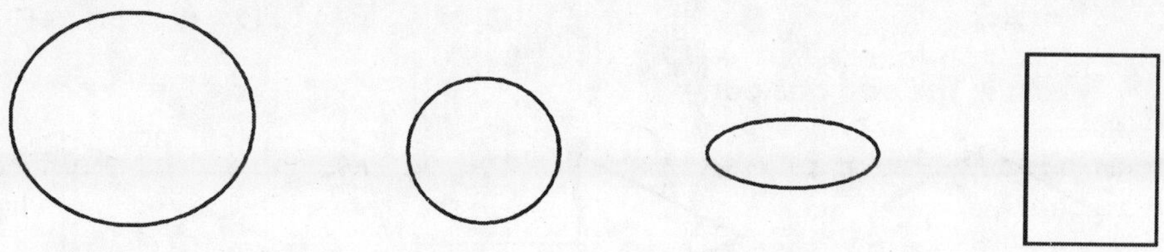

A B C D

2. Which comes next?

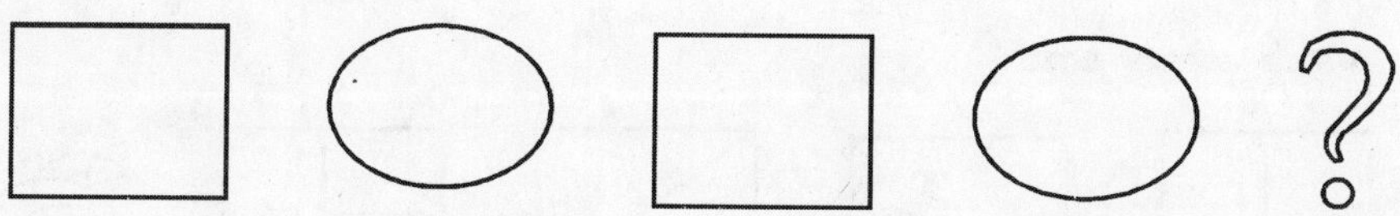

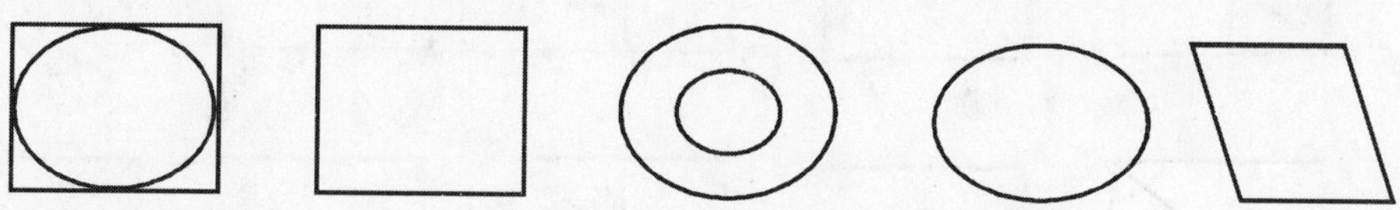

A B C D E

3. Which is the odd one out?

A B C D

4. Which comes next?

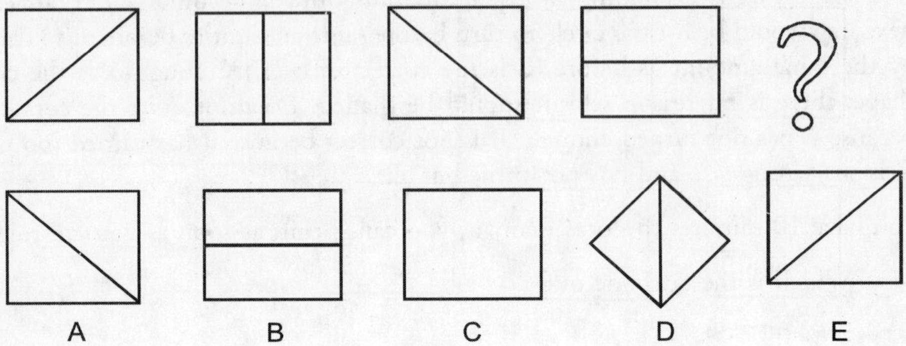

5. Which is the odd one out?

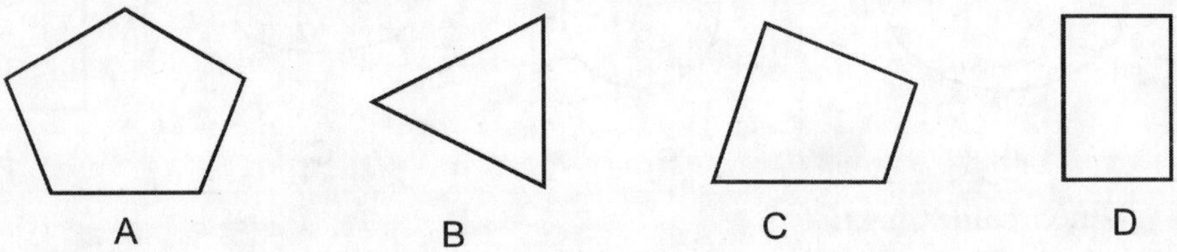

6. Which comes next?

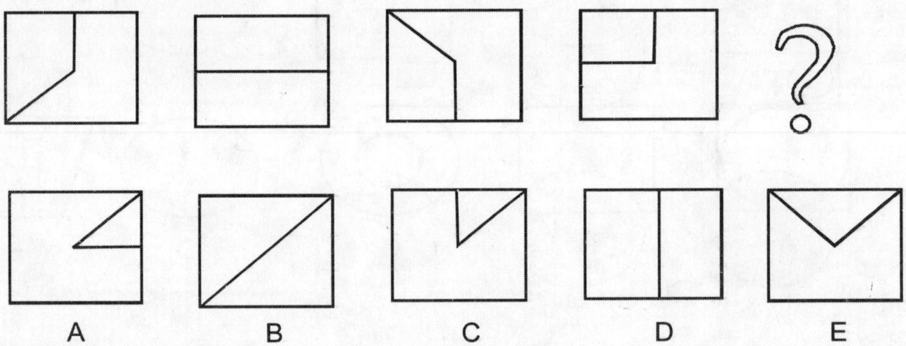

7. Which is the odd one out?

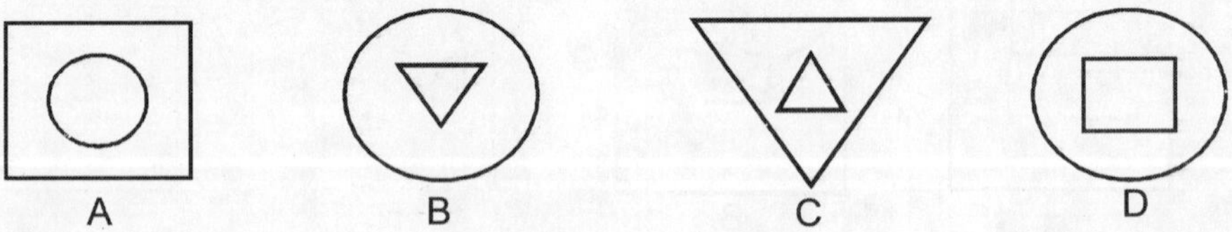

8. Which comes next?

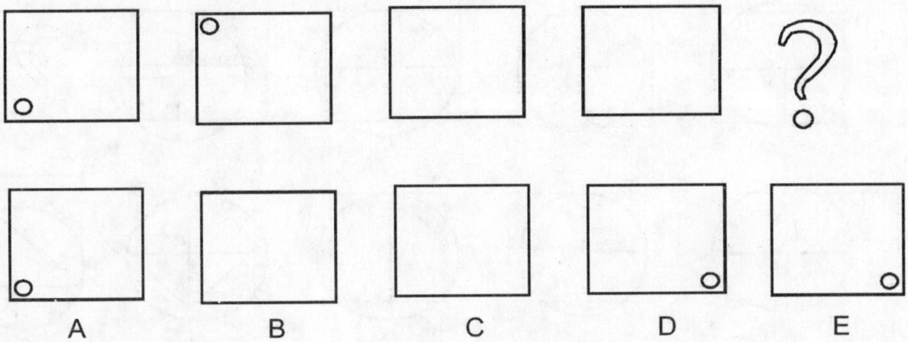

9. Which is the odd one out?

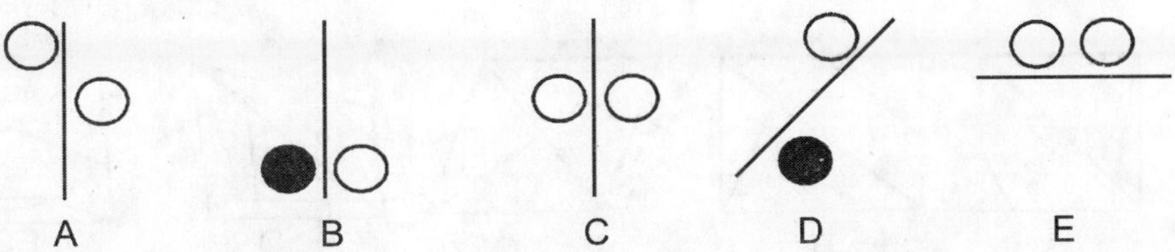

10. Which comes next?

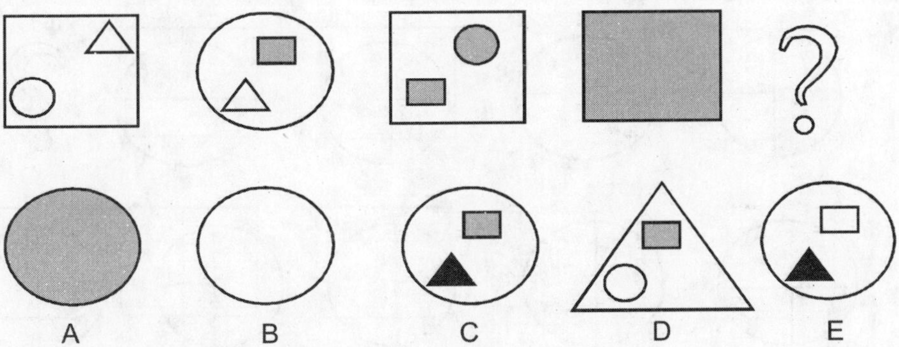

11. Which is the odd one out?

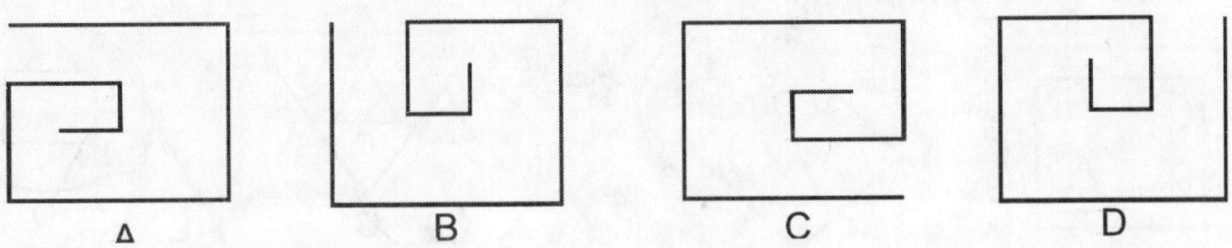

12. Which comes next?

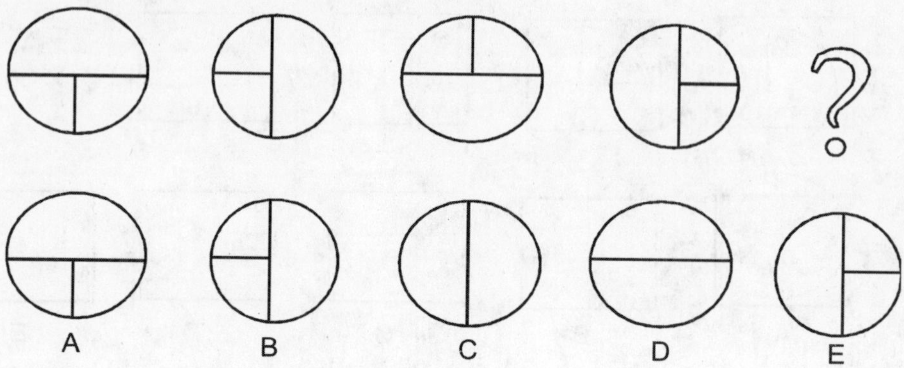

13. Which is the odd one out?

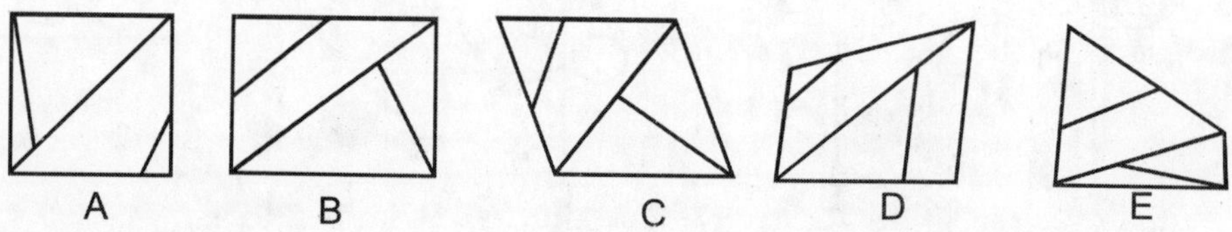

14. Which comes next?

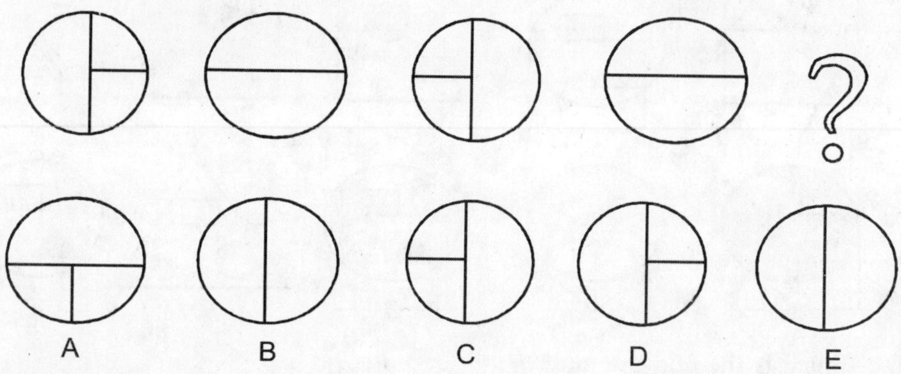

15. Which is the odd one out?

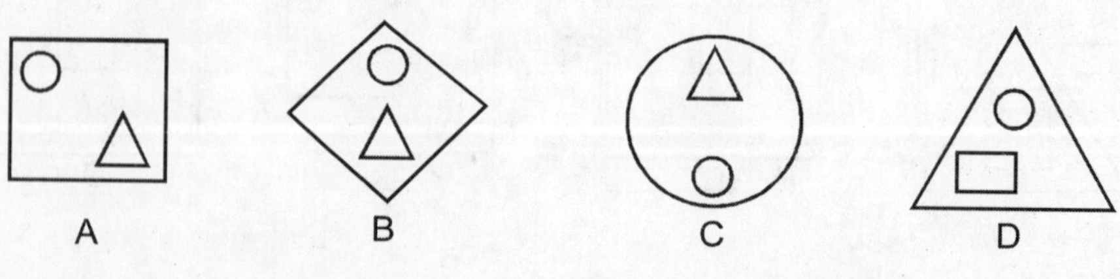

16. Which comes next?

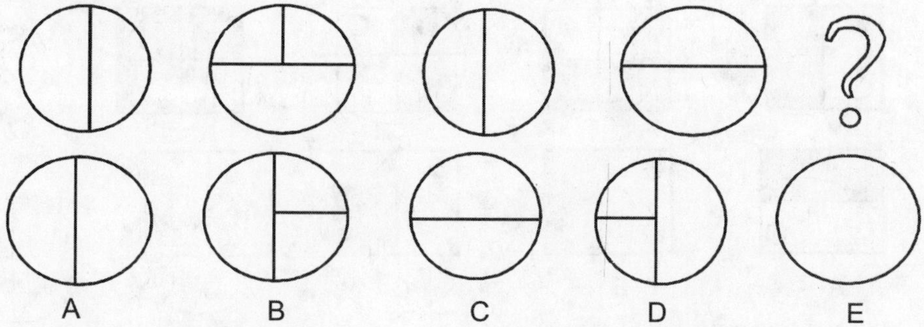

17. Which is the odd one out?

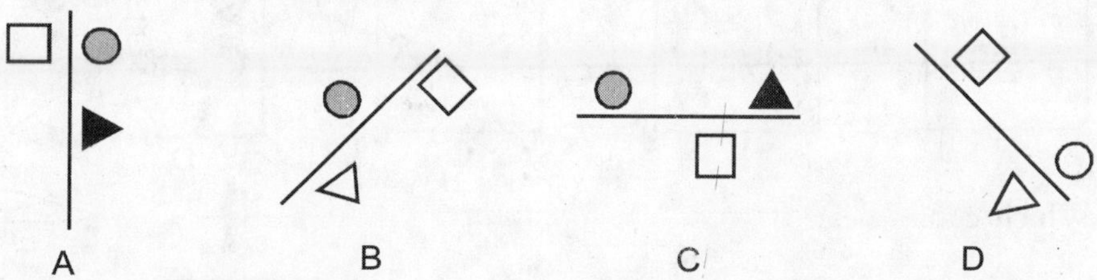

18. Which comes next?

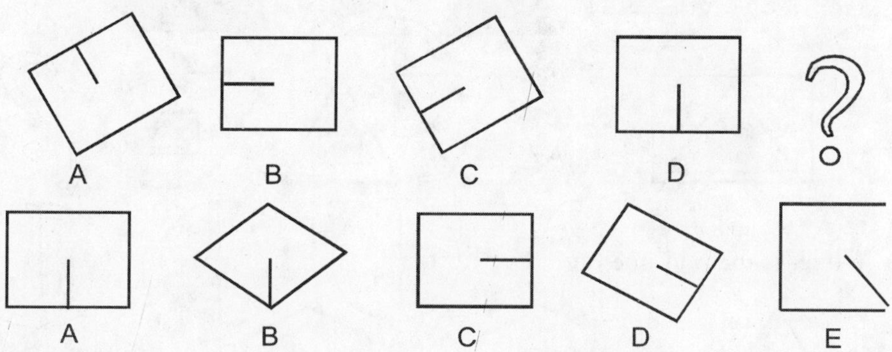

19. Which is the odd one out?

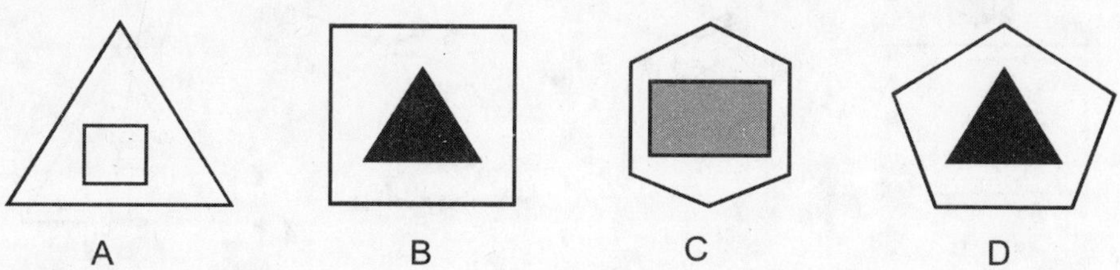

20. Which comes next?

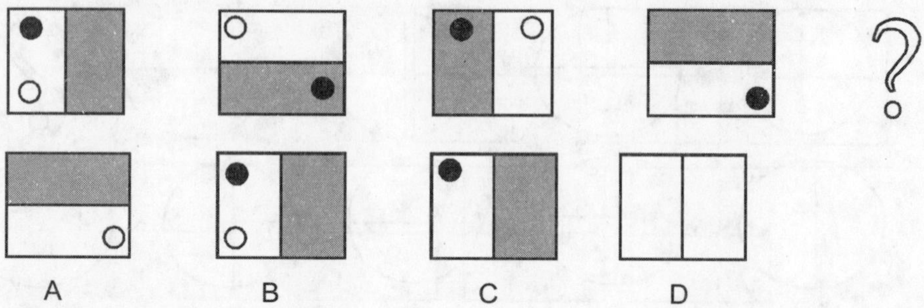

21. Which is the odd one out?

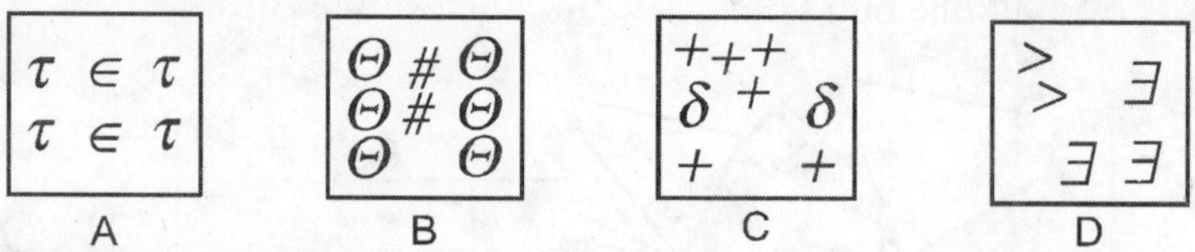

22. Which comes next?

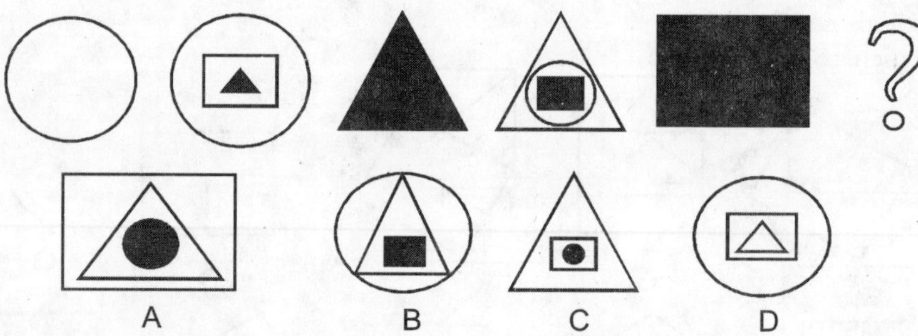

23. Which is the odd one out?

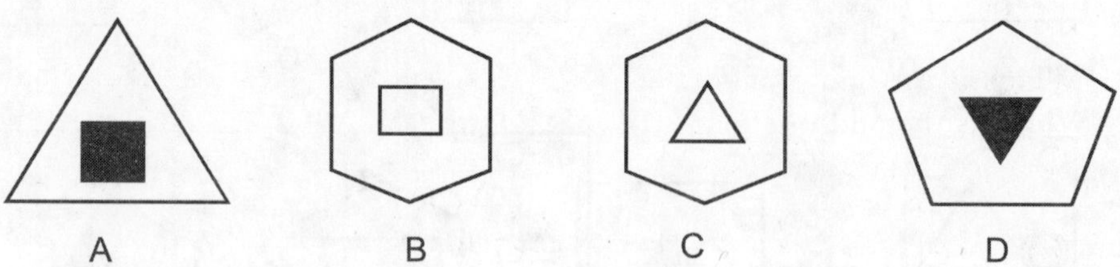

24. Which comes next?

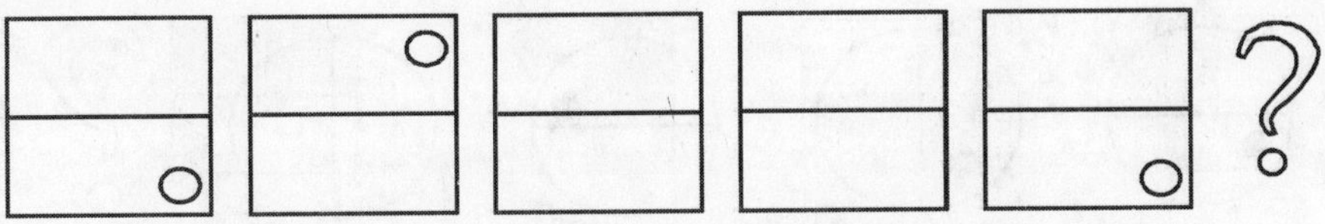

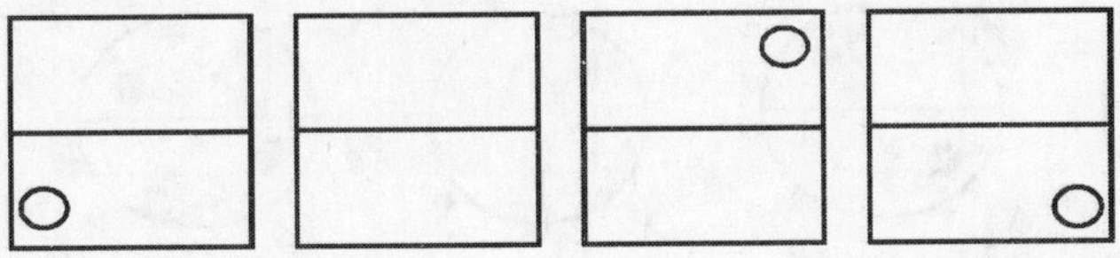

A B C D

25. Which is the odd one out?

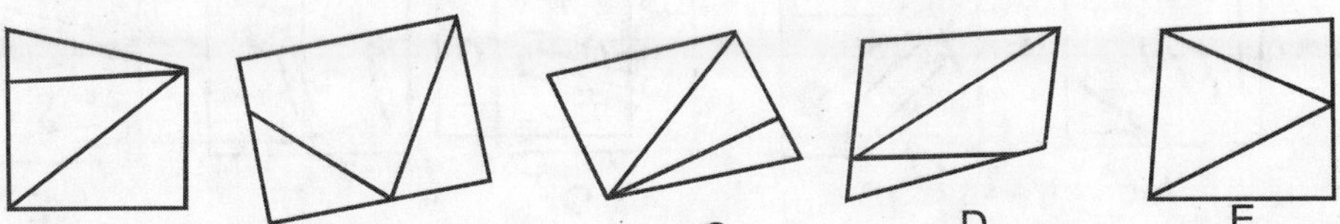

A B C D E

26. Which comes next?

A B C D E

27. Which is the odd one out?

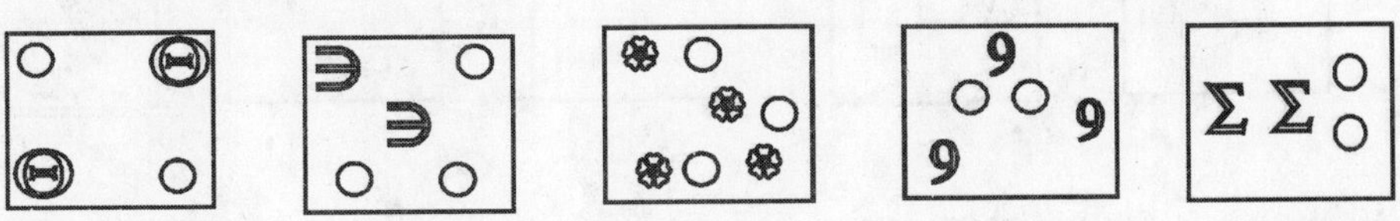

A B C D E

28. Which comes next?

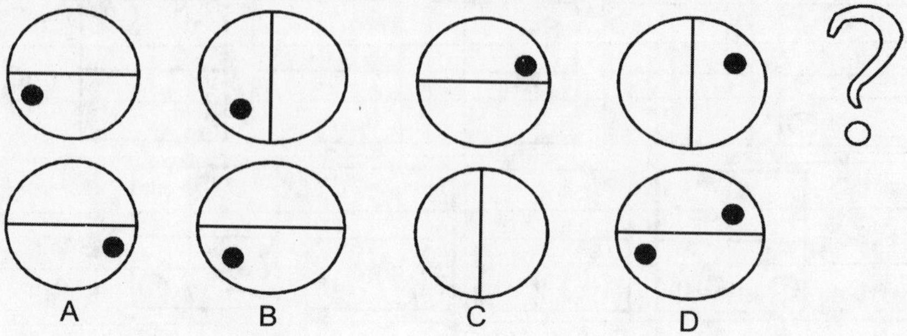

29. Which is the odd one out?

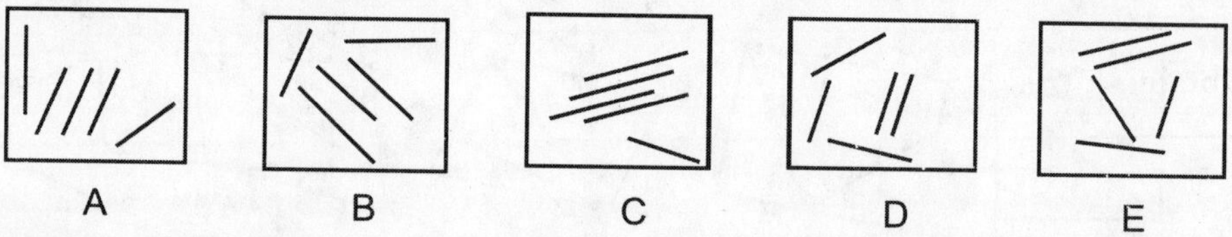

30. Which comes next?

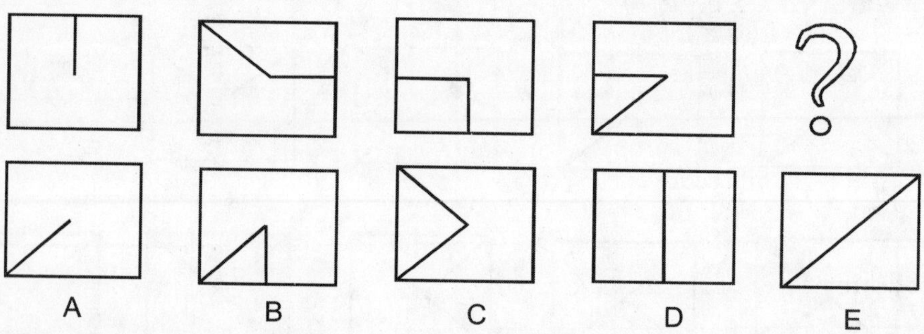

31. Which is the odd one out?

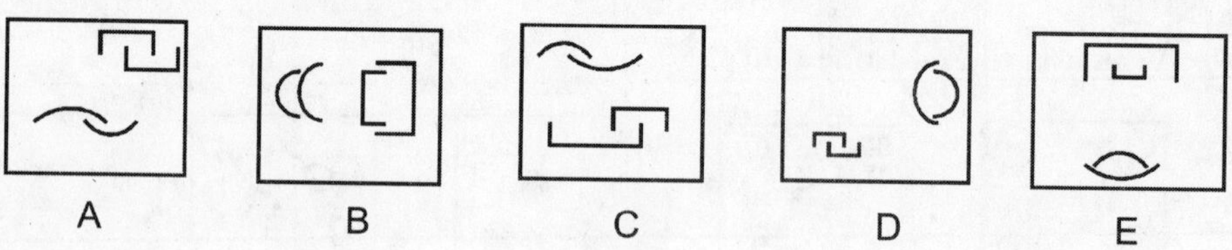

32. Which is the odd one out?

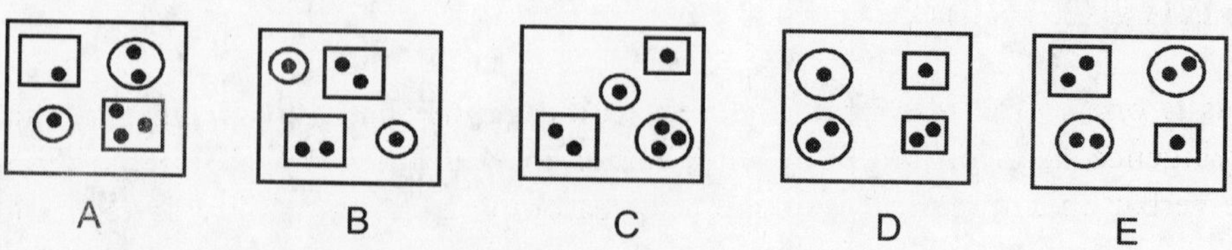

Answers to Visual Reasoning Test

1-d	9-e	17 - d	25 - e
2-b	10 - a	18 - d	26 - b
3-a	11 - b	19 - a	27 - b
4-e	12 - a	20 - b	28 - b
5-c	13 - d	21 - d	29 - c
6 - a	14 - d	22 - a	30 - d
7-c	15 - c	23 - a	31 - b
8-a	16 - a	24 - b	32 - d

Obtaining the total score

Number correct =	________
Plus 3 if no mistakes	+3 ________
Total score =	________

Establishing level of potential

Average	Above average	Well above average	Exceptional
1-6	7-13	14-20	21+

INTERPRETATION

This is one of the tests that is closest to measuring 'natural' intelligence, that is, intelligence that you are born with, rather than abilities you acquired. Although the verbal and numerical tests are also reasoning tests, the ability to read and to work with numbers has had to be learnt. Therefore, the visual test is one of the 'purer' measures of aptitude, testing your reasoning with clues that do not have words or numbers. However, it is not the 'best measure of innate intelligence, since some highly intelligent people do not do well on this test—they may require words or numbers to express their intelligence.

If you do better on the visual test than on the verbal or numerical reasoning tests, it often follows that you have a leaning towards science. When aptitude on the visual test is not accompanied by success on the numerical test as well, the leaning is towards those sciences that are less obviously numerical, such as the biological sciences. When numerical reasoning is also strong, the leaning tends more towards the physical and chemical sciences, as well as technology and engineering. When verbal reasoning accompanies strong visual reasoning, the preference is often to move more towards the social sciences.

People who do well on the visual test are often good at detail and at researching information, whether it is in science or in areas such as historical research.

9 CHAPTER

Numerical Reasoning Test

LEARNING OBJECTIVE

- To explain numerical reasoning test.

NUMERICAL REASONING TESTS

In this test you are given numbers that connect in some way. They connect along the row, but there is also a relationship with the numbers that are above or below each other. Sometimes a number is missing and a space mark, or line, (–), has been put in its place.

One of the numbers has been replaced by a question mark (?). From the information given, you have to find the number that would replace the question mark.

Example

1	_	3	?	Answer
_	4	6	8	

The most logical answer is 4; it fits the sequence 1, 2, 3, 4 because 2 could replace the space mark. Also, 4 is half of 8, in the same way that 3 is half of 6, 2 is half of 4, and 1 is half of 2. The answer 4, makes all the numbers fit together logically.

1	2	3	4
2	4	6	8

Example

1	_	9	?	Answer = 54
2	6	_		

(The numbers in the lower line are always twice the number in the line above. Also, from left to right, each number is multiplied three times.)

1	3	9	27	Answer = 27
2	6	18	54	

❖ Testing Numerical Reasoning

Working out the correct numbers for the empty spaces can help you find the number that can replace the question mark. You have eight minutes to do as many as you can. It is important to work as quickly as possible in order to get as many right as possible in the time allowed.

Begin as soon as you are ready.

1.	4	3	2	?	
	4	_	2	1	Answer =

Contd...

2.	2	4	6	_			
	4	?	12	16			Answer =
3.	1	?	5	7	_		
	_	6	_	_	18		Answer =
4.	_	_	8	4	?		
	64	32	_	_	4		Answer =
5.	2	3	?	_	12		
	_	_	5	8	12		Answer =
6.	3	6	9	12			
	9	?	_	36			Answer =
7.	25	16	9	4			
	_	4	?	2			Answer =
8.	3	7	?	_			
	4	8	16	32			Answer =
9.	7	12	22	_	82		
	4	9	19	?	_		Answer =
10.	13	14	16	?	28		
	1	_	4	_	8		Answer =
11.	3	7	16	35	?		
	1	2	3	_	5		Answer =
12.	11	14	_	?			
	33	42	60	87			Answer =
13.	3	6	5	8	7	_	
	7	11	11	15	15	?	Answer =
14.	?	5	7	12	_		
	3	_	8	13	21		Answer =
15.	4	5	8	10	?	20	
	10	8	20	16	40	_	Answer =

Contd...

16.	3	7	5	?	7	11	
	_	4	2	4	2	_	Answer =
17.	5	10	7	12	_		
	10	30	?	60	54		Answer =
18.	6	13	20	_	34		
	?	24	37	_	63		Answer =
19.	0	5	3	13	11	?	
	5	_	10	2	20	_	Answer =
20.	13	?	22	31	53		
	78	45	_	93	_		Answer =

Answers to numerical reasoning test

1-1	6-18	11-74	16-9
2-8	7-2	12-29	17-28
3-3	8-15	13-21	18-11
4-2	9-39	14-2	19-31
5-5	10-20	15-16	20-9

Obtaining the total score

Number Correct =	
Plus 2 if no mistakes	+2
Total score =	

Establishing level of potential

Average	Above average	Well above Average	Exceptional
1-4	5-7	8-12	13+

INTERPRETATION

The numerical test is much more than a test of arithmetic, since it involves working out the relationship between numbers and detecting a pattern. Although some arithmetical skills are required, the test measures mathematical potential in a broader way than the skill of arithmetic does. Often people who do well on this test say that they have never done particularly well with mathematics, whereas it is only lack of practice involving the 'rules of numbers'—how to subtract, divide, and so on — that has made mathematics difficult for them.

Potential in this area could point to many careers where the analysis of quantitative data is important. Such areas might be as diverse as marketing and science, because both/involve the use of statistics. If you have a high score, you would probably readily grasp financial information in business, even though you may be somewhat slow or careless with accounting.

If your score is much higher than those for visual and verbal reasoning, you will probably prefer a career that specifically uses this potential in the first instance. You would probably prefer to follow courses that have a mathematical element, depending upon your motivation. If your interests are commercial, then economics or business studies might suit you. If your interests are more technical, then courses in science, engineering or computing might suit you.

If your score is accompanied by high verbal reasoning, then you might prefer a career where you can use numerical as well as verbal ability, so commerce, business or teaching would be some of the possibilities for you to consider. When your numerical score is accompanied by visual reasoning potential, your leaning is likely to be more scientific or technical, at least at the outset of your career, though your eventual direction will be influenced by your personality.

10

CHAPTER

Verbal Analysis Test

LEARNING OBJECTIVE

❖ To know detailed analysis & verbal analysis test.

INTRODUCTION

In this test, we are looking at the way you can draw logical conclusions from the information you have been given. There is always sufficient information for you to work out the correct answer. You should not draw upon any previous experience or information you suppose might be relevant. You are given some facts and some possible answers. Tick the letter that corresponds to the correct answer.

Example 1

The town of Newport is further west than the town of Flatpeak, although not so far west as the town of Daybridge.

Which town is furthest east?

Answer: (a) Newport (b) Daybridge (c) Flatpeak

The answer cannot be (a) because Newport is west of Flatpeak. It cannot be (b) because Daybridge is even further west. So Flatpeak must be to the east of both other towns. The answer is (c).

Example 2

Fred, Mack and John all have two different cars each. One of them does not have a Ford. Mack is the only one to have a Ferrari. John has a Ford. Fred and Mack have Buicks.

Who has a Rolls-Royce?

Answer: (a) Fred (b) Mack (c) John

The answer is (c). It cannot be (a), because Fred has a Ford and a Buick. It cannot be (b), because Mack has a Ferrari and a Buick.

Because of the amount of information you are sometimes asked to deal with, it is recommended that you have a piece of scrap paper so that you can, if you wish, draw and make notes or plans. Diagrams, like the following, are often helpful:

CAR:	Fred	Mack	John
Ferrari	X	✓	X
Buick	✓	✓	X
Ford	✓	X	✓
Rolls -Royce			

❖ Testing Verbal Analysis

You have ten minutes to do as much of the test as you can. Get your scrap paper and pencil ready in case you need it. Work as accurately and as fast as you can. When you are ready, start the dock and begin.

1. Emma lives further up the hill than Jane. Pauline lives further up the hill than Emma. Who lives furthest up the hill?

   (a) Emma (b) Jane (c) Pauline

2. All the girls like sports. Sue and Josie like tennis, while Sally and Anne like running. Both Sue and Anne like swimming.

   (i) Who likes tennis and swimming?

   (a) Sue (b) Josie (c) Sally (d) Anne

   (ii) Who likes swimming and running?

   (a) Sue (b) Josie (c) Sally (d) Anne

3. Mr. Everton and Mr. Soames have longer holidays that Mr. Francke. Mr. Porter has a shorter holiday than Mr. Francke, while Mr. Peters has a longer holiday than Mr. Francke. Who has the shortest holiday?

   (a) Mr. Everton (b) Mr. Soames (c) Mr. Francke (d) Mr. Porter (e) Mr. Peters

4. Toby, Rob and Frank all take a holiday by the sea, while Sam, Jo and Tony go hiking in the mountains. Frank, Sam and Jo travel by air. Jo, Rob and Tony do not enjoy their holiday.

   (i) Who goes to the sea and does not enjoy their holiday?

   (a) Toby (b) Rob (c) Frank (d) Sam (e) Jo (f) Tony

   (ii) Who does not travel by air and goes hiking?

   (a) Toby (b) Rob (c) Frank (d) Sam (e) Jo (f) Tony

5. In reverse order, the most popular holiday tours offered by a travel company are Toronto, Florida, Rome and Paris, although Rome is extremely popular whatever the time of year. After a marketing promotion, Toronto becomes more popular than Rome, but less popular than Florida.

   (i) Which tour is most popular after the marketing promotion?

   (a) Toronto (b) Florida (c) Rome (d) Paris

(ii) Which tour is least popular after the marketing promotion?

(a) Toronto (b) Florida (c) Rome (d) Paris

6. Fred, John, Garth and Joe all have children. Fred and John are the only two to have boys. John and Joe take their children to school by bus, while it is short enough to school for the others to walk. To be fair, Fred and Joe are car owners, and sometimes do use their cars to get the children to school.

(i) Who owns a car, but usually goes to work by bus?

(a) Fred (b) Joe (c) John (d) Garth

(ii) Who does not own a car and has a daughter?

(a) Fred (b) Joe (c) John (d) Garth

7. In a museum, Modern Sculpture is to be found on the floor below Watercolours. Greek Pottery is on the floor above the Oil Paintings. The top floor contains the Italian Collection. Watercolours are on the same floor as South American Art, whereas the Oil Paintings are on the floor below Modern Sculpture.

(i) What is to be found on the lowest floor?

(a) Modern Sculpture (b) Watercolours

(c) Greek Pottery (d) Oil Paintings

(e) Italian Collection (f) South American Art

(ii) Which two are on the same floor?

(a) Modern Sculpture and Greek Pottery (b) Watercolours and Oil Paintings

(c) Oil Paintings and South American Art (d) None of these

8. Casey, Stuart, Ritchie, Billie and Colin all buy their own vehicles. Casey and Colin have room for three passengers as well as themselves. The others have room for only one passenger besides themselves. Ritchie and Casey have good front tyres, though the other tyres on all of the other vehicles are dangerous. Casey and Billie have vehicles that take diesel fuel. The others have vehicles that take petrol.

(i) Who can take three passengers in their diesel vehicle?

(a) Casey (b) Stuart (c) Ritchie (d) Billie (e) Colin

(ii) How many people have dangerous tyres on diesel vehicles that have room for only one passenger?

(a) 5 (b) 4 (c) 3 (d) 2 (e) 1 (f) None

(iii) Who can take only one passenger, but has some good tyres?

(a) Casey (b) Stuart (c) Ritchie (d) Billie (e) Colin

9. Mrs. Booth has difficulty feeding her four children, as each one will eat only certain foods. Sharon and Robina will eat rice and lamb. Kelly and Sharon are the only ones who like bread and cheese. Kelly and Sam both eat chicken and bread.

(i) Which is the only food that Sharon does not eat?

(a) bread (b) chicken (c) lamb (d) rice (e) cheese

(ii) Who eats cheese, chicken and bread?

(a) Sharon (b) Kelly (c) Robina (d) Sam

(iii) Who does not eat cheese, but does eat lamb and rice?

(a) Sharon (b) Kelly (c) Robina (d) Sam

(iv) Which food will be acceptable to most of the children?

(a) bread (b) rice (c) lamb (d) cheese (e) chicken

10. Mr. Marx's and Mr. Bagshaw's cars are black. The others have red ones. Mr. Bagshaw and Mrs. Chance have a white stripe on the sides of their cars. Miss Jenkins has a blue stripe on the side of her car. Mr. Fleming and Mr. Marx have silver stripes on the sides of their cars. Miss Jenkins and Mr. Fleming's have blue upholstery; while the others have white.

(i) Who has a car with blue upholstery and a silver stripe?

(a) Mr. Bagshaw (b) Miss Jenkins (c) Mrs. Chance

(d) Mr. Fleming (e) Mr. Marx

(ii) Who has a car with a silver stripe and white upholstery?

(a) Mr. Bagshaw (b) Miss Jenkins (c) Mrs. Chance

(d) Mr. Fleming (e) Mr. Marx

(iii) Who has the red car with a blue stripe and matching upholstery?

(a) Mr. Bagshaw (b) Miss. Jenkins (c) Mrs. Chance

(d) Mr. Fleming (e) Mr. Marx

11. In a 'knockout basketball competition, Centurions are beaten by Raiders. Saracens beat Centurions. Saracens are beaten by Raiders and Aztecs. Centurions and Raiders are beaten by Aztecs.

(i) How many games do Saracens win?

(a) 1 (b) 2 (c) 3 (d) 4 (e) 0

(ii) How many games do Raiders win?

(a) 1 (b) 2 (c) 3 (d) 4 (e) 0

(iii) Who emerges as the champions?

(a) Raiders (b) Saracens (c) Aztecs (d) Centurions

12. Stopping at the shop, on the way to school, Cheryl and Tom are the only ones not to buy chocolate. Of the five children, four of them, including Laura, buy fudge. Unlike the others, Sally, Cheryl and Sandy do not buy any toffee. In fact, Cheryl only buys fruit gums, as she does not like other kinds of sweets.

(i) Who only had a piece of toffee and a piece of fudge?

(a) Sally (b) Cheryl (c) Laura (d) Tom (e) Sandy

(ii) Who had three sweets?

(a) Sally (b) Cheryl (c) Laura (d) Tom (e) Sandy

(iii) Who are the two people who took the same number and type of sweets?

(a) Sally and Laura (b) Sally and Tom

(c) Laura and Tom (d) Tom and Sandy

(e) Sandy and Sally

(iv) In total, how many sweets were taken by the group?

(a) 7 (b) 8 (c) 9 (d) 10 (e) 11 (f) 12

13. Jane, Rachel and Tessa are girls who are wearing a jacket, coat or skirt in blue, green or red. None of these articles of clothing are in the same colour and each girl is wearing something of each colour. The coat belonging to Tessa is not

green. Rachel's jacket and Jane's skirt are the same colour. Tessa's skirt is red. Her jacket, Rachel's skirt and Jane's coat are all the same colour.

(i) What colour is Tessa's coat?

(a) blue (b) green (c) red

(ii) What colour is Jane's jacket?

(a) blue (b) green (c) red

(iii) Which girt has the green coat?

(a) Jane (b) Rachel (c) Tessa

(iv) Which girl has the blue jacket?

(a) Jane (b) Rachel (c) Tessa

Answers to verbal analysis test

1-c	(ii)-d	(iii)-c	12(i)-d
2(i)-a	7(i)-d	(iv)-a	(ii)-c
(ii)-d	(ii)-a	10(i)-d	(iii)-e
3-d	8(i)-a	(ii)-e	(iv)-d
4(i)-b	(ii)-e	(iii)-b	13(i)-a
(ii)-f	(iii)-c	11(i)-a	(ii)-c
5(i)-d	9(i)-b	(ii)-b	(iii)-a
(ii)-b	(ii)-b	(iii)-c	(iv)-b
6(i)-b			

Obtaining the total score

Number correct =	______
Plus 3 if no mistakes	+3 ______
Total score =	______

Establishing level of potential

Average	Above average	Well above average	Exceptional
1-7	8-11	12-15	16+

INTERPRETATION

It requires a critical analysis of the facts given, but it also demands that you make logical assumptions about information that can only be derived from what you have been given so far, since vital information is not given to you directly. In this test, you need the ability to be able to 'put two and two together'.

In the same way as the other reasoning tests, the verbal test requires you to analyze the situation with which you are presented. The verbal test assesses whether you can reason using words, as opposed to numbers or visual information. If you do better on this test than the other reasoning tests, you will almost inevitably be drawn towards careers where you are involved with communications in some form. High verbal as well as numerical reasoning or visual reasoning is frequently a good indicator of 'academic' potential across the humanities, social sciences and biological sciences.

Obviously, the verbal reasoning test requires some amount of vocabulary, but the complexity of the words themselves is not what is being measured. Often, people whose second language is English do well on this test because they have the logical mind to enable them to achieve with it, even though their level of vocabulary is much lower. It is worth comparing your own score on the verbal reasoning test with the vocabulary test. If you obtain high scores on both, it really does seem that a career involving words and communications would suit you. If you are high on verbal reasoning, but low on vocabulary, you will probably use your ability in talking with people, perhaps in management or in some other form of direct, person-to-person communications. If your vocabulary is higher, you will probably do well in some written or more formal communications.

11

CHAPTER

Sequential Reasoning Test

LEARNING OBJECTIVES

- To discuss testing sequential reasoning.
- To understand through interpretation.

INTRODUCTION

You are given a string of shapes. You have to work out which two shapes are missing from the string. The missing shapes have been replaced with 1 and 2. Choose the correct answers from the possible answers provided on the page. Write in the correct letter that goes with the missing shape. There is space to write in your answers on the right of the page.

Possible answers:

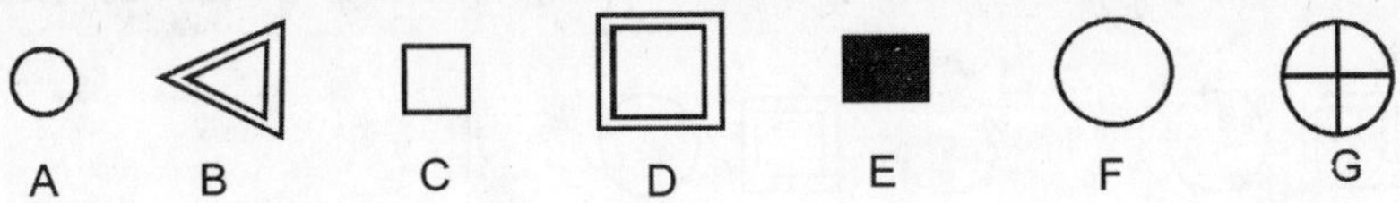

Example 1

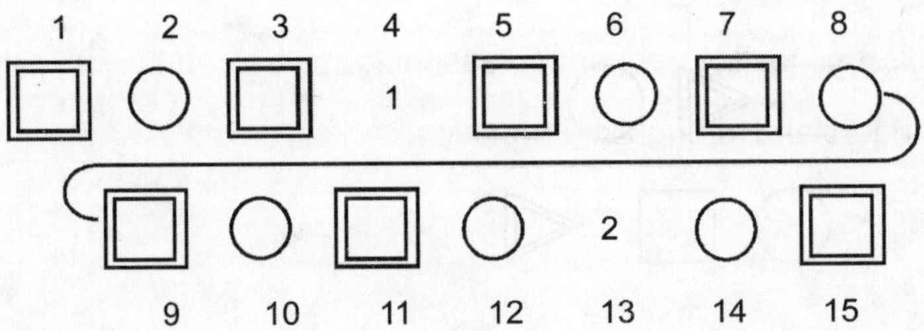

Answers

1 = F

2 = D

Example 2

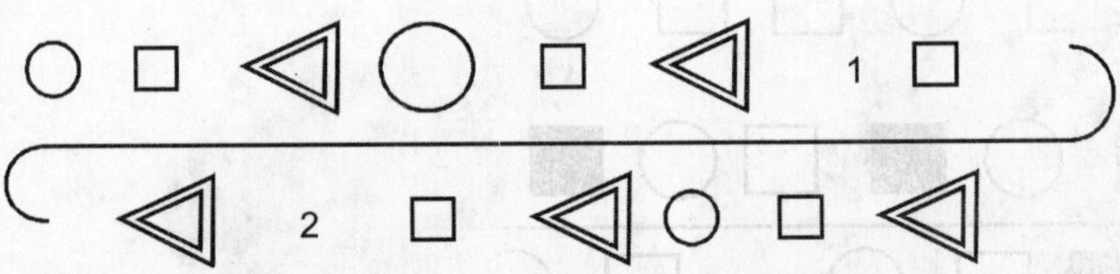

Answers

1 = A

2 = F

In Example 1, there is a sequence of alternate squares and circles. The fourth in the sequence is a missing circle, so F is correct from the possible answers. Number 13 in the sequence, where 2 has been placed, should have a square, so D has been written in as the correct answer.

In Example 2, the sequence is triangle, circle, and square. A small, white circle would go where the 1 has been placed, so A has been written in. In the sequence, the circles are alternately small and large. A large circle would go where the 2 has been placed, so F has been written in.

❖ Testing Sequential Reasoning

The real test is done in just this way. Find the correct answer from those given on each page and write in the letter in the space provided for answers. Both parts must be correct to score.

You have 15 minutes to do as many as you can.

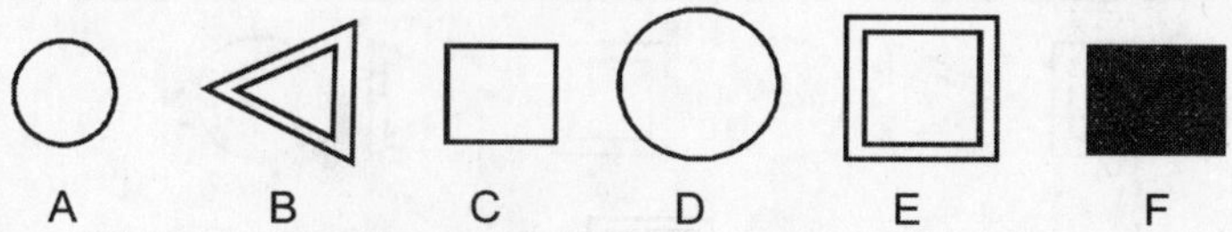

1.

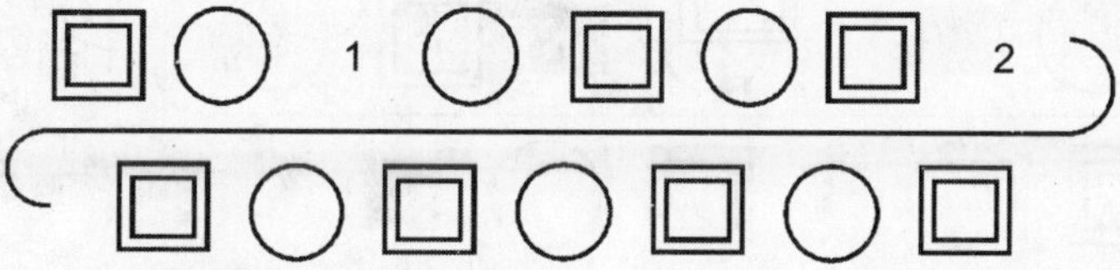

1 =

2 =

2.

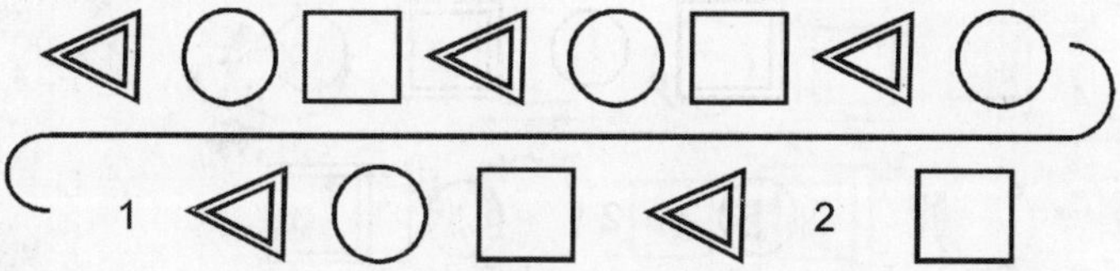

1 =

2 =

3.

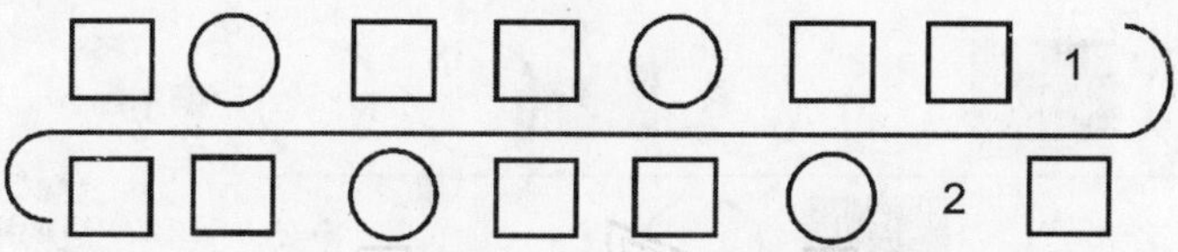

1 =

2 =

4.

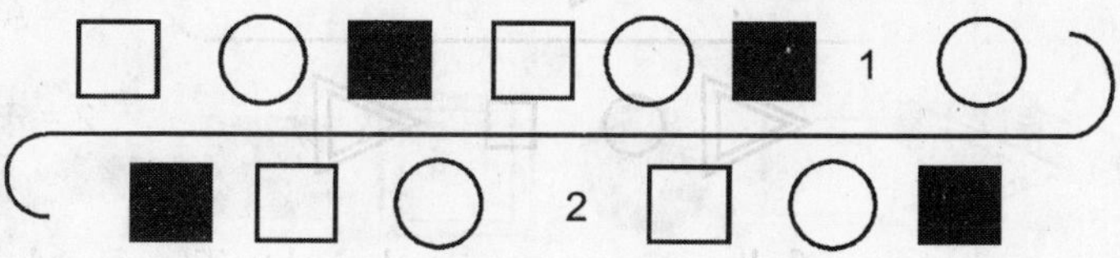

1 =

2 =

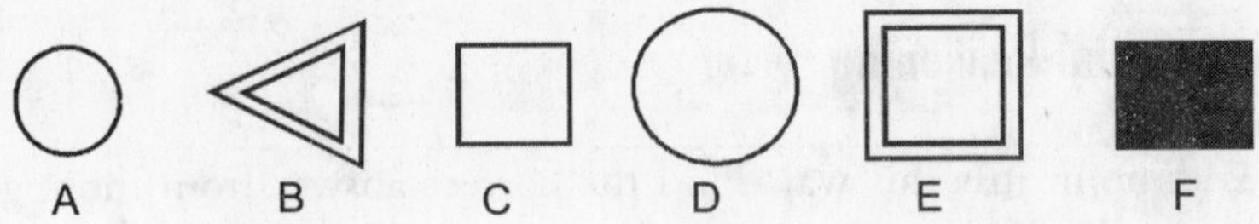

5.
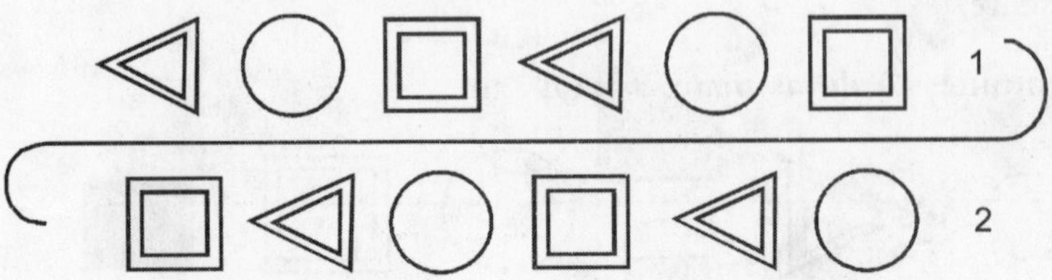

1 =
2 =

6.
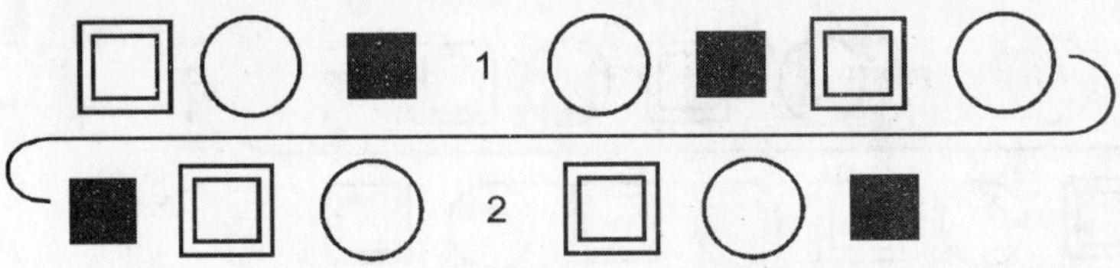

1 =
2 =

7.
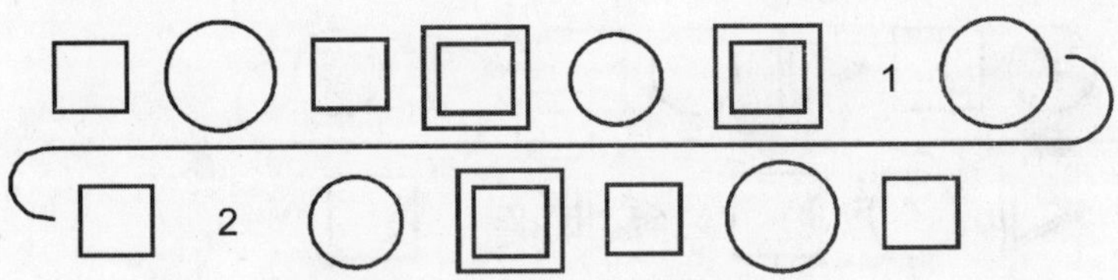

1 =
2 =

8.
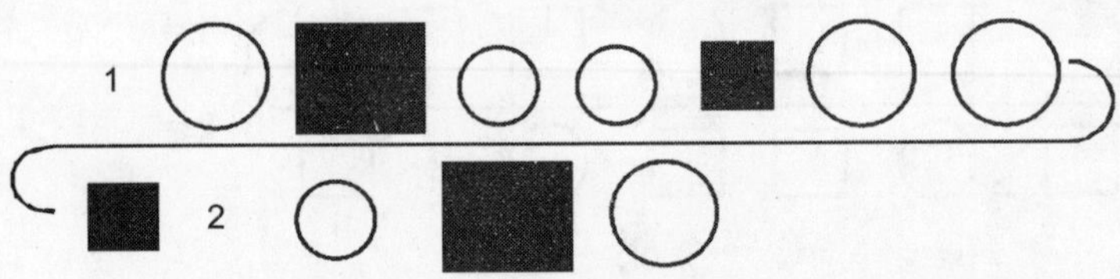

1 =
2 =

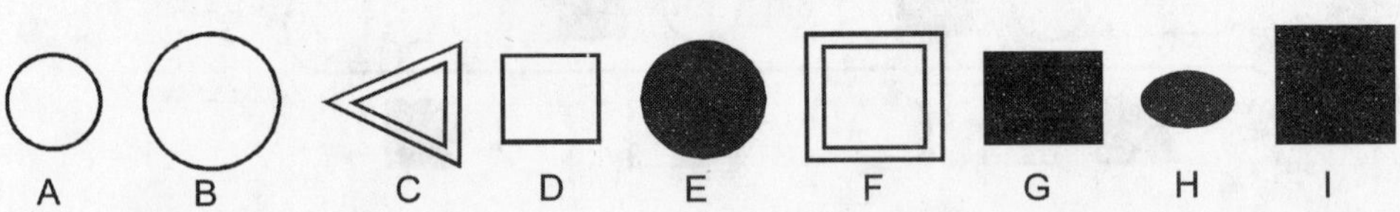

9.
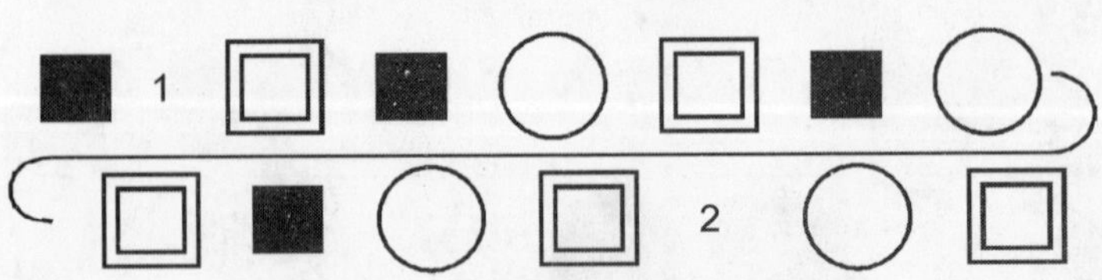

1 =
2 =

10.

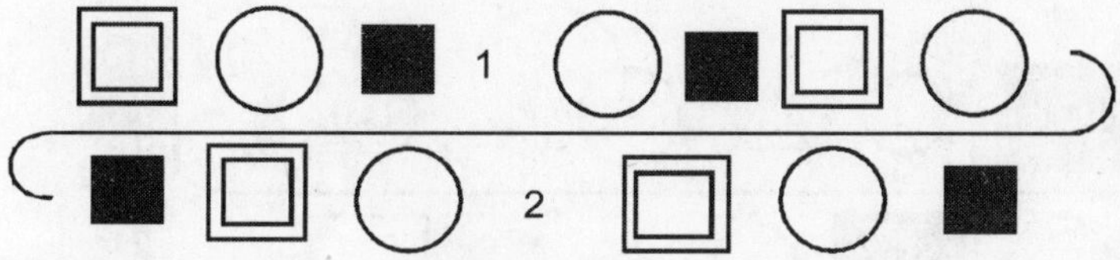

1 =
2 =

11.

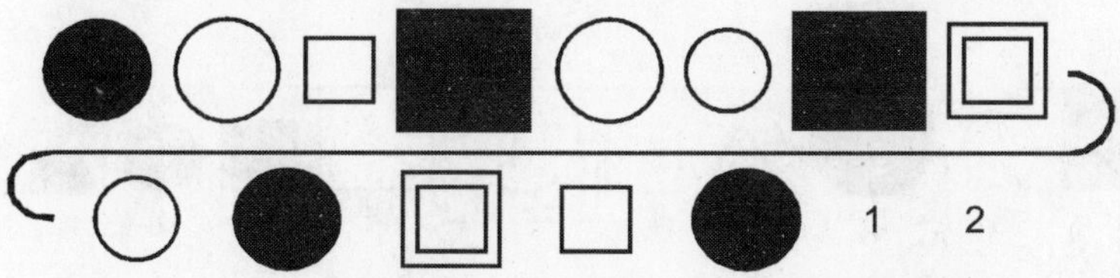

1 =
2 =

12.

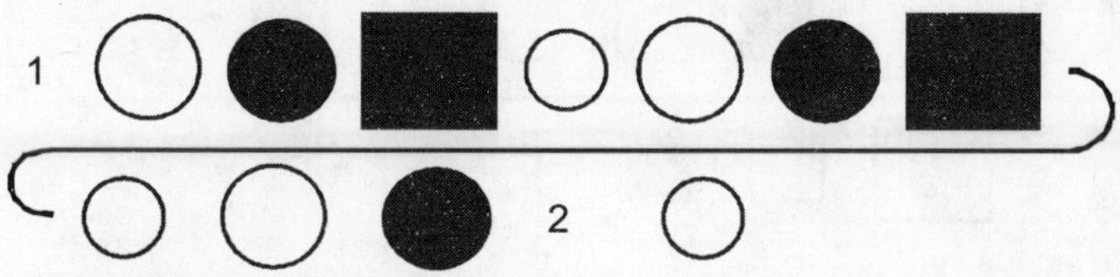

1 =
2 =

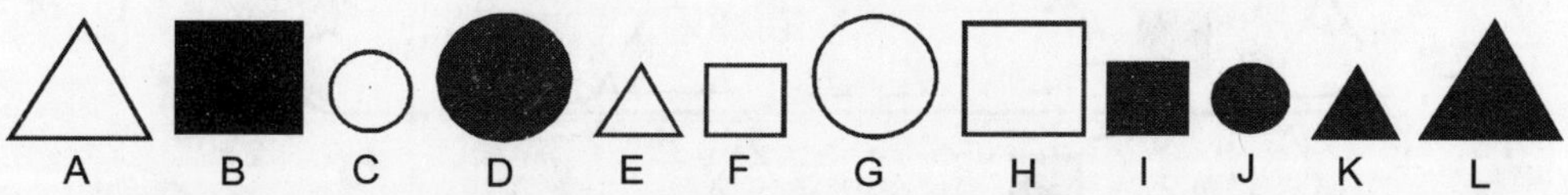

13.

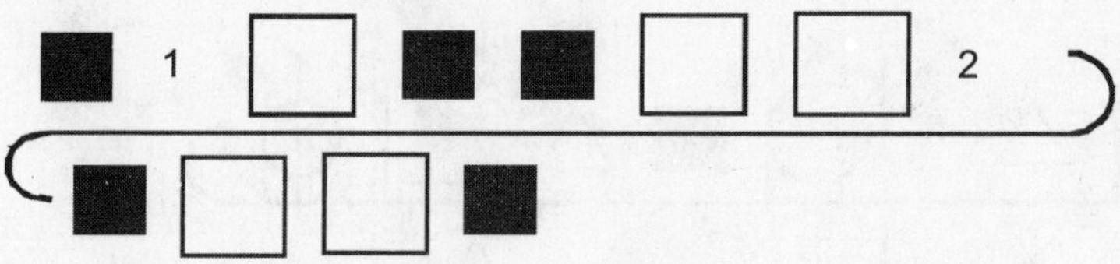

1 =
2 =

14.

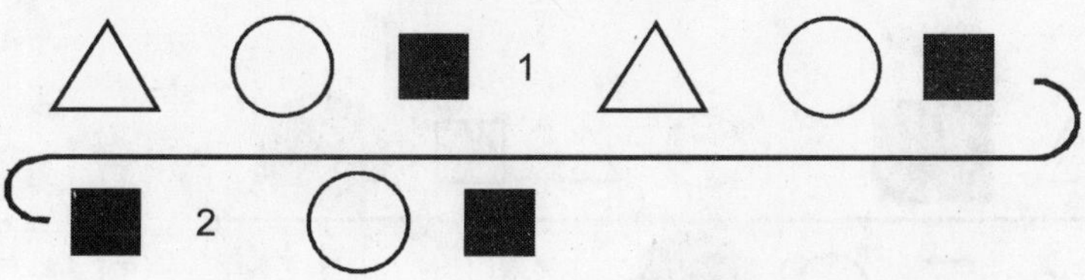

1 =
2 =

15.

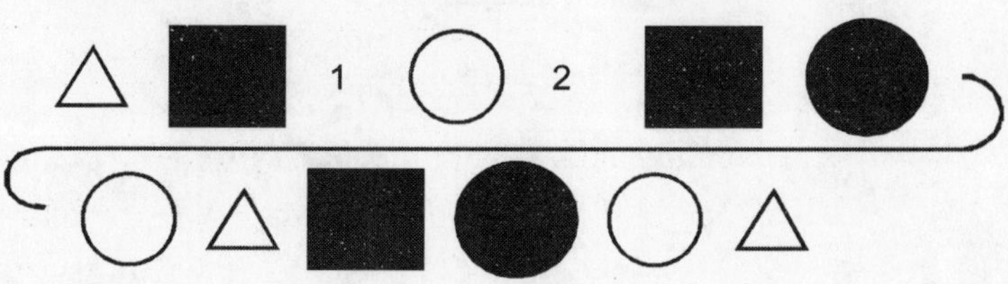

1 =
2 =

16. 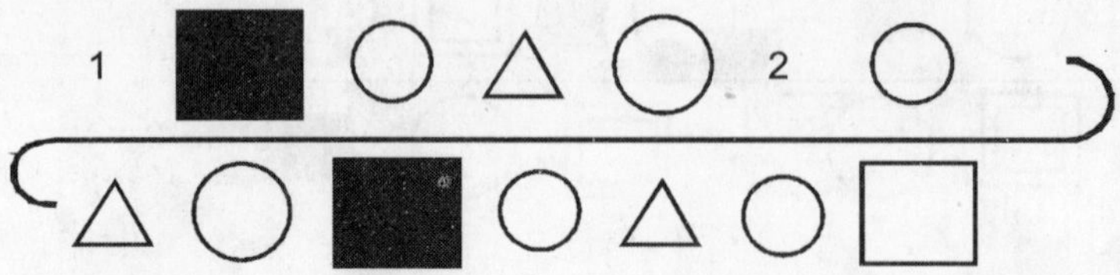

1 =

2 =

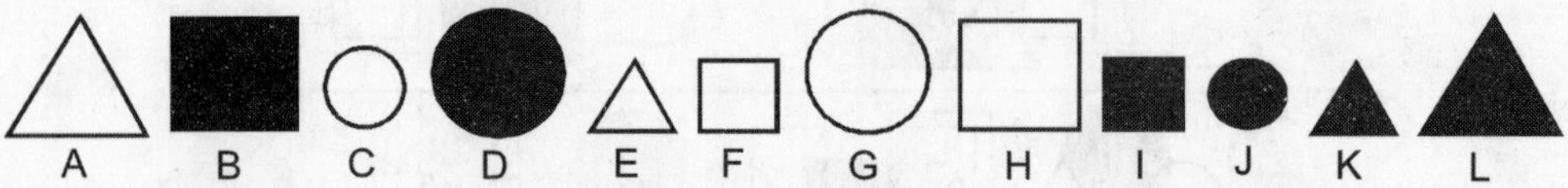

17. 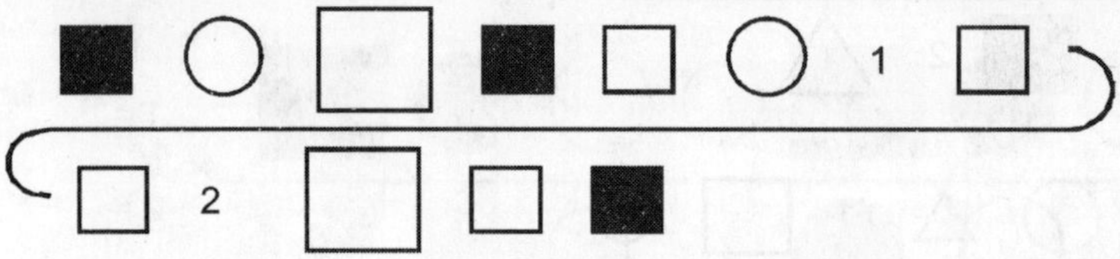

1 =

2 =

18. 

1 =

2 =

19. 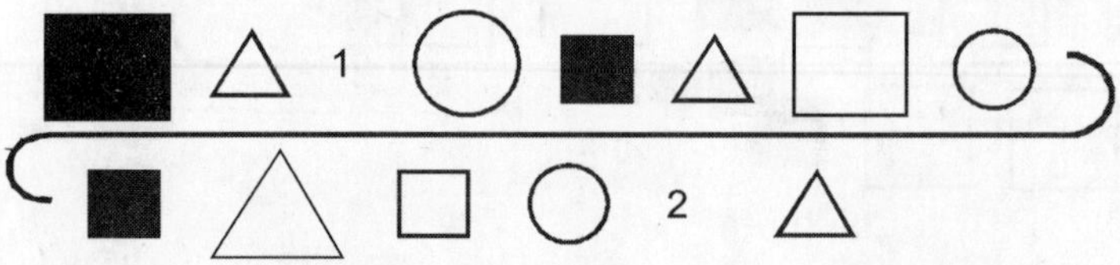

1 =

2 =

20. 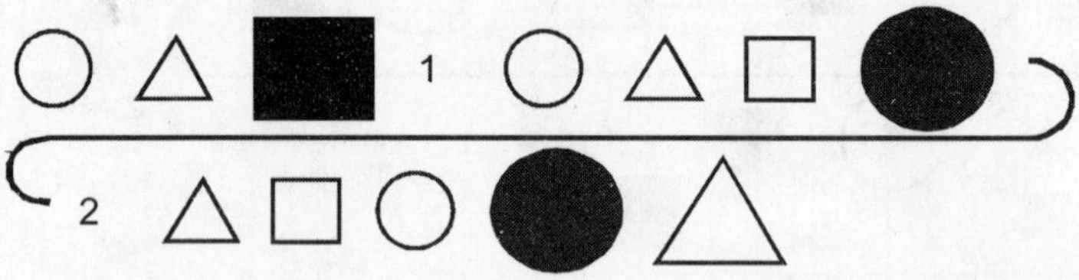

1 =

2 =

A B C D E F G H I J K L M N O P Q R

21. 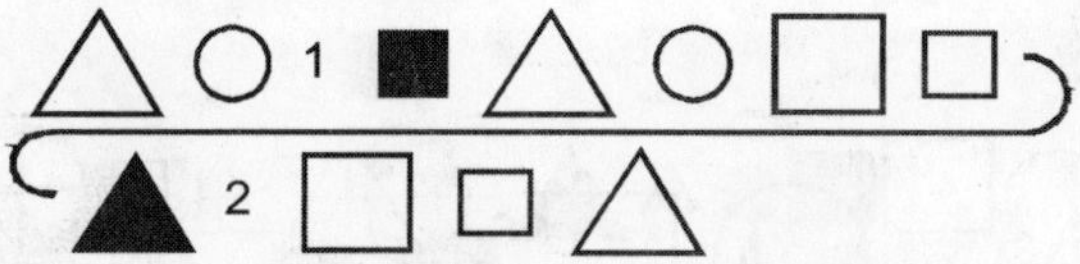

1 =

2 =

22. 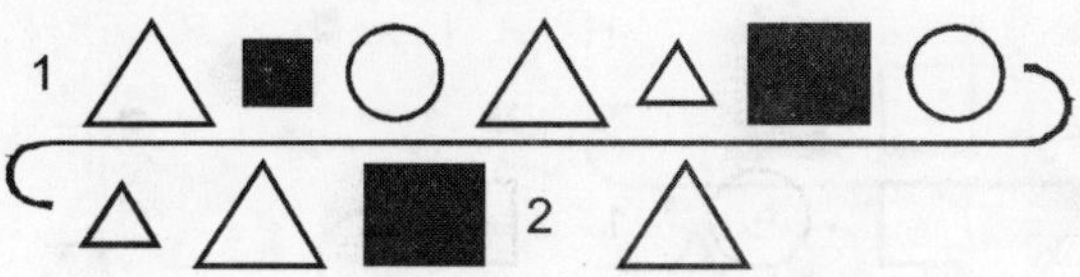

1 =

2 =

23. 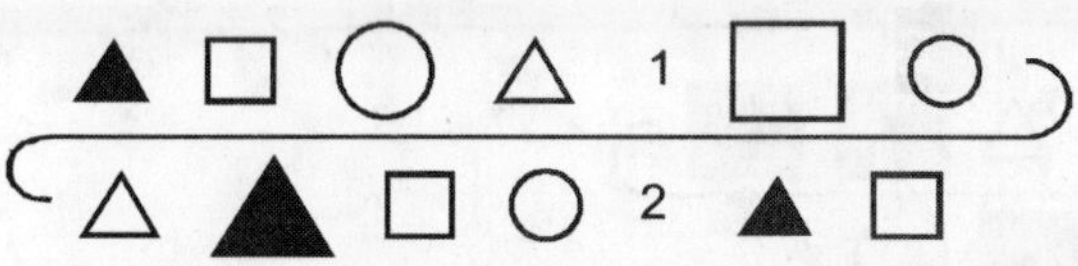

1 =

2 =

24. 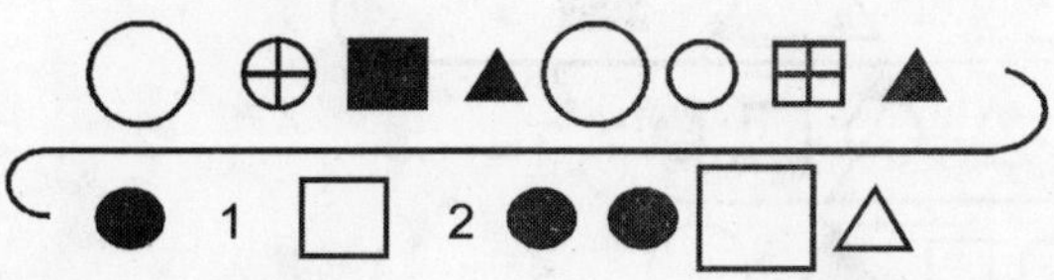

1 =

2 =

A B C D E F G H I J K L M N O P Q R

25. 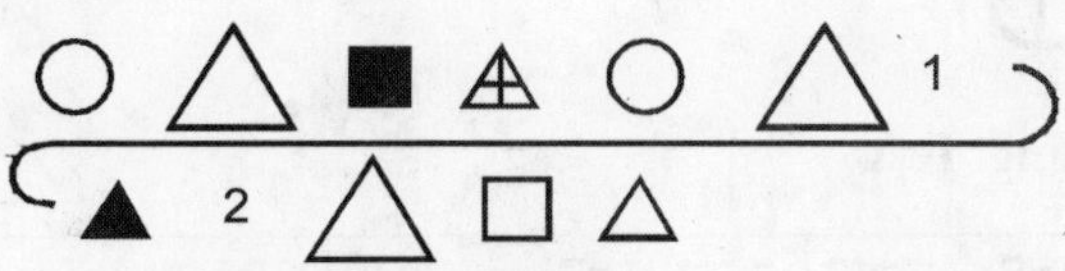

1 =

2 =

26. 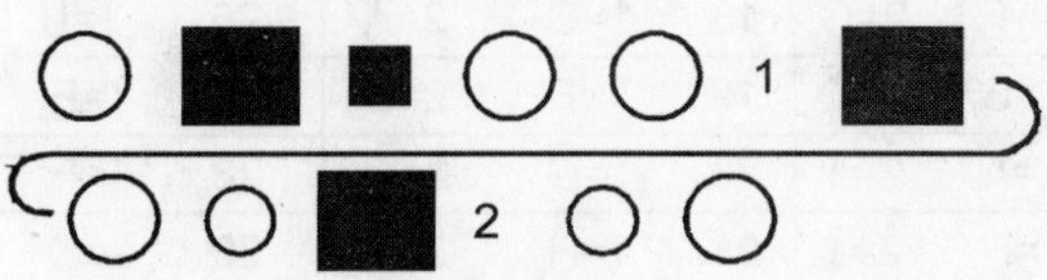

1 =

2 =

27. 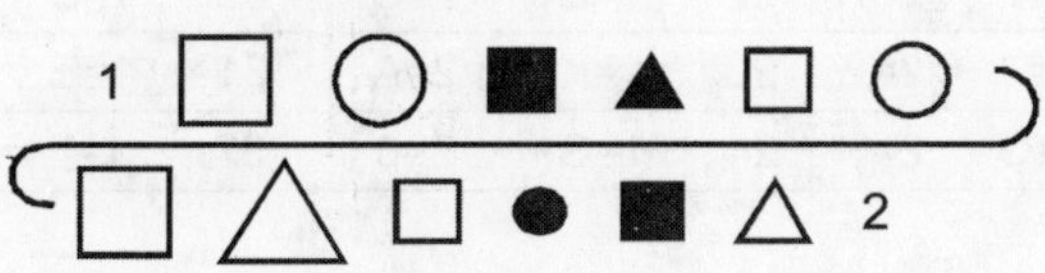

1 =

2 =

28. 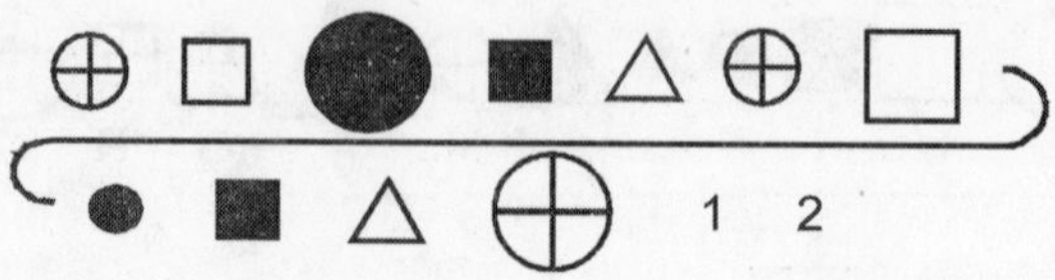
1 =
2 =

29. 
1 =
2 =

30. 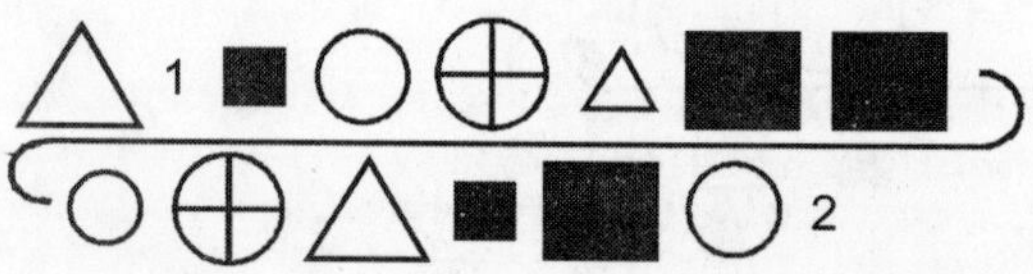
1 =
2 =

31. 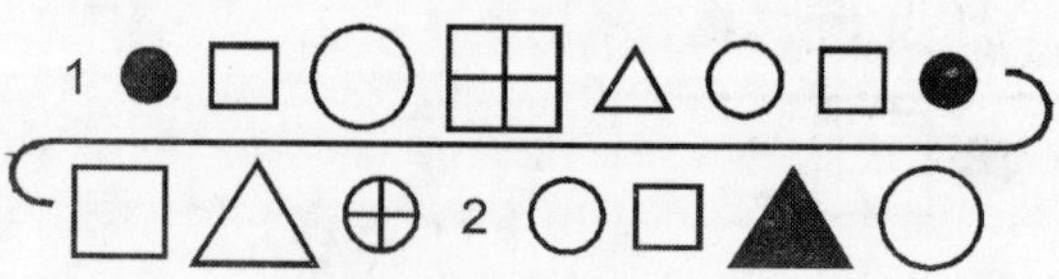
1 =
2 =

32. 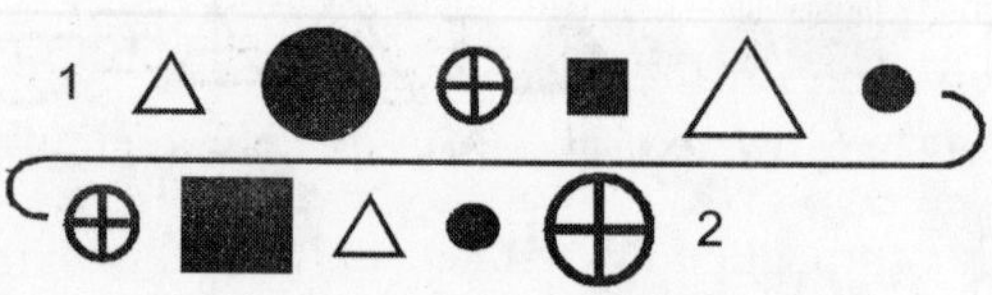
1 =
2 =

Answers to Sequential Reasoning Test

1	1=E	2=0	9	1=B	2=G	17	1=B	2=J	25	1=F	2=M
2	1=C	2=0	10	1=F	2=G	18	1=G	2=A	26	1=I	2=B
3	1=A	2=C	11	1=B	2=0	19	1=F	2=B	27	1=E	2=H
4	1=C	2=F	12	1=A	2=1	20	1=G	2=G	28	1=F	2=J
5	1=D	2=E	13	1=H	2=1	21	1=H	2=C	29	1=C	2=J
6	1=E	2=F	14	1=I	2=A	22	1=E	2=C	30	1=B	2=M
7	1=C	2=E	15	1=D	2=E	23	1=K	2=A	31	1=E	2=F
8	1=A	2=A	16	1=G	2=H	24	1=G	2=0	32	1=I	2=I

Obtaining the Total Score

Number correct =	
Plus 3 if no mistakes	+ 3
Total score =	

Establishing Level of Potential

Average	Above average	Well above average	Exceptional
1-8	9-12	13-18	19+

INTERPRETATION

In this test a number of sequences thread through each other. It is a complex matter to be able to detect each thread and see how they overlap in order to detect the missing components. In the sense that it contains only visual information, the sequential reasoning test seems to be similar to the perceptual test. However, the way of reasoning in this test is qualitatively different.

The purpose of the sequential reasoning test serves as a further check on your underlying potential. Although most people find this test very demanding indeed, if not downright difficult, it can often reveal potential that does not appear on the visual, numerical or verbal reasoning tests. In other words, if you obtain a higher score on the sequential reasoning test than on the other reasoning tests, you can be sure that you have potential that you have not used so far.

Often, people with this type of result turn out to be much more successful in their careers than their merely academic results might have predicted. If your score is well above average, compared with your other reasoning scores, you will probably find yourself eventually in a career where you work at the same level or above the level of many graduates or professional people, even though you have no qualifications to speak of yourself. You will probably 'work your way up' in your career, getting promoted because you prove you have initiative and capability, rather than because you have passed examinations that have tested formal skills. You can think quickly and are probably most effective in dealing with practical situations involving people.

Where potential seen on the sequential reasoning test is accompanied by high scores on the other reasoning tests, this would indicate strong and broad abilities that would probably be expressed by success in a career involving management.

CHAPTER 12

Spatial Recognition Test

LEARNING OBJECTIVE

- To discuss various aspects of spatial recognition test.

INTRODUCTION

This test explores how easily you can 'see' and turn around objects in space.

You will be shown a shape in the middle of the page. Below it are five other shapes. Each of these is numbered. You have to decide whether each of the alternatives is identical to the original shape. A shape will be the same as the original if it has been turned over or around. It will not be the same as the original if the proportions or parts have been changed. You are to answer each question with a 'Y' for Yes and 'N' for No.

Remember, shapes that are identical to the original, but have been turned around or have been turned over, are marked 'Y'. If it is not the same or a 'mirror image' you mark 'N'. Try to 'see' the result in your mind.

Example

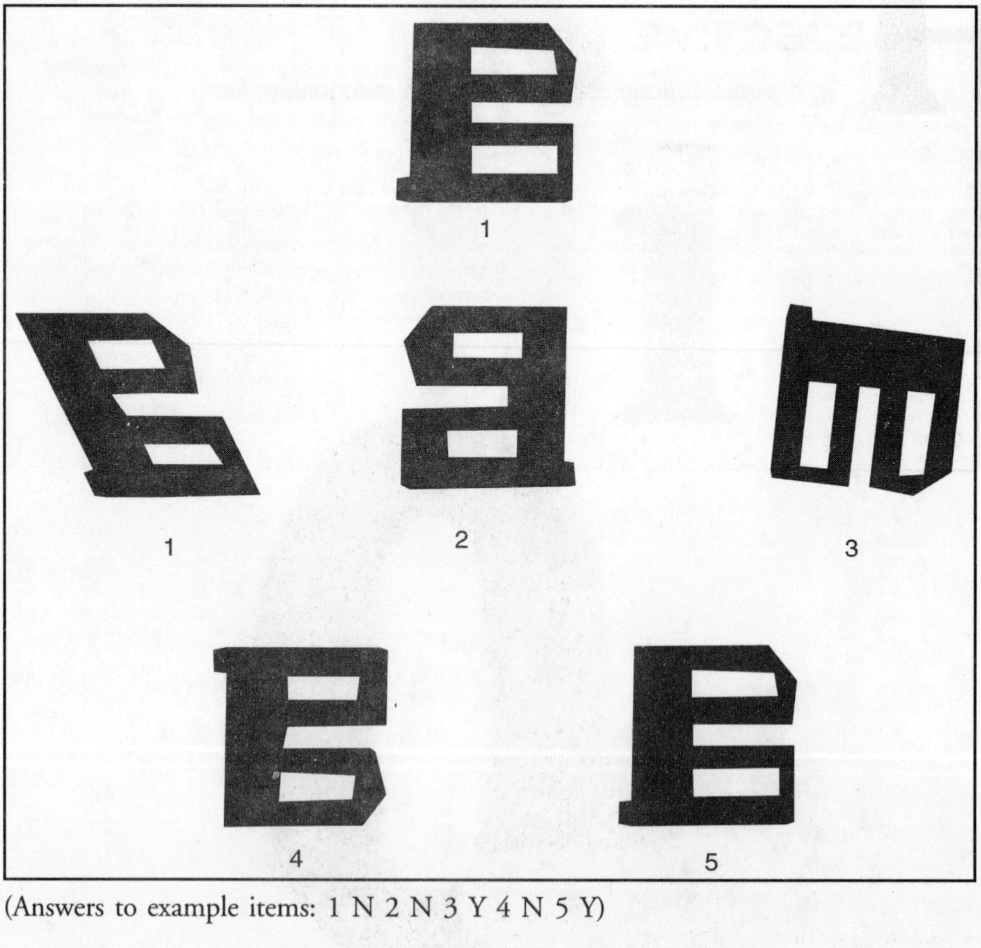

(Answers to example items: 1 N 2 N 3 Y 4 N 5 Y)

You have to work as quickly and as accurately as you can. You have 10 minutes. Start as soon as you are ready.

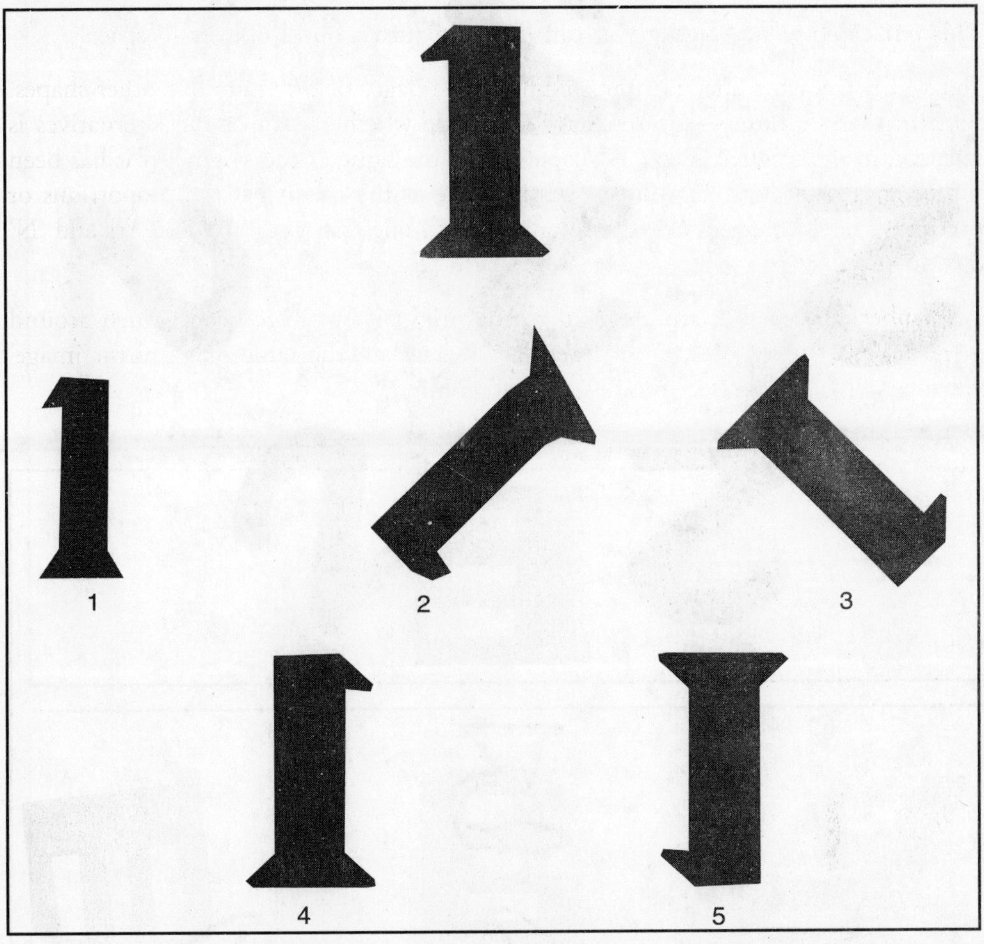

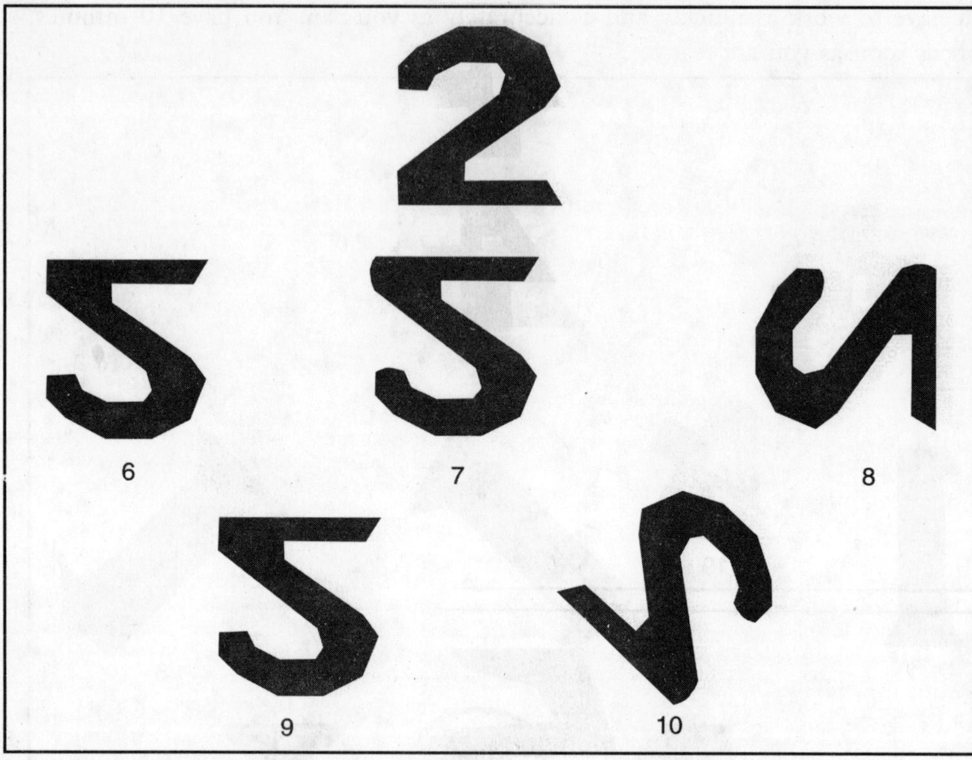
6
7
8
9
10

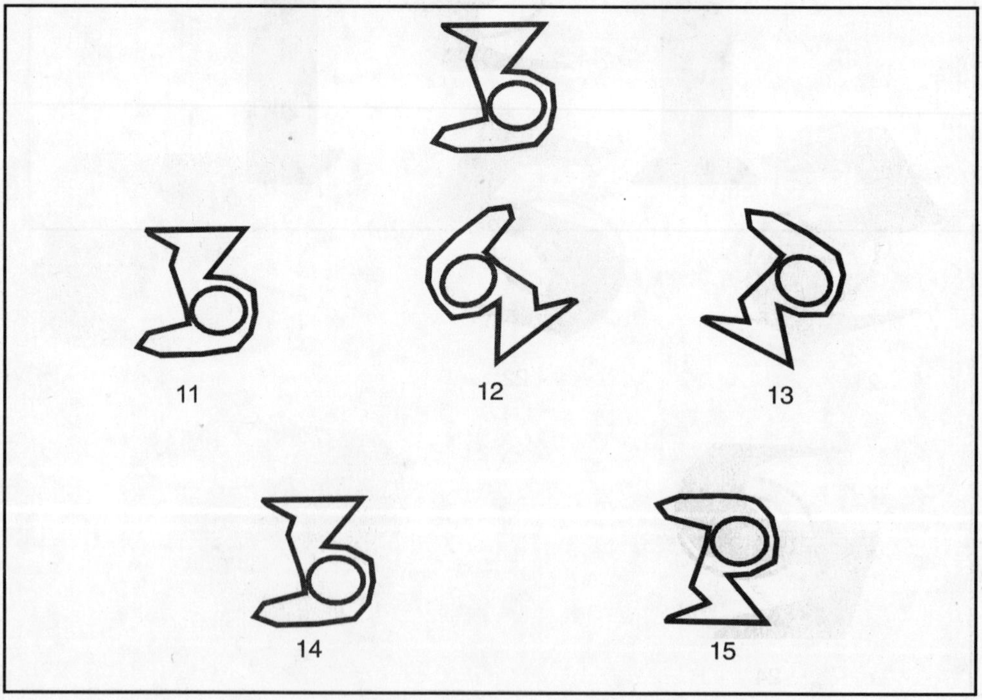
11
12
13
14
15

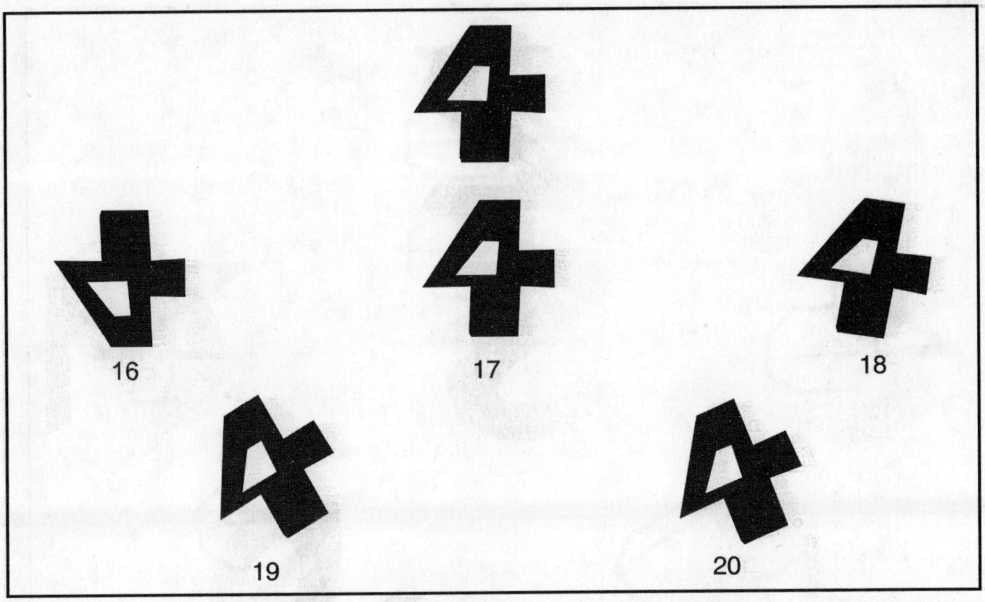
16
17
18
19
20

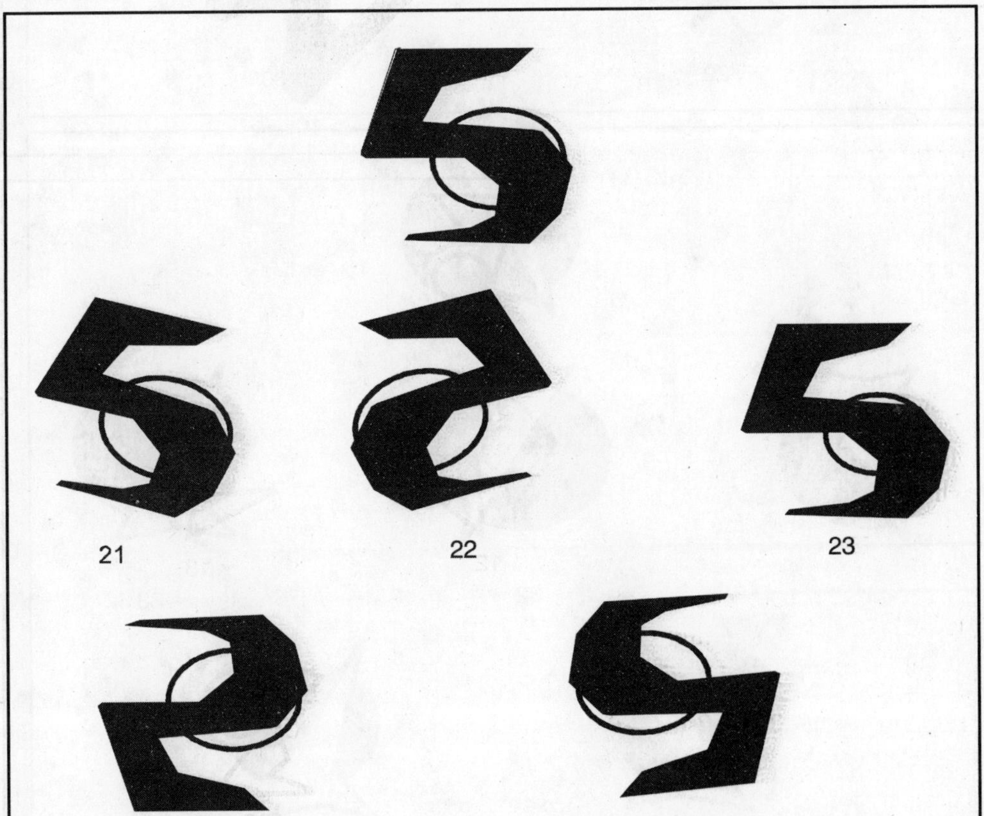
21
22
23
24
25

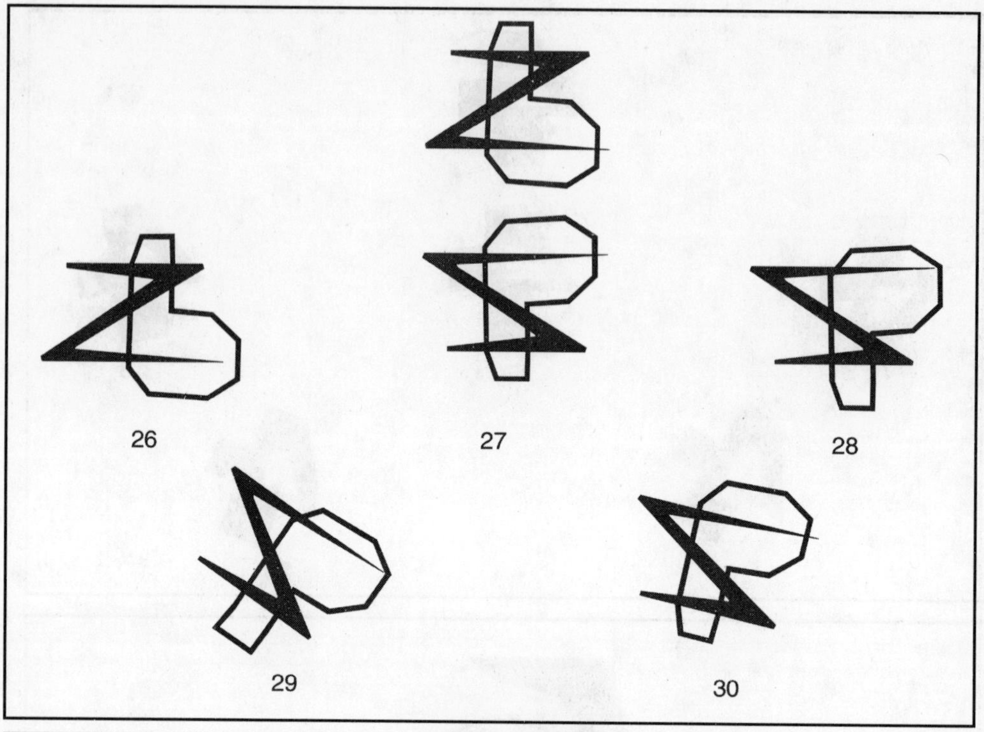
26
27
28
29
30

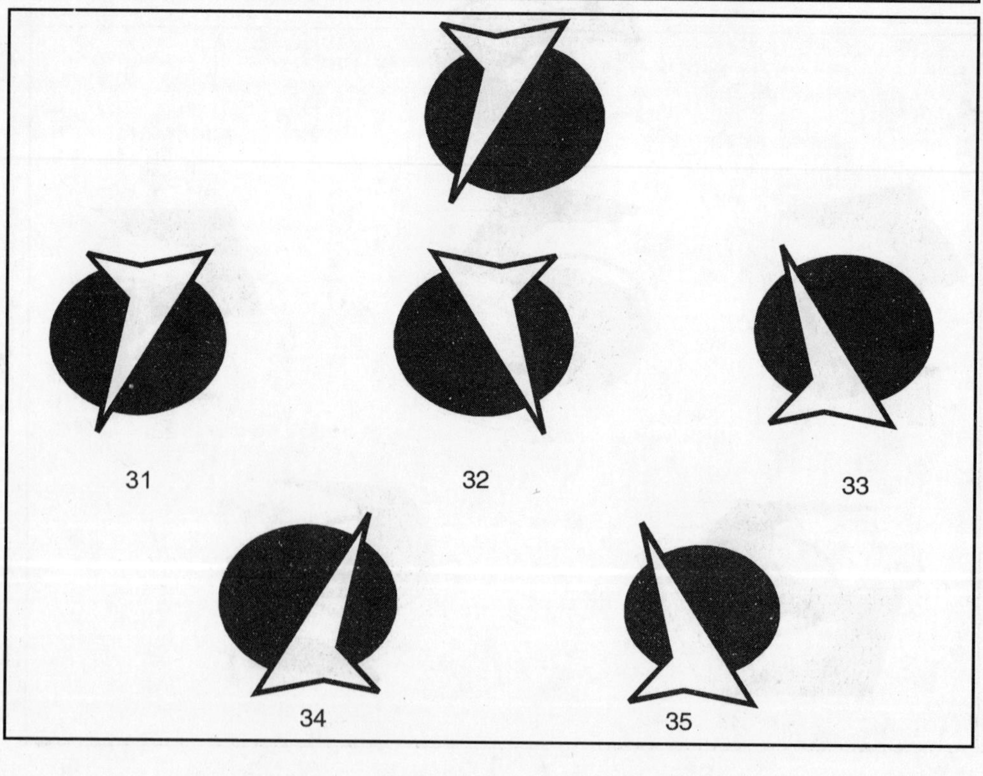
31
32
33
34
35

36

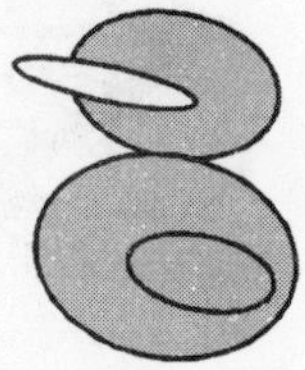

37

38

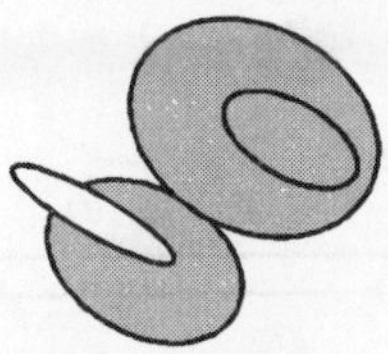

39

40

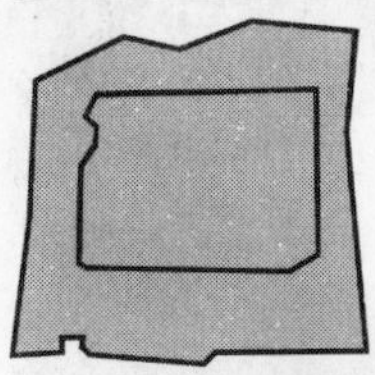

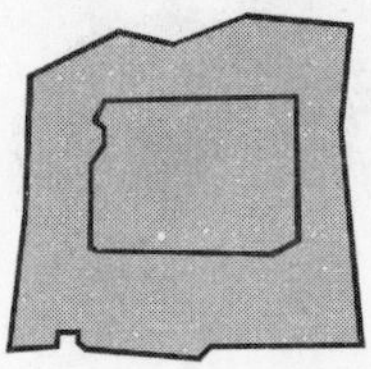

41

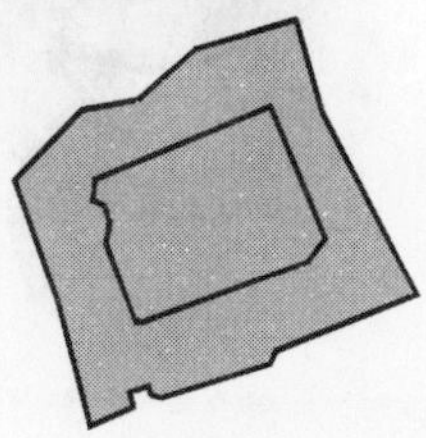

42

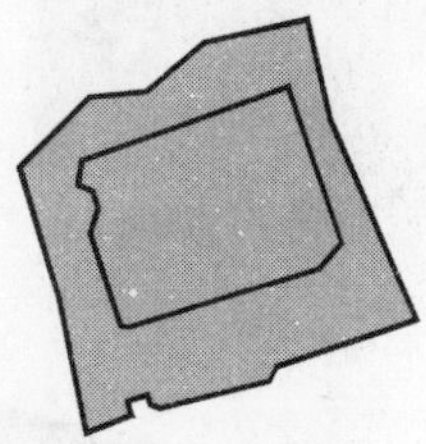

43

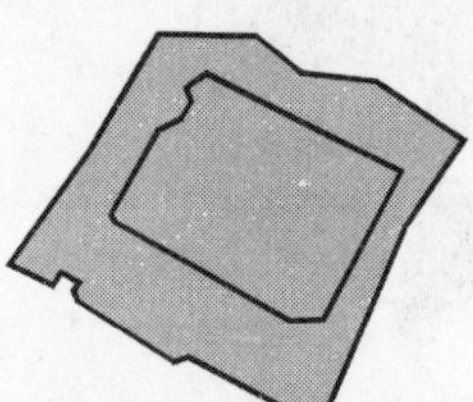

44

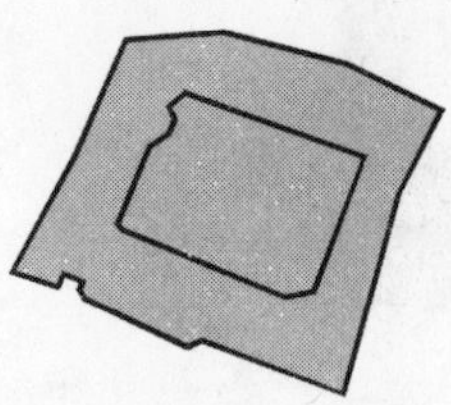

45

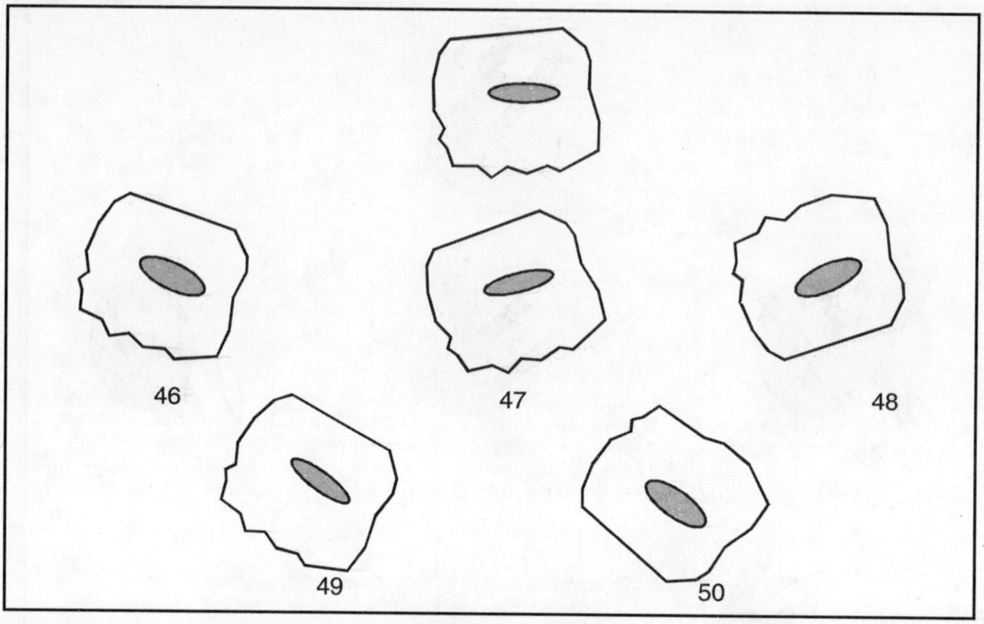
46
47
48
49
50

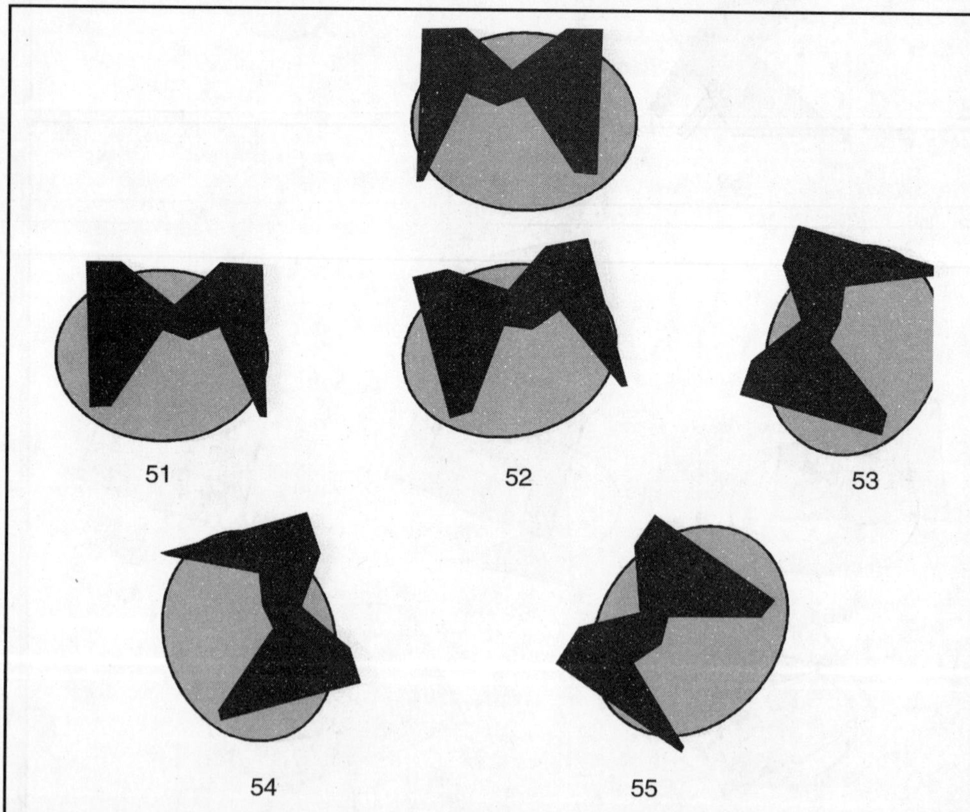
51
52
53
54
55

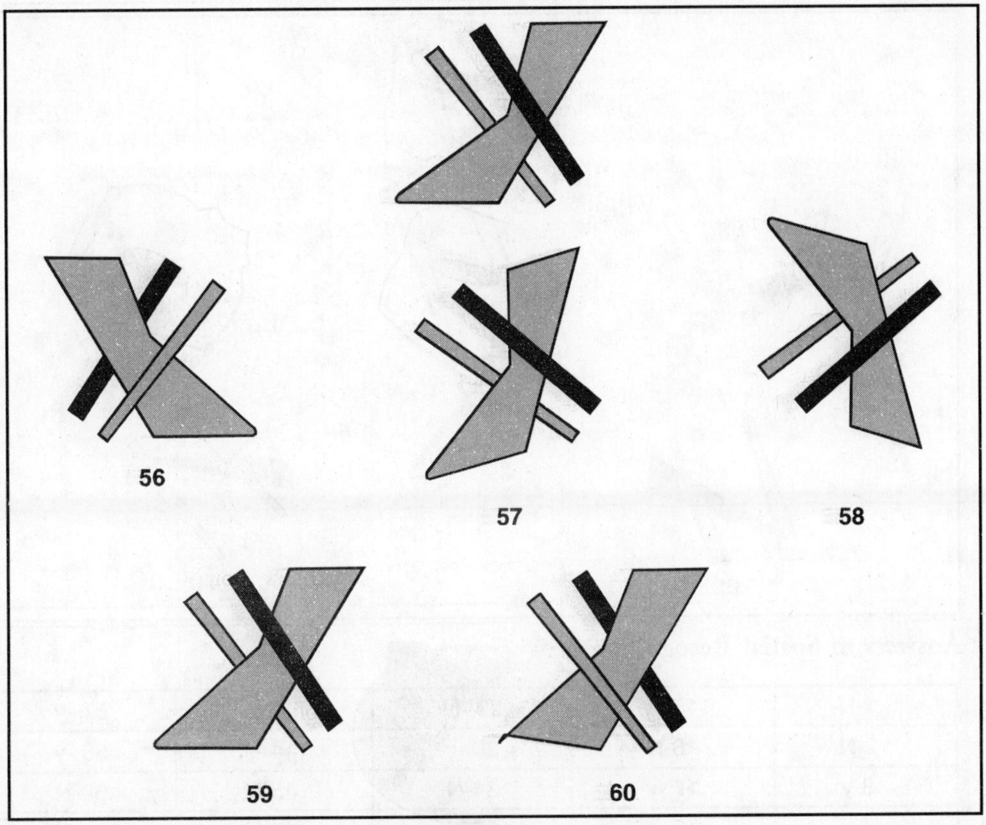
56
57
58
59
60

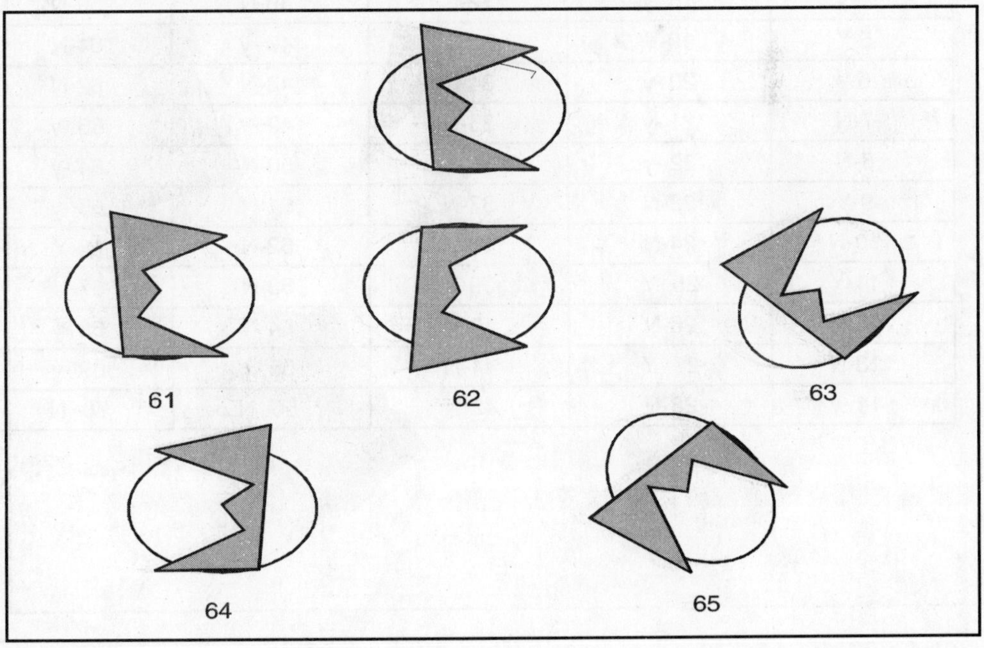
61
62
63
64
65

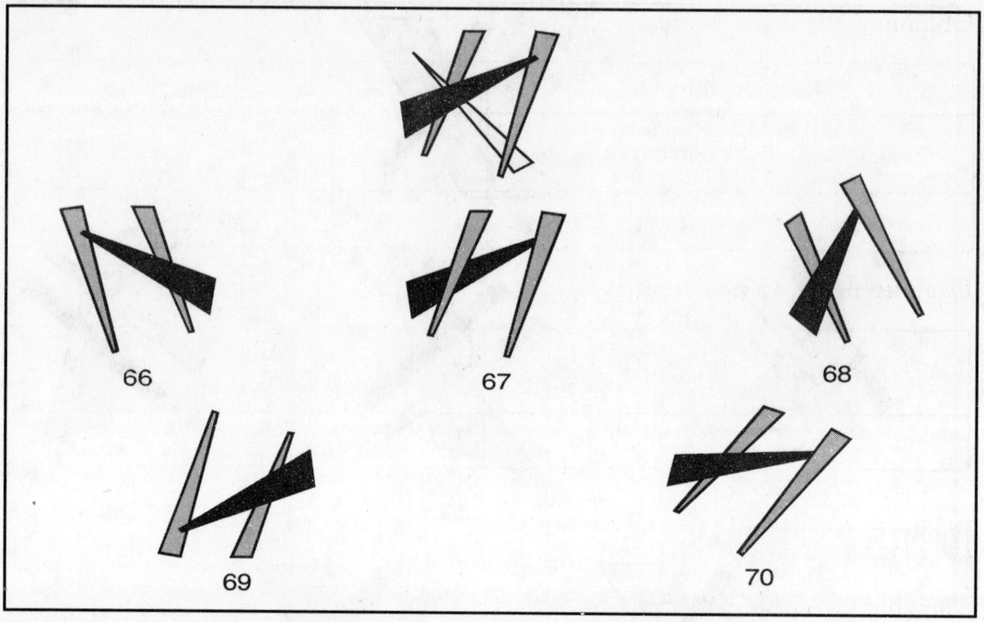

Answers to Spatial Recognition Test

1-N	15-N	29- N	43 -y	57 -y
2-N	16-N	30 -y	44 -y	58 -y
3-y	17 -y	31-N	45-N	59-N
4-y	18 -y	32-N	46-N	60-N
5-Y	19-Y	33 -y	47 -y	61-N
6-y	20 -y	34-N	48-N	62-N
7-N	21 -y	35-N	49 -y	63 -y
8-N	22 -y	36 -y	50-N	64 -y
9-Y	23-N	37-N	51-N	65 -y
10-N	24-N	38-N	52-N	66-Y
11-Y	25 -Y	39-Y	53-N	67-N
12-N	26-N	40 -y	54-N	68 -y
13-N	27 -Y	41-N	55 -y	69 -y
14 -y	28-N	42-N	56- N	70- N

Obtaining the Total Score

Number correct =	______________
Take away half the number of errors	- ______________
Total score =	______________

Establishing Level of Potential

Average	Above average	Well above Average	Exceptional
1-26	27-34	35-42	43+

INTERPRETATION

The ability to cope with rotating shapes is in some way the equivalent of, turning things over in the mind'—an ability that is relevant to many areas of endeavour where flexibility of thinking is important. Often, people who do well on this test are: seen as original or imaginative because they seem to create new possibilities or outcomes. If you can do well on this test you may well be perceived as someone who comes up with ideas that are new or different.

How this potential expresses itself is usually determined by how it combines with other areas of potential. It may reveal a purely artistic potential, but could also appear in subjects such as computing and systems, technology, and geography. If accompanied by verbal ability, you may well be drawn to careers where you can be involved with ideas and cultural activities, such as writing or media work.

CHAPTER 13

Three-D Test

LEARNING OBJECTIVES

- To understand pros and cons of Three-D Test.
- To show the methods of the test.

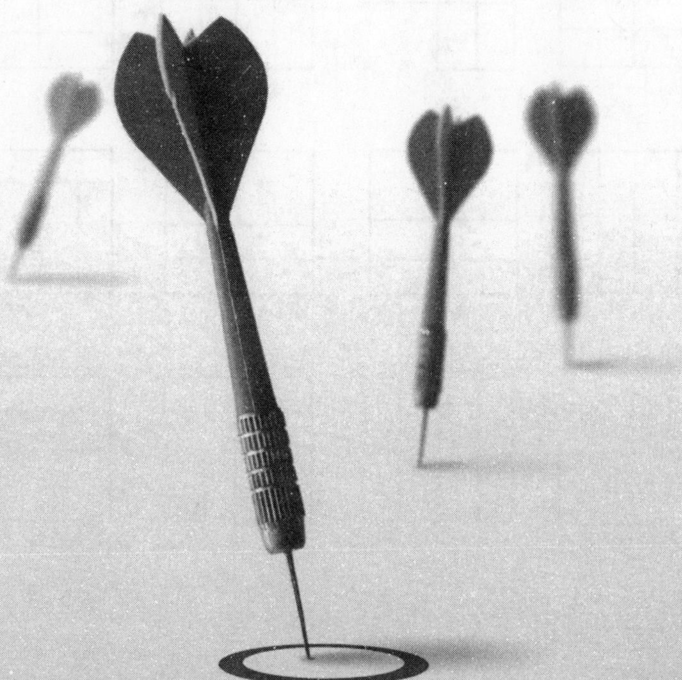

THREE-D TEST

In this test you are asked to discover the hidden sides of objects. You are shown a stack of blocks. Each block is exactly the same size. You can see the front, or facing, sides. You can also see the top side. But you cannot see the two sides that are hidden from your view. Nor can you see the bottom, or underneath, side. However, you can imagine what the hidden sides and underneath must look like.

In the example given below, there is a stack of five blocks. You have to imagine, out of the five possibilities you are given, which one is the view from side A. Only one of the five is correct. Then, do the same for sides B and C. In each set of possibilities, only one is correct, even though it may have been turned around. Tick the correct one.

Example

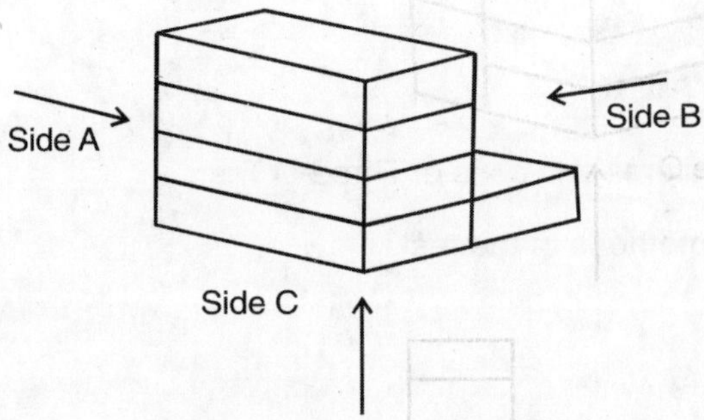

Side A

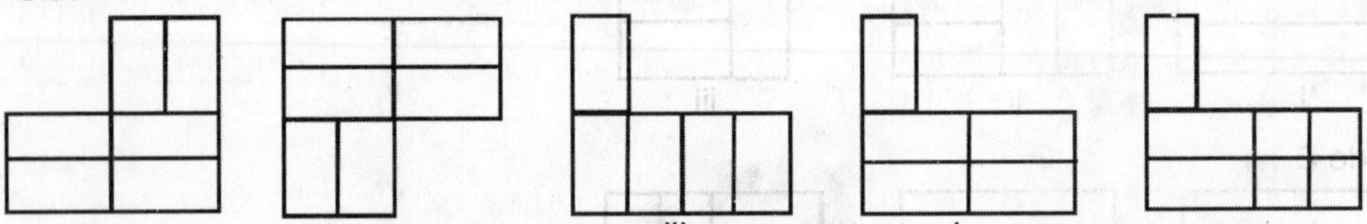

i ii iii iv v

Side B

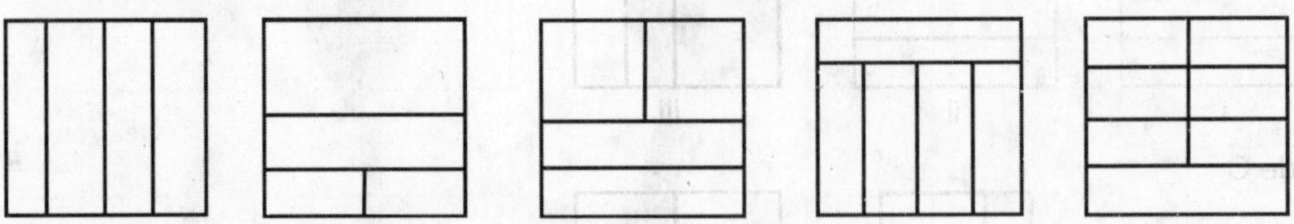

i ii iii iv v

Side C

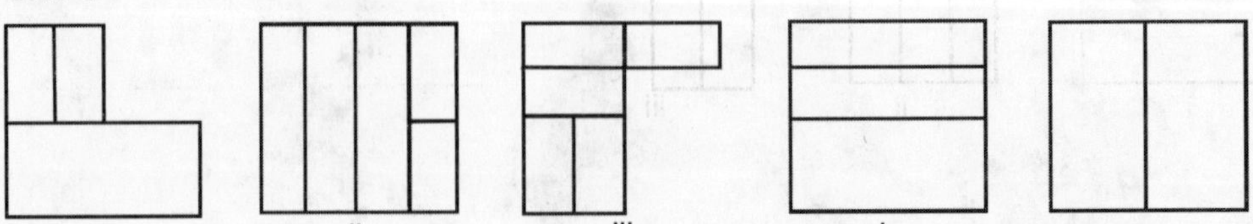

i ii iii iv v

For the example, the answer is number (iii) for side A, even though it has been turned around. For side B, number (i) is the correct answer. Number (v) is the correct answer for side C.

❖ Testing

You may find it helpful to have spare paper available. For each example, tick the correct choice out of the five options given for each side. Be careful, as the view may have been turned around. You have five minutes to do as many as you can.

1.

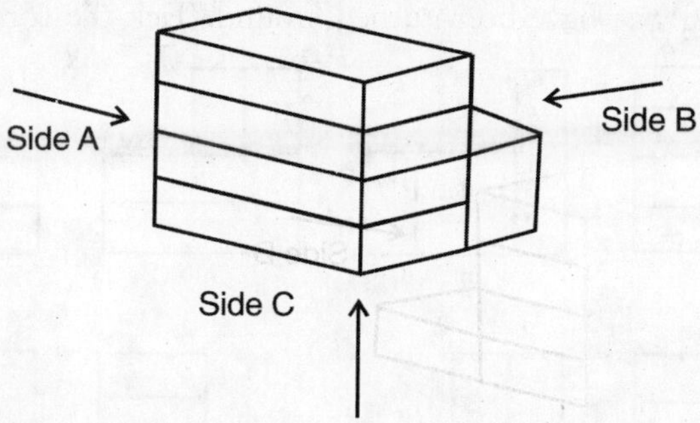

Side A

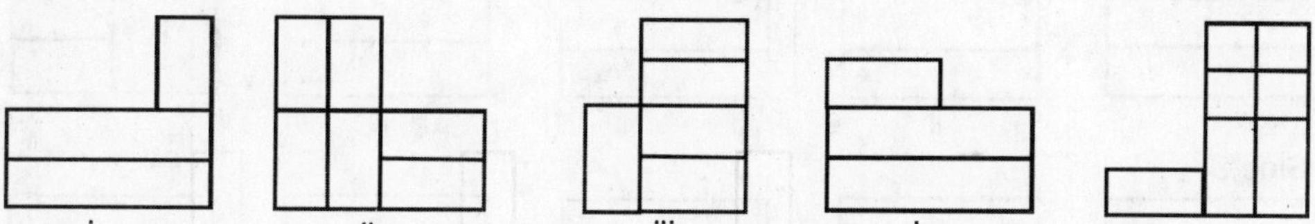

i ii iii iv v

Side B

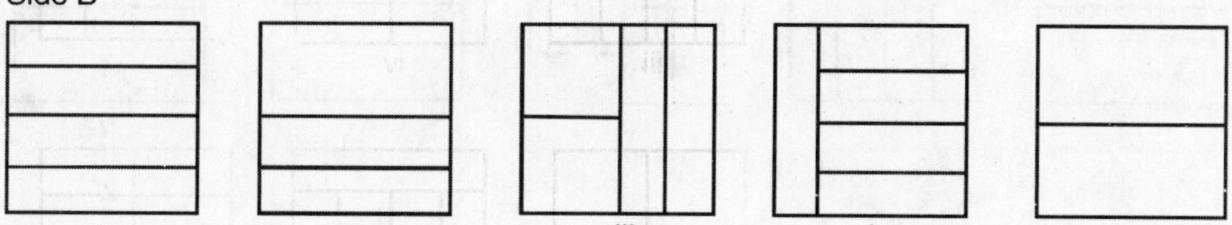

i ii iii iv v

Side C

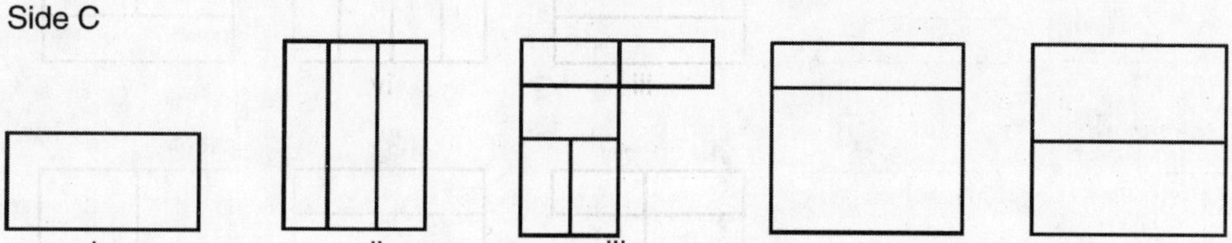

i ii iii iv v

2.

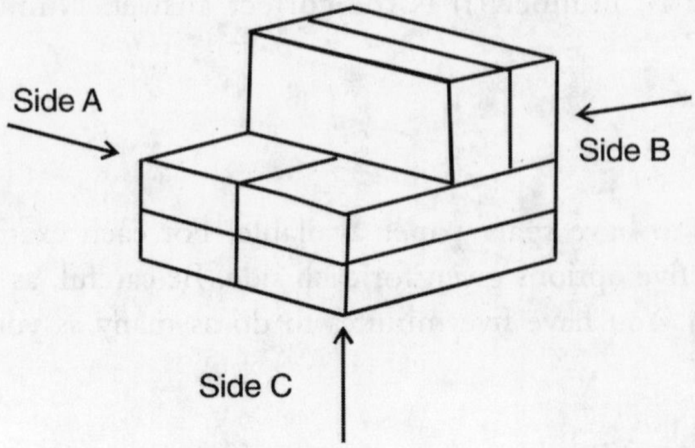
Side A
Side B
Side C

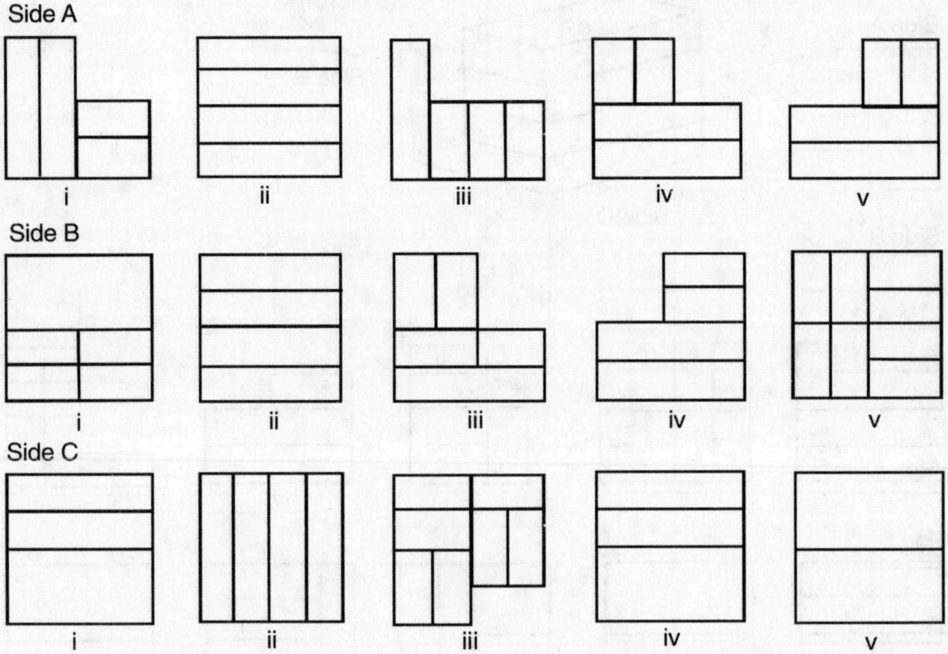
Side A
i
ii
iii
iv
v
Side B
i
ii
iii
iv
v
Side C
i
ii
iii
iv
v

3.

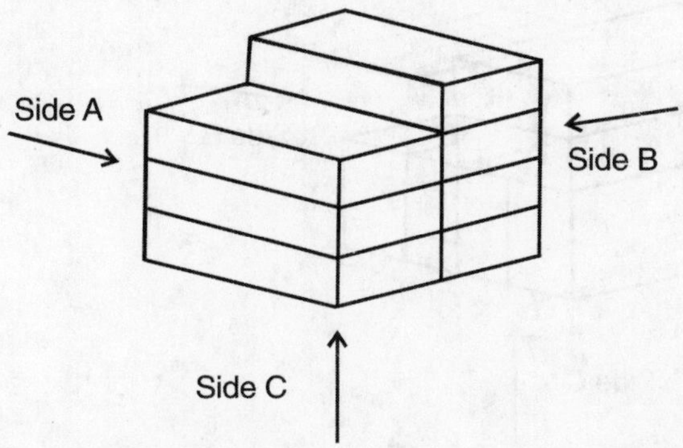

Side A

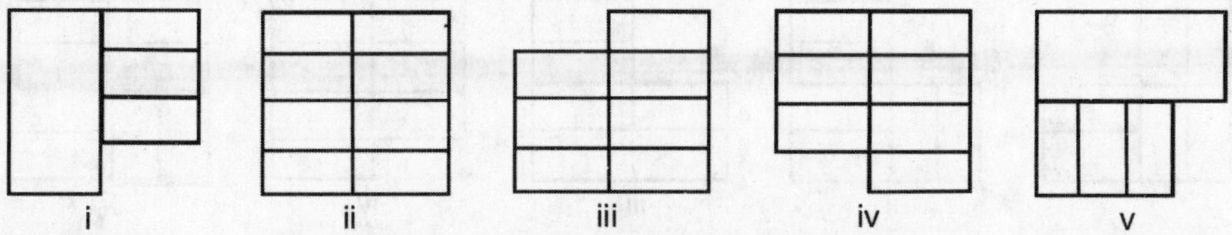

Side B

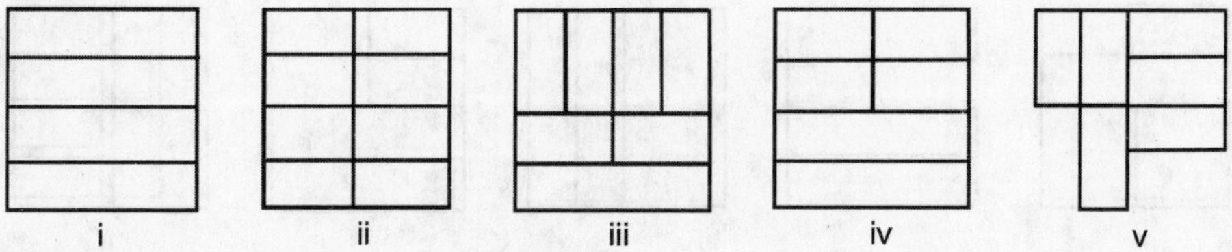

Side C

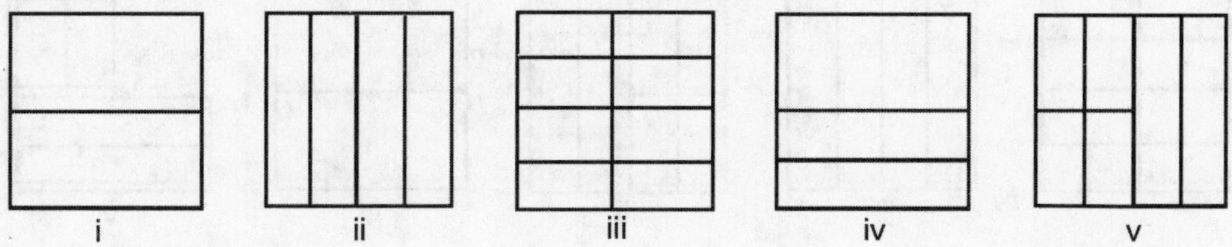

4.

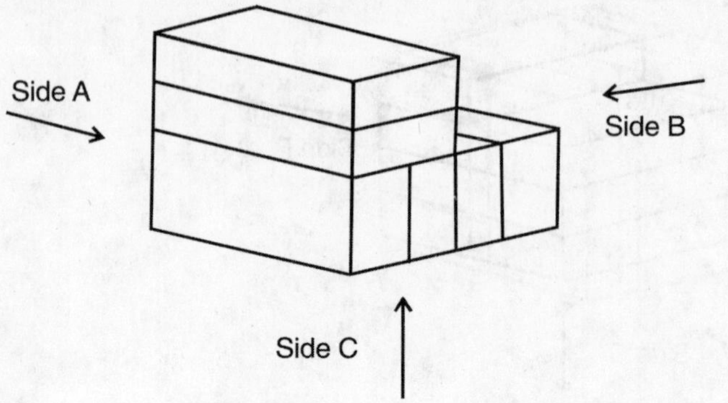

Side A

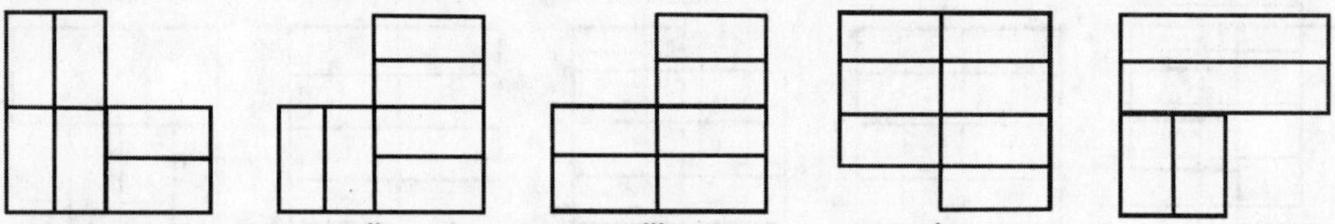

i ii iii iv v

Side B

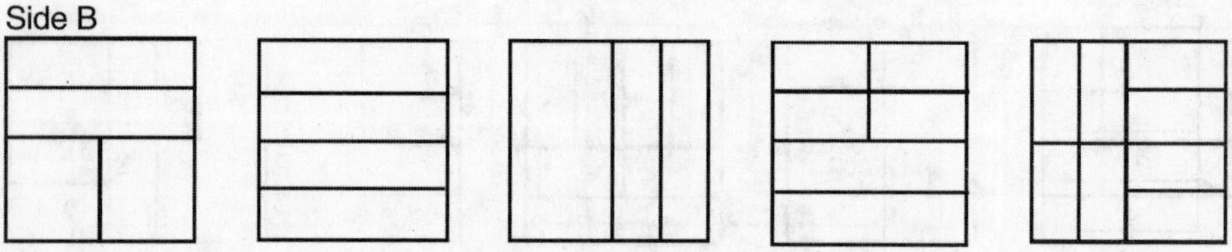

i ii iii iv v

Side C

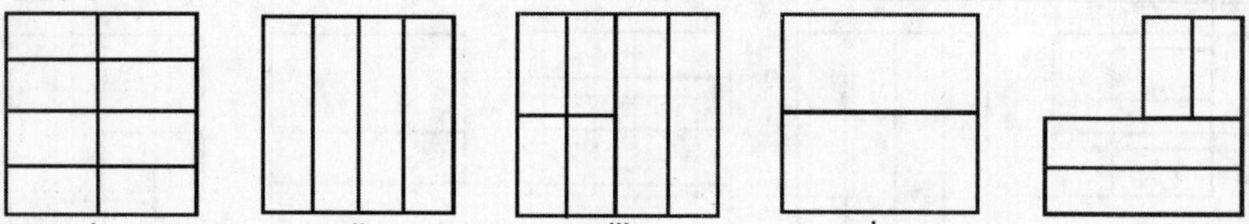

i ii iii iv v

5.

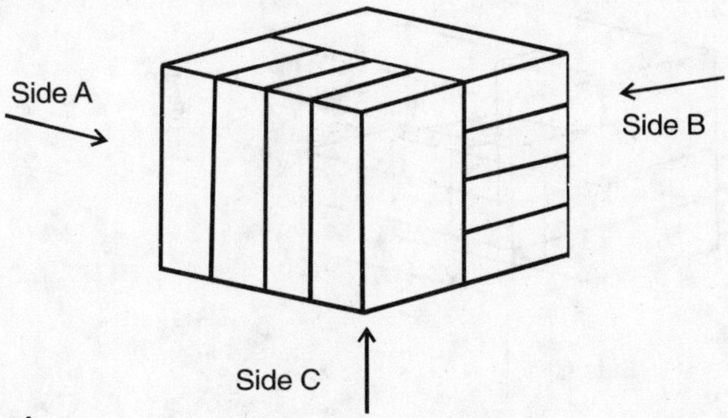

Side A

Side B

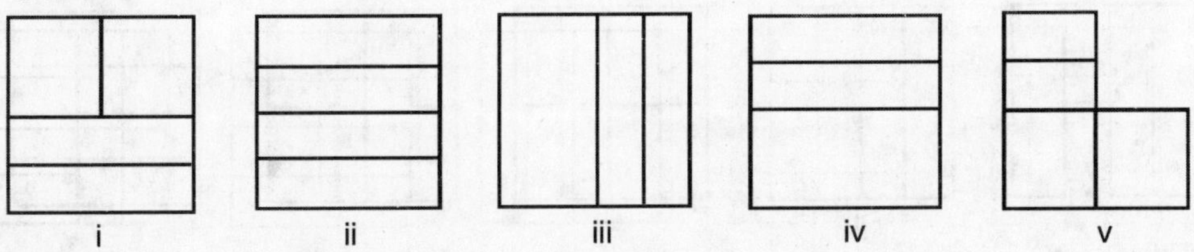

Side C

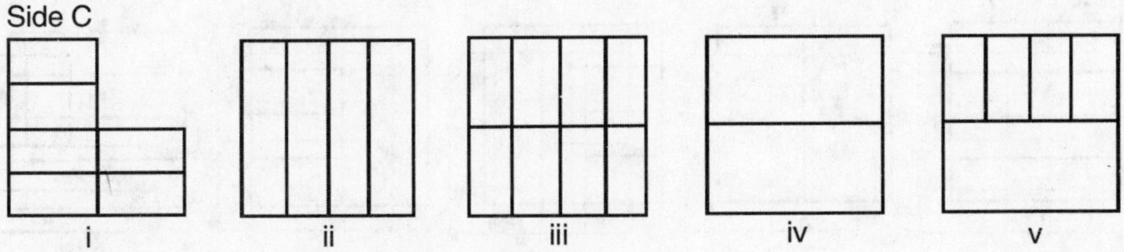

6.

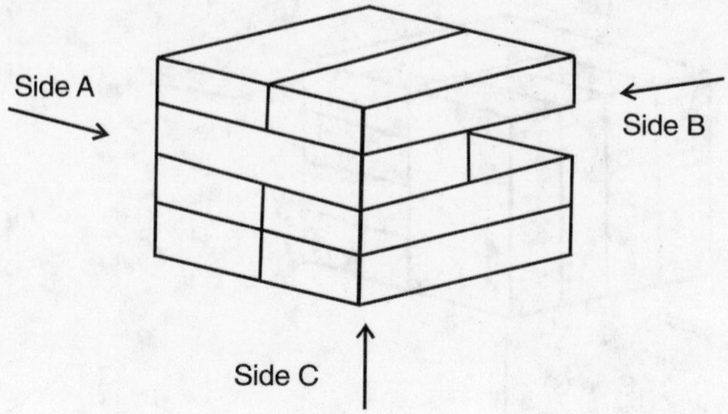

Side A

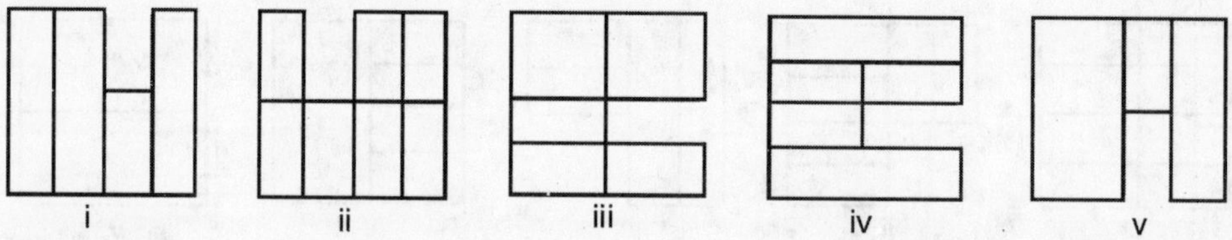

Side B

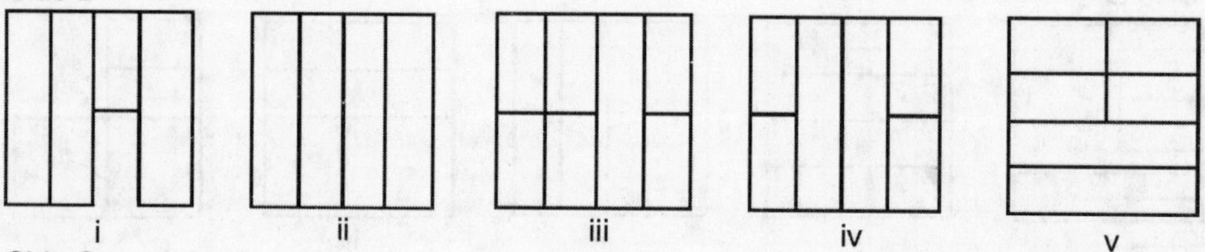

Side C

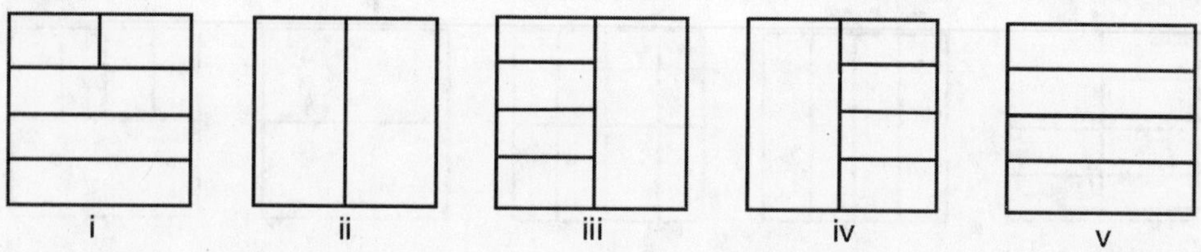

7.

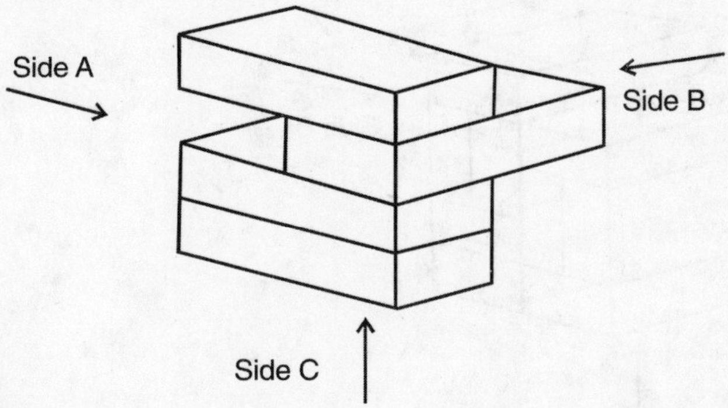

Side A

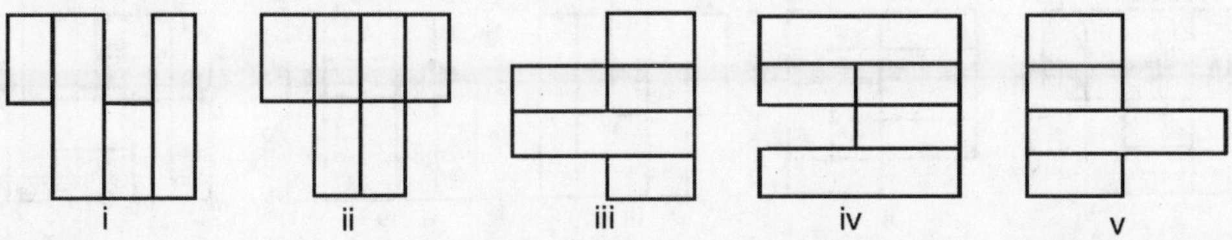

Side B

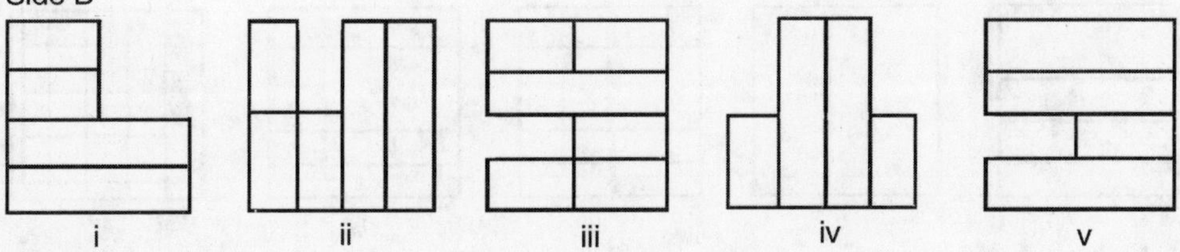

Side C

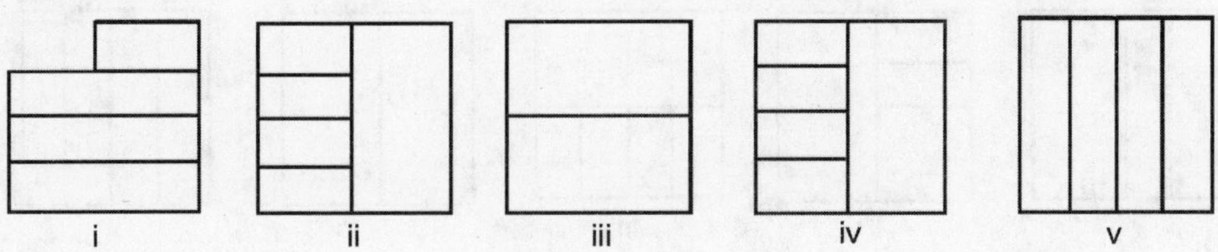

8.

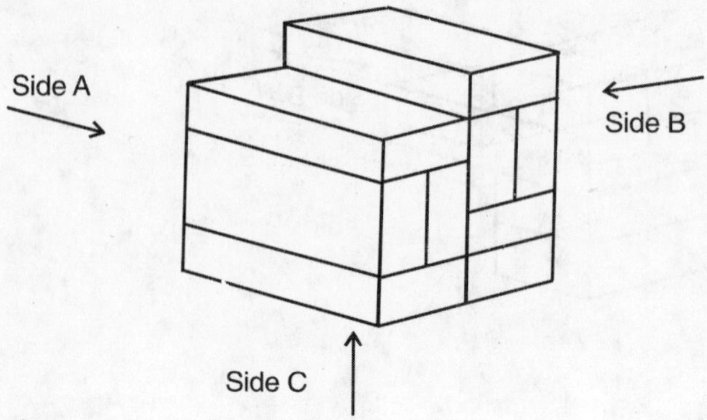

Side A

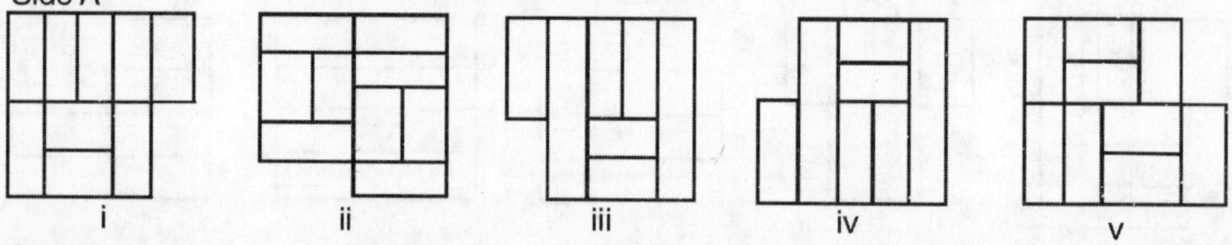

Side B

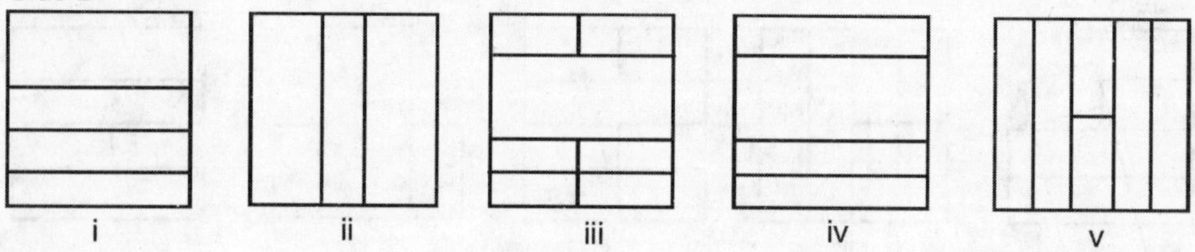

Side C

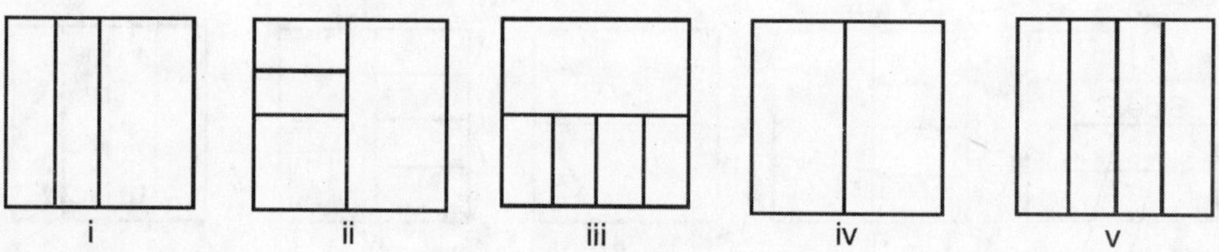

9.

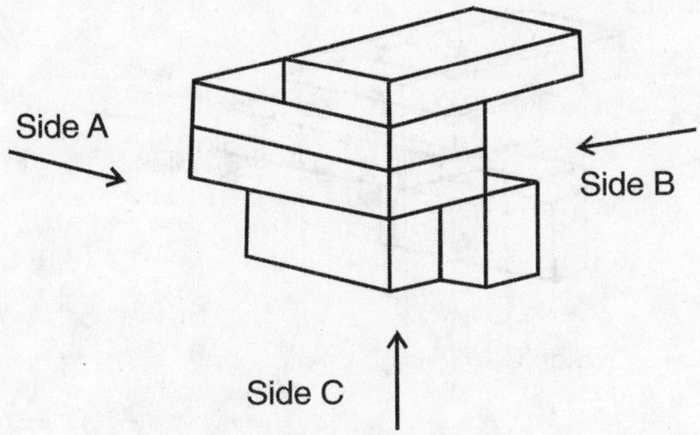

Side A

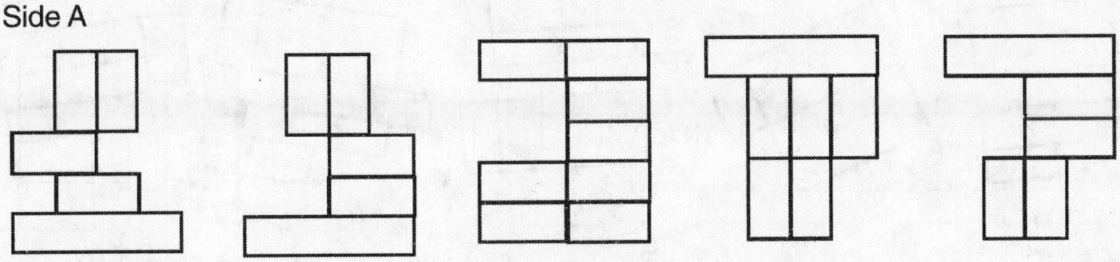

i ii iii iv v

Side B

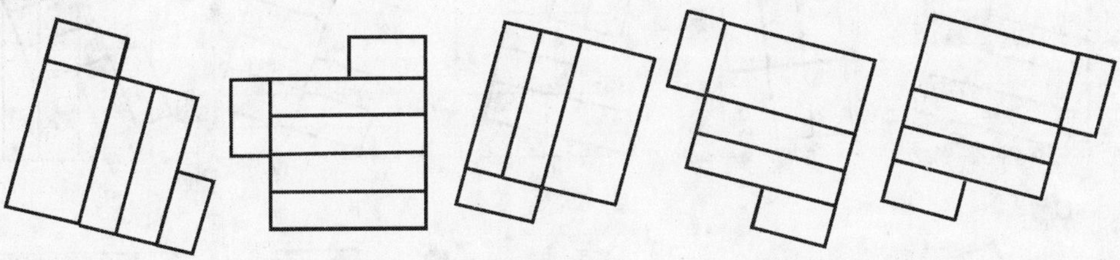

i ii iii iv v

Side C

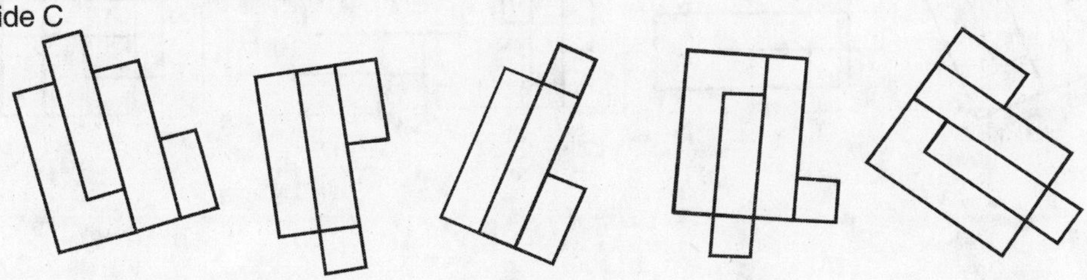

i ii iii iv v

10.

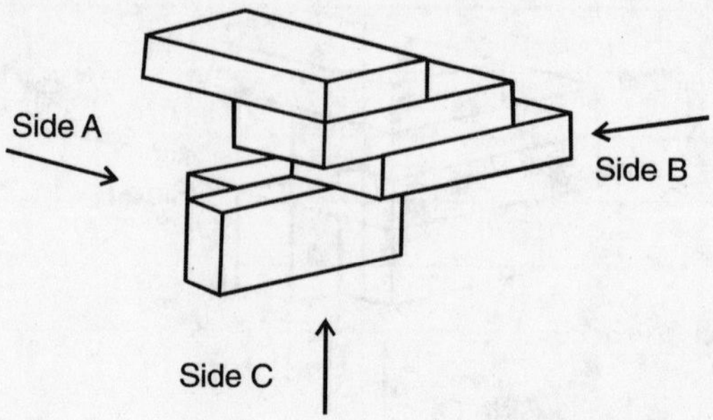

Side A

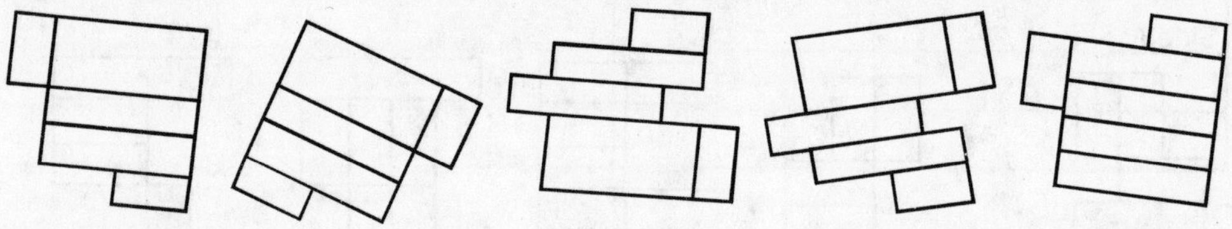

i ii iii iv v

Side B

i ii iii iv v

Side C

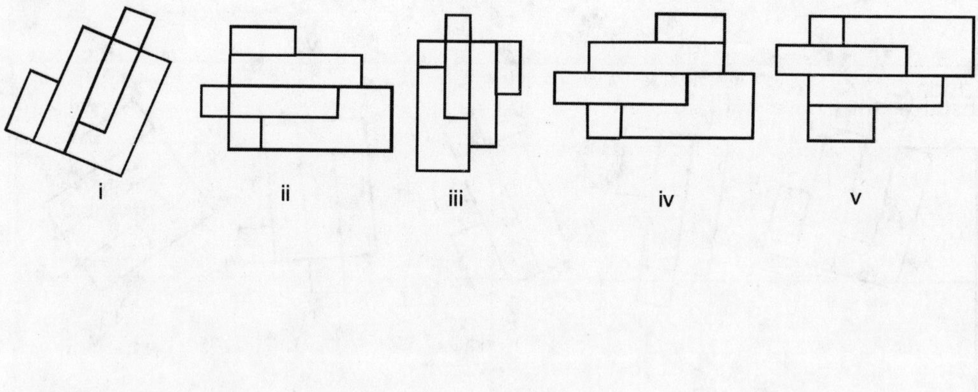

i ii iii iv v

Answers to Three-D test

1	A-iii	B-ii	C-v
2	A-iv	B-i	C-v
3	A-iv	B-i	C-i
4	A-ii	B-iii	C-ii
5	A-iv	B-ii	C-v
6	A-i	B-iii	C-ii
7	A-v	B-v	C-iii
8	A-ii	B-iv	C-iv
9	A-v	B-iv	C-i
10	A-iii	B-iii	C-v

Obtaining the Total Score

Number correct =	________
Plus 3 if no mistakes	+3
Total score =	________

Establishing Level of Potential

Average	Above average	Well above average	Exceptional
1-12	13-16	17-21	22+

INTERPRETATION

This test demands many of the same attributes as the test of spatial recognition. However, it does not distort the shapes in the same way, and the shapes themselves are regular.

Though the three-D is often an indicator of creative potential in the same way as the spatial recognition tests, it is usually predictive of success in areas that are more formal and require a more structured, technical approach, as in architecture and many forms of planning, for example.

This test is also different from the spatial recognition test, because the objects are specifically three-dimensional, not flat. This has implications for the way you think. Psychologically, it requires that you are able to 'look behind what appears on the surface of things'. You have to form a representation in your mind of what is on the other side. Literally, you have to conceive a diagram or picture that exists nowhere but in your own mind, which you infer from the original presented to you.

Possibly because the test demands that you bring an image together in your mind to form a unified whole, it was once thought that this type of test was the purest measure of intelligence. There is no doubt that it is another good measure of hard, natural intelligence. It will come to the surface in some way, even though it is not accompanied by the more formal verbal, numerical or visual aptitudes. People who have this type of potential are almost always recognized as intelligent, even though they may not necessarily do as well as expected in educational settings; they often do better when they have left formal schooling.

However, this aptitude by itself may express itself in design, drawing and craft skills. With numerical reasoning, it would suggest professional training in areas connected with engineering and technology.

CHAPTER 14

Systems Test

LEARNING OBJECTIVES

- To explain systems test.
- To know how to conduct systems test.

SYSTEMS TEST

In this test you are given a series of letters and symbols at the top of each page. Each letter goes with a particular symbol. The letter is in the top box of each pair and the symbol is at the bottom.

Your task is to write in the letter that goes with each symbol. The example below shows you how. The first nine have been done already. Complete the last three yourself.

Example

A	B	C	D	E	F	G	H	I	J	K	L
✈	⌖	☜	🕯	❄	✡	✞	✋	⚐	💣	☯	☪

Sample Answer

1	2	3	4	5	6	7	8	9	10	11	12
D	G	J	H	D	F	A	K	C	D	A	B
🕯	✞	💣	✋	🕯	✡	✈	☯	☜	🕯	✈	⌖

The answers to 10, 11 and 12 are D, A and B

On each page, look at the symbols that go with each letter (the top of the page). Then write in the missing letter that goes with each symbol for each of the test items. It is important to go as quickly as possible without making mistakes. You have exactly four minutes and you must get as many correct as possible in the time allowed.

A	B	C	D	E	F	G	H	I	J	K	L
✈	⌖	☜	🕯	❄	✡	✞	✋	⚐	💣	☯	☪

1	2	3	4	5	6	7	8	9	10	11	12
☪	✈	💣	✋	⚐	❄	✈	✋	☪	⌖	✈	🕯

13	14	15	16	17	18	19	20	21	22	23	24
🏳	🖐	🕯	☯	🏳	✡	☪	☜	🏳	🕈	❄	✡

25	26	27	28	29	30	31	32	33	34	35	36
☪	☯	☜	✡	☪	✈	🏳	❄	✞	🖐	💣	✈

37	38	39	40	41	42	43	44	45	46	47	48
✡	💣	✞	☪	🕯	🕈	☯	💣	❄	✡	🕯	☜

49	50	51	52	53	54	55	56	57	58	59	60
☯	❄	🏳	🕯	☯	✡	✈	☜	✞	☪	💣	✞

A	B	C	D	E	F	G	H	I	J	K	L
✈	🕈	☜	🕯	❄	✡	✞	🖐	🏳	💣	☯	☪

61	62	63	64	65	66	67	68	69	70	71	72
✞	✡	🖐	☯	☯	🕈	💣	🕯	☪	✞	✈	☜

73	74	75	76	77	78	79	80	81	82	83	84
🕯	🖐	✞	🏳	🕈	☪	☯	❄	☪	🏳	✡	🕯

85	86	87	88	89	90	91	92	93	94	95	96
✡	💣	✈	✋	☪	☯	❄	✈	⌖	✋	🕯	✞

97	98	99	100	101	102	103	104	105	106	107	108
✋	✡	🏳	⌖	☪	🕯	🏳	☪	✈	⌖	💣	✋

109	110	111	112	113	114	115	116	117	118	119	120
☯	💣	⌖	✈	✞	🏳	❄	💣	✋	✡	🕯	✞

A	B	C	D	E	F	G	H	I	J	K	L
✈	⌖	☞	🕯	❄	✡	✞	✋	🏳	💣	☯	☪

M	N	O	P	Q	R	S	T	U	V	W	X
❖	♌	■	●	&	♒	♎	♋	📫	♓	⍓	◆

121	122	123	124	125	126	127	128	129	130	131	132
✋	🏳	💣	☯	☪	♋	📫	♓	⍓	◆	✈	⌖

133	134	135	136	137	138	139	140	141	142	143	144
&	✡	✞	■	✋	🏳	💣	☯	☪	♌	✞	♒

145	146	147	148	149	150	151	152	153	154	155	156
♌	♒	✈	✈	🕈	📪	&	☜	❖	◆	■	💣

157	158	159	160	161	162	163	164	165	166	167	168
&	📪	■	✈	☜	✈	❖	◆	💣	♌	🕈	♒

169	170	171	172	173	174	175	176	177	178	179	180
&	☪	♒	📪	♌	&	■	🏳	💣	✡	🖐	♎

181	182	183	184	185	186	187	188	189	190	191	192
◆	✡	✞	🖐	■	✈	☪	🕯	❄	&	❖	☜

193	194	195	196	197	198	199	200	201	202	203	204
📪	♌	♎	☜	❖	☪	◆	♒	🖐	🏳	💣	■

205	206	207	208	209	210	211	212	213	214	215	216
◆	❖	☜	📪	♎	✈	☜	🕯	☪	🕯	❄	♒

Answers to Systems Test

It is rare for people to make more than the odd or occasional mistake on this test. You can check, if you wish, for absolute accuracy, but the number of items you have attempted is likely to provide a reliable overall answer. If, however, you think you may have been guessing, and have therefore probably made some mistakes, you should go back and check what you have done, and take the number of errors you have made away from the number attempted.

Obtaining the Total Score

Number correct =

Establishing Level of Potential

Average	Above average	Well above average	Exceptional
1 - 100	101-132	133-165	166+

INTERPRETATION

This is a demanding test because it can become tedious while at the same time demanding absolute concentration. The way you attempted the test can be revealing. Most people check off symbols one by one as they appear. A variant of this approach is to take one symbol at a time, checking off all the same symbols on the page. If you have approached the test in one of these ways you are measuring your aptitude for checking and organization.

Another method is more conceptual, involving memorizing each one of the items as they become familiar. In this process the letter becomes identified with the symbol and takes its place. People who use this method eventually are quick on this test because they eliminate the time required for checking. If, you made use of this method you are also measuring your aptitude for the memorization and recognition of information.

This aptitude is essential where attention to detail is required, as in many administrative situations. However, people who use the 'memory approach' may be at a disadvantage if they are presented with constantly new information to check, because this gives them no opportunity to form a concept they can retain in their memory to help them. They come into their own in dealing with information where they are expected to impose some sort of system or conceptual framework upon the information. In other words, they may be more adept at sorting out problems of order rather than checking the correctness of items.

Precision is usually appreciated in careers involving financial transactions and in legal work. The same type of ability is demanded in computer programming and analysis.

CHAPTER 15

Vocabulary Test

LEARNING OBJECTIVES

- To discuss Vocabulary Test.
- To understand the importance of the test.

VOCABULARY TEST

This is a test of your understanding of words. You are given a word and have to say which one of the alternatives is closest in meaning to it. You have to place a tick in the correct box. Look at the examples below.

Examples

1. OWN	2. ADD
☑ (a) Possess	☐ (a) Subtract
☐ (b) Unpaid	☑ (b) Count
☐ (c) Disown	☐ (c) Duke
☐ (d) Landlord	☐ (d) New

In Example 1, to possess means the same as to own. If you think of a sentence with the word own in it, you will find that the word possess could replace it. For example, 'I own a car—I possess a car'. Unpaid means owing, not to own. Disown means the opposite of to own. Landlord means an owner, not to own. Own and possess are verbs, while unpaid is an adjective, disown is a verb, but means the opposite of own and landlord is a noun.

In Example 2, subtract is the opposite of add, although it is a verb, as add is a verb. Duke is a noun, but does not mean add. New means fresh, and therefore could be added, but it would not be able to replace the word add in a sentence. In any case, fresh is an adjective. Both add and count are verbs. Count is the answer, because it is almost identical in meaning to add and could easily replace it in a sentence, for example, 'You should ADD up your money—You should count up your money.' It does not matter that count can have other meanings, for example, as a noun in 'The Count and Countess were invited to the palace.'

You can have as much time as you want to do this test, but it is probably not worth spending any longer than five minutes, as you will find that you either know the meanings of the words, or you do not.

Place a tick in the box of the alternative that is closest in meaning to the word in capitals.

1. **BAD**
- ☐ (a) evil
- ☐ (b) angel
- ☐ (c) good
- ☐ (d) ban

2. **WET**
- ☐ (a) appetite
- ☐ (b) strong
- ☐ (c) watery
- ☐ (d) dry

3. **CHIEF**
- ☐ (a) mainly
- ☐ (b) minor
- ☐ (c) head
- ☐ (d) unimportant

4. **CHOP**
- ☐ (a) rough
- ☐ (b) duty
- ☐ (c) stormy
- ☐ (d) divide

5. **SOFT**
- ☐ (a) harsh
- ☐ (b) undemanding
- ☐ (c) contact
- ☐ (d) comfort

6. **GOWN**
- ☐ (a) sack
- ☐ (b) shout
- ☐ (c) robe
- ☐ (d) about

7. **IMAGINARY**
- ☐ (a) realistic
- ☐ (b) bleak
- ☐ (c) trance
- ☐ (d) dreamy

8. **ACTIVE**
- ☐ (a) mobile
- ☐ (b) baffle
- ☐ (c) rigid
- ☐ (d) motion

9. **PIERCE**
- ☐ (a) puncture
- ☐ (b) stung
- ☐ (c) loud
- ☐ (d) stabbing

10. **INVALUABLE**
- ☐ (a) worthless
- ☐ (b) valuable
- ☐ (c) variable
- ☐ (d) cheap

11. ADAPT
- ☐ (a) convert
- ☐ (b) flexible
- ☐ (c) inflexible
- ☐ (d) transformation

12. IMPARTIAL
- ☐ (a) connected
- ☐ (b) detached
- ☐ (c) involved
- ☐ (d) unconcern

13. REPUTABLE
- ☐ (a) infamous
- ☐ (b) supposed
- ☐ (c) good
- ☐ (d) stature

14. LIGHTEN
- ☐ (a) discover
- ☐ (b) darken
- ☐ (c) illumine
- ☐ (d) weak

15. GROUNDLESS
- ☐ (a) justified
- ☐ (b) background
- ☐ (c) basis
- ☐ (d) absurd

16. FASTEN
- ☐ (a) affix
- ☐ (b) untie
- ☐ (c) holder
- ☐ (d) thin

17. BARGAINING
- ☐ (a) trafficking
- ☐ (b) anticipate
- ☐ (c) promise
- ☐ (d) agree

18. WORRISOME
- ☐ (a) reassuring
- ☐ (b) unworried
- ☐ (c) annoy
- ☐ (d) perturbing

19. UNDERCURRENT
- ☐ (a) undercharge
- ☐ (b) atmosphere
- ☐ (c) undermine
- ☐ (d) belittle

20. SATANIC
- ☐ (a) divine
- ☐ (b) devil
- ☐ (c) inhuman
- ☐ (d) biting

21. PRICELESS

☐ (a) prized

☐ (b) cheap

☐ (c) menu

☐ (d) expense

22. MUTINOUS

☐ (a) defiance

☐ (b) uprising

☐ (c) obedient

☐ (d) turbulent

23. HOMELY

☐ (a) mother

☐ (b) domestic

☐ (c) formal

☐ (d) revered

24. FUNCTIONAL

☐ (a) plain

☐ (b) official

☐ (c) decorative

☐ (d) gathering

25. EXEMPT

☐ (a) spared

☐ (b) liable

☐ (c) except

☐ (d) illustrate

26. GALLANT

☐ (a) cowardly

☐ (b) escort

☐ (c) courageousness

☐ (d) polite

27. EXPRESSLY

☐ (a) assert

☐ (b) energetic

☐ (c) particularly

☐ (d) vaguely

28. DAPPER

☐ (a) sloppy

☐ (b) spry

☐ (c) be speckled

☐ (d) dappled

29. COGNIZANT

☐ (a) unaware

☐ (b) apprehension

☐ (c) acquainted

☐ (d) perception

30. PORTEND

☐ (a) presage

☐ (b) insignificant

☐ (c) presentiment

☐ (d) emblazon

31. **BENEDICTION**

- ☐ (a) anathema
- ☐ (b) benevolence
- ☐ (c) munificence
- ☐ (d) blessing

32. **CONCOMITANT**

- ☐ (a) coincidental
- ☐ (b) accidental
- ☐ (c) incidental
- ☐ (d) compressed

33. **GUILELESS**

- ☐ (a) artful
- ☐ (b) shame
- ☐ (c) innocent
- ☐ (d) transparent

34. **CULMINATE**

- ☐ (a) crown
- ☐ (b) peak
- ☐ (c) begin
- ☐ (d) pursue

35. **EXONERATE**

- ☐ (a) absolution
- ☐ (b) inflate
- ☐ (c) incriminate
- ☐ (d) vindicate

36. **ICONOCLASTIC**

- ☐ (a) denunciatory
- ☐ (b) credulity
- ☐ (c) uncritical
- ☐ (d) optimistic

37. **IMPLICIT**

- ☐ (a) innuendo
- ☐ (b) explicit
- ☐ (c) latent
- ☐ (d) stated

38. **PENURIOUS**

- ☐ (a) paucity
- ☐ (b) indigent
- ☐ (c) dearth
- ☐ (d) meditative

39. **SPURIOUS**

- ☐ (a) authentic
- ☐ (b) specious
- ☐ (c) sordid
- ☐ (d) disheveled

40. **TRANSMOGRIFY**

- ☐ (a) attitudinize
- ☐ (b) traverse
- ☐ (c) mutation
- ☐ (d) metamorphose

Answers to Vocabulary Test

1 - a	9 - a	17 - a	25 - c	33 - d
2 - c	10 - b	18 - d	26 - d	34 - b
3 - c	11 - a	19 - b	27 - c	35 - d
4 - d	12 - b	20 - c	28 - b	36 - a
5 - b	13 - c	21 - a	29 - c	37 - c
6 - c	14 - c	22 - d	30 - a	38 - b
7 - d	15 - d	23 - b	31 - d	39 - b
8 - a	16 - a	24 - a	32 - c	40 - d

Obtaining the Total Score

	Number correct =	______
Plus 4 if you are aged under 16	Plus 2 if aged 17-20	+ ______
	Total score =	______

Establishing Level of Potential

Average	Above average	Well above average	Exceptional
1-19	20-25	26-30	31+

INTERPRETATION

The vocabulary test may be regarded as a test of knowledge like any learnt skill, and therefore, different from the other tests, which look at more abstract, underlying potential. It is true that the vocabulary is not measuring innate intelligence, that is, what you were born with. However, it is measuring a means by which intelligence is choosing to express itself. Through the use of words, bearing in mind that words form concepts, there is scope for clear analysis and expression of information as well as abstract ideas. It is certainly an area of potential that is relevant to career success.

Lack of a strong vocabulary will probably not hold you back in your career, provided you have other areas of potential that are more important for the task or type of work on which you are engaged. It will obviously hold you back in areas of communication in which a high vocabulary is expected. Typically, students of technically-oriented courses do less well on vocabulary tests than those who are pursuing arts courses such as English, history, languages or philosophy. All these demand that words be used correctly and precisely.

Although a comparatively weak vocabulary may not necessarily be essential to success, many people gain promotion to a level where they believe that lack of vocabulary is a serious disadvantage. If your vocabulary is lower than your other test scores, you can certainly take it that you have the potential to improve your vocabulary.

CHAPTER 16

Aptitude Profiling and IQ

LEARNING OBJECTIVES

- To discuss level of score and aptitude profile and career options.
- To explain intelligence test.

LEVEL OF SCORE

'Average' means that you scored about as well as most other people on a test. Therefore, no especial aptitude has been detected on this occasion. You may have an aptitude for a type of problem solving that has not been detected by the specific test. It could be that the areas of work that may be predicted by this test may be less suited to you than those suggested by other tests where there is stronger evidence. Areas of work suggested by results providing the strongest evidence are the ones that will most likely be where you will find it easiest to be successful.

Given below is a chart titled 'Your aptitude profile'. Place your own scores in the chart by circling your own score in the appropriate place.

If you connect up the scores, you should have a graph that looks something like the example:

Example Profile

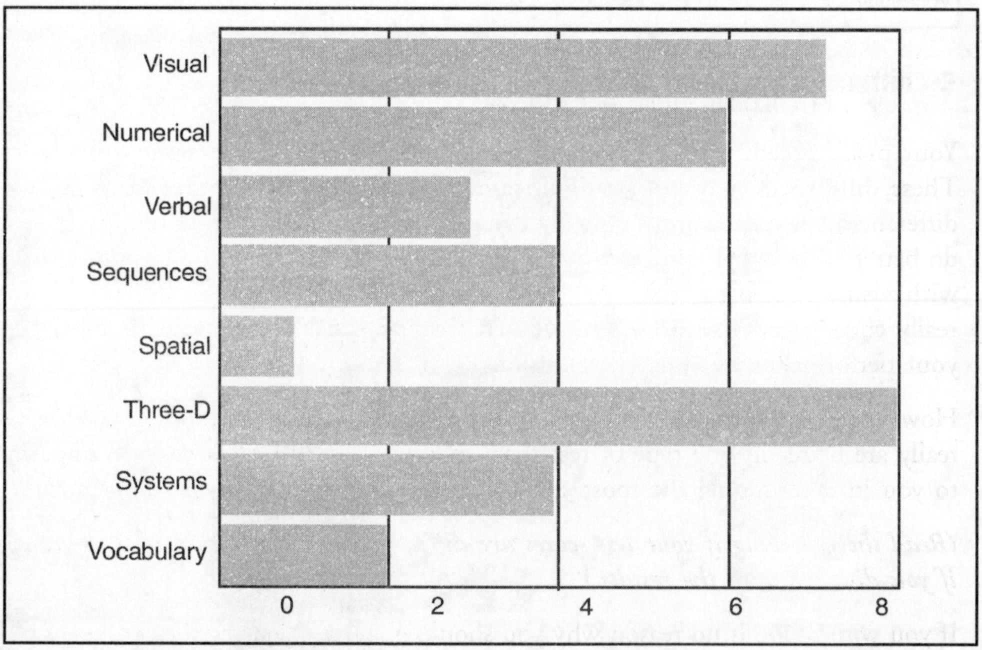

Your Aptitude Profile

Mark the place where each of your test results falls in the chart. You can draw a bar from the left of the chart to your score, to form a bar line, as in the example profile above.

Your aptitude profile

Test	Average		Above average		Well above average		Exceptional	
Point on scale	1	2	3	4	5	6	7	8
Visual	1-3	4-6	7-9	10-13	14-17	18-20	21-24	25+
Numerical	1-2	3-4	5	6-7	8-10	11-12	13-16	17+
Verbal	1-3	4-7	8-9	10-11	12-13	14-15	16-18	19+
Sequences	1-4	5-8	9-10	11-12	13-16	17-18	19-21	22+
Spatial	1-12	13-26	27-30	31-34	35-38	39-42	43-48	49+
Three-D	1-6	7-12	13-14	15-16	17-18	19-21	22-24	25+
Systems	1-50	51-100	101-116	117-132	133-149	150-165	166-183	184+
Vocabulary	1-9	10-19	20-22	23-25	26-27	28-30	31-34	35+

❖ Differences between Scores

Your profile readily enables you to see possible differences between your scores. These differences may not be significant. For example, on another occasion, your differences between scores might be reversed, so that on one occasion you seem to do better with verbal than with visual reasoning, but on the next occasion do better with visual reasoning than with verbal reasoning. This may be because you are really equally good on both tests. It may be that tiredness, or other reasons, affect your performance on different occasions.

However, the greater the difference between tests, the more likely it is that you really are better in one type of test than another. This difference may be important to you in determining the most suitable area of study or what career to pursue.

(Read the following if your test scores are different from what you had assumed and if you disagree with the results.)

If you wish, there is no reason why you should not place your own estimates of your potential, if these are different from your test results, in the chart. It depends on how far you agree that the test results are fully and accurately assessing you. There is always room for some doubt. As discussed in the introduction, your results on the tests might be affected by all sorts of issues relating to:

1. The efficiency with which you test yourself;

2. The conditions in which you test yourself;

3. Who you compare yourself with; and
4. Whether the tests themselves have reliably detected your potential.

Therefore, your own estimates might be based upon your progress at school and upon other experiences.

As a rough guide, take it that if there is a clear section between two scores, there may be a significant difference in your aptitude. For example, if your score on one test is in the upper section of good evidence and another score is in the upper part of some evidence, there will be a section (clear score area) between the two scores. You can become more certain, the more sections there are between the two scores. To make this clear, each of your scores on the tests will fall under a number 1-8 written in the chart at the top. So, for example, there may not be any real difference between a score of 5 and 6, but there is likely to be a real difference in your potential if the scores are 5 and 7. The greater the difference between scores, the greater the difference in your potential. How much weight you place upon the difference between any two scores is, in the end, for you to judge.

Interpretation of your profile is reasonably easy if you have one result that stands out from the others. There remains the difficulty of relating this aptitude to a career —even a distinct aptitude may translate into numerous career options.

Most people will obtain a pattern where there is no single, distinguishable aptitude, but rather a pattern that appears to consist of relative 'highs and lows'. Your highest score might be the best indication, but also look at any other relatively high scores.

Do your scores seem to group themselves in any way? How are your high scores different from your lower scores? What, broadly, do the relative highs and lows tell you? Some people do better with all the word and numerical types of test, but not visual types and spatial types. This would be interpreted as more of an administrative as opposed to an artistic pattern. Others may do well in both the numerical and visual tests, but not so well on the verbal side. This might indicate more of a scientific bias. There are, of course, many possible patterns for you to interpret.

The level of the various scores is not particularly relevant and you may have other high scores besides those that are frequently indicative of potential in certain areas. Your own pattern is most unlikely to be identical to the following common patterns, but you may find them useful for general guidance.

APTITUDE PROFILE AND CAREER OPTIONS

Accountancy and Finance

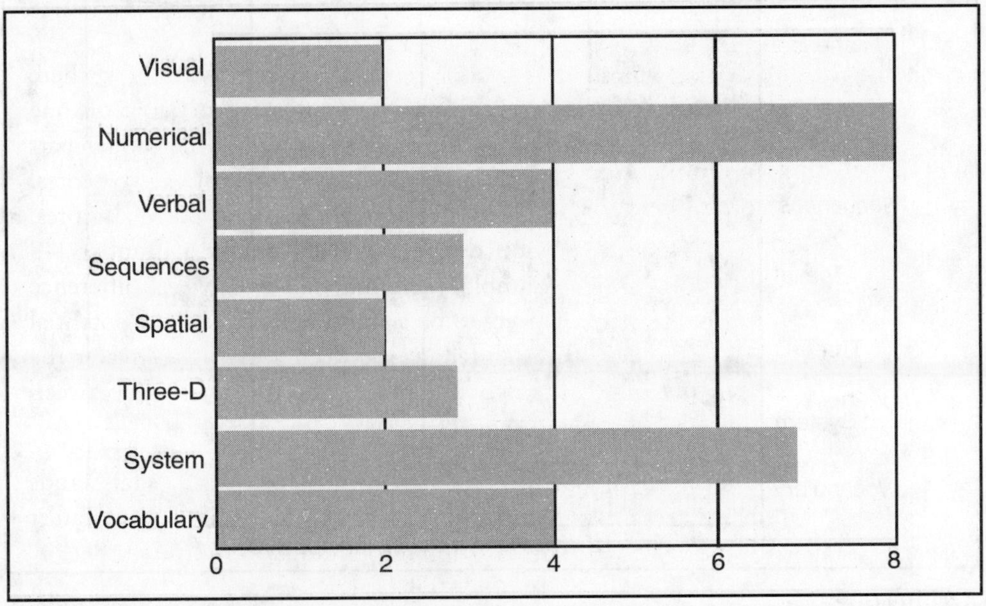

Agriculture and Land Management

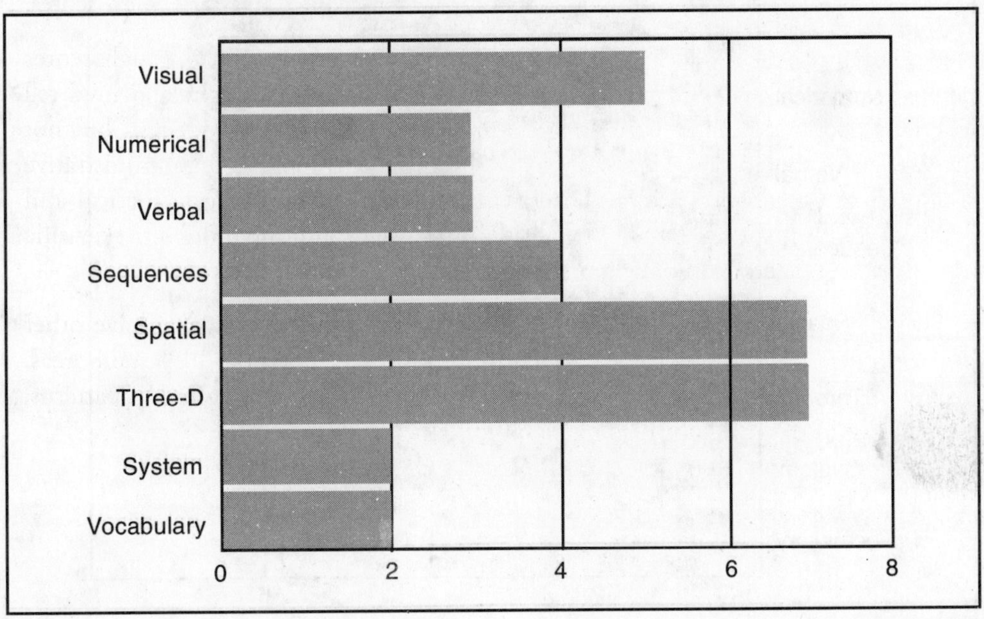

Archaeology and Anthropology

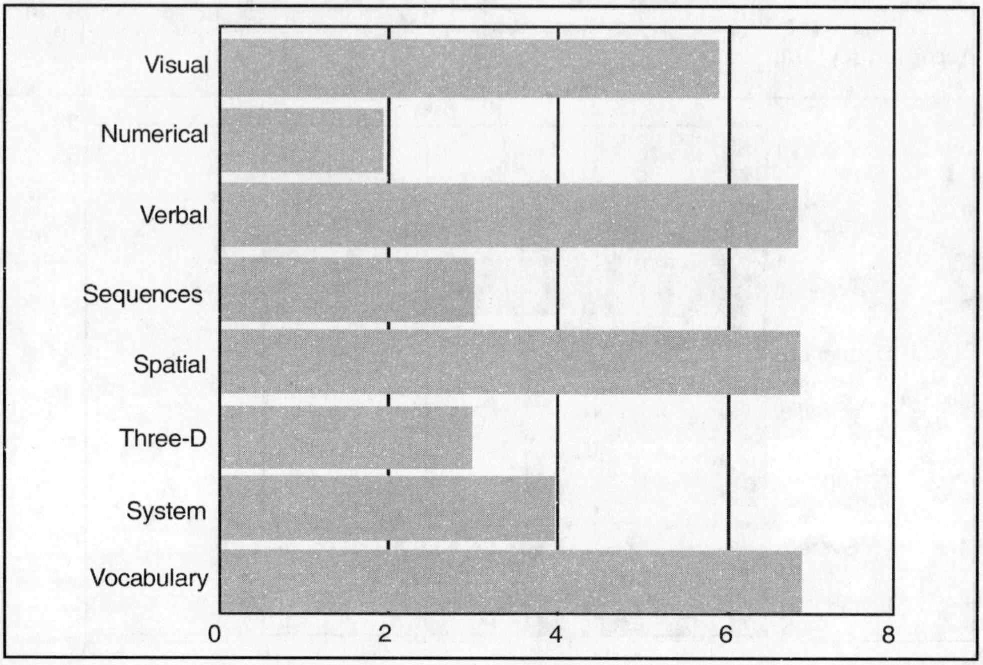

Architecture

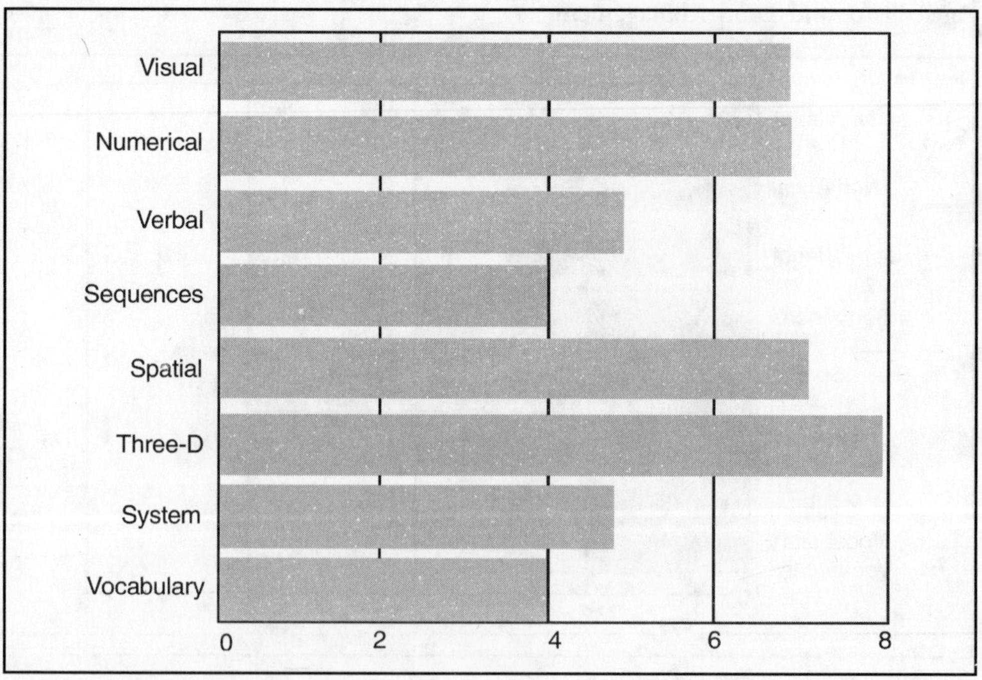

Art and Design

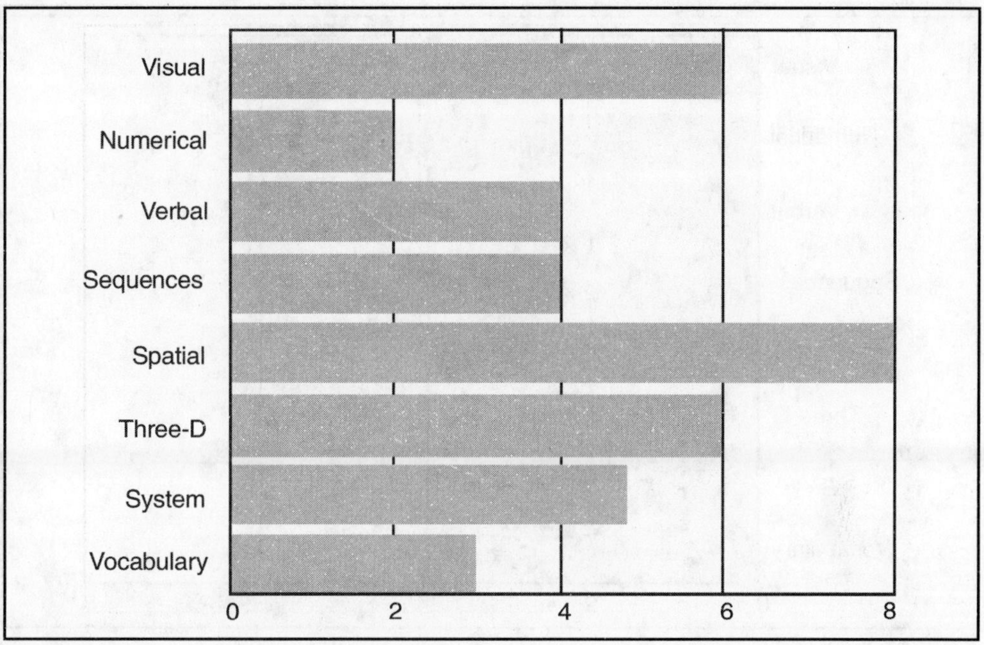

Art History

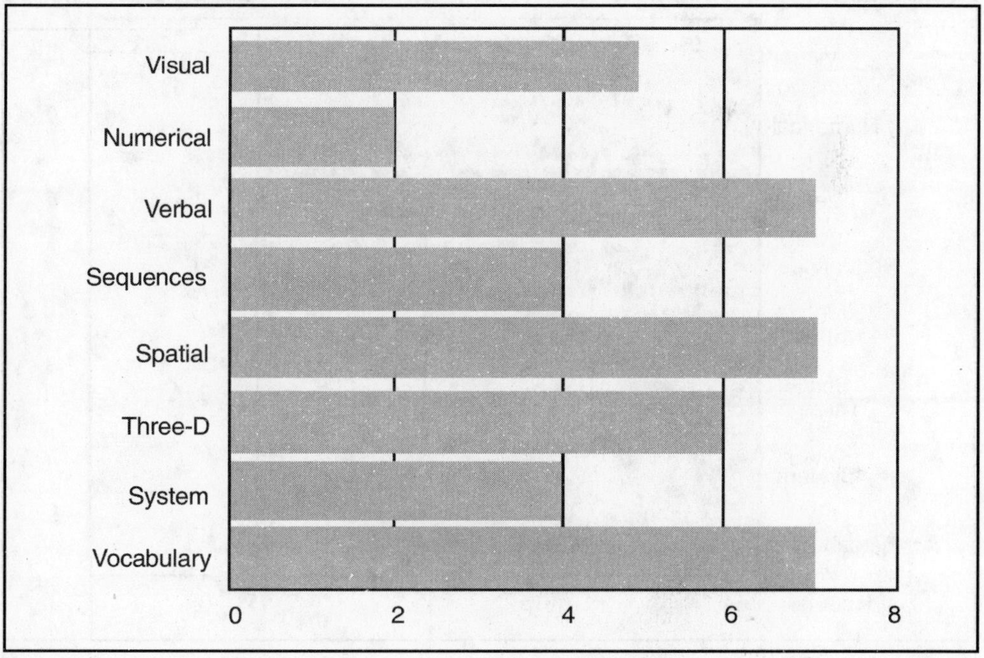

Biology and the Biological Sciences

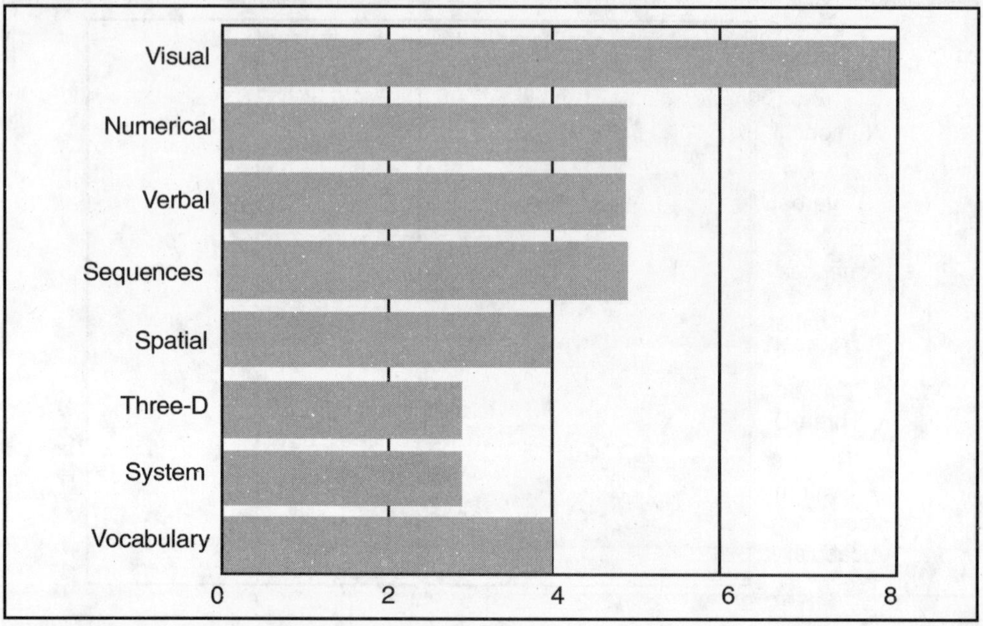

Business, Management and Marketing

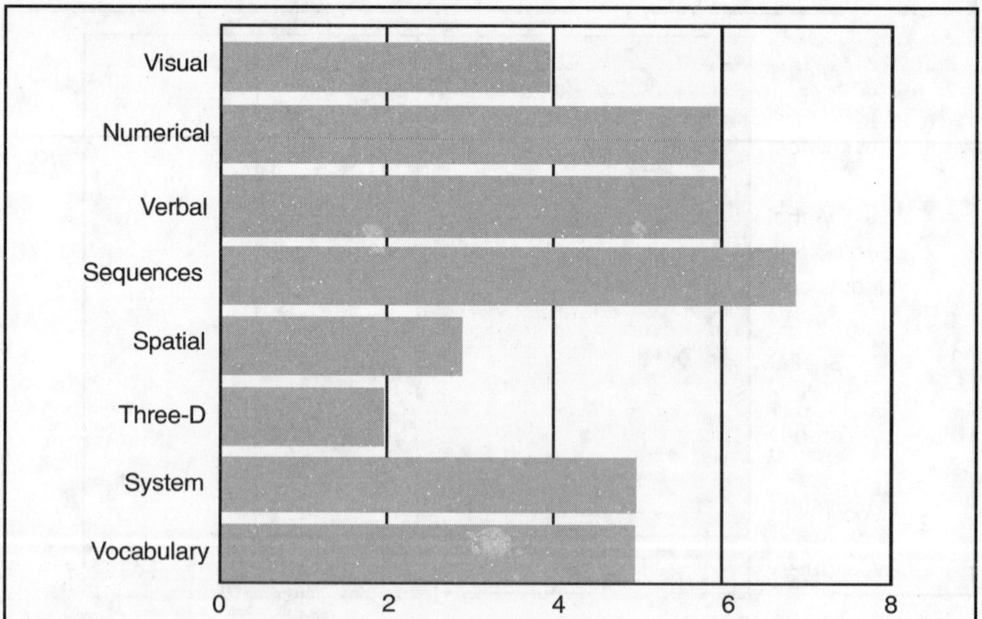

Catering

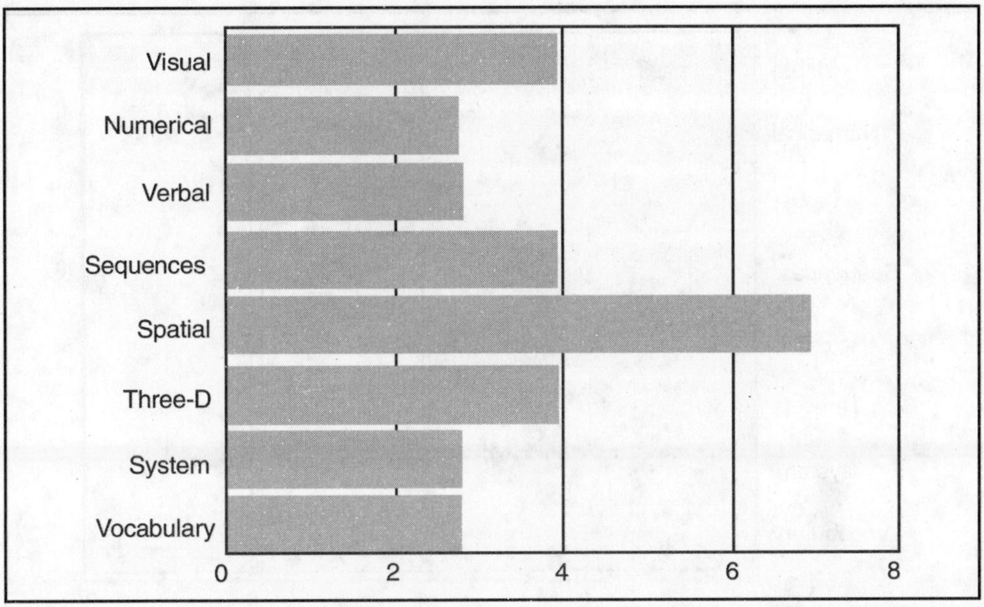

Chemistry

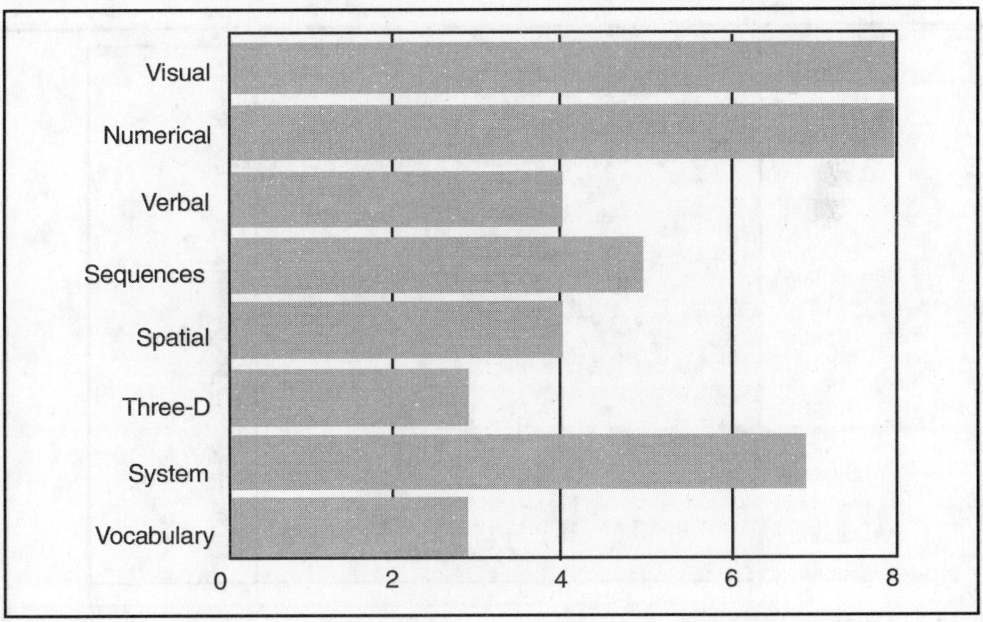

Classics

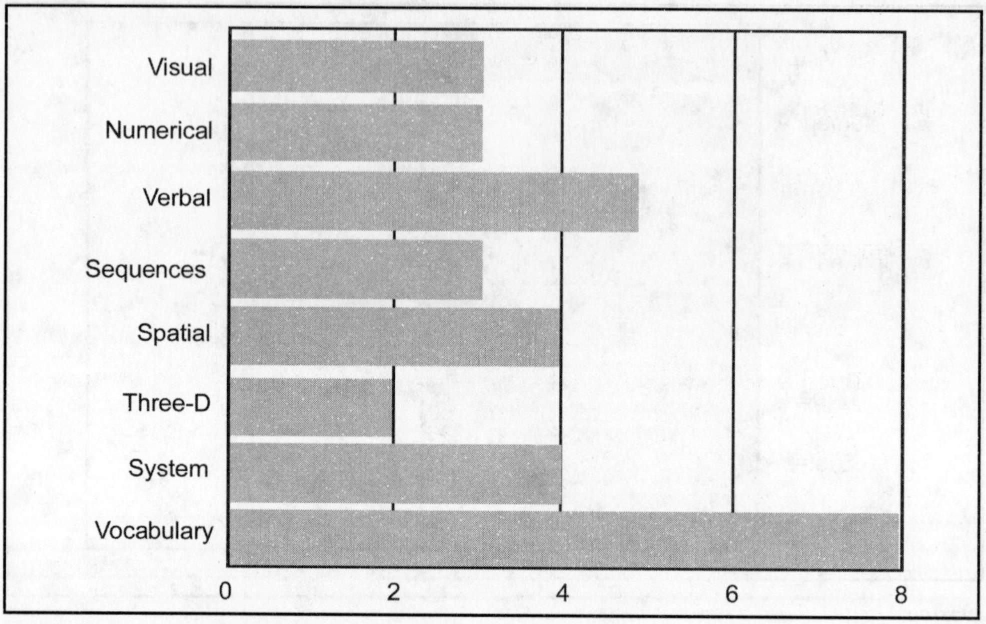

Computing and IT

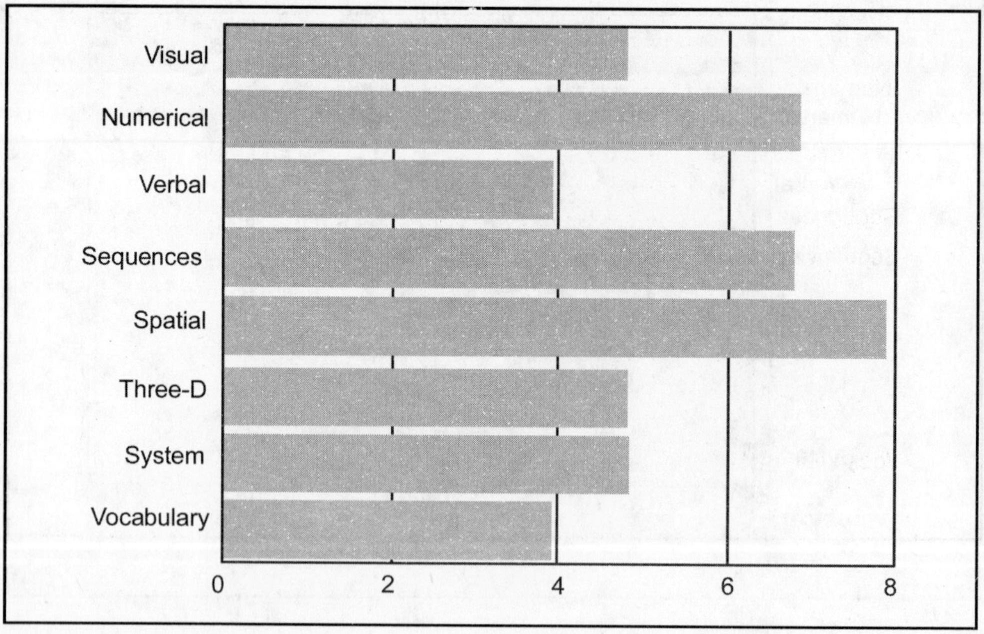

Craft

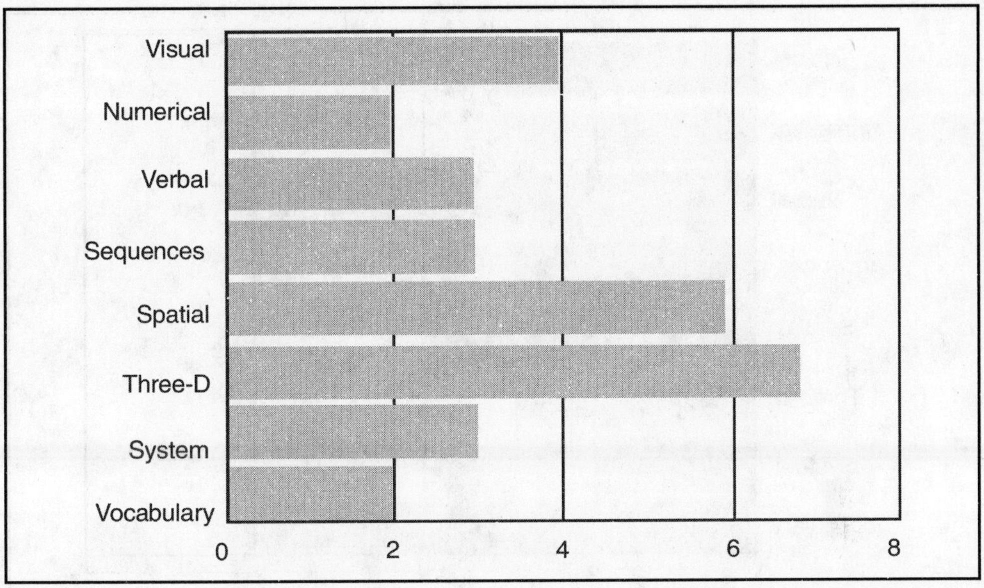
Visual
Numerical
Verbal
Sequences
Spatial
Three-D
System
Vocabulary
0
2
4
6
8

Dance

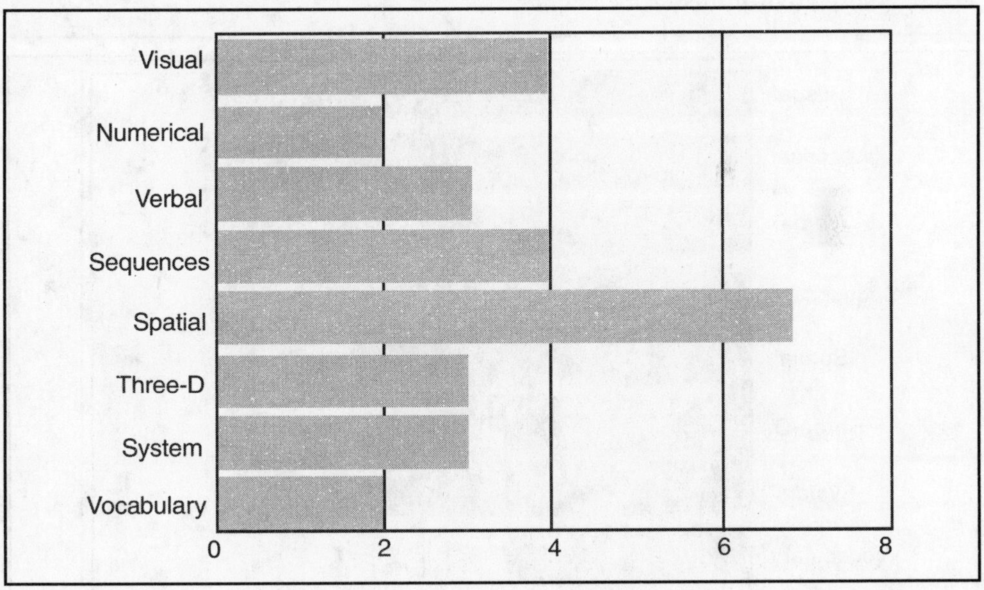
Visual
Numerical
Verbal
Sequences
Spatial
Three-D
System
Vocabulary
0
2
4
6
8

Drama

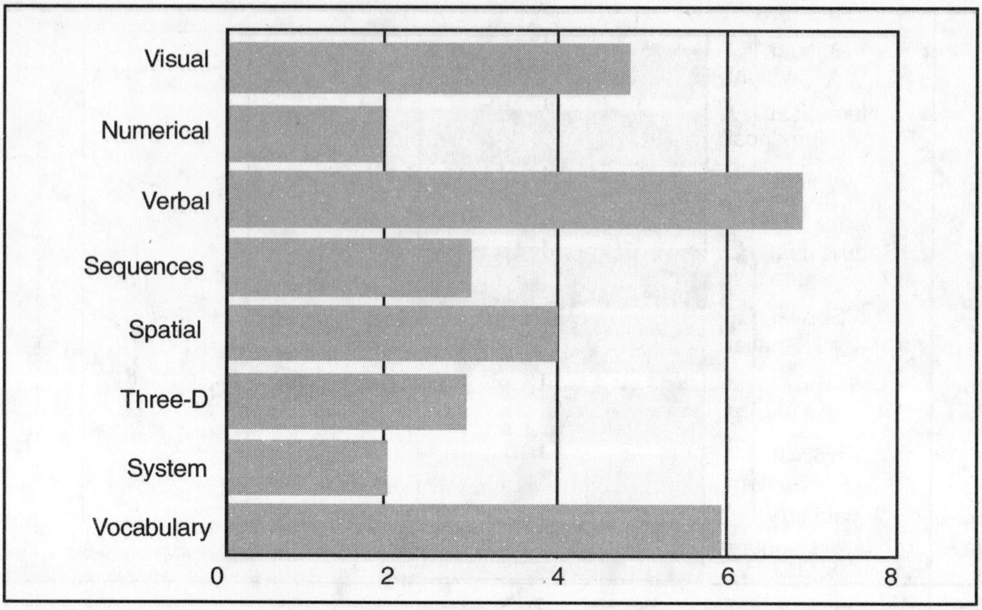

Ecology and Environmental Sciences

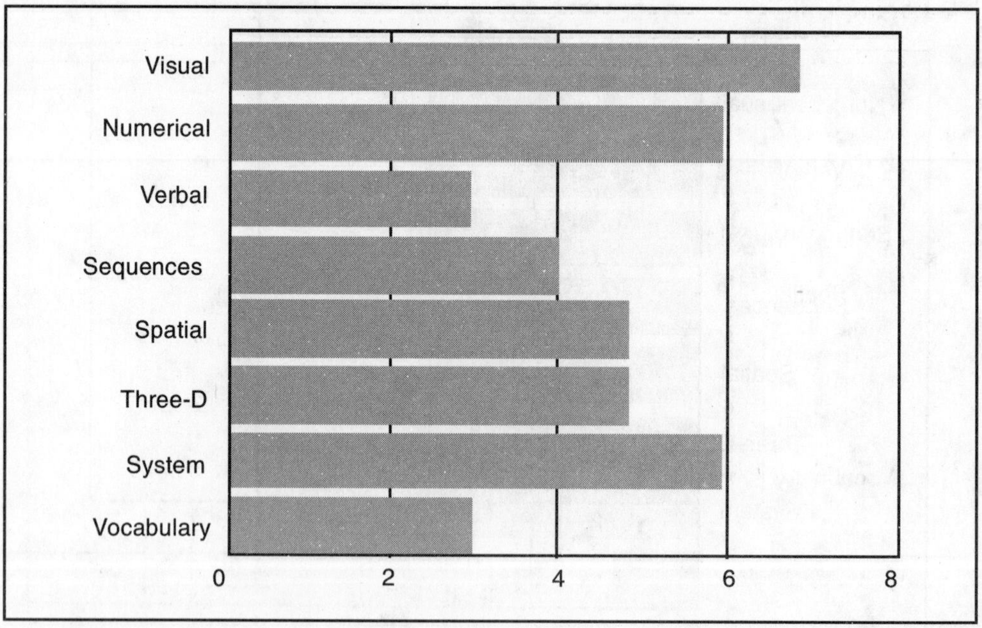

Economics

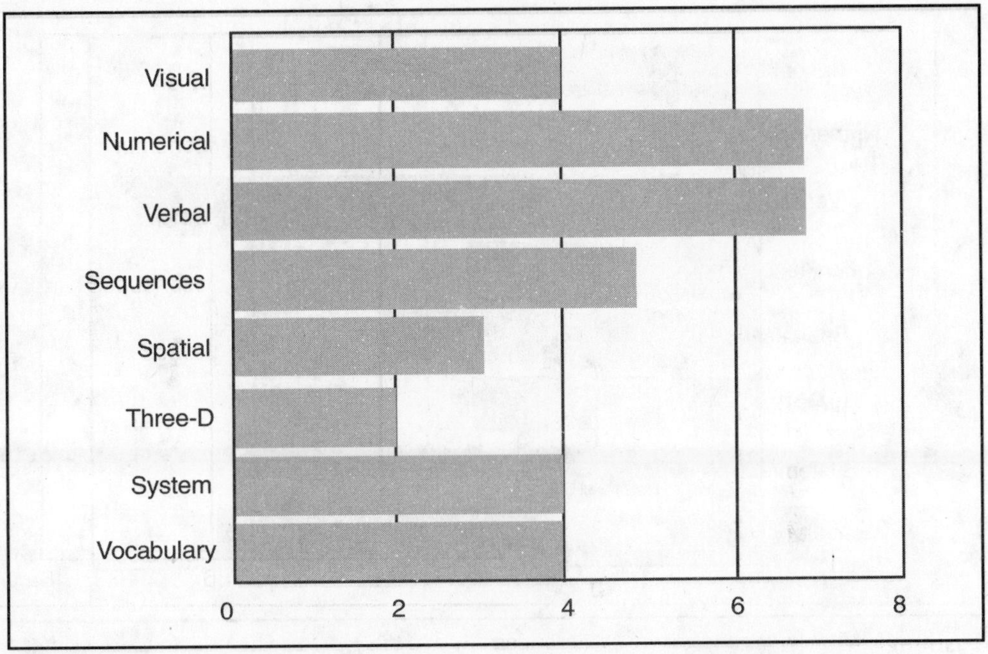

Engineering

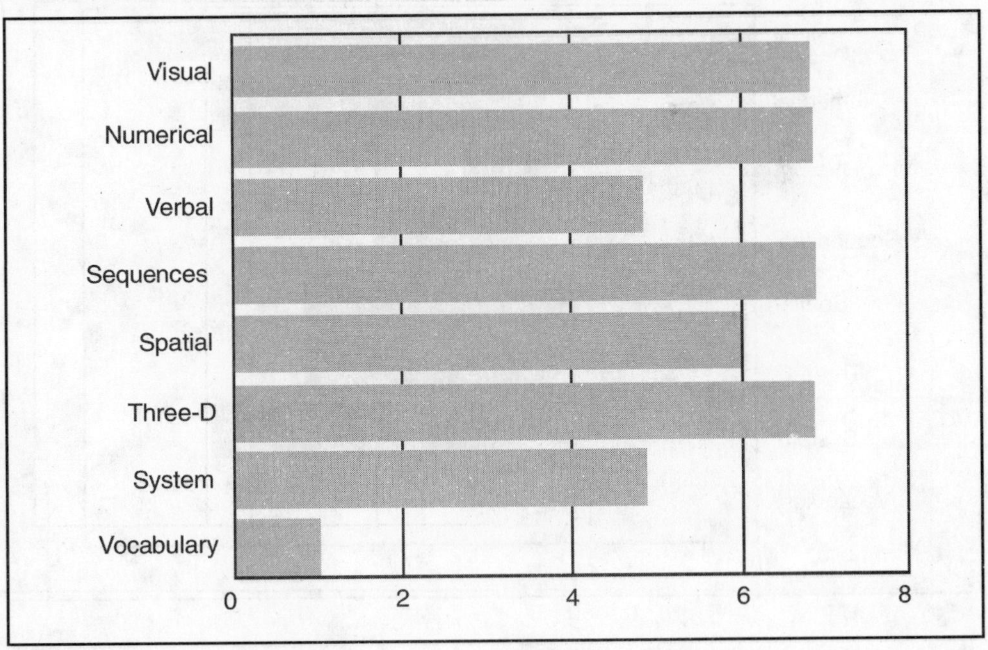

English

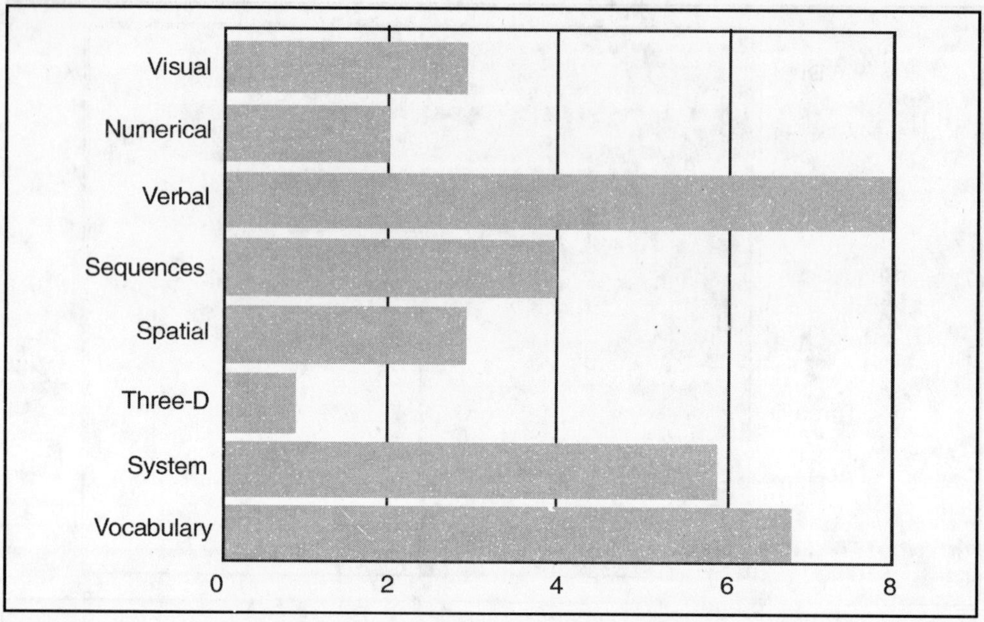

Fashion

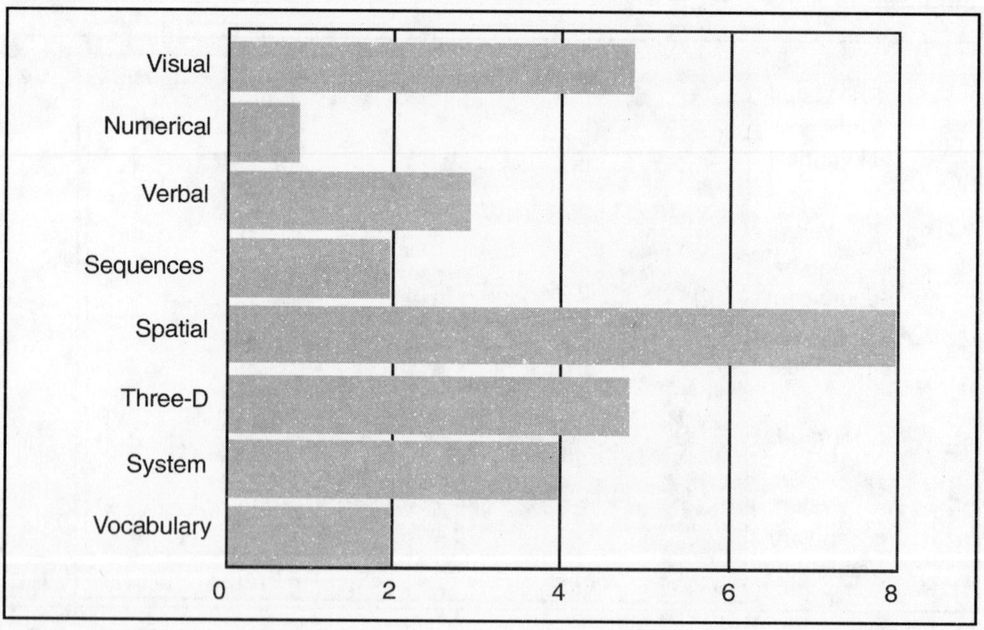

Geography

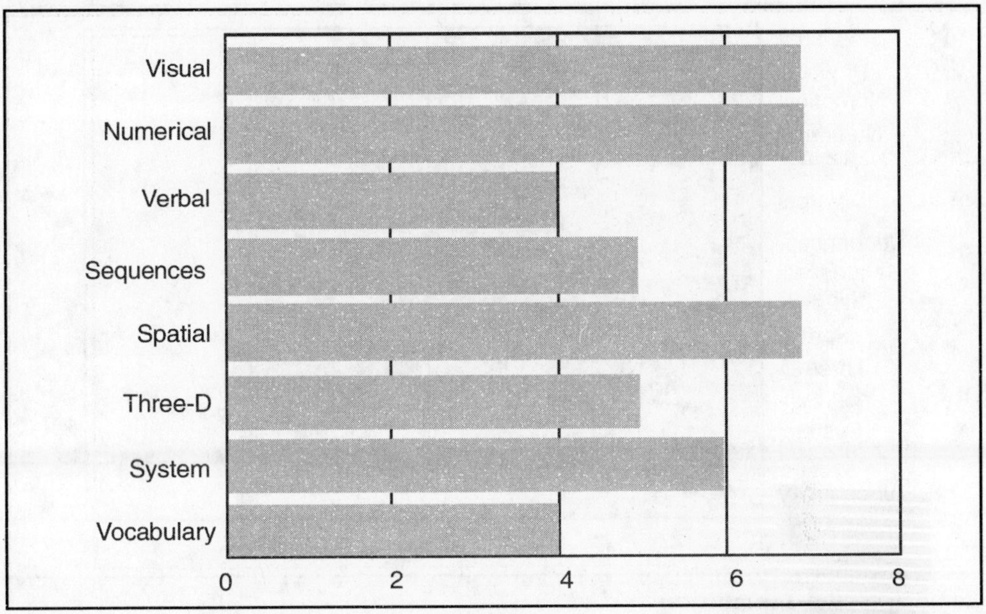

History

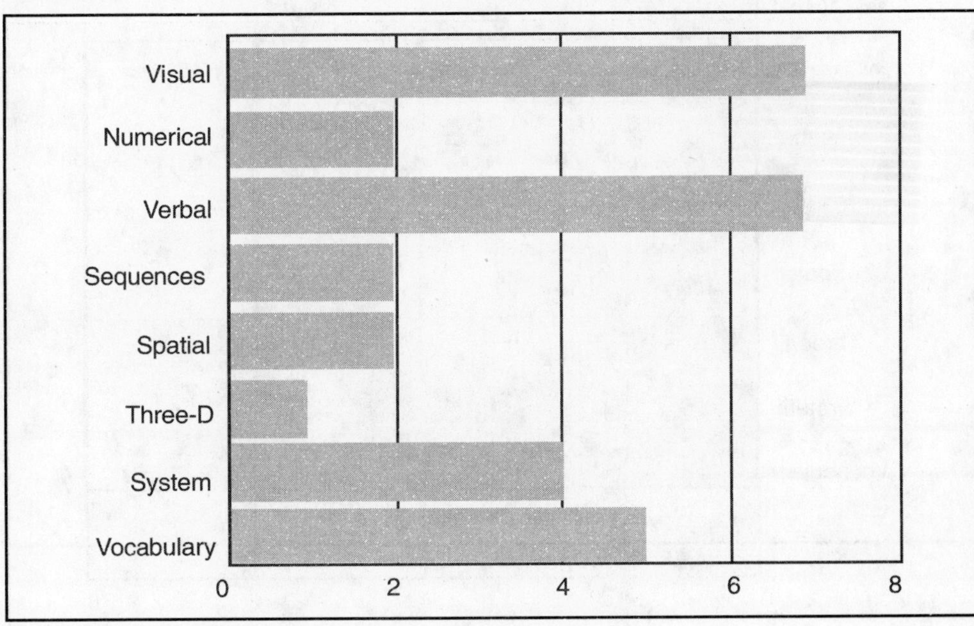

Hotel Management

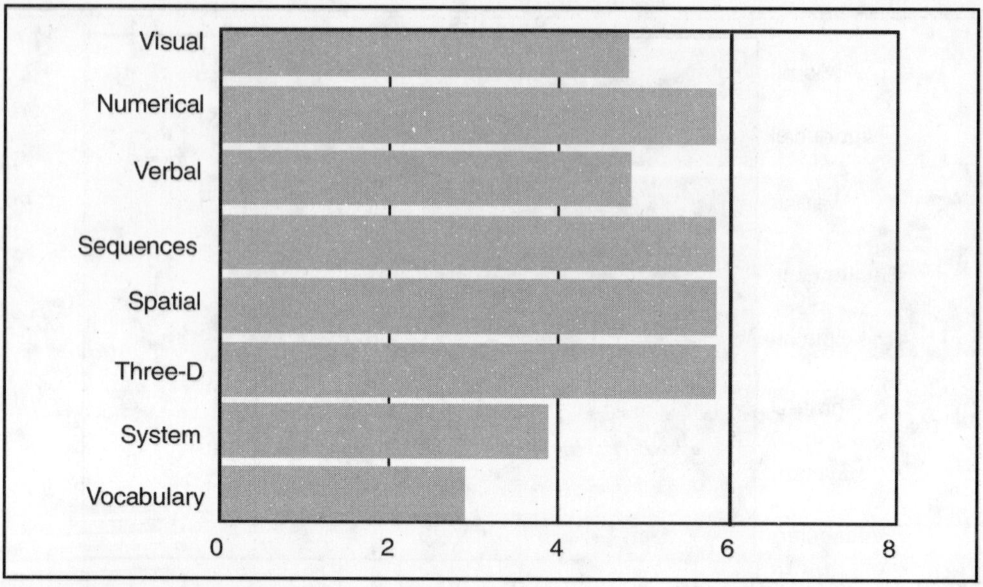

Languages and Linguistics

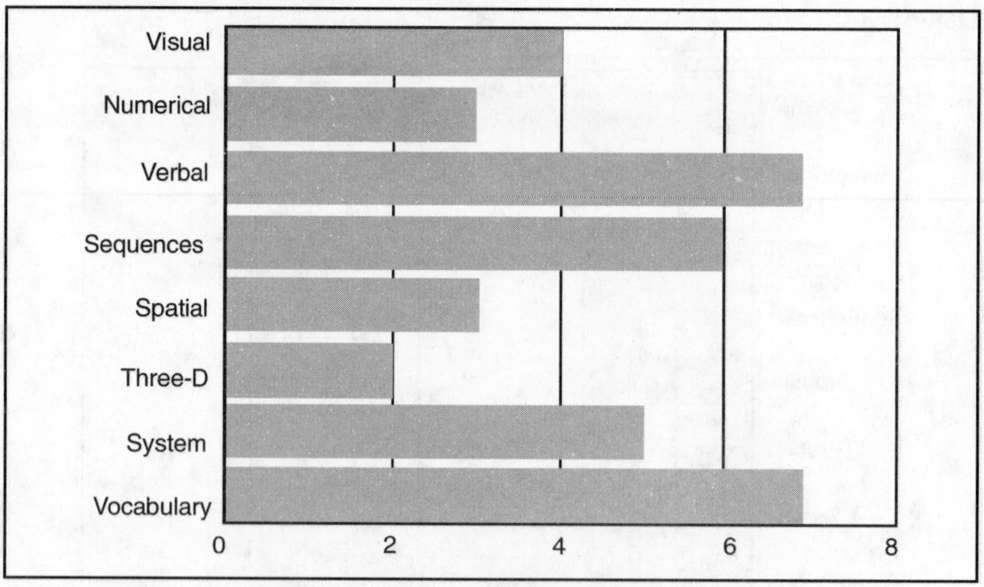

Law

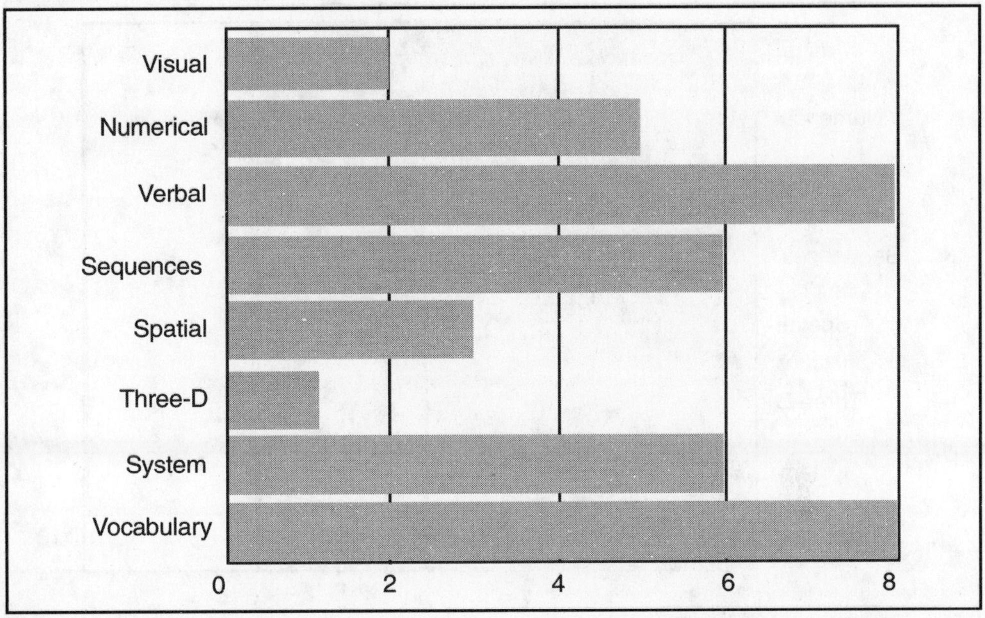

Library and Information Science

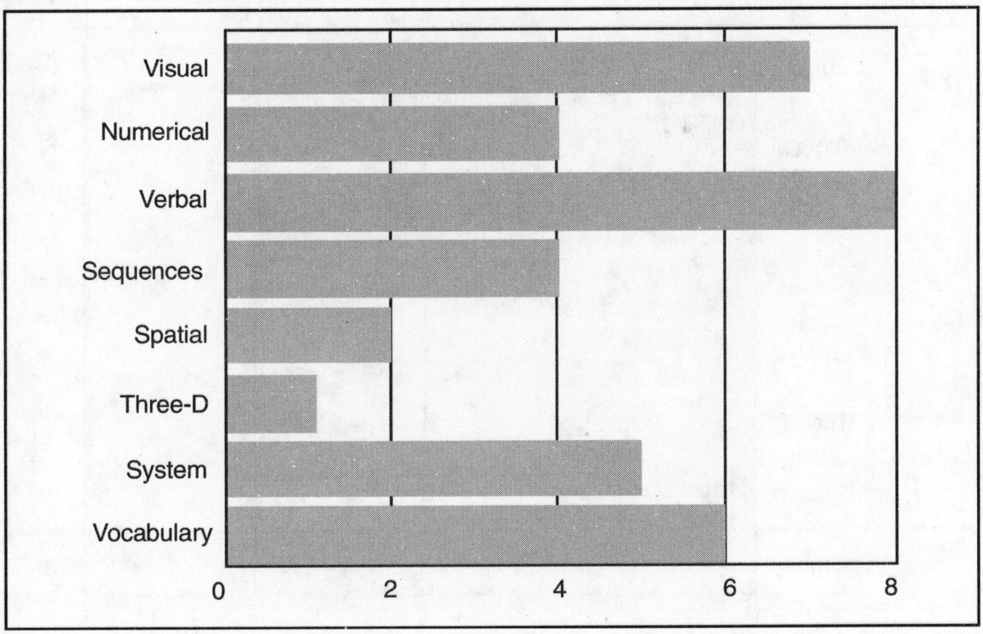

Mathematics and Statistics

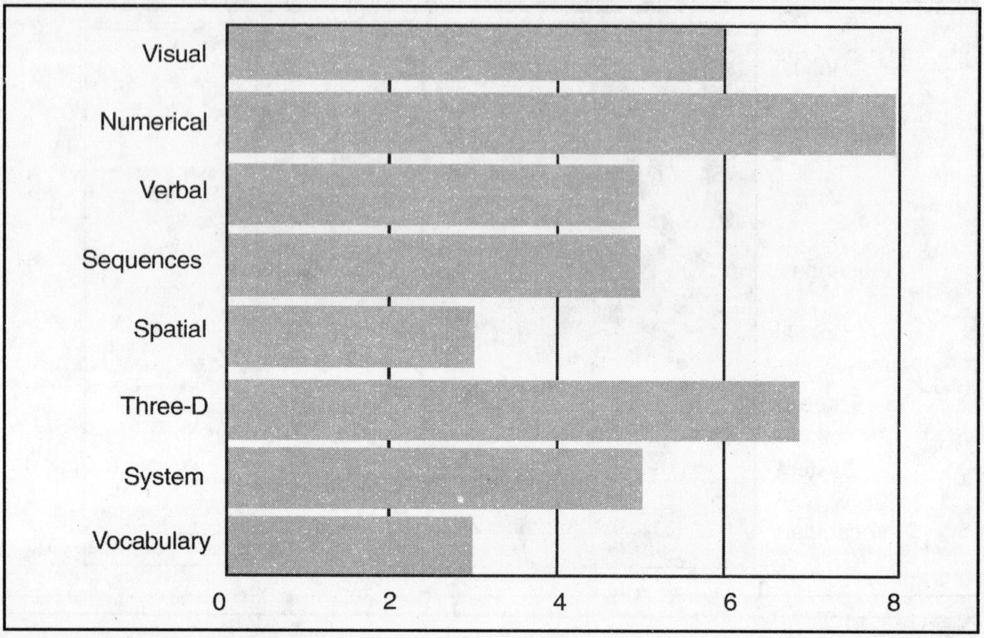

Media and Communication

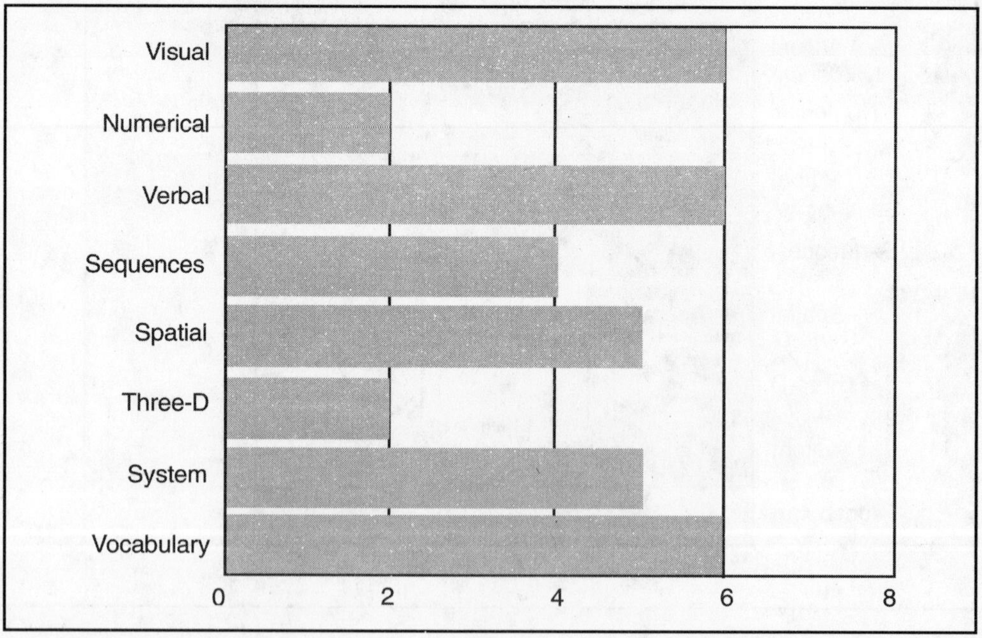

Music

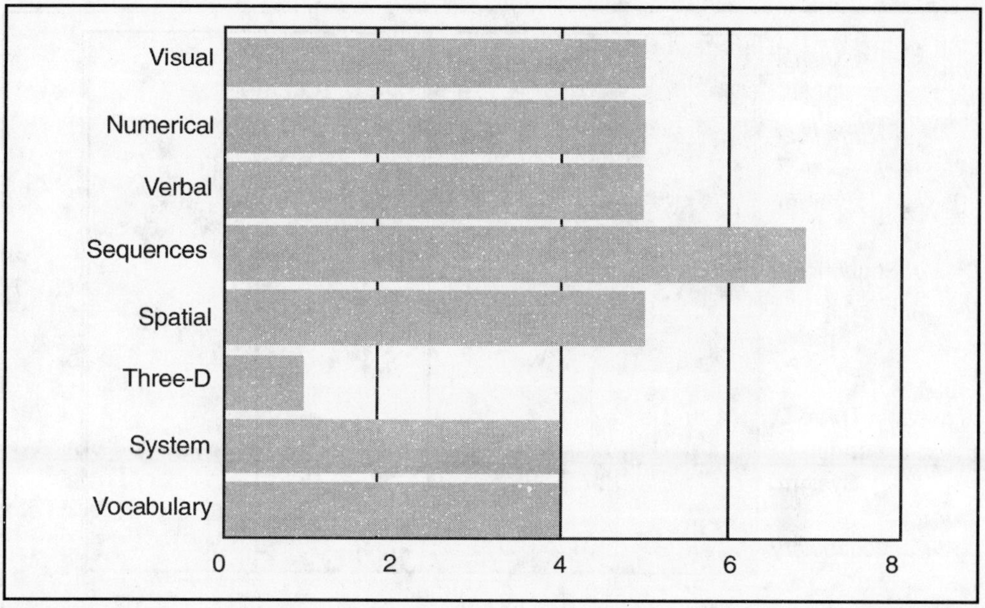

Nursing

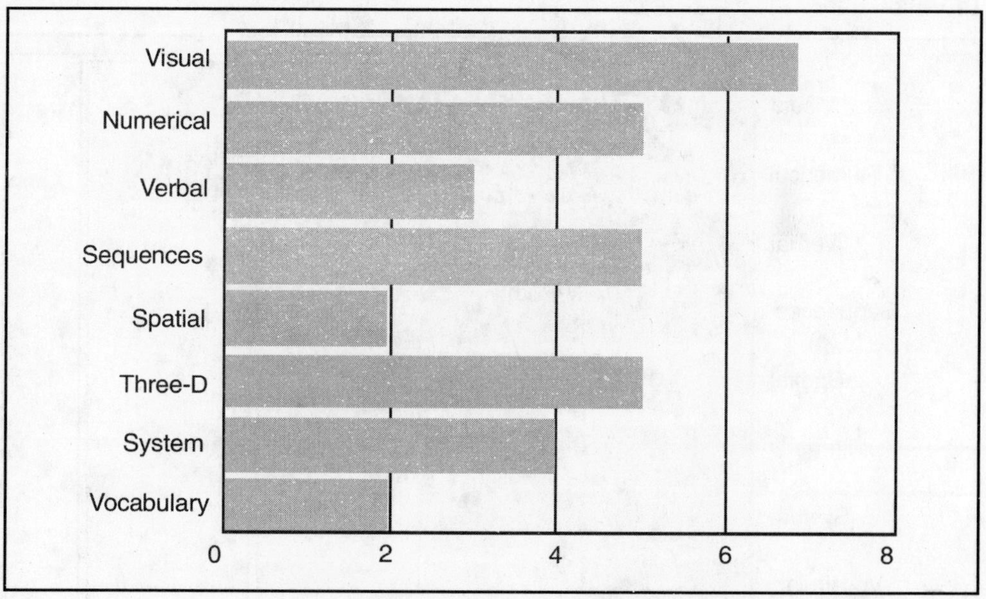

Philosophy and Religious Studies

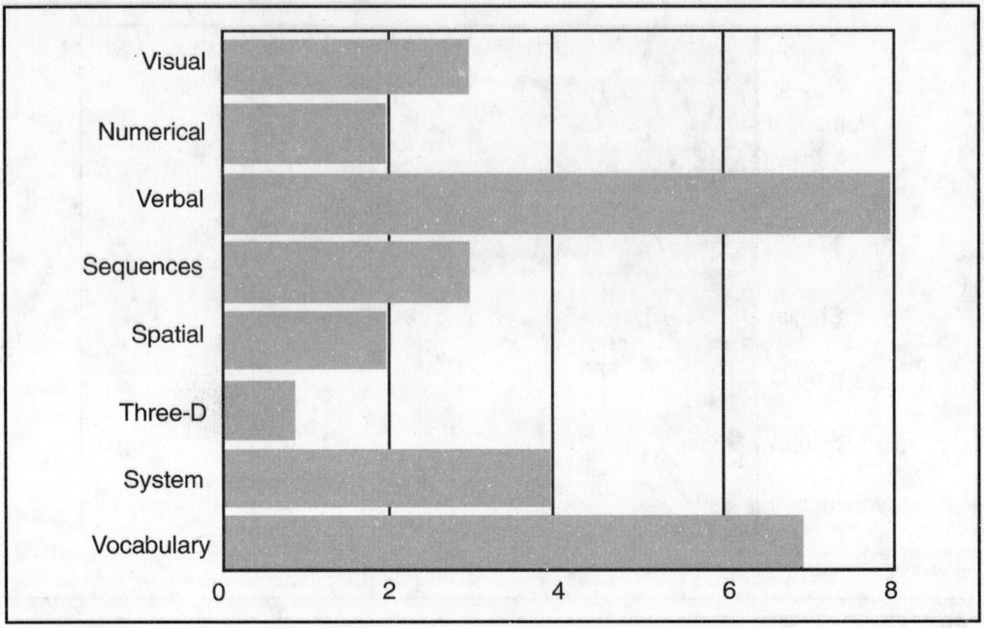

Physics

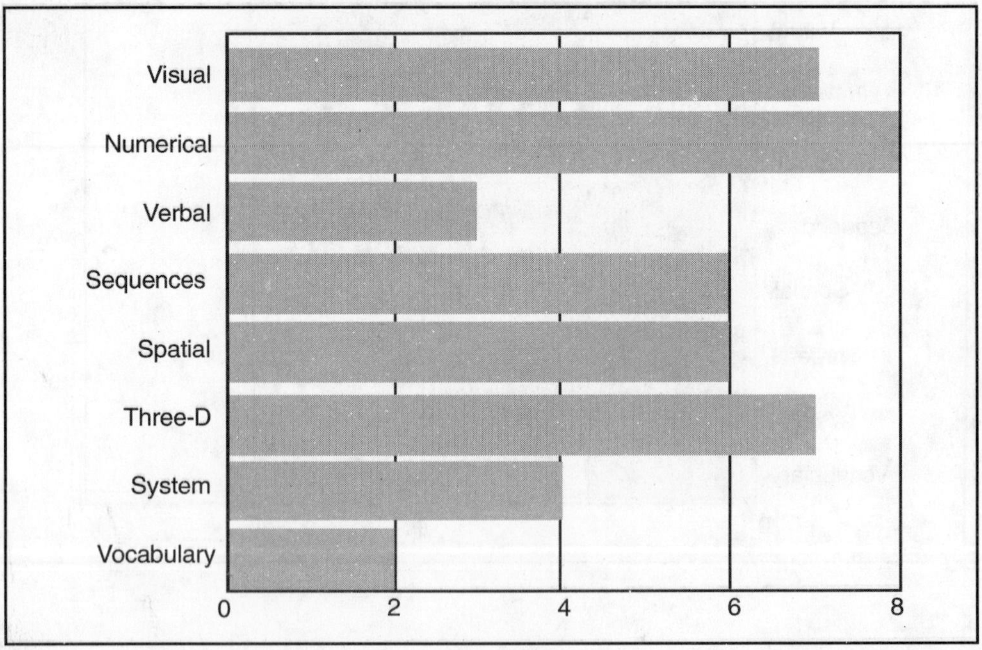

Politics and International Relations

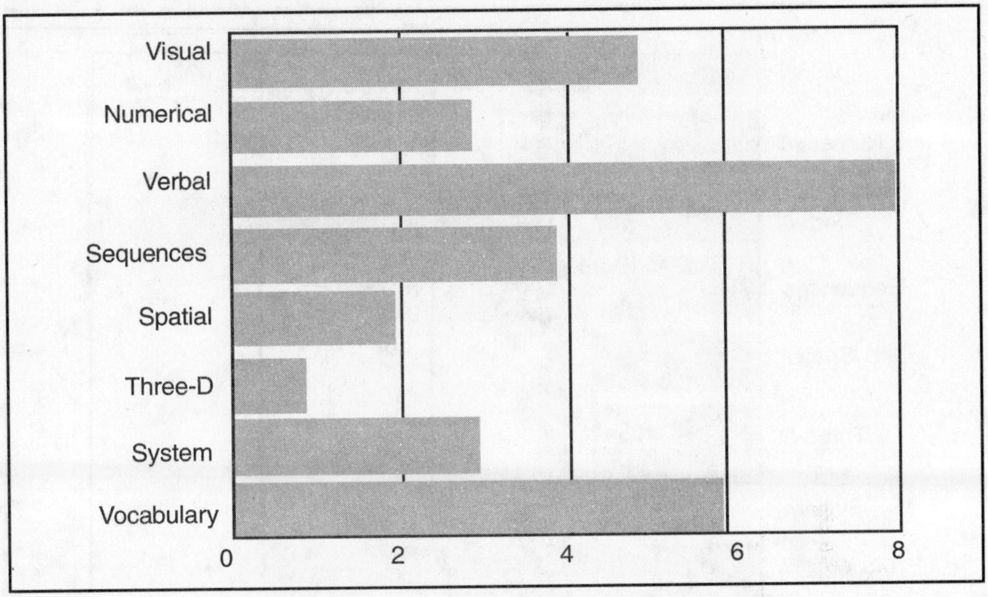

Psychology

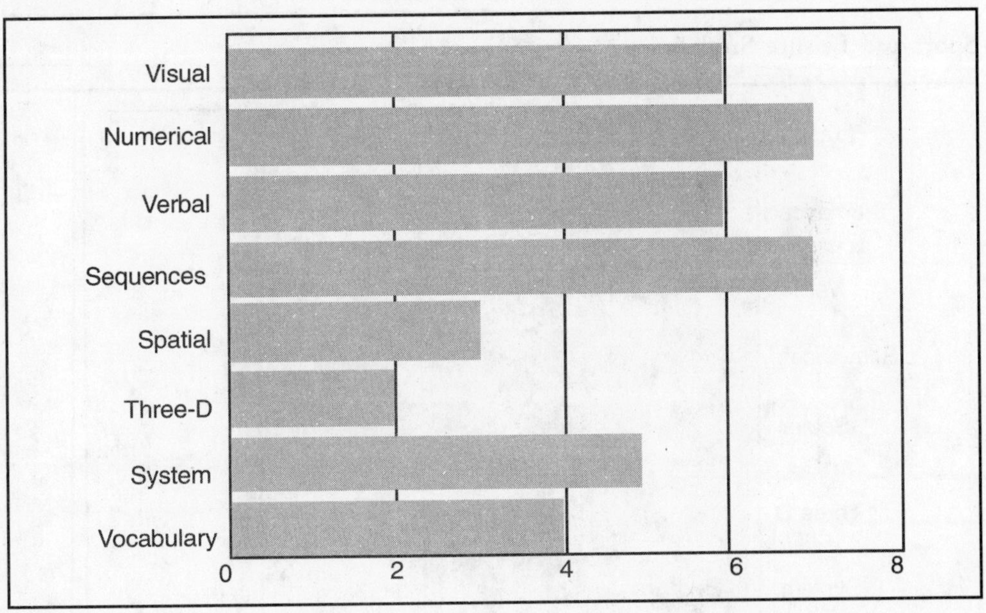

Sociology

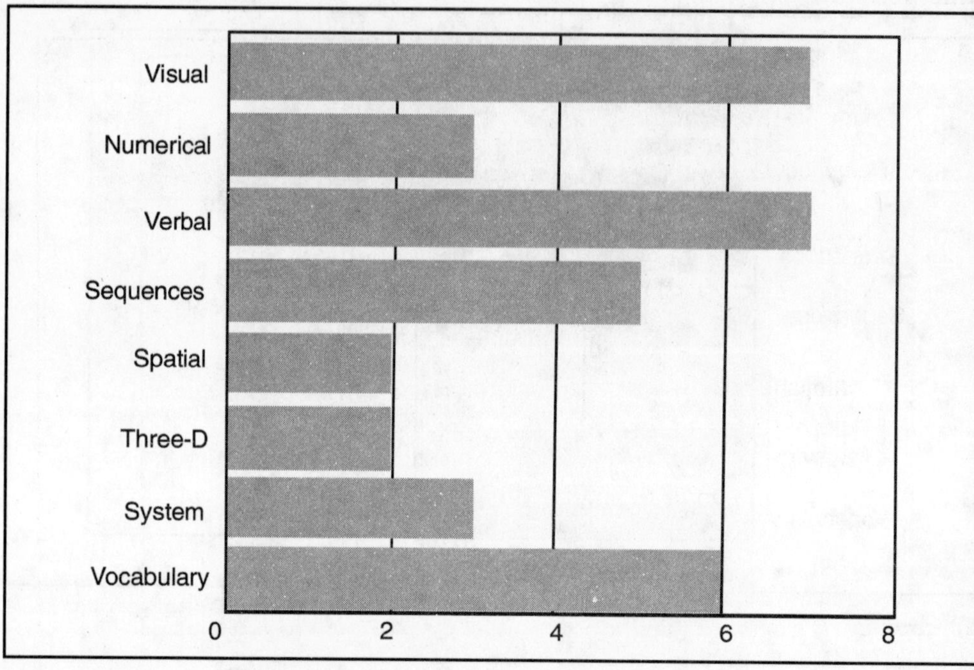

Sport and Leisure Studies

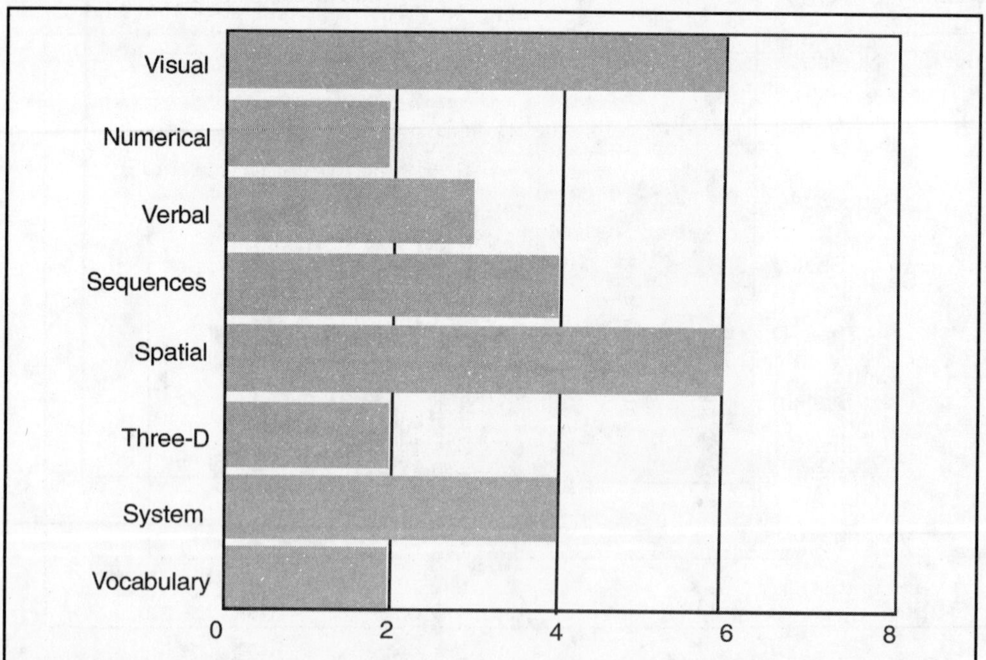

Textile Technology

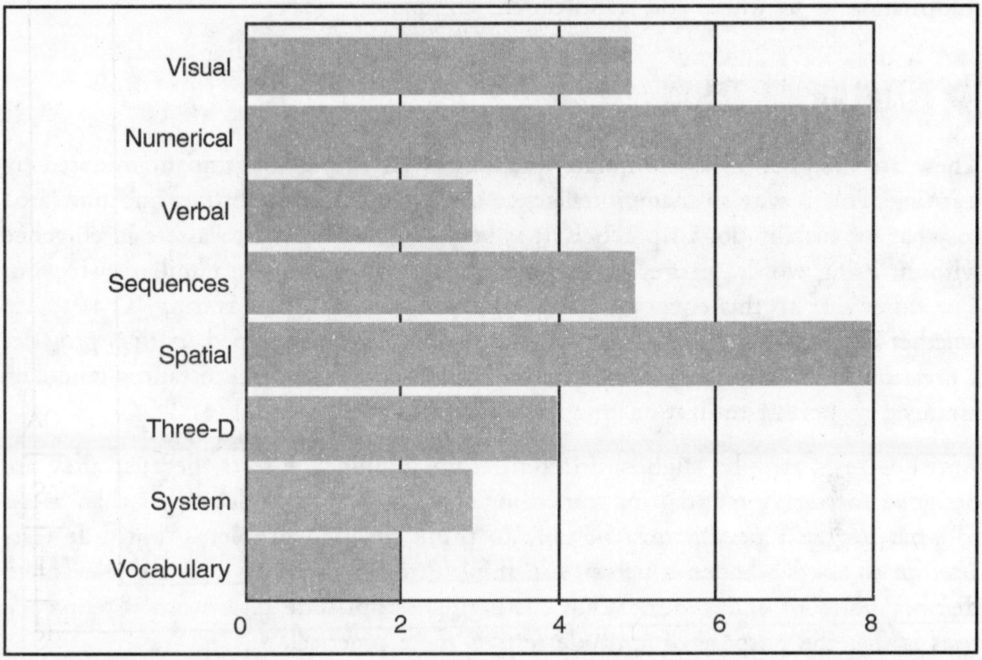

Veterinary Medicine

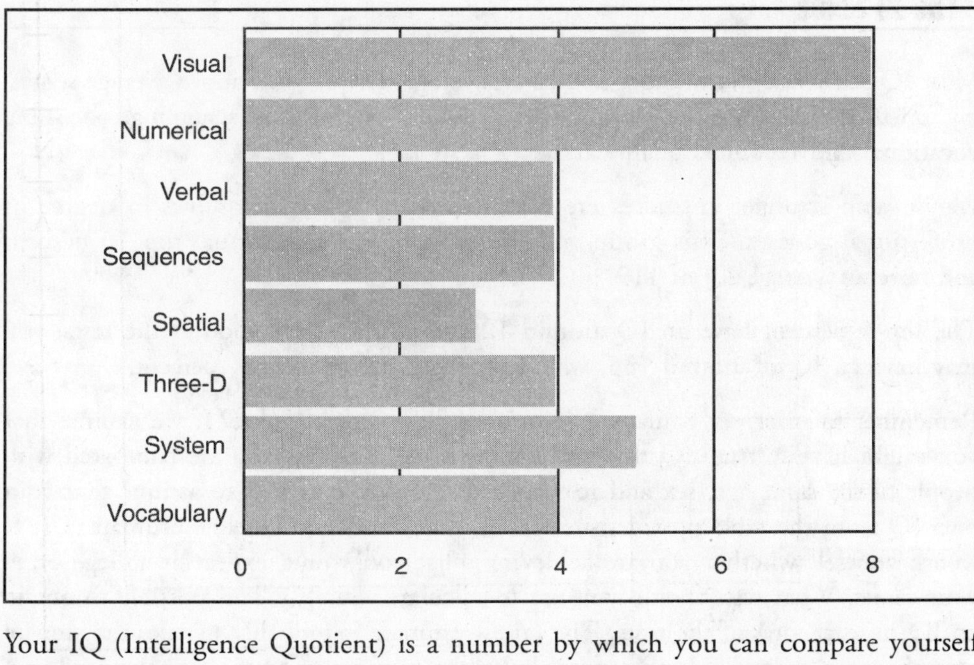

Your IQ (Intelligence Quotient) is a number by which you can compare yourself with other people. In an indirect way, you have already been doing this with your test results in this book. All that an IQ does is attempt to give you more precise information as to where you stand on the comparative scale.

INTELLIGENCE TESTS

These are designed to assess innate qualities as far as possible uncontaminated by learning. This is why so many intelligence tests seem to be so abstract and unrelated to what we usually do. In practice, it is very difficult indeed to assess intelligence without using words, figures or shapes that have at least some familiarity to you. The other side to this equation is that the whole point of measuring IQ is to see whether a person has intelligence that has not yet been developed. It thus provides a measure of how much more a person could achieve, if circumstances could be arranged to permit realization of that person's innate potential.

Aptitude tests may be slightly different from intelligence tests, because they are designed to assess potential for something specific. For example, rather than assess to what degree a person may be able to think through problems, aptitude tests attempt to assess whether a person can think through problems that are relevant to distinct fields of endeavour. What distinguishes aptitude tests from intelligence tests is that the purpose of aptitude tests is more practical.

The IQ Scale

Most IQ scales use the number 100 as an average. People with above average scores, say, up to about 115 on appropriate tests, usually extend their schooling, obtaining vocational and technical qualifications.

People with stronger aptitudes are usually able to apply themselves to degree or professional courses. This group will, roughly, be the intellectual top 10 percent and have an average IQ of 119.

The top 5 percent have an IQ around 125. If you are very good at the tests, you may have an IQ of around 135, which puts you into the top 1 percent.

Remember to interpret your own score only as a general guide. If we assume that you might have a 'true' IQ this will not be revealed unless you are compared with people of the same age, sex and relevant background. It is best to assume that your own IQ from the table provided here is likely to be only a baseline estimate. Use it to ask yourself whether you are achieving what you would expect at college or in your career. What tests should you use to calculate your IQ? It is possible to obtain an IQ on each one of the tests. The fairest estimate is probably to take the sum of several scores, then divide that number by the number of tests you have used.

❖ Your IQ

	100	105	110	115	120	125	130	135	140	145
Visual	1-6	7-9	10-13	14-17	18-20	21-24	25-26	27-28	29-30	31-32
Numerical	1-4	5	6-7	8-10	11-12	13-16	17-18	19	20	21
Verbal	1-7	8-9	10-11	12-13	14-15	16-18	19-20	21-22	23-26	27-33
Sequences	1-8	9-10	11-12	13-16	17-18	19-21	22-24	25-28	29-30	31-32
Spatial	1-26	27-30	31-34	35-38	39-42	43-48	49-54	55-60	61-65	66-70
Three-D	1-12	13-14	15-16	17-18	19-21	22-24	25-26	27-28	29	30
Systems	1-100	111-116	117-132	133-149	150-165	166-183	184-200	201-208	209-214	215-218
Vocabulary	1-19	10-12	23- 25	26-27	28-30	31-34	35-36	37-38	39	40

❖ Calculating Your IQ

('X' equals the number of tests used.)

Total 'IQ/' score from X tests = ______________

Divide by X tests / ______________

IQ = ______________

Aptitudes and Career Profiles

CODE

V	Visual
N	Numerical
Ve	Verbal
S	Sequential
Sp	Spatial

Contd...

3D	Three-D
Sy	Systems
Vo	Vocabulary

Note: Where it has been considered that a career may be suitable on the basis of aptitude on any of the tests, no ticks have been placed.

	V	N	Ve	S	Sp	3D	Sy	Vo
Accident assessor			✓		✓	✓		
Accountant		✓					✓	
Accounting technician		✓					✓	
Actor			✓					✓
Actuary	✓	✓		✓			✓	
Acupuncturist	✓				✓			
Administrator							✓	✓
Advertising copywriter			✓					✓
Advertising executive		✓	✓	✓	✓			✓
Aerobics instructor					✓			
Aeronautical engineer	✓	✓			✓	✓		
Aeronautical technician		✓				✓		
Agricultural mechanic			✓		✓			
Agricultural secretary							✓	
Agriculturalist		✓			✓			
Airline cabin staff							✓	
Air traffic controller	✓	✓		✓				
Ambulance crew								
Anesthetist	✓	✓						
Animal keeper								
Animal nurse								
Anthropologist	✓		✓	✓				
Antique dealer					✓			
Appliance repairer					✓	✓		
Arborist					✓			
Aroma therapist	✓							
Architect	✓	✓			✓	✓		
Architectural technician	✓				✓	✓		

Contd...

Archivist			✓				✓	✓
Armed forces officer	✓	✓						
Armed forces personnel								
Art dealer					✓			
Art restorer					✓			
Art therapist					✓			
Artist					✓			
Arts administrator		✓					✓	
Astronaut	✓	✓					✓	
Astronomer	✓	✓			✓			
Auctioneer					✓			
Audiologist technician	✓					✓		
Auditor		✓		✓			✓	
Author			✓					✓
Automobile technician					✓	✓		
Bacteriologist	✓	✓					✓	
Baggage handler								
Baker								
Ballet dancer					✓			
Bank clerk		✓					✓	
Bank manager		✓					✓	
Barperson								
Barrister		✓	✓					✓
Beautician					✓			
Bicycle repairer						✓		
Bilingual secretary			✓				✓	✓
Biologist	✓	✓						
Biomedical engineer		✓				✓		
Blacksmith/furrier					✓			
Boat builder					✓	✓		
Bookbinder						✓		
Book critic			✓					✓
Book illustrator								
Bookseller		✓			✓			
Botanist	✓							

Contd...

Brewer								
Bricklayer						✓		
Broker		✓						
Builder's merchant		✓						
Building demolition expert				✓	✓			
Building inspector						✓		
Building society assistant		✓					✓	
Building society manager		✓					✓	
Building surveyor					✓	✓		
Bursar		✓						
Bus driver								
Business consultant		✓		✓				
Buyer		✓			✓		✓	
Cabinet maker					✓			
Camera repairer						✓		
Car body designer					✓			
Careers adviser								
Carpenter						✓		
Cartographer					✓		✓	
Cartoon animator					✓			
Cashier		✓					✓	
Caterer					✓			
CD-ROM producer		✓			✓			
Chef	✓				✓			
Chemical technician	✓							
Chemical technologist	✓	✓						
Chemist	✓	✓					✓	
Chief executive		✓	✓	✓				✓
Child care worker								
Chimney sweep	✓					✓		
Chiropodist	✓					✓		
Choreographer					✓			
Cinema manager								
Civil engineer		✓				✓		
Civil servant		✓	✓				✓	✓

Contd...

Clerk							✓	
Clinical psychologist	✓	✓	✓	✓				
Clown					✓			
Club manager								
Coastguard								
College admissions counsellor						✓		
Comic illustrator					✓			
Commercial account manager	✓					✓		
Community social worker								
Community warden								
Company secretary		✓					✓	✓
Compositor						✓		
Computer animator		✓						
Computer game designer	✓				✓	✓	✓	
Computer hardware designer		✓			✓	✓		
Computer systems analyst	✓			✓				
Computer technician	✓				✓			
Confectioner								
Conference organizer								
Conservation officer	✓							
Copywriter			✓					✓
Coroner	✓	✓						
Cost accountant		✓					✓	
Counsellor								
Courier								
Court reporter							✓	✓
Crane operator								
Criminologist	✓			✓				
Cruise director								
Cryptographer	✓			✓	✓	✓	✓	✓
Cultural anthropologist	✓		✓					
Curator			✓		✓			
Currency trader		✓						
Customer services manager								
Customs officer								

Contd...

Dance instructor								
Dancer								
Deaf interpreter								
Decorator					✓			
Demonstrator								
Dental assistant	✓							
Dental hygienist	✓							
Dental nurse	✓							
Dental technician	✓					✓		
Dentist	✓	✓			✓	✓		
Dermatologist	✓							
Design engineer		✓				✓		
Designer					✓			
Dietician	✓					✓		
Director (media)			✓	✓				✓
Disc jockey								
Dispensing optician	✓							
Display artist					✓			
Diver						✓		
Doctor of medicine	✓	✓				✓	✓	
Drama teacher			✓					✓
Draughtsperson		✓				✓	✓	
Dresser (stage)					✓			
Dressmaker					✓			
Driver								
Drug and alcohol counsellor								
Drycleaner								
Ecologist	✓							
Economist		✓	✓					✓
Editor			✓				✓	✓
Editor (newspapers)			✓	✓			✓	✓
Editorial cartoonist			✓		✓			
Educational psychologist	✓	✓	✓					
Electrical engineer		✓				✓		
Electrician						✓		

Contd...

Electronics engineer		✓				✓		
Elementary school teacher					✓		✓	✓
Embalmer					✓			
Employment officer								
Engineering pattern maker		✓				✓		
Engineering technician		✓				✓		
English language teacher			✓					✓
Engraver					✓			
Entertainments officer								
Environmental health officer	✓							
Equestrian		✓			✓	✓		
Ergonomist		✓			✓	✓		
Estate agent								
Estate manager								
Exhibition organizer								
Explosives expert	✓			✓	✓	✓	✓	
Farm manager		✓				✓		
Farmer						✓		
Farm worker					✓			
Fashion buyer		✓			✓			
Fashion designer					✓			
Film projectionist						✓		
Film reviewer			✓		✓			✓
Financial analyst		✓					✓	
Financial controller		✓					✓	
Firefighter						✓		
Fisheries officer								
Fisherman								
Fitter						✓		
Flight attendant								
Florist					✓			
Fly person (theatre)					✓			
Food hygiene inspector	✓							
Food service worker								
Foreign correspondent			✓					✓

Contd...

Foreign language teacher			✓					✓
Forensic pathologist	✓	✓			✓	✓		
Forensic psychologist	✓			✓				✓
Forensic scientist	✓	✓			✓	✓		
Forester								
Freelance writer			✓					✓
Fund raiser								
Funeral director								
Furniture maker		✓			✓			
Gamekeeper								
Gardener								
Genealogist	✓						✓	
Geneticist	✓	✓						
Geochemist	✓	✓						
Geologist		✓			✓			
Glassblower						✓		
Glazier						✓		
Golf professional								
Graphic designer					✓			
Grocer								
Groundsperson								
Guard								
Gunsmith					✓	✓		
Hairdresser					✓			
Head teacher	✓	✓	✓	✓				✓
Health services administrator							✓	
Health visitor	✓							
Heating engineer						✓		
Historian			✓					✓
Homeopath	✓							
Horologist								
Horticulturalist		✓				✓		
Hospital physicist	✓	✓		✓		✓		
Hospital porter								
Hostel warden								

Contd...

Hotel manager		✓			✓			
House parent								
Housing manager							✓	
Human resources manager			✓				✓	✓
Hydrographic surveyor		✓				✓		
Hydrologist		✓				✓		
illustrator					✓			
Immunologist	✓	✓						
Importer/exporter		✓						
Industrial designer					✓			
Industrial nurse	✓							
Industrial relations officer								
Information officer								✓
Information scientist	✓							✓
Instrument and control engineer	✓			✓				
Instrument maker						✓		
Insurance adjuster		✓					✓	
Insurance agent							✓	
Interior designer					✓			
Interpreter			✓					
Interviewer			✓					
Jewellery maker					✓			
Jockey								
Joiner						✓		
Journalist			✓					✓
Judge			✓	✓				✓
Justices Clerk							✓	
Laboratory technician	✓					✓		
Landscape architect	✓	✓			✓			
Language teacher			✓					✓
Lawyer			✓	✓				✓
Legal executive	✓		✓				✓	✓
Leisure centre staff								
Liberal studies teacher	✓							
Librarian	✓						✓	✓

Contd...

Library assistant							✓	✓
Lighthouse keeper								
Lighting technician						✓		
Linguist			✓					✓
Literary agent			✓					✓
Literary critic			✓					✓
Lock keeper								
Locksmith						✓		
Locomotive engineer		✓				✓		
Lorry driver								
Machinist								
Maintenance technician						✓		
Maitre d'								
Make-up artist					✓			
Management consultant		✓		✓				
Managing director		✓	✓	✓				
Marine biologist	✓							
Market gardener								
Market researcher		✓					✓	
Marketing manager		✓			✓			✓
Masseur/masseuse					✓			
Materials scientist		✓			✓	✓		
Mathematician		✓			✓			
Mechanic						✓		
Mechanical engineer		✓				✓		
Medical illustrator					✓			
Medical records officer							✓	
Medical representative	✓							
Medical secretary							✓	
Mental nurse	✓							
Merchandiser		✓						
Merchant seaman								
Metallurgist		✓						
Meteorologist					✓			
Microbiologist	✓	✓						

Contd...

Midwife	✓							
Milkman								
Miller								
Milliner					✓			
Miner								
Minister of religion								✓
Model (fashion)								
Model maker					✓	✓		
Museum assistant								
Music producer								
Music therapist								
Musician								
Nanny								
Nature conservancy warden								
Navigating officer	✓	✓			✓		✓	
Negotiator								
Neurosurgeon	✓	✓		✓	✓	✓		
Notary public			✓				✓	✓
Novelist			✓					✓
Nuclear physicist	✓	✓			✓	✓		
Nurse	✓							
Nursery nurse								
Nutritionist	✓							
Obstetrician	✓	✓			✓			
Occupational psychologist	✓	✓	✓					
Occupational therapist					✓	✓		
Office cleaner								
Office machinery mechanic						✓		
Office manager		✓					✓	✓
Oil rig worker						✓		
Operational researcher	✓	✓		✓	✓		✓	
Ophthalmic optician	✓					✓		
Optician (dispensing)	✓					✓	✓	
Organization and methods officer	✓	✓	✓					

Contd...

Orthodontist	✓				✓	✓		
Orthoptist	✓				✓	✓		
Osteopath					✓			
Outplacement consultant	✓							✓
Panel beater						✓		
Paramedic	✓							
Patent agent	✓	✓		✓		✓	✓	✓
Patent examiner	✓	✓		✓		✓	✓	✓
Pathologist	✓	✓						
Pattern cutter						✓		
Personal trainer								
Pharmacist	✓						✓	
Pharmacologist	✓				✓	✓		
Philosopher			✓	✓				✓
Photographer					✓			
Photographic technician	✓				✓			
Physical education teacher	✓							
Physicist		✓			✓	✓		
Physiotherapist	✓				✓			
Piano teacher								
Piano tuner								
Picture framer						✓		
Pilot (airplane)		✓			✓	✓		
Pilot (coastal)					✓	✓		
Plasterer		✓			✓			
Play leader								
Plumber						✓		
Poet			✓					✓
Police dog handler								
Police officer				✓		✓		
Political agent							✓	✓
Politician			✓					
Pool and spa operator								
Post office clerk							✓	
Poster designer					✓	✓		

Contd...

Postman/woman								
Potter					✓			
Press agent			✓					
Principal nursing officer	✓							
Printer						✓		✓
Prison officer								
Probation officer								
Producer (films)		✓			✓			✓
Production manager					✓			
Programmer		✓		✓	✓	✓	✓	
Property negotiator								
Prosthetics engineer		✓				✓		
Psychiatric social worker	✓						✓	
Psychiatrist	✓		✓					✓
Psychoanalyst	✓		✓					
Psychologist	✓	✓	✓					
Psychotherapist	✓							
Public relations executive			✓					
Publican								
Publicity agent			✓					
Publisher			✓					✓
Purchasing manager		✓			✓		✓	
Purser		✓					✓	
Quality controller		✓				✓	✓	
Quality inspector		✓				✓	✓	
Quantity surveyor	✓	✓			✓	✓	✓	
Racing car driver								
Radiographer	✓					✓		
Railway guard								
Rating valuation officer	✓	✓					✓	
Receptionist								
Recording engineer		✓			✓			
Reflexologist	✓							
Remedial teacher								
Renovator					✓			

Contd...

Reporter			✓					✓
Restorer					✓			
Retail assistant								
Retail manager								
Roofer						✓		
Saddler					✓			
Sailor								
Sales executive								
Sales manager		✓		✓			✓	✓
Sales trainer			✓	✓				
Salesperson								
Science teacher	✓	✓						
Science writer	✓	✓						
Scientific instrument maker	✓				✓			
Scriptwriter			✓					✓
Sculptor					✓			
Secretary/PA							✓	
Senilities analyst		✓					✓	
Security officer								
Session musician								
Set designer					✓	✓		
Shepherd								
Shipping and forwarding officer	✓					✓		
Shop fitter						✓		
Sign writer					✓			
Silversmith					✓			
Social scientist	✓							
Social worker								
Soldier								
Solicitor			✓				✓	✓
Sound engineer		✓				✓		
Space salesperson								
Speech therapist	✓							
Sports coach								
Sports official (referee)								

Contd...

Stage hand								
Stage manager					✓			✓
Statistician		✓		✓				
Stock controller		✓					✓	
Stockbroker		✓						
Stone mason					✓			
Studio assistant								
Stunt performer								
Surgeon	✓	✓		✓	✓	✓		
Surveyor		✓			✓			
Systems analyst		✓			✓		✓	
Tailor					✓			
Tax inspector		✓	✓				✓	
Taxi driver					✓			
Taxidermist					✓			
Teacher	✓	✓	✓					
Teacher of art/craft					✓	✓		
Teacher of handicapped								
Technical illustrator					✓	✓		
Technical representative						✓		
Technical writer						✓		✓
Telecommunications engineer	✓				✓			
Telephonist								
Television engineer						✓		
Television production assistant							✓	
Thatcher					✓			
Theatre administrator	✓	✓					✓	
Tyler					✓			
Tool maker					✓	✓		
Toy maker					✓			
Tracer						✓	✓	
Traffic warden								
Train driver								
Training officer			✓			✓		
Translator			✓				✓	

Contd...

Transport manager								
Travel agent							✓	
Truck driver								
Third accountant		✓						
Umpire								
Underwriter		✓					✓	
Union negotiator								
Upholsterer					✓			
Urban planner	✓					✓	✓	
Veterinary nurse								
Veterinary surgeon	✓	✓			✓	✓		
Vision mixer						✓		
Vocational counsellor				✓				✓
Waiter/waitress								
Watch repairer						✓		
Welder						✓		
Window dresser					✓			
Word processor operator							✓	
Work study officer	✓			✓			✓	
Writer			✓					✓
Youth worker								
Zookeeper					✓			
Zoologist	✓	✓						

CHAPTER 17

Multi-Dimensional Assessment of Personality (MAP): A Unique Psychometric Test

LEARNING OBJECTIVES

- ❖ To discuss about origin, background and purpose of MAP.
- ❖ To explain personality dimensions.

ORIGIN AND BACKGROUND OF THE SCALE

The Multi-dimensional Assessment of Personality Series (MAP Series) should orient the alert reader to the fact that he has in the Series something very different from the majority of other test constructions. The MAP Series construction belongs in the realm of structured tests, i.e., tests that are shaped to the structures that basic research has shown to be essential elements of human personality in our culture.

Structured tests are a necessary requirement for functional testing and assessment, i.e., diagnostic testing, where the natural history, the age curves, the degree of inheritance, and the response to therapy of the dimensions measured is understood. With many older tests, e.g., the Rorschach, T.A.T., etc., one depends only on empirical statistical relations between some bit of test behaviour and some diagnostic category, e.g., schizophrenia. With structured tests, by contrast, one gets an evaluation of the dimension understood in a tested theory of personality assessment. For example, we know that the dimension of 'Emotional Stability (Maturity)', is significantly lower in neurotics and psychotics than in normals; that its hereditary determination is relatively unimportant; that it is high in people capable of meeting emergencies, such as airlines pilots, electricians, and nurses; that it is lowered by chronic conflict and fatigue; that it has some physiological association; and so on.

Along with the measures on other dimensions, in a total profile, this means that the psychologist with his theoretical insight, is able to make predictions and take remedial steps that go beyond the mere statistical estimate he is normally able to make between a raw score and some criterion which is valid only for a day. Since these measures have been born out of a slow process, of adequate, programmatic basic research, it is not surprising that the full scientific implication in applied psychology are yet to come. The several basic dimensional patterns are firm enough, as seen from occupational profiles established on these scales. But they stand relatively stark in terms of theoretical embellishment because psychologists have been all too prone, in the past, to build theories around clinical entities, rather than these real, replicable, and objectively measurable broad personality dimensions. They are real because they emerge from sophisticated multivariate experimental techniques—such as microbes emerged from microscopic and staining techniques in which most physicians were untrained. However, it is not necessary to get immersed in the theoretical origins in order to understand, logical and insightfully, the personality theory now growing from the discovery of personality dimensions.

Discovery of behaviour index values for an increasing number of clinical, industrial, social and educational situations can be left to applied psychology, providing it measures dimensions well and meaningfully. It is the 'meaningful' aspect with which we are here concerned. The MAP Series is the psychologist's answer to these considerations, in the questionnaire realm, to the demand for a test giving fullest information in the shortest time about most personality dimensions' indexes. It is not merely concerned with some narrow concept of neuroticism or "adjustment", or some special kind of ability, but sets out to cover planfully and precisely all the main dimensions along which people can differ.

In applied fields such as clinical, educational, and industrial psychology, the practitioner usually has a feeling that certain behavioural dimensions, e.g., maturity, competitiveness, enthusiasm (according to the nature of the adjustment involved), will be more important and predictive than others. He may be right; but the verdict of many years of research indicates that in nine cases out of ten, he will overlook some other, unconsidered personality dimensions that are equally important. The best way to begin is to take cognizance of the total personality, in all its main dimensions. Similarly, in research design, the investigator often begins with an interest in one concept only, e.g., anxiety, extraversion, superego strength; yet he would generally be wise, in his first attack in field, to discover what is happening on other personality dimensions at the same time.

The busy psychometrist may sometimes feel that twenty sub-scores is a lot, but if such is the real complexity of human nature, and if, as studies show, the majority of these personality characteristics are involved in most criterion predictions, a much better multiple correlation is to be obtained by respecting the complexity than by indulging in a fool's paradise of over-simplification. To simplify, personality assessment is useful in some circumstances, but in most situations it looses some of the possible predictive power and some of the insight into the personality structure.

It is for these prevalent and important conditions that the present MAP series is intended. Its vocabulary is that of the daily newspaper, and since no writing is required it can be used as a group or individual test, for a age range of 5 years and above.

There are three special considerations which raise the utility of the MAP Series, for most personnel managers, clinical, educational, and research psychologist.

1. Some of the finest statistical research has been devoted to its construction on a very broad sampling of the area of personality responses;
2. The statistical treatment resulted in a true personality structure, revealing functionally inter-independent items for each dimensions;
3. A standardization on a proper variety of occupational groups, teenagers, school students, and young children, to accumulate relations of important criteria.

Regarding the last, the possible statistical predictions from the dimensions, and the psychological grasp of their modes of action, are continually increasing.

Organized research is establishing patterns for various clinical diagnostic and prognostic groups, and regression coefficients on criteria of occupational and educational success and adjustment.

Although innumerable questionnaires and inventories have been published in the last few years, only one or two have been well founded on factor statistical showing that the separate traits or dimensions of personality which they claim to measure are real, functionally unitary, and psychologically significant dimensions. The questionnaires in the present series meet a long-standing demand for a personality – measuring instrument properly validated with respect to the primary personality dimensions that are rooted in general personality research. It is at present unique in: (a) having every item possessed of a demonstrated saturation with respect to each of the dimensions which it sets out to measure, and, (b) having proof that each of the dimension corresponds to a primary personality dimension found elsewhere, i.e., beyond the questionnaire realm, notably in ratings in real-life behaviour situations.

A full description of the psychological meaning of each one of these dimensions is given later. At this point, it is suffice to summarize that these are the main dimensions (a) that have been found necessary and adequate to cover all kinds of individual differences of personality found in common speech and psychological literature (they leave out no important aspect of the total personality); (b) that they are independent of one another, so that it is possible for a person to combine any score whatever on one with any score on others (in other words, they do not overlap in meaning, or waste scores by partially repeating the same measure under a new name, as many arbitrary questionnaire scales do, but represent clear functional unities.); (c) that these are known to be important in the sense of each having a wide area of influence on behaviour, and in which the influence can be understood in terms of psychological processes of maturation, learning, and interaction with physiological conditions.

It is now appropriate to proceed to explain the way in which the actual test is designed, scored, and administered. After that, you will be better prepared to follow a fuller discussion of the nature of the actual dimensions and the final use of scores in understanding and predicting with respect to a given case.

DESIGN AND PURPOSE OF THE SCALE

Although the questionnaire type of personality test is a mistake to assume that it is a universally valid instrument. Its results differ somewhat as between cooperative and uncooperative, well-educated and poorly educated, honestly and ulteriorly-motivated subjects. Questionnaires have so far been shown to have their most valid application with students or with cooperative, anonymous subjects, under research conditions, and it is recommended that where honesty, in sight, and cooperation are poor, or wherever opportunities exist to test the subject at greater length, objective tests should be used.

However, the majority of questions in the MAP Series are indirect, asking about interests which the subject would not necessarily perceive to be related to the trait in question, so that it escapes some of the distortions described. Moreover, in the MAP Series, we do not interpret the dimensions from the nature of the subject's statements about himself, but from the known correlations between these 'mental interiors' as found in questionnaire dimensions and the dimensions established in behaviour. In other words, the question responses are treated as behaviour, not as valid self ratings.

Increasingly, nowadays, we recognize that major directions of adult life are decided in childhood: that "the child is father of the man." This being so, it becomes all the more important to know the child, to study him via meaningful, accurate, and standard measurements. Accordingly, in the MAP Series a special emphasis is placed on development of testing instrument for children, which are organically linked to adult tests by psychological continuity of concepts.

Fortunately, it has proved possible to understand adults in terms of essentially the same personality structures as are applied in children's tests. Except for one or two special dimensions, our information on the child form need not be lost or arduously lost recast and re-interpreted as he becomes a man. Such continuity of score meaning over wide age ranges is a unique and valuable feature of the MAP Series, thus, filling a real need in current research and practice. For one of the most important guides to reliable counselling is having records of earlier exact measurement on the personality dimensions of the child, extending over a number of years.

In development research, measurements on a child at one age must be compared with measurements on the same child some years later. Most previous work of this kind has been hampered by lack of tests which refer to the same dimension reliably at different ages. For example, a score on a verbal intelligence test at one age cannot be accurately compared with a score on another type of culturally-contaminated test at another age.

The design of the MAP Series, which keeps these long-distance goals in view, is meant to cater the psychologists who wants this kind of constancy in their assessments. The MAP Series provides a sequence of scales, which measure the same demonstrated personality dimensions at different ages. The various Forms: Form-A (for Adults), Form-T (for Teenagers), Form-C (for Children), and Form-P (for Primary level), cover essentially the same dimensions from ages 5 and above. Thus, those counsellors and school psychologists, who follow through with structured tests of this type in their routine testing at different age periods will now be able to draw more insightful and systematic conclusions than hitherto about developmental changes in individuals as they progress through the school system, from elementary school through college and adult life. All the Forms are intended for administration in both group and individual situations, for clinical work the latter is preferable. The subjects make their responses on the booklet itself. This booklet can be hand-scored with the help of scoring stencils.

Three alternative answers to each item are provided to the subject, in Form A and T, as these are for an older age group. In Form C and P, two category responses are provided as the younger age group is prone to get confused with the middle category response of 'in between', 'uncertain', or 'undecided'.

FORM - A (for ADULTS)

The Form A of the MAP Series is based on several years of research in which every item has been subjected to statistical investigation, thus providing an unusually sound foundation of proof that the twenty scales are stable and independent. This form has been revised, modernized in scoring, and intensified in validity several times since last few years.

The Form A has a wide range of applications. In vocational guidance and industrial selection practice there are extremely few tests for which actual optimum job profiles exist to guide the psychologist. The MAP FORM A has more than fifty job profiles including those of salesmen, electricians, pilots, teachers, nurses, business executives, managers, etc., to objectively index a candidate's fitness. Thus, the Form A can comfortably be used in industry and business for selection, placement, and promotion of personnel by predicting important job-related characteristics, such as length of time an employee is likely to remain with the company, sales effectiveness, work efficiency, tolerance for routine, and several measures relevant to specific occupations.

In clinical and counselling settings, the MAP FORM A provides psychologists with measures of anxiety, emotional stability, mental health and other behavioural trends that help counsellors make diagnostic decisions and plan treatment strategies.

❖ Psychological Descriptions of the Dimensions Measured by Map Form - A

A test of normal, adult personality, the MAP FORM A measures 20 dimensions covering Adaptability, Achievement, Motivation, Boldness, Competition, Enthusiasm, General Ability, Guilt Proneness, Imagination, Innovation, Leadership, Maturity, Mental Health, Morality, Self-Control, Sensitivity, Shrewdness, Suspiciousness, Social Warmth, and Tension.

Table 17.1 presents a brief summary of the MAP Form A and their high score meanings. In this figure and the following descriptions, the term 'high score' is generally reserved for sten score range of 8-10, which places the individual in the upper 20% with respect to their reference population. However, this does not suggest that the low scores are of no significance. The dimensions with low score (sten range 1-3) represent important interpretable departures from the norm, placing the individual in the bottom 20th percentile or lower, with respect to the reference population. Sten scores of 4-7 represent deviations in the indicated direction from the norm, but are less significant features of the profile than the upper and lower sten ranges.

PERSONALITY DIMENSIONS

Adaptability (Ad)

This dimension refers to the ability to make appropriate responses to changed or changing circumstances. Those individuals who score high readily accept any beneficial change to meet the environmental demands are said to be highly adaptable. They settle down to the conditions for work or learning with the elimination of unnecessary preparatory behaviour.

The *Ad* dimension is a collection of various other personality dimensions consisting of emotional maturity, uninhibited behaviour, trustworthiness, self-assurance, strong will power, social preciseness and following self image. Low scoring individuals do not have a harmonious relationship in their environment and are unable to obtain satisfaction for most of their needs. They usually fail to meet the demands of their physical and social surroundings.

Achievement Motivation (Am)

This is a sentimental dimension consisting mainly of two attitudes: "learning skills" and "keeping the job". It seems to reflect the amount of actual experience the individual has had and the degree to which he is currently interested and concerned. *Am* is a collection of various other personality dimensions referred to as general intelligence, dominance, imagination, radicalism, self-sufficiency and discipline. High scoring individuals may be described as ambitious, overtly interested in their career and realistically involved in various aspects of life. Low scores indicate regressive behaviour, escapism and unwillingness to accept responsibility. Feelings of failure may also tend to decrease this score.

Boldness (Bo)

High scoring individuals on dimension *Bo* are typically adventurous, bold and energetic with good insight. They enjoy being the focus of attention in a group situation and have no problem with stage fright. Thus, with the consequent, it is not unusual to find successful salespeople generally above average on this dimension. High scorers are reported to feel that enjoying is more important than winning the game. They also describe themselves as quick decision makers, but it should be pointed out that they do not necessarily make the correct decision. It is seen that competitive athletes are generally significantly above average on this dimension.

Clinically speaking, high *Bo* individuals, like well-insulated building, are able to withstand external pressures passively without expending much energy in doing so. Low *Bo* individuals, on the other hand have little 'insulation', therefore, external stresses can penetrate them more easily. Consequently, they expend more energy to maintain equilibrium.

Competition (Co)

High *Co* indicates that the individual is self-assertive, dominant and aggressive. Such individuals describe themselves as forceful and are generally very direct in their relations with other people. They like to put their own ideas into practice and enjoy having things their own way. Occupationally, sportsmen and judges are found to be significantly above average on this dimension. High *Co* is also important in many sales occupations.

Co also plays an important role in marital compatibility. When both the partners tend to be competitive and dominant, they fail to channel their interests in non-competitive directions resulting in more conflicts. Regarding clinical implications, extremely high *Co* scores (sten 9 or 10) are sometimes associated with aggression and stubbornness that frequently masks covert feelings of inferiority. Low *Co* individuals tend to be submissive, mild, humble and accommodating.

Enthusiasm (En)

High scoring individuals on dimension *En* are generally happy go-lucky, lively and enthusiastic. In their self reports they admit to having more friends than most people. They enjoy parties, shows and jobs that offers change, variety and travel. Therefore, airline attendants, travel agents, and sales personnel score significantly above average on this dimension. Whereas, research scientists are found to be significantly below average.

The low score on this dimension need not be confused with depression. Low *En* simply indicates that the person is serious, prudent and sober. This dimension may be treated as a behavioural control indicator in which high score indicates that the individual will externalize or 'act out' inner conflicts. On the other hand, low *En* simply indicates that the person will internalize (or control) his inner conflicts.

General Ability (Ga)

High scoring individuals on *Ga* have a greater mental capacity to learn. They are insightful, fast learning, and intellectually adaptable. They are also inclined to have more intellectual interests and show better judgements in their observations. Low scoring individuals on the other hand, have a poor mental capacity to learn and are unable to handle abstract problems. They act to be less well-organized and show poor judgement in their observations.

There may be some clinical significance to low scores on *Ga*, particularly for individuals who, on the basis of other available evidence, could be expected to perform reasonably well. Since the items themselves are not extraordinarily difficult, an otherwise capable individual who answers too many of them incorrectly may not be paying sufficient attention to the test.

Guilt-proneness (Gp)

The high *Gp* person feels over-fatigued by exciting situations, is unable to sleep through worrying, feels inadequate to meet the rough daily demands of life, is easily downhearted and remorseful, feels that people are not as moral as they should be, is inclined to piety, prefers books and quiet interests to people and noise, and shows a mixture of hypochondriacal and neurasthenic symptoms, with phobias and anxieties most prominent.

Occupationally, high *Gp* scores occur in senior clerks, writers, waitresses, and editorial workers, and low in professional athletes, electricians, firemen, nurses, priests (but not some other clerical denominations), and salesmen. In group dynamics, high *Gp* persons do not feel accepted or free to participate, are considered shy, ineffective speakers, and hinderers, but remain religiously task oriented in their remarks. They select few peers as friends, and have high standards of group conformity to rules. High *Gp* dimension is strongly weighted against successful leadership in face to face situations and is correlated significantly with accident proneness in automobile driving.

Clinically, *Gp* is very important, first as one of the largest contributor in anxiety, appearing centrally in the depressive anxiety syndrome, and secondly, as tending to be generally high in neurotics and many psychotics.

It is very low in convicts and mostly distinguishes those who "act out" their maladjustment from those who suffer it as internal conflict. Consequently, it is not to be confused with simple super ego strength or a 'psychological weakness', it represents a "guilt proneness" and "poorness in spirit" sometimes associated with piousness.

Imagination (Im)

Essentially, it is seen that the high *Im* person has an intense subjectivity and inner mental life. Although cheerful and irresponsible' on practical matters he actually has higher internal anxiety, tensions than the low *Im* person. He may walk and talk in his sleep, and alternates periods of placid disregard of practical considerations with hysteroid episodes of relatively childishly dependent behaviour.

High *Im* individuals in groups tend to feel unaccepted, but unconcerned. They participate and make original leadership suggestions, and are not immediately ignored, but their suggestions turn out to be rejected. They express significantly more dissatisfaction with the group unity and its regard for rules of procedure. Occupationally high *Im* occurs in artists, researchers, planning executives, and editors. Low *Im* is seen in occupations requiring mechanical sense, realism and alertness.

Innovation (In)

Individuals with high score on this dimension tend most frequently to be analytical, liberal and innovative. High *In* persons are more well-informed, more inclined to experiment with problem solutions, less inclined to moralize, etc. They feel that society should throw out traditions, they trust logic rather than feelings, favour relaxed divorce laws, and prefer to break with established ways of doing things.

Occupationally, it is high in executives and directors, progressive politicians, and especially, scientific researchers. It is low in priests, nurses, many semiskilled and unskilled worker groups, and in more (as contrasted with less) successful psychiatric technicians. Neurotics tend to run low on *In*. In group dynamics, the high *In* person contributes significantly more remarks to discussion, a high percentage being of a critical nature.

Leadership (Ld)

A person who scores high on *Ld* has the ability to direct and control the attitude or actions of others. This is specially true when this person exhibits such influence on a group. High *Ld* individuals usually occupy such positions in a group that commands a certain authority or potential for controlling the behaviour of this group. High leadership qualities consists of various other personality characteristics such as self-confidence, controlled and strong will power. They are also adventurous and responsive to people, persevering, determined and responsible, and are usually quick and alert in their surroundings.

Subjectively, the high *Ld* person views himself as a guardian of manners and morals. They are planful and are able to concentrate, interested in analyzing people and prefer efficient people to other companions. Low scoring individuals are undependable, obstructive and prefer to be sound followers. They are group dependent and impatient and are likely to escape when faced with responsibility.

Maturity (Ma)

This dimension is the first of those involved in the anxiety pattern. Its contribution is negative, i.e., higher anxiety is generally reflected in low scores on *Ma*. This dimension is one of dynamic integration and maturity as opposed to general emotionality. In its positive sense it seems to be what the psychoanalysts are attempting to describe by the notion of ego strength. The individuals level on *Ma* may be taken as an index of his stress tolerance. The higher the *Ma* score, the more resources the individual has available to meet the challenges of the day. The low *Ma* person is easily annoyed by things and people, is dissatisfied with the world situation, his family, the restrictions of life, and his own health. He shows generalized neurotic responses in the form of phobias, psychosomatic disturbances, sleep disturbances, hysterical and obsessional behaviour.

High *Ma* individuals are frequently chosen as leaders than are low *Ma* individuals. It should be noted that criminals also score high on dimension *Ma* ("ego strength") which agrees with their psychoanalytic contrast to neurotics. Clinically, the outstanding observation is that most disorders show low *Ma* scores, though neurotics and psychotics do not differ only in having low *Ma*, but in other dimensions also.

Occupationally, individuals having to adjust to difficulties thrown upon them from outside, e.g., teachers, engineers, salesmen, firemen, run well above average on dimension *Ma*, while in occupations not demanding sudden adjustments, or in which the individual can set his own pace, e.g., postmen, clerks, writers, show lower ego strength.

Mental Health (Mh)

High scoring individuals on *Mh* are in a relatively enduring state in which they are well adjusted, have a zest for living, and are attaining self-actualization or self-realization. This is a positive state, and not mere absence of mental disorder. It includes all measures aimed at preventing mental disorder and at improving the psychological adjustment of individuals and their capacity for harmonious relationship in groups. The *Mh* dimension consists of various other personality characteristics such as emotional stability, impulsivity, self-security and low tension.

At the level of self-report, high *Mh* individuals report that they are generally able to reach personal goals without much difficulty. They do not seem to be easily distracted when working on something and have general satisfaction with the way they have lived their lives.

Occupationally, administrator groups have scored significantly above average on this particular dimension. It has been found to be significantly below average in the chronically unemployed. *Mh* is also important in accident proneness, the low *Mh* individuals are more prone to accidents as compared to high *Mh* individuals. Low *Mh* is also associated with physical illness, specially coronary problems.

Morality (Mo)

Individuals who score high on this dimension tend to be more persistent, more respectful of authority, and more conforming to the standards of the group. The hypothesis may be set up that this factor corresponds to the superego as in psychoanalysis. On the whole, it would seem that this dimension best depicts the regard for moral standards, the tendency to drive the ego and to restrain the id, which are most frequently regarded as marks of the super-ego.

In their self-reports, high *Mo* individuals describe themselves as being disgusted by sloppy people and messy rooms. They generally follow rules to the letter. Low scores on *Mo* occasionally signals sociopathic tendencies. Extremely high scores on *Mo* are also associated with rigidity and unrealistic high standards for themselves, and, as a result experience guilt and feeling of inadequacy when they fail to meet their standards. Thus, flexibility is not a part of the high scoring individuals behaviour and this may lower the individuals ability to cope with extreme stress.

Occupationally, military cadets appear to score significantly above average on this dimension. Real estate agents and salesmen score below average on this dimension.

Self-Control (Sc)

This dimension may be treated as the ability to bind anxiety. High-scoring individuals generally have strong control over emotional life and behaviour in general. The high *Sc* person shows socially approved character responses, behaviour control, persistence, foresight, considerateness of others, and conscientiousness.

In group dynamics, high *Sc* score especially picks out persons who will be chosen as leaders, but even more so those who are effective rather than merely popular leaders. They make more remarks than others, especially problem-raising and solution-offering, receive fewer votes as hinderers, and fewer rejections at the end of the sessions. High *Sc* is associated with success in mechanical, mathematical, and productive organizational activities. It is high in executives, electricians, and psychiatric technicians, in all of which objectivity, balance and decisiveness are required. It is significantly related to freedom from automobile accidents.

Clinically, low *Sc* is a major contributor to the anxiety pattern and serves as a important clinical sign, signaling the individual's inability to keep his/her emotions in order. But at the same time, if *Sc* is extremely high (sten 9-10) in combination with elevations on dimension *Gp* (guilt proneness) and *Tn* (tension – to be discussed later), there is a tendency to excess compulsivity, resulting in obsessional types of behaviour.

Sensitivity (Se)

Descriptions associated with high scores on this dimension include tender-minded, dependent, overprotected, fidgety, clinging, and insecurity among individuals. High *Se* scorers prefer to use reason rather than force in getting things done. The high *Se* person shows a fastidious dislike of "crude" people and rough occupations, a liking for travel and new experiences, a labile (indeed, unstable), imaginative aesthetic mind, a love of dramatics, and a certain impracticality in general affairs. There are indications that artists score high on this dimension. Group performances tend to be poorer with high *Se*, while they receive significantly more descriptions as fussy, slowing-up group performance in arriving at decisions, and making social-emotional negative (morale upsetting) remarks. Low *Se* on the other hand, represents some sort of tough, masculine, practical, mature, group-solidarity generating, and realistic ("no-nonsense") temperamental dimension.

Occupationally, it distinguishes interior decorators, musicians, and artists from engineers and surgeons — and perhaps sensitive clinicians from psychometrists. Available evidence points out that psychiatric technician, artists, waitresses, and women preferring home to profession score high, and electricians and mechanics score low. As mentioned above, high *Se* tends to be significantly associated with mental break down, both – psychotic, neurotic, and psychosomatic complaints. Low *Se* individuals have a history of fewer illnesses and operations, more aggressiveness, and significantly greater participation in athletics and sports.

Shrewdness (Sh)

High scoring individuals report that they prefer being around 'polished', sophisticated people. They say that their feelings are not easily swayed and that they are polite and diplomatic about handling other people. They prefer to keep problems to themselves. High *Sh* individuals may also be described as ingenious, good at clinical diagnosis, flexible in viewpoint, alert to manners, to social obligations, and to the social reactions of others. The pattern represents some form of intellectual-educational development, not to be confused with intelligence, though it correlates both with intelligence and dominance.

Although this dimension thus looks like a socially acquired pattern of skills, there is curious initial evidence in the clinical field that it is associated with a generalized mental alertness, health, and efficiency. Occupationally, the highest groups are the skilled professions and precision occupations, e.g., civil engineers, scientists, pilots, and the lowest are priests, nurses, psychiatric technicians and convicts. In group dynamics high *Sh* individuals are recorded with significantly greater frequency as leading in-analytical, goal-oriented discussion, and in providing constructive solutions, while low *Sh* individuals receive more checks as slowing and hindering proceedings. Among married couples *Sh* may be an important relationship factor. Individuals who are extremely high (sten 9 or 10) on this dimension may be to detached and unable to respond appropriately to the emotional needs of the other partner.

Self-Sufficiency (Ss)

High scoring individuals on this dimension prefer to be alone. They do not need the support of groups. In describing themselves, they prefer to work alone rather than with committees and are good at problem solving themselves. High scorers also appear to be related to success at school, particularly at the upper educational levels.

Occupationally, *Ss* is found very high for executive, scientists, explorers and criminals. Social workers and teachers score significantly below average on this dimension.

Clinically speaking, extremely high scores on *Ss* are probably not directly indicative of any underline pathology, but in combination with low Social Warmth (*Sw* - to be discussed later) and Enthusiasm (*En*) or high Guilt Proneness (*Gp*) and Tension (*Tn*) may lead to pathological withdrawal from the society. High scorers may also be associated with the incidence of coronary heart disease and hypertension.

Suspiciousness (Su)

The descriptions associated with high scorers on this dimension include suspecting, jealous, dogmatic, critical, and irritable. However, it is important to note that *Su* is a normal personality dimension, which is not to be confused with paranoia – which comes under the pathological domain. Self reports of high *Su* scorers include the notation that they do not forget mistakes easily, they say their parents were strict and demanding. They are bothered about what others say behind their backs and they tend to be critical of others' work.

Occupationally, engineers, mechanics, nurses, school counsellors and others who work in public related jobs score significantly below average, whereas accountants, lawyers, executives and policemen score above average.

Clinically, high *Su* indicates higher frequencies of general illness particularly peptic ulcers and high blood pressure. Low scores on *Su* must be regarded as a healthy sign, regardless of how extreme it may be.

Social Warmth (Sw)

High *Sw* scorers are usually found to be very warm hearted, personable, and easy to get along with. Their self-reports indicate that they like to give presents to others even without any occasion. If given a choice, they would rather sell than develop an invention. They are most satisfied and successful in occupations where public relations or interpersonal contact is essential, such as sales positions. High *Sw* individuals prefer to adapt to other people's schedule rather than require others to adapt to their schedules. They are also more likely to share their feelings with others.

Occupationally, sales personnel, social workers, middle managers and teachers are found to score significantly above average. Artists and research scientists, who are typically more oriented to things and ideas than to people, tend to score below average.

Clinically, extremely low scores (sten 1 or 2) may indicate unsatisfied interpersonal relationships. In combination with other dimensions such as low Enthusiasm (*En*), and Boldness (*Bo*) or high Self-sufficiency (*Ss*) may point to a pathological dislike and avoidance of others. On the other hand, extremely high scores (sten 9 or 10) may suggest an unhealthy and overriding need for approval by others.

Tension (Tn)

High *Tn* scorers are irritated by small things, are short tempered and may suffer from sleep disturbances. Extreme cases involve being irrationally worried, tense, irritable, anxious, and in turmoil. In group situations, high scorers rarely achieve leadership and have a poor concept of group unity and orderliness. It is seen that high score on *Tn* is an important indicator that signals an unmistakable S-O-S on the part of the individual.

Occupationally, waiters, housewives, news persons, and people in jobs which permit little self-expression and face more environmental demands score high; while executives, engineers, and salesmen score low.

On the clinical front, high *Tn* along with high Guilt-proneness (*Gp*) is a clear indicator of general anxiety and differentiates normal from neurotic. It also contributes significantly to automobile accident proneness.

TABLE 17.1: HIGH SCORE DESCRIPTION OF MAP FORM-A DIMENSIONS

Dimensions	Symbols	High Score Description
Adaptability	Ad	Accommodating, accepts and adjusts to situations easily.
Achievement Motivation	Am	Ambitious, overtly interested in career, and realistic involvement in life.
Boldness	Bo	Socially bold, adventurous, responsible and friendly.
Competition	Co	Independent minded, stern and assertive.
Enthusiasm	En	Cheerful, talkative, expressive and candid.

Contd...

General Ability	Ga	Intelligent, high abstract thinking, sensitive to minute details.
Guilt Proneness	Gp	Escapist, shirking responsibility, insecured and depressed.
Imagination	Im	Self-absorbed, impractical, untraditional in ideas.
Innovation	In	Experimental thinking, liberal ideas, can analyze concepts swiftly.
Leadership	Ld	Controls, directs and initiates actions for a group. Power to influence others, achieves goals.
Maturity	Ma	Realistic about life and emotionally stable.
Mental Health	Mh	Zestful, well adjusted, has a positively harmonious state of mind.
Morality	Me	High sense of duty, attentive to people, emotionally disciplined and responsible.
Self-control	Sc	High self-image, socially conscious, strong will power.
Sensitivity	Se	Over protected, dependent, impatient, and attention seeking.
Shrewdness	Sh	Calculating, immaculate, and socially alert.
Self-sufficiency	Ss	Independent, manipulating, enterprising.
Suspiciousness	Su	Living on frustration, skeptical, jealous and irritable.
Social Warmth	Sw	Outgoing, participative, good natured and warm hearted.
Tension	Tn	Excited, tense, anxious and frustrated.

ADMINISTRATION

The present scale is printed on a test booklet given at the end of the chapter. The first page contains the instructions for answering questions with few examples. This booklet contains the actual test items to be answered by the subject. Since this scale is a power test (i.e. there is no time limit), the average subject takes approximately 25-30 minutes to complete the test in full. It can be given both individually or in group situations.

The MAP Form A has been designed for self-administration with little supervision required. The examiner should not indicate to the subject that the scale is a "personality" scale, nor that the MAP Form A printed on the booklet stands for 'Multidimensional Assessment of Personality'. If at all any statement must be made about the nature of the scale, it should be referred to as attitude or interest scale.

If the subjects can read a newspaper, they can understand the instructions on the first page and work out the practice problems themselves. No further instructions are required, because if they understand these questions and answer them by checking one of the three possible answers, they will be able to answer the actual questions themselves.

It is necessary to distinguish between the clinical use of the test, usually individual, and the educational and industrial use, typically group. In group testing or individual testing the normal subjects are simply asked to read the first page and to fill in name, etc., on the top of the test booklet and wait until they receive further instructions. When everybody has read the instructions the examiner says; "Please turn over the page. Are their any questions about marking the answers or about anything else?"

He deals with questions, if any, and may then, according to discretion and the nature of the group of subjects, briefly reemphasize certain points in the instructions. For example, with a group of prospective employees, he may say: “It is to your own interest to answer as correctly and truthfully as you can.” Or, “Remember not to use the ‘Not Sure’, ‘Uncertain’, or ‘Undecided’ type of choices more than it is absolutely necessary. In general, it is good to remind everyone preferably five minutes after starting; “Be sure never to miss a question. You can erase and make corrections if you wish; but make your final pencil marks quite clear.”

It helps most subjects to know the rate at which they should be working. There tends to be a skewed distribution in the time people take to do the test, such that the last few, in a group of a hundred, will take three or four times as long as the average, unless reminded. Thus, after 20 minutes, most subjects will be at about the half way mark, or beyond. We recommend calling out at three points; after 10 minutes, say, “You should now be at item 40 or beyond. Answer more quickly if you have not reached 40”. After 20 minutes, say, “You should be now at about item 90. Remember to give the first answer that comes to you. If you have not reached 90 you are deciding too slowly.” After 30 minutes, say, “you should be now about to finish the test. Please hand in your test booklet here as soon as you finish.” Add, when most people are about to finish:

“Glance over your test booklet to make sure you have not missed any question, and that your name, etc., are on the top of the test booklet.” There is, of course, no absolute time limit; but after 30 minutes, stragglers should be encouraged to finish as soon as possible.

SCORING

The scoring procedure in MAP Form-A is quite objective and simple. Transparent stencil scoring key is available for this purpose.

Please follow the steps mentioned below to do the scoring:

1. Before starting the scoring procedure, examiner should ensure that the subject has answered all the questions in the booklet. If more than 15 questions are skipped, the test is invalid and should not be scored. This should, however, be checked and corrected during administration of the test.
2. Please also ensure that each question has one and only one answer.
3. Please note the each answer scores either 2 or 1 as indicated by the numbers printed above the boxes, only exception being the 'Ga' dimension where the answers are scored either 2 or 0.
4. Add the scores vertically for each dimension and write it down at the bottom of the answer sheet in the space provided for that dimension.
5. Each item in this test measures some dimension as indicated in the sheet.
6. For dimension "Vi", add the scores seen in the shaded boxes at the bottom of the scoring key and note it down in the right hand corner of the answer sheet.
7. Now, convert these raw scores to sten scores by the procedure mentioned later in the norm tables.
8. Plot these scores on the profile sheet provided with the test materials.

STANDARDIZATION

The MAP Form A has only 147 items, which cover twenty normal personality dimensions. The detailed description with the psychological meaning of these dimensions has already been discussed earlier. The test items have been selected from a total pool of more than 2000 items that had been tested and refined in programmatic studies on personality structure. Each of the items in the questionnaire has three choices from which the subject may select one answer. Generally, the last response (C) is an "uncertain", or "somewhat", or "undecided" type of category. The instructions specifically urge the subject not to use this category very frequently, and keep it as a last resort when both (A) and (B) are not suitable. All of the items were carefully screened, and several criteria were considered in the final item selection.

The standardization of MAP Form A is based on more than 3000 protocols tested at more than 15 locations throughout the country. Various research scholars, assistants and psychologists participated in this standardization. The sample included college students, normal adults and occupational groups from various industries. Table 17.2 provides a demographic profile of these groups. The primary sampling considerations were geographical locations (mainly town and cities), occupations (to reflect socio-economic status), and age.

TABLE 17.2: DEMOGRAPHIC DESCRIPTION OF THE STANDARDIZATION SAMPLES (ALL FIGURES ARE GIVEN IN PERCENTAGES)

	Total Sample	College Students	Normal Adults	Occupational Groups
Place of Data Collection				
Eastern Region	17.3	21.7	18.6	16.6
Western Region	27.4	27.3	26.9	19.9
Northern Region	38.2	28.6	31.6	34.6
Southern Region	17.1	22.4	22.9	28.9
Occupations				
Accountants	-	-	-	4.12
Administrative	-	-	-	4.40
Athletes	-	-	-	2.60
Clerical	-	-	-	5.25
Computer Professionals	-	-	-	5.00
Counsellors/Psychologists	-	-	-	3.10
Doctors	-	-	-	4.80
Editorial/Newsmen	-	-	-	2.40
Electricians	-	-	-	2.15
Engineers	-	-	-	3.70
Executives (Business)	-	-	-	4.72
Fire Fighters	-	-	-	1.70
Housewives	-	-	-	5.34
Lawyers	-	-	-	4.10
Mechanics	-	-	-	2.75
Nursing Staff	-	-	-	3.80
Pilots	-	-	-	2.10
Policemen	-	-	-	4.21
Priests	-	-	-	1.60
Researchers	-	-	-	2.63
Salesmen	-	-	-	6.03
Scientists	-	-	-	2.70
Secretaries	-	-	-	5.40

Contd...

Teachers	-	-	-	5.20
Technicians	-	-	-	4.95
Waiters	-	-	-	1.65
Others	-	-	-	2.60
Age				
Mean	29.4	20.4	42.1	31.6
Range	18-62	18-22	21-62	23-40

NORMS

In many research applications, the examiner will have no need to convert the raw scores obtained from the test to sten scores. However, commonly the test users would like to know where an individual stands in relation to a defined population. For this purpose the raw scores are converted into sten scores. The term 'sten' comes from "standard ten". The sten score is distributed over ten equal intervals of standard score points, from 1 to 10. The use of sten scores has been found to be very satisfactory, especially, with people inexperienced in statistical techniques involved in psychological testing.

Once the test administrator has decided which table will be most appropriate, the use of norm table is quite straightforward. For example, to convert raw score of dimension Bo, find the raw score of dimension Bo in the row Bo and read the corresponding sten score on the top or bottom column of 'Sten' scores. Do likewise for other dimensions. Please note that the values within the table (i.e., in the body of the table) are "raw scores"—the values obtained from the scoring key; and the values on the top and bottom columns are corresponding "sten scores". The sten scores are plotted on the MAP Form A profile sheet, which is provided separately.

Since, significant differences were found between males and females on some of the dimensions, the norms for each group were prepared separately. The norm tables given here are therefore separate for both males and females. The basic set of norms consists of Normal Adults and College Students.

A normative group data for various occupations is also available, but is not published here due to the size and complexity involved in the comparison and analysis of the same manually. This normative data is inbuilt in the computer software program available for this scale. These special norms are meant for comparison of the individual's profile with relation to specific job areas. The computer software package also offers a computerized narrative report, consisting of automated interpretations of the MAP Form A test results. This report and computer software package is available through the Computer Applications Division of M/s PSY-COM SERVICES.

To use norm tables the test user must note that the sten scores derived from these tables are n-stens or normalized stens, i.e., they do not result from a linear transformation of the raw score distribution, but instead, from an area transformation of the raw scores designed to produce a more normal distribution. For test users who wish to convert a group mean raw-score profile to s-sten (standard-deviation stens), the means and standard deviations of the norm group are given at the bottom of the tables.

The sten of 4-7 indicates average score, sten 8-10 indicates high and extremely high score and sten of 1-3 indicates low and extremely low scores.

TABLE 17.3: NORMS FOR GENERAL ADULT POPULATION (MALES)

DIMENSION	1	2	3	4	5	6	7	8	9	10		MEAN	SD
	Sten Scores												
Ad	0-2	3	4	5	6-7	8	9	10	11	12-14	Ad	7.11	1.78
Am	0-2	3	4-5	6	7	8	9	10-11	12	13-14	Am	7.51	1.88
Bo	0-2	3	4-5	6	7	8-9	10	11-12	13	14	Bo	7.82	2.88
Co	0-2	3-4	5	6	7-8	9	10-11	12	13	14	Co	8.33	2.08
En	0-3	4	5	6-7	8	9	10	11	12-13	14	En	8.85	2.25
DIMENSION	**1**	**2**	**3**	**4**	**5**	**6**	**7**	**8**	**9**	**10**		**MEAN**	**SD**
	Sten Scores												
Ga	0-6	7	-	8	9	-	10	11	12	13-14	Ga	9.25	1.49
Gp	-	1	2	3	4-5	6	7	8	9-10	11-14	Gp	5.13	1.28
Im	0-3	4	5	6	7	8	9	10-11	12	13-14	Im	7.70	1.92
In	0-1	2-3	4	5	6-7	8	9	10-11	12	13-14	In	7.14	1.78
Ld	0-2	3-4	5	6	7-8	9	10	11-12	13	14	Ld	8.34	2.08
DIMENSION	**1**	**2**	**3**	**4**	**5**	**6**	**7**	**8**	**9**	**10**		**MEAN**	**SD**
	Sten Scores												
Ma	0-4	5	6	7-8	9	10	11	12	13	14	Ma	9.61	1.95
Mh	0-2	3	4-5	6	7	8	9-10	11	12	13-14	Mh	7.62	2.34
Mo	0-4	5	6	7	8-9	10	11	12	13	14	Mo	9.12	1.98
Sc	0-3	4	5-6	7	8	9	10-11	12	13	14	Sc	8.01	2.41
Se	-	0-1	2-3	4	5	6-7	8	9-10	11	12-14	Se	5.98	1.49
DIMENSION	**1**	**2**	**3**	**4**	**5**	**6**	**7**	**8**	**9**	**10**		**MEAN**	**SD**
	Sten Scores												
Sh	0-2	-	3	4	5	6	7	8	9	10-14	Sh	5.85	1.46
Ss	0-1	2-3	4	5-6	7	8	9-10	11	12-13	14	Ss	7.81	2.71

Contd...

Su	0-3	4	5	6	7	8	9	10	11	12-4	Su	**7.59**	**1.90**
Sw	0-1	2-3	4	5	6	7	8-9	10	11	12-14	Sw	**6.65**	**2.09**
Tn	-	0-1	2	3-4	5	6-7	8	9-10	11	12-14	Tn	**5.79**	**1.45**
Vi	0-2	3	4	5	6	7	8	9	10	11-14	Vi	**6.52**	**2.03**
DIMENSION	**1**	**2**	**3**	**4**	**5**	**6**	**7**	**8**	**9**	**10**		**MEAN**	**SD**
	Sten Scores												

Age Range: 21-62 Years, N = 845

TABLE 17.4: NORMS FOR GENERAL ADULT POPULATION (FEMALES)

DIMENSION	**1**	**2**	**3**	**4**	**5**	**6**	**7**	**8**	**9**	**10**		**MEAN**	**SD**
	Sten Scores												
Ad	0-2	3-4	5	6	7	8-9	10	11	12-13	14	Ad	**7.97**	**2.63**
Am	0-2	3	4	5	6-7	8	9	10	11	12-14	Am	**7.07**	**2.33**
Bo	-	0-2	3	4-5	6	7-8	9	10-11	12-13	14	Bo	**6.85**	**3.08**
Co	-	0-1	2-3	4	5-6	7	8-9	10	11-12	13-14	Co	**6.19**	**3.03**
En	0-2	3	4	5-6	7	8	9	10-11	12	13-14	En	**7.41**	**2.59**
DIMENSION	**1**	**2**	**3**	**4**	**5**	**6**	**7**	**8**	**9**	**10**		**MEAN**	**SD**
	Sten Scores												
Ga	0-6	7	-	8	9	-	10	11	12	13-14	Ga	**9.25**	**1.49**
Gp	0-1	2	3-4	5	6-7	8	9-10	11	12-13	14	Gp	**7.23**	**2.90**
Im	0-3	4-5	6	7	8	9	10	11-12	13	14	Im	**8.58**	**2.31**
In	0-3	4	5	-	6	7	8	9	10	11-14	In	**6.94**	**1.89**
Ld	0-2	3	4-5	6	7	8-9	10	11	12	13-14	Ld	**7.82**	**2.58**
DIMENSION	**1**	**2**	**3**	**4**	**5**	**6**	**7**	**8**	**9**	**10**		**MEAN**	**SD**
	Sten Scores												
Ma	0-5	6	7	8	9	10	11	12	13	14	Ma	**9.31**	**1.99**
Mh	0-2	3	4-5	6	7	8	9-10	11	12	13-14	Mh	**7.71**	**2.54**
Mo	0-4	5	6	7	8-9	10	11	12	13	14	Mo	**9.75**	**1.87**
Sc	0-3	4	5	6	7-8	9	10	11	12	13-14	Sc	**8.04**	**2.42**
Se	0-4	5	6	7	8	9	10	11	12-13	14	Se	**8.64**	**2.23**
DIMENSION	**1**	**2**	**3**	**4**	**5**	**6**	**7**	**8**	**9**	**10**		**MEAN**	**SD**
	Sten Scores												
Sh	0-2	3	4	5	6	7	8	9	10	11-14	Sh	**6.91**	**2.01**
Ss	0-2	3	4	5-6	7	8	9	10	11-12	13-14	Ss	**7.36**	**2.38**
Su	0-3	4	5	6	7	8	9	10-11	12	13-14	Su	**7.79**	**2.16**

Contd...

Sw	0-4	5	-	6	7	8	9	10	11	12-14	Sw	**7.84**	**1.84**
Tn	0-1	2	3-4	5	6	7-8	9	10-11	12	13-14	Tn	**6.89**	**2.88**
Vi	0-2	3	4	5	6	7	8	9	10	11-14	Vi	**6.52**	**2.03**
DIMENSION	**1**	**2**	**3**	**4**	**5**	**6**	**7**	**8**	**9**	**10**		**MEAN**	**SD**
	Sten Scores												

Age Range: 21-62 Years, N = 764

TABLE 17.5: NORMS FOR GENERAL ADULT POPULATION (COMBINED)

DIMENSION	**1**	**2**	**3**	**4**	**5**	**6**	**7**	**8**	**9**	**10**		**MEAN**	**SD**
	Sten Scores												
Ad	0-2	3	4	5-6	7	8	9-10	11	12	13-14	Ad	**7.54**	**2.64**
Am	0-2	3	4	5-6	7	8	9	10	11	12-14	Am	**7.29**	**2.32**
Bo	0-1	2	3-4	5	6-7	8	9-10	11-12	13	14	Bo	**7.41**	**3.13**
Co	0-1	2	3-4	5	6-7	8	9-10	11	12-13	14	Co	**7.26**	**3.28**
En	0-2	3-4	5	6	7	8-9	10	11	12	13-14	En	**7.84**	**2.51**
DIMENSION	**1**	**2**	**3**	**4**	**5**	**6**	**7**	**8**	**9**	**10**		**MEAN**	**SD**
	Sten Scores												
Ga	0-6	7	-	8	9	-	10	11	12	13-14	Ga	**9.25**	**1.49**
Gp	-	0-1	2-3	4	5-6	7	8-9	10	11	12-14	Gp	**6.18**	**2.89**
Im	0-3	4	5	6	7-8	9	10	11	12	13-14	Im	**8.14**	**2.31**
In	0-2	3	4	5	6-7	8	9	10	11	12-14	In	**7.04**	**2.32**
Ld	0-2	3	4-5	6	7-8	9	10	11-12	13	14	Ld	**8.08**	**2.86**
DIMENSION	**1**	**2**	**3**	**4**	**5**	**6**	**7**	**8**	**9**	**10**		**MEAN**	**SD**
	Sten Scores												
Ma	0-3	4	5-6	7	8	9	10-11	12	13	14	Ma	**8.72**	**2.50**
Mh	0-2	3	4	5-6	7	8	9-10	11	12-13	14	Mh	**7.64**	**2.71**
Mo	0-4	5	6	7	8	9-10	11	12	13	14	Mo	**8.90**	**2.23**
Sc	0-3	4	5-6	7	8	9	10-11	12	13	14	Sc	**8.61**	**2.58**
Se	0-1	2-3	4	5	6-7	8	9-10	11	12	13-14	Se	**7.31**	**2.80**
DIMENSION	**1**	**2**	**3**	**4**	**5**	**6**	**7**	**8**	**9**	**10**		**MEAN**	**SD**
	Sten Scores												
Sh	0-2	3	4	5	6	7	8	9	10	11-14	Sh	**6.38**	**2.02**
Ss	0-2	3	4	5-6	7	8	9-10	11	12	13-14	Ss	**7.43**	**2.65**
Su	0-3	4	5	6	7	8	9	10	11	12-14	Su	**7.68**	**2.07**

Contd...

Sw	0-2	3-4	5	6	7	8	9	10	11	12-14	Sw	7.29	2.16
Tn	-	0-1	2-3	4	5-6	7	8-9	10	11-12	13-14	Tn	6.34	2.97
Vi	0-2	3	4	5	6	7	8	9	10	11-14	Vi	6.52	2.03
DIMENSION	**1**	**2**	**3**	**4**	**5**	**6**	**7**	**8**	**9**	**10**		**MEAN**	**SD**
	Sten Scores												

Age Range: 21-62 Years, N = 1601

TABLE 17.6: NORMS FOR COLLEGE STUDENTS (MALES)

DIMENSION	**1**	**2**	**3**	**4**	**5**	**6**	**7**	**8**	**9**	**10**		**MEAN**	**SD**
	Sten Scores												
Ad	0-4	5	6	7	8	9	10-11	12	13	14	Ad	8.84	2.25
Am	0-3	4	5	6-7	8	9	10	11	12-13	14	Am	8.35	2.38
Bo	0-2	3	4	5-6	7	8-9	10	11-12	13	14	Bo	7.82	2.88
Co	0-2	3	4	5	6-7	8	9	10-11	12	13-14	Co	7.26	2.62
En	0-4	5	6	7	8	9	10-11	12	13	14	En	8.85	2.25
DIMENSION	**1**	**2**	**3**	**4**	**5**	**6**	**7**	**8**	**9**	**10**		**MEAN**	**SD**
	Sten Scores												
Ga	0-6	7	-	8	9	10	11	12	13	14	Ga	9.75	1.81
Gp	0-1	2	3	4-5	6	7	8	9	10	11-14	Gp	6.19	2.35
Im	0-3	4	5	6-7	8	9	10	11	12	13-14	Im	8.12	2.19
In	0-3	4	5-6	7	8	9	10	11	12	13-14	In	8.38	2.26
Ld	0-3	4	5-6	7	8	9	10-11	12	13	14	Ld	8.69	2.52
DIMENSION	**1**	**2**	**3**	**4**	**5**	**6**	**7**	**8**	**9**	**10**		**MEAN**	**SD**
	Sten Scores												
Ma	0-5	6	7	8	9	10	11	12	13	14	Ma	9.61	1.95
Mh	0-2	3-4	5	6	7	8	9	10-11	12	13-14	Mh	7.62	2.34
Mo	0-5	6	7	8	9	10	11	12	13	14	Mo	9.12	1.98
Sc	0-3	4	5	6	7-8	9	10	11	12	13-14	Sc	8.01	2.41
Se	0-1	2	3-4	5	6	7-8	9	10-11	12	13-14	Se	6.99	2.73
DIMENSION	**1**	**2**	**3**	**4**	**5**	**6**	**7**	**8**	**9**	**10**		**MEAN**	**SD**
	Sten Scores												
Sh	0-2	3	4	5	6	-	7	8	9	10-14	Sh	6.09	1.82
Ss	0-2	3	4-5	6	7	8-9	10	11	12-13	14	Ss	7.81	2.71
Su	0-4	5	6	7	8	9	-	10	11	12-14	Su	8.01	1.99
Sw	0-2	3	4	5	6	7	8	9	10	11-14	Sw	6.65	2.09
Tn	0-2	3	4	5	6	7	8	9	10	11-14	Tn	6.33	2.00
Vi	0-2	3	4	5	6	7	8	9	10	11-14	Vi	6.52	2.03
DIMENSION	**1**	**2**	**3**	**4**	**5**	**6**	**7**	**8**	**9**	**10**		**MEAN**	**SD**
	Sten Scores												

Age Range: 21-62 Years, N = 873

TABLE 17.7: NORMS FOR COLLEGE STUDENTS (FEMALES)

DIMENSION	1	2	3	4	5	6	7	8	9	10		MEAN	SD
	Sten Scores												
Ad	0-2	3-4	5	6	7-8	9	10	11-12	13	14	Ad	8.06	2.65
Am	0-2	3	4	5-6	7	8	9	10-11	12	13-14	Am	7.38	2.43
Bo	0-2	3	4	5	6	7-8	9	10	11	12-14	Bo	6.98	2.30
Co	-	0-2	3	4-5	6	7	8-9	10	11	12-14	Co	6.42	2.73
En	0-3	4	5-6	7	8	9	10	11	12-13	14	En	8.46	2.33
DIMENSION	1	2	3	4	5	6	7	8	9	10		MEAN	SD
	Sten Scores												
Ga	0-6	7	-	8	9	10	11	12	13	14	Ga	9.75	1.81
Gp	0-2	3	4	5-6	7	8	9	10-11	12	13-14	Gp	7.42	2.58
Im	0-4	5	6	7	8	9	10	11-12	13	14	Im	8.79	2.19
In	0-3	4	5	6-7	8	9	10	11	12	13-14	In	8.25	2.40
Ld	0-2	3	4-5	6	7	8	9-10	11	12	13-14	Ld	7.61	2.51
DIMENSION	1	2	3	4	5	6	7	8	9	10		MEAN	SD
	Sten Scores												
Ma	0-5	6	7	8	9	10	11	12	13	14	Ma	9.32	1.90
Mh	0-2	3-4	5	6	7-8	9	10	11	12-13	14	Mh	8.01	2.64
Mo	0-6	7	8	9	-	10	11	12	13	14	Mo	9.97	1.87
Sc	0-2	3-4	5	6	7	8	9-10	11	12	13-14	Sc	7.72	2.44
Se	0-3	4	5-6	7	8	9-10	11	12	13	14	Se	8.71	2.64
DIMENSION	1	2	3	4	5	6	7	8	9	10		MEAN	SD
	Sten Scores												
Sh	0-2	3	4	5	6	7	8	9	10	11-14	Sh	6.58	2.03
Ss	0-2	3	4	5-6	7	8	9-10	11	12	13-14	Ss	7.64	2.66
Su	0-4	5	6	7	-	8	9	10	11	12-14	Su	8.00	1.88
Sw	0-3	4	5	6	7	8	9	10	-	11-14	Sw	7.28	1.86
Tn	0-1	2	3-4	5	6	7-8	9	10	11	12-14	Tn	6.85	2.57
Vi	0-2	3	4	5	6	7	8	9	10	11-14	Vi	6.52	2.03
DIMENSION	1	2	3	4	5	6	7	8	9	10		MEAN	SD
	Sten Scores												

Age Range: 21-62 Years, N = 708

TABLE 17.8: NORMS FOR COLLEGE STUDENTS (COMBINED)

DIMENSION	1	2	3	4	5	6	7	8	9	10		MEAN	SD
	Sten Scores												
Ad	0-3	4	5	6	7	8-9	10	11	12	13-14	Ad	7.84	2.37
Am	0-2	3	4-5	6	7	8	9-10	11	12	13-14	Am	7.53	2.48
Bo	0-1	2	3-4	5	6-7	8	9-10	11	12-13	14	Bo	7.40	2.96
Co	0-1	2-3	4	5	6-7	8	9-10	11	12	13-14	Co	7.34	2.81
En	0-4	5	6	7	8	9	10-11	12	13	14	En	8.66	2.28
DIMENSION	**1**	**2**	**3**	**4**	**5**	**6**	**7**	**8**	**9**	**10**		**MEAN**	**SD**
	Sten Scores												
Ga	0-6	7	-	8	9	10	11	12	13	14	Ga	9.75	1.81
Gp	0-1	2-3	4	5	6	7-8	9	10	11	12-14	Gp	6.81	2.52
Im	0-4	5	6	7	8	9	10	11	12	13-14	Im	8.46	2.19
In	0-3	4	5	6-7	8	9	10	11	12	13-14	In	8.32	2.32
Ld	0-2	3-4	5	6	7-8	9	10	11-12	13	14	Ld	8.05	2.65
DIMENSION	**1**	**2**	**3**	**4**	**5**	**6**	**7**	**8**	**9**	**10**		**MEAN**	**SD**
	Sten Scores												
Ma	0-6	7	8	9	-	10	11	12	13	14	Ma	9.97	1.85
Mh	0-2	3-4	5	6	7-8	9	10	11-12	13	14	Mh	8.07	2.66
Mo	0-5	6	7	8	9	10	11	12	13	14	Mo	9.55	2.04
Sc	0-3	4	5	6	7	8-9	10	11	12	13-14	Sc	7.87	2.41
Se	0-2	3	4-5	6	7	8-9	10	11-12	13	14	Se	7.85	2.80
DIMENSION	**1**	**2**	**3**	**4**	**5**	**6**	**7**	**8**	**9**	**10**		**MEAN**	**SD**
	Sten Scores												
Sh	0-2	3	4	5	6	7	8	9	10	11-14	Sh	6.34	1.92
Ss	0-2	3	4-5	6	7	8-9	10	11	12-13	14	Ss	7.73	2.67
Su	0-4	5	6	7	8	-	9	10	11	12-14	Su	8.01	1.94
Sw	0-3	-	4	5	6	7	8	9	10	11-14	Sw	6.97	1.98
Tn	0-1	2	3-4	5	6	7	8-9	10	11	12-14	Tn	6.59	2.55
Vi	0-2	3	4	5	6	7	8	9	10	11-14	Vi	6.52	2.03
DIMENSION	**1**	**2**	**3**	**4**	**5**	**6**	**7**	**8**	**9**	**10**		**MEAN**	**SD**
	Sten Scores												

Age Range: 21-62 Years, N = 1581

A WORD ABOUT FAKING

Since MAP Form A was designed for students, general adult population and various occupational groups, it was assumed that the subjects are motivated towards showing themselves in the most favourable light. In order to check this error a validity index or 'lie' index was developed. It is recognized that the questionnaire method is not the best approach for the measurement of personality traits, particularly in an unmotivated situation. However, the majority of questions in the MAP Form A are indirect, asking about interests which the subjects would not necessarily perceive to be related to the dimension in question. Moreover, dimensions measured are not interpreted from the nature of the subject's responses about himself, but from the known correlations between these "mental interiors" as found in scale dimensions, and the dimensions as actually established in behaviour.

The MAP Form A consists of 147 items, out of these, some questions are overlapping or similar in nature. These questions are "Validity Index" questions to give Validity Indicator Score (Vi score). The validity items are cross-checked for response consistency with each other so that the subject's overall faking pattern can be assessed. That is, for instance, item no.1 is cross checked for the same response with item no. 135. If the subject responds to 'a' in No.1 and also 'a' in No.135 (or 'b' in both the items) we conclude that there is consistency in his/her responses. This cross-checking is done for about 50 items. If such consistency is found in more than 50% of the total Vi items then the benefit of 'honesty' is given to the subject.

The limit of 50% has been found to be statistically sound when this form was given to the subjects under two conditions: (1) 'anonymity', where the test was said to have no connection whatsoever with their careers, and (2) 'strongly motivated' conditions, where subjects believed that their job/course depended on their replies. These questions, out of the 50 studied, which showed the greatest 'distortion' were correlated with the distortion on the total test. Here also it was found that even under 'strongly motivated' conditions subjects do not show 'total honesty' probably because they always want to give the best possible impression of themselves.

Further, lower the "Vi" score, the greater the chances that the scores on anxiety related dimensions (such as *Gp*, *Ma*, *Se*, *Su* and *Tn*) and extraversion related dimensions (such as *Bo*, *Co*, *En* and *Sw*) are more distorted. The distortion is generally in the direction of "socially acceptable" responses, which lead to lower anxiety and slightly elevated extraversion related dimension scores. We suggest the following interpretation of "Vi" score for test users.

TABLE 17.9: INTERPRETATION OF VI SCORE

"Vi" Sten Score	Interpretation
10	**No distortion.** There is little or no distortion—responses are quite consistent.
5-9	**Low distortion.** Scores are fairly accurate and retesting not required.
1-4	**High distortion.** Scores are not very reliable, as it is possibly one or more sten scores higher or lower on some dimensions than they should be. Desirable for the individual to take the test again after some time, with emphasis on Rule 1 of the test instructions.

RELIABILITY

The reliability or internal consistency is important to study, i.e., the agreement of dimension scores with itself under some change of conditions. Therefore, the reliabilities of the MAP Form A were calculated as split-half reliability and test-retest reliability coefficients with one week interval. The results obtained are shown in the table given here.

For calculating the split-half reliability, a trial run of the present scale was conducted. The reliability were computed for over 1000 individuals using Spearman-Brown formula. The scale was divided into two parts using odd-even method and care was taken to ensure that each half contained more or less the same number of questions.

The test-retest reliability was also calculated for the present scale by calculating the correlation of coefficient between two sets of scores of the same individual on the same scale, with one weeks time interval. The sample size for test-retest reliability was approximately 600 subjects.

TABLE 17.10: TEST-RETEST AND SPLIT-HALF RELIABILITY COEFFICIENTS

Dimension	Test-retest (one week interval)	Dimension	Split-half
Ad	.69	Ad	.72
Am	.63	Am	.68
Bo	.72	Bo	.76
Co	.71	Co	.75
En	.70	En	.73
Ga	.58	Ga	.62
Gp	.65	Gp	.69
Im	.62	Im	.65
In	.68	In	.75
Ld	.68	Ld	.73
Ma	.65	Ma	.70
Mh	.70	Mh	.73
Mo	.72	Mo	.75
Sc	.61	Sc	.66
Se	.72	Se	.75
Sh	.65	Sh	.68
Ss	.68	Ss	.72
Su	.72	Su	.75
Sw	.74	Sw	.77
Tn	.72	Tn	.76

VALIDITY

The basic definition of validity is that it is an index of how well a scale measures what it purports to measure. In the case of an ability test or an achievement test, this can be done directly and more easily. But this may not be possible with a personality test.

Now, the question here is, what was MAP Series designed to measure? As mentioned earlier the MAP Form A was conceived primarily as a device to measure 20 independent personality dimensions that resulted from a set of items administered on normal adults, occupational groups, and clinical groups. The items in this final form are the survivors from several thousands of items originally tried, and constitute only those which continue to have significant validity against the dimensions. The factor analysis verified the existence and structure of these 20 independent personality dimensions. More formally, to understand the concept of validity used here we must know the background theory of factorial validity.

Factorial validity is a technique which uses factor analyses in order to show the independence of each dimension. Most tests of mental ability and personality, sample a composite behaviour or ability such as verbal knowledge, numerical and quantitative reasoning, memory span, and concept formation. These and other abilities, specially when represented by a single composite index (such as mental age or IQ), are not functional unities. Further, they are not measures of a "pure" ability, i.e., one type of ability uncomplicated by others. Thus, a test is said to have high factorial validity if it is a measure of one functional unity (for example, word knowledge), to the exclusion of other elements as far as possible. The ultimate goal is to device tests, which will measure only one functional unity, relatively independent of others, i.e., low inter-correlations. Such pure tests can then be used as subtests in a comprehensive measuring instrument.

In the MAP Series, these functional unities are identified by analyzing the intercorelations among a number of separate, relatively restricted measures, which identify the common factors for obtained coefficients. Factor analysis, therefore, is intended to reduce the number of variables, or test categories, needed to represent an individual's traits for specified purposes. Factorial validity here, is therefore, determined by the weights (called, 'loadings') contributed to the total-test scores by each of derived scores. It is determined by the relative independence of one another (low inter-correlations). Thus, to be true to its design, each dimension should have one 'important' loading—on the dimension that it was intended to measure—and 19 'unimportant' loadings. These factorial validity coefficients are shown in Table 17.11 below.

TABLE 17.11: FACTORIAL VALIDITY COEFFICIENTS OF THE MAP FORM-A

Dimension	Validity Coefficients	Dimension	Validity Coefficients
Ad	.83	Ma	.80
Am	.79	Mh	.83
Bo	.84	Mo	.84
Co	.84	Sc	.78
En	.83	Se	.84
Ga	.76	Sh	.80
Gp	.80	Ss	.82
Im	.78	Su	.84
In	.82	Sw	.86
Ld	.82	Tn	.84

Perhaps the best interpretation of these values is that they represent an upper limit of predictive potential of any single dimension. For example, dimension Ad by itself is unlikely to correlate higher than 83 with any external or 'real' criterion. The reason behind this is that the pure factor underlying each dimension is the most important systematic source of influence on that particular dimension.

MAP (MULTI-DIMENSIONAL ASSESSMENT OF PERSONALITY) ADULT FORM

Name: ______________________________________ Date: __________

Age:____________ Sex:___________Occupation:________ _______

(write M or F)

In this booklet, there are some questions to see what interests you have and how you feel about certain situations. There are no 'right' or 'wrong' answers because people have the right to their own views. All you have to do is answer what is true for you.

Some sample questions are given below which you will answer for practice, to see that you understand what you have to do. There are three possible answers to each question. You should answer either "Yes" or "No", (or "A" or "B"), by marking a (X) in the appropriate box. Mark the last answer or "C" only when it is impossible to say "Yes" or "No". Now answer the four practice questions given below:

EXAMPLES:

1.	I prefer friends who are:	quiet ☐	lively ☐	can't decide ☐
2.	People say I'm impatient.	true ☐	false ☐	uncertain ☐
3.	I like to watch team games.	yes, often ☐	no, never ☐	sometimes ☐
4.	I would like to be: (A) a mechanic, (B) a salesman (C) undecided.	(A) ☐	(B) ☐	(C) ☐

Ask now if something is not clear.

In the following pages; you will find more questions similar to those above. As you answer the questions, keep these four rules in mind:

1. Give only answers that are true for *you*. It is best to say what you really think.
2. You may have as much time as you need, but try to go fairly fast. It's best to give the *first* answer that comes to you and not spend too much time on any one question.
3. Answer *every* item one way or the other. Don't skip any item.
4. You should mark the (a) or (b) answer most of the time. Mark the last (c) answer *only* when you feel you have to, because neither (a) nor (b) seems to be right for you.

TEST BOOKLET

1.	If I could get the right training, I would rather be: (A) a manager in a company, (B) a guidance counsellor with young people, (C) none of the above.	(A) ☐	(B) ☐	(C) ☐
2.	There are times when I do, what I want and pay no attention to rules and regulations.	yes,true ☐	no, never ☐	uncertain ☐
3.	It is embarrassing for me if I suddenly become the centre of attention at a social gathering. (A) yes, very much, (B) no, not at all, (C) slightly.	(A) ☐	(B) ☐	(C) ☐
4.	I feel too disgusted to eat even if the plates are slightly dirty.	yes, often ☐	no, never ☐	sometimes ☐
5.	I am worried about my actions when I am doing things independently.	yes, often ☐	Rarely ☐	occasionally ☐
6.	I am active in large gatherings, such as parties or public meetings.	yes, always ☐	no, never ☐	sometimes ☐
7.	I am careful of people who get more friendly and familiar very easily. (A) yes, always, (B) no, not necessarily, (C) sometimes.	(A) ☐	(B) ☐	(C) ☐
8.	A person should take action fast when deciding a practical matter.	true, always ☐	not as a rule ☐	sometimes ☐
9.	I get "stage-fright" when I come into a room full of people.	often ☐	hardly ever ☐	sometimes ☐
10.	I am quite frank in telling people my feelings and ideas, and I never have regrets for it.	True ☐	False ☐	uncertain ☐
11.	I am never disturbed by threats.	true, never ☐	false, I do ☐	sometimes ☐
12.	I feel uncomfortable if several people watch me at work.	yes ☐	no ☐	uncertain ☐
13.	I can put worries and responsibilities out of my mind whenever I want to.	yes ☐	no ☐	sometimes ☐
14.	I usually feel my way to a decision slowly rather than decide quickly by logic or reason.	true ☐	false ☐	uncertain ☐
15.	I consider myself as a very sociable, outgoing person.	yes ☐	no ☐	can't decide ☐
16.	Raising funds for a helping cause is: (A) quite enjoyable for me, (B) an unpleasant job for me, (C) undecided.	(A) ☐	(B) ☐	(C) ☐

Contd...

17.	It is more important to: (A) get along smoothly with people, (B) practice your own ideas, (C) uncertain.	(A) ☐	(B) ☐	(C) ☐
18.	In a small group, I prefer to sit back and let others do most of the talking.	yes, mostly ☐	no, never ☐	sometimes ☐
19.	I would enjoy more being: (A) an office manager, (B) an architect, (C) uncertain	(A) ☐	(B) ☐	(C) ☐
20.	Society should be guided by logical thinking rather than by sentimental beliefs.	yes, always ☐	no, never ☐	sometimes ☐
21.	I like to join clubs and social groups. (A) true, (B) false, (C) not very keen.	(A) ☐	(B) ☐	(C) ☐
22.	I think my memory has improved and is better than before.	yes ☐	no ☐	can't decide ☐

23.	I'm uncomfortable when others are waiting on something that needs quick action.	very much so ☐	not at all ☐	Somewhat ☐
24.	I prefer to stay away from public meetings.	usually ☐	never ☐	sometimes ☐
25.	"Rope" is to "tie" as "knife" is to:	cut ☐	sharp ☐	point ☐
26.	There are ways in which I honestly consider myself better than most people.	yes, many ☐	hardly, any ☐	a few ☐
27.	To be cautious and not expect too much is better than to be over-cheerful, and always expect success.	true ☐	false ☐	uncertain ☐
28.	Which one of the following things is different from the others?	candle ☐	electric light ☐	moon ☐
29.	I like to direct others in their work.	yes, usually ☐	no, never ☐	occassionally ☐
30.	In reading, I prefer to read light, family stories rather than war or adventure stories.	true ☐	false ☐	uncertain ☐
31.	Which one of the following fractions is not the same kind as the others? (A) 3/1, (B) 3/9, (C) 3/11	(A) ☐	(B) ☐	(C) ☐
32.	In an arguement, my mind does not seem to work too well. (A) true, I get confused, (B) false, I am always cool, (C) uncertain.	(A) ☐	(B) ☐	(C) ☐

Contd...

33.	I would prefer to dress up: (A) in something everyone will notice, (B) neatly and quietly, (C) uncertain.	(A) □	(B) □	(C) □
34.	"Large" means the same as:	fat, □	tall, □	big. □
35.	If I were to disagree with my boss, I would probably: (A) keep it to myself, (B) come out and say so, (C) uncertain.	(A) □	(B) □	(C) □
36.	I like to spend an evening: (A) at a lively party, (B) with a quiet hobby, (C) undecided.	(A) □	(B) □	(C) □
37.	Which one of the following should come next at the end of this row of letters: xooooxxoooxxx?	(A)oxxx □	(B)xooo □	(C)ooxx □
38.	When I have to convey my disapproval or disagreement, I stay calm and I am not nervous.	true □	false □	uncertain □
39.	"Size" is ,to "length" as "dishonest" is to: (A) Prison, (B) Sin, (C) Stealing	A □	B □	C □
40.	Being waited on by a servant or someone like that: (A) embarresses me, (B) makes me feel little, (C) uncertain.	A □	B □	C □
41.	I like to play practical jokes on people without any ill-feeling in them.	(A) □	(B) □	(C) □
42.	Which one of the following words does not belong with the others? (A) Zigzag, (B) Wide, (C) Straight	A □	B □	C □
43.	I have sometimes, had hateful feelings towards my parents.	Yes □	No □	Sometimes □
44.	I would rather spend time fishing or gardening than watching horse or car races.	yes □	no □	sometimes □

45.	If my boss called me in his room, I would: (A) be afraid I had done something wrong, (B) make it a chance to ask for something I want, (C) get confused.	(A) □	(B) □	(C) □
46.	I am usually not very particular about details, for example, remembering particular names of roads or shops in the city.	true, I am not □	false, I am □	undecided □

Contd...

47.	As a teenager, if my opinion was different from what my parents thought, I/usually: (A) accepted their authority, (B) kept my own opinion, (C) undecided.	(A) ☐	(B) ☐	(C) ☐
48.	If friends or neighbours treat me badly and show they dislike me: (A) I tend to get downhearted, (B) it doesn't upset me a bit, (C) can't decide.	(A) ☐	(B) ☐	(C) ☐
49.	I like to have friends who: (A) are efficient and practical, (B) seriously think out their attitude toward life, (C) uncertain.	(A) ☐	(B) ☐	(C) ☐
50.	The glamour of any big national ceremony should be preserved.	yes, always ☐	very rarely ☐	sometimes ☐
51.	I get depressed if I think seriously about my responsibilities.	quite often ☐	no, never ☐	occasionally ☐
52.	When I am talking, I hardly ever walk up and down, or use my arms to express my ideas.	true, never ☐	false, I do ☐	uncertain ☐
53.	When our reason tells us old customs and traditions are out of date, we should drop them.	agree ☐	disagree ☐	uncertain ☐
54.	I rarely lie awake because of unhappy, disturbing ideas.	true ☐	false, I do lie ☐	sometimes ☐
55.	I would enjoy being a newspaper writer on drama, concerts, plays, etc.	Yes ☐	no ☐	uncertain ☐
56.	It is easy to change people's ideas by logic and reason.	I agree ☐	I disagree ☐	undecided ☐
57.	If I know that an operation is being done on an animal (for a good reason), it does not upset me. (A) true, I treat it as a common-sense matter, (B) false, it gives me horrors, (C) uncertain.	true ☐	false ☐	perhaps ☐
58.	Members of my family quickly show their irritation over small things. (A) yes, quite a lot, (B) no,not at all, (C)sometimes.	(A) ☐	(B) ☐	(C) ☐
59.	Most people will fool themselves and give silly reasons in order to keep comfortable privileges or gain a profit.	true ☐	false ☐	uncertain ☐
60.	Even in times of trouble, my spirits are generally high.	true ☐	false ☐	uncertain ☐
61.	I like vivid, true-to-life love scenes in a movie.	true ☐	false ☐	uncertain ☐

Contd...

62.	To get an interesting argument going, I believe in gently telling people what is wrong with their ideas.	generally ☐	never ☐	occasionally ☐
63.	I have a feeling that my friends don't need me so much as I need them.	true ☐	False ☐	uncertain ☐
64.	I don't enjoy long discussions with people who have ideas about serious, intellectual things.	true, don't ☐	false, I do ☐	undecided ☐
65.	Sometimes I feel like starting an argument or picking up a fight with someone just for the sake of doing it.	yes, I do ☐	no, never ☐	can't decide ☐
66.	It's hard for me to admit it when I am wrong.	yes ☐	no ☐	sometimes ☐

67.	I am considered by others as a stable and a confident person.	yes, certainly ☐	no ☐	sometimes ☐
68.	When the time comes to do something I have planned and looked forward to, I don't feel up to doing it.	often ☐	almost never ☐	sometimes ☐
69.	I like to go to shows and social outings.	yes, often ☐	very rarely ☐	sometimes ☐
70.	I am not scared or shy of speaking in front of large groups. (A) true, I am never bothered by it, (B) false, I find it very hard, (C) sometimes it bothers me.	(A) ☐	(B) ☐	(C) ☐
71.	Thunder and lightening hardly ever upset me. (A) true, they don't, (B) false, they do, (C) sometimes.	(A) ☐	(B) ☐	(C) ☐
72.	I hardly ever get impatient and angry with people. (A) true, I almost never do, (B) false, I get angry. quickly, (C) uncertain.	(A) ☐	(B) ☐	(C) ☐
73.	I am able to concentrate on one job or plan for as long as possible.	yes, always ☐	no, never ☐	sometimes ☐
74.	I seldom get so excited that I say things I am sorry for. (A) true, I don't, (B) false, I do say such things, (C) uncertain.	(A) ☐	(B) ☐	(C) ☐
75.	Disturbing and troubling thoughts sometimes race through my head.	true, a lot ☐	not at all ☐	not much ☐

Contd...

76.	While making my decisions I give more value on: (A) what is right and wrong, (B) what is practicable or workable, (C) can't decide.	(A) ☐	(B) ☐	(C) ☐
77.	In a dark house, I cannot control my fears.	true ☐	false ☐	sometimes ☐
78.	I am not given to big "ups" and "downs" of mood.	true, I am not ☐	false, I am ☐	sometimes ☐
79.	I like a job with variety, even if it has a bit of risk.	yes ☐	no ☐	at times ☐
80.	If I meet drunken people, I: (A) stay cool and relaxed (B) get very nervous and embarrassed, (C) am slightly nervous.	(A) ☐	(B) ☐	(C) ☐
81.	I believe in: (A) "Don't worry be happy", (B) being sober in everyday matters, (C) undecided moods.	(A) ☐	(B) ☐	(C) ☐
82.	When one small thing after another goes wrong, I: (A) carry on as usual, (B) feel discouraged, (C) uncertain.	(A) ☐	(B) ☐	(C) ☐
83.	I see many emotional dreams that leave me disturbed when I wake up.	often ☐	almost never ☐	sometimes ☐
84.	In my next life, I would prefer to lead: (A) the same kind of life, (B) a more comfortable life, (C) can t say.	(A) ☐	(B) ☐	(C) ☐
85.	I enjoy organizing a social group, such as a club or a team.	yes, often ☐	never ☐	occasionally ☐
86.	My mood and efficiency are generally not affected by the changes in the weather.	true ☐	false ☐	sometimes ☐
87.	I often lose control over my emotions and feelings.	true ☐	false ☐	uncertain ☐
88.	When I know I am doing the right thing, I find my task easy.	always ☐	never ☐	sometimes ☐
89.	I think that being free to do what I like is more important than good manners and respect for the law.	very true ☐	no, false ☐	uncertain ☐
90.	My actions get influenced while experiencing feelings of jealousy.	yes, always ☐	no, never ☐	sometimes ☐

Contd...

91.	In school, I had a keen interest in (or still prefer): (A) music, (B) handicrafts, (C) none of the above.	(A) ☐	(B) ☐	(C) ☐
92.	I am a fairly strict person who always wants to see the right things done.	yes, always ☐	no, not always ☐	sometimes ☐
93.	In an arguement, I: (A) make sure what I say is right, (B) say what I feel like saying, (C) can't decide.	(A) ☐	(B) ☐	(C) ☐
94.	For reading I usually enjoy: (A) true-to-life action stories. (B) light, imaginative things, (C) nothing in particular.	(A) ☐	(B) ☐	(C) ☐
95.	While working, I: (A) try to plan ahead (B) expect problems will be taken care of by themselves when they come, (C) can't decide.	(A) ☐	(B) ☐	(C) ☐
96.	Without thinking first, I say hateful things to people I usually love.	often ☐	hardly ever ☐	sometimes ☐
97.	If I worked on a newspaper, I would rather deal with: (A) politics and sports, (B) society news and reviewing movies, (C) uncertain.	(A) ☐	(B) ☐	(C) ☐
98.	People think I am too careless and casual, even then they like me.	true ☐	false ☐	uncertain ☐
99.	When I talk, I like: (A) to say things just as they come to me, (B) to get my thoughts organized first, (C) can't say.	(A) ☐	(B) ☐	(C) ☐
100.	I often feel that I should go away and travel like a gypsy.	true ☐	false ☐	perhaps ☐
101.	If people are clever enough to twist the roles without breaking them, they should: (A) certainly do so, (B) not do it anyway, (C) do so if unavoidable.	(A) ☐	(B) ☐	(C) ☐
102.	I always believe in doing the socially acceptable thing and to ask how my actions look to others.	true, ☐	false ☐	uncertain ☐
103.	I get excited about plays and novels.	yes ☐	no ☐	not really ☐
104.	In school, I never had trouble with teachers because of bad behaviour. (A) true, I almost never had trouble, (B) false, I had plenty of trouble, (C) sometimes.	(A) ☐	(B) ☐	(C) ☐

Contd...

105.	I have trained myself to be very patient with people.	Yes always, ☐	no, not often ☐	sometimes ☐
106.	In school, I preferred (or still prefer): (A) arithmatic or mathematics, (B) literature or English, (C) uncertain.	(A) ☐	(B) ☐	(C) ☐
107.	If my banker made a careless mistake, and didn't charge me for something I should have paid, (A) it wouldn't be my business to tell them, (B) I would feel I had to point it out and pay, (C) uncertain.	(A) ☐	(B) ☐	(C) ☐
108.	If I am left out by my friends I: (A) make a fuss out of it, (B) take it calmly, (C) uncertain.	(A) ☐	(B) ☐	(C) ☐
109.	I am more sensitive to art and surroundings than most people.	true ☐	false ☐	uncertain ☐
110.	My mind doesn't work very clearly all the time.	True ☐	False ☐	sometimes ☐

111.	In situations when politeness does not work, I get tough and sharp.	often ☐	rarely ☐	sometimes ☐
112.	I like to do team-work with lot of other people involved.	yes ☐	no ☐	sometimes ☐
113.	Regular newspaper issues are not interesting for me. (A) yes true, (B) no, they are interesting for me, (C) it's difficult to decide.	(A) ☐	(B) ☐	(C) ☐
114.	It is more important to bring up children with kindness than to teach them to be self-reliant or successful in life.	yes ☐	no ☐	uncertain ☐
115.	In designing something, I would prefer to work:	on my own ☐	in a team ☐	can't decide ☐
116.	Nobody gets angry in my family.	true ☐	false ☐	very rarely ☐
117.	I resent aggressive people more than I dislike people who talk a lot about their troubles.	true ☐	false ☐	uncertain ☐
118.	I like to socialize even if I am not a prominent figure in the group.	true ☐	false ☐	not always ☐
119.	People who brag or show they think too much of themselves, irritate me a lot. (A)	(A) ☐	(B) ☐	(C) ☐

Contd...

	yes, always, (B) no, hardly ever, (C) sometimes.			
120.	Certain animals make me nervous.	yes, often ☐	no, never ☐	occasionally ☐
121.	I like to do my own planning, without any interruptions and suggestions from others.	yes ☐	no ☐	it depends ☐
122.	I don't get worked up or show my emotions in my voice as much as most people do.	true, I don't ☐	false, I do ☐	uncertain ☐
123.	I feel need to go in for some heavy physical activity.	quite often ☐	never ☐	occasionally ☐
124.	When I do what I want, I find I am generally: (A) understood only by close friends, (B) doing what most people think is okay, (C) undecided.	(A) ☐	(B) ☐	(C) ☐
125.	I never get bored or annoyed with poorly educated people.	true ☐	false ☐	uncertain ☐
126.	I enjoy the company of some animals like – cats, dogs, horses, etc.	true ☐	false ☐	uncertain ☐
127.	I don't like people to say I am different or peculiar.	true, I don't ☐	false, I do ☐	Uncertain ☐
128.	Most people would try to get away with as much as they could if they were not afraid of being caught.	true ☐	false ☐	perhaps ☐
129.	I value good manners and social 'know-how' more than certain other traits present in people.	yes ☐	no ☐	uncertain ☐
130.	I would rather enjoy life quitely in my own "way" than be admired for my achievements.	true ☐	false ☐	uncertain ☐
131.	If I make a silly mistake I soon forget it.	yes, easily ☐	no, I cannot ☐	sometimes ☐
132.	I am not very considerate of other people.	true ☐	false ☐	sometimes ☐

133.	I would prefer to be a: (A) high school teacher, (B) a forester, (C) uncertain.	(A) ☐	(B) ☐	(C) ☐
134.	I just can't stand those people, who talk nonsense.	true ☐	false ☐	uncertain ☐

Contd...

135.	If the income were the same, I would prefer to be: (A) a navigatot or pilot, (B) a lawyer, (C) none of the above.	(A) ☐	(B) ☐	(C) ☐
136.	I get irritated over small setbacks very easily.	yes, often ☐	no, never ☐	sometimes ☐
137.	If I had an idea for a new kitchen gadget, I would prefer: (A) working on it in the laboratory, (B) selling it to the people, (C) I am uncertain about it.	(A) ☐	(B) ☐	(C) ☐
138.	While playing a game, it doesn't irritate me if others pass their comments. (A) true, it doesn't, (B) false, it does, (C) sometimes.	(A) ☐	(B) ☐	(C) ☐
139.	It would be more interesting to be: (A) an artist or sculptor, (B) a social club secretary, (C) none of the above.	(A) ☐	(B) ☐	(C) ☐
140.	People seem to get in my way and frustrate me a lot.	yes, often ☐	almost never ☐	sometimes ☐
141.	On special holidays and birthdays, I: (A) like to give presents, (B) feel that buying presents is a nuisance, (C) not concerned.	(A) ☐	(B) ☐	(C) ☐
142.	The noise of a nail on glass, and similar screechy sounds, set my nerves on edge. (A) unbearably, (B) not at all, (C) somewhat.	(A) ☐	(B) ☐	(C) ☐
143.	If I am asked to work for a charity, I would: (A) generally accept, (B) say "I am too busy", (C) occasionally accept It.	(A) ☐	(B) ☐	(C) ☐
144.	When something really makes me furious, I calm down again quite quickly.	yes ☐	no ☐	undecided ☐
145.	I have never done daring things just for fun. (A) true, I never have, (B) False, I have, (C) sometimes..	(A) ☐	(B) ☐	(C) ☐
146.	I feel restless as if I want something but do not know what.	often ☐	very rarely ☐	occasionally ☐
147.	I may deceive people by being friendly when I really dislike them.	true ☐	false ☐	sometimes ☐

STOP HERE, MAKE SURE YOU HAVE ANSWERED EVERY QUESTION.

Sw =	Tn =	Vi =

MAP Series - Adult Form

PROFILE SHEET

Name: ______________ Age:________ Sex:________ Date: ______________

Occupation: _________________ Remarks: _________________

Raw Score	Sten Score	Dimensions	Standard Ten Scores 1	2	3	4	5	6	7	8	9	10	Description
		Ad	〈	〈	〈	〈	〈	〈	〈	〈	〈	〈	Adaptability
		Am	〈	〈	〈	〈	〈	〈	〈	〈	〈	〈	Achievement Motivation
		Bo	〈	〈	〈	〈	〈	〈	〈	〈	〈	〈	Boldness
		Co	〈	〈	〈	〈	〈	〈	〈	〈	〈	〈	Competition
		En	〈	〈	〈	〈	〈	〈	〈	〈	〈	〈	Enthusiasm
		Ga	〈	〈	〈	〈	〈	〈	〈	〈	〈	〈	General Ability
		Gp	〈	〈	〈	〈	〈	〈	〈	〈	〈	〈	Guilt Proneness
		Im	〈	〈	〈	〈	〈	〈	〈	〈	〈	〈	Imagination
		In	〈	〈	〈	〈	〈	〈	〈	〈	〈	〈	Innovation
		Ld	〈	〈	〈	〈	〈	〈	〈	〈	〈	〈	Leadership
		Ma	〈	〈	〈	〈	〈	〈	〈	〈	〈	〈	Maturity
		Mh	〈	〈	〈	〈	〈	〈	〈	〈	〈	〈	Mental Health
		Me	〈	〈	〈	〈	〈	〈	〈	〈	〈	〈	Morality
		Sc	〈	〈	〈	〈	〈	〈	〈	〈	〈	〈	Self Control
		Se	〈	〈	〈	〈	〈	〈	〈	〈	〈	〈	Sensitivity
		Sh	〈	〈	〈	〈	〈	〈	〈	〈	〈	〈	Shrewdness
		Ss	〈	〈	〈	〈	〈	〈	〈	〈	〈	〈	Self Sufficiency
		Su	〈	〈	〈	〈	〈	〈	〈	〈	〈	〈	Suspiciousness
		Sw	〈	〈	〈	〈	〈	〈	〈	〈	〈	〈	Social Warmth
		Tn	〈	〈	〈	〈	〈	〈	〈	〈	〈	〈	Tension

Answer Sheet for MAP Series

Adult Form

Examples:

1. a ☐ b ☐ c ☐ 3. a ☐ b ☐ c ☐
2. a ☐ b ☐ c ☐ 4. a ☐ b ☐ c ☐

Name: ______________________ Date: ____________

Age: ____________ Sex: ____________ (Write M or F) Occupation: ____________

PAGE 2		PAGE 3		PAGE4		PAGE 5		PAGE 6		PAGE7		PAGE 8	
1.	a ☐ b ☐ c ☐	23.	a ☐ b ☐ c ☐	45.	a ☐ b ☐ c ☐	67.	a ☐ b ☐ c ☐	89.	a ☐ b ☐ c ☐	111.	a ☐ b ☐ c ☐	133.	a ☐ b ☐ c ☐
2.	a ☐ b ☐ c ☐	24.	a ☐ b ☐ c ☐	46.	a ☐ b ☐ c ☐	68.	a ☐ b ☐ c ☐	90.	a ☐ b ☐ c ☐	112.	a ☐ b ☐ c ☐	134.	a ☐ b ☐ c ☐
3.	a ☐ b ☐ c ☐	25.	a ☐ b ☐ c ☐	47.	a ☐ b ☐ c ☐	69.	a ☐ b ☐ c ☐	91.	a ☐ b ☐ c ☐	113.	a ☐ b ☐ c ☐	135.	a ☐ b ☐ c ☐
4.	a ☐ b ☐ c ☐	26.	a ☐ b ☐ c ☐	48.	a ☐ b ☐ c ☐	70.	a ☐ b ☐ c ☐	92.	a ☐ b ☐ c ☐	114.	a ☐ b ☐ c ☐	136.	a ☐ b ☐ c ☐
5.	a ☐ b ☐ c ☐	27.	a ☐ b ☐ c ☐	49.	a ☐ b ☐ c ☐	71.	a ☐ b ☐ c ☐	93.	a ☐ b ☐ c ☐	115.	a ☐ b ☐ c ☐	137.	a ☐ b ☐ c ☐
6.	a ☐ b ☐ c ☐	28.	a ☐ b ☐ c ☐	50.	a ☐ b ☐ c ☐	72.	a ☐ b ☐ c ☐	94.	a ☐ b ☐ c ☐	116.	a ☐ b ☐ c ☐	138.	a ☐ b ☐ c ☐
7.	a ☐ b ☐ c ☐	29.	a ☐ b ☐ c ☐	51.	a ☐ b ☐ c ☐	73.	a ☐ b ☐ c ☐	95.	a ☐ b ☐ c ☐	117.	a ☐ b ☐ c ☐	139.	a ☐ b ☐ c ☐
8.	a ☐ b ☐ c ☐	30.	a ☐ b ☐ c ☐	52.	a ☐ b ☐ c ☐	74.	a ☐ b ☐ c ☐	96.	a ☐ b ☐ c ☐	118.	a ☐ b ☐ c ☐	140.	a ☐ b ☐ c ☐
9.	a ☐ b ☐ c ☐	31.	a ☐ b ☐ c ☐	53.	a ☐ b ☐ c ☐	75.	a ☐ b ☐ c ☐	97.	a ☐ b ☐ c ☐	119.	a ☐ b ☐ c ☐	141.	a ☐ b ☐ c ☐
10.	a ☐ b ☐ c ☐	32.	a ☐ b ☐ c ☐	54.	a ☐ b ☐ c ☐	76.	a ☐ b ☐ c ☐	98.	a ☐ b ☐ c ☐	120.	a ☐ b ☐ c ☐	142.	a ☐ b ☐ c ☐
11.	a ☐ b ☐ c ☐	33.	a ☐ b ☐ c ☐	55.	a ☐ b ☐ c ☐	77.	a ☐ b ☐ c ☐	99.	a ☐ b ☐ c ☐	121.	a ☐ b ☐ c ☐	143.	a ☐ b ☐ c ☐
12.	a ☐ b ☐ c ☐	34.	a ☐ b ☐ c ☐	56.	a ☐ b ☐ c ☐	78.	a ☐ b ☐ c ☐	100.	a ☐ b ☐ c ☐	122.	a ☐ b ☐ c ☐	144.	a ☐ b ☐ c ☐
13.	a ☐ b ☐ c ☐	35.	a ☐ b ☐ c ☐	57.	a ☐ b ☐ c ☐	79.	a ☐ b ☐ c ☐	101.	a ☐ b ☐ c ☐	123.	a ☐ b ☐ c ☐	145.	a ☐ b ☐ c ☐
14.	a ☐ b ☐ c ☐	36.	a ☐ b ☐ c ☐	58.	a ☐ b ☐ c ☐	80.	a ☐ b ☐ c ☐	102.	a ☐ b ☐ c ☐	124.	a ☐ b ☐ c ☐	146.	a ☐ b ☐ c ☐
15.	a ☐ b ☐ c ☐	37.	a ☐ b ☐ c ☐	59.	a ☐ b ☐ c ☐	81.	a ☐ b ☐ c ☐	103.	a ☐ b ☐ c ☐	125.	a ☐ b ☐ c ☐	147.	a ☐ b ☐ c ☐
16.	a ☐ b ☐ c ☐	38.	a ☐ b ☐ c ☐	60.	a ☐ b ☐ c ☐	82.	a ☐ b ☐ c ☐	104.	a ☐ b ☐ c ☐	126.	a ☐ b ☐ c ☐		
17.	a ☐ b ☐ c ☐	39.	a ☐ b ☐ c ☐	61.	a ☐ b ☐ c ☐	83.	a ☐ b ☐ c ☐	105.	a ☐ b ☐ c ☐	127.	a ☐ b ☐ c ☐		
18.	a ☐ b ☐ c ☐	40.	a ☐ b ☐ c ☐	62.	a ☐ b ☐ c ☐	84.	a ☐ b ☐ c ☐	106.	a ☐ b ☐ c ☐	128.	a ☐ b ☐ c ☐		
19.	a ☐ b ☐ c ☐	41.	a ☐ b ☐ c ☐	63.	a ☐ b ☐ c ☐	85.	a ☐ b ☐ c ☐	107.	a ☐ b ☐ c ☐	129.	a ☐ b ☐ c ☐		
20.	a ☐ b ☐ c ☐	42.	a ☐ b ☐ c ☐	64.	a ☐ b ☐ c ☐	86.	a ☐ b ☐ c ☐	108.	a ☐ b ☐ c ☐	130.	a ☐ b ☐ c ☐		
21.	a ☐ b ☐ c ☐	43.	a ☐ b ☐ c ☐	65.	a ☐ b ☐ c ☐	87.	a ☐ b ☐ c ☐	109.	a ☐ b ☐ c ☐	131.	a ☐ b ☐ c ☐		
22.	a ☐ b ☐ c ☐	44.	a ☐ b ☐ c ☐	66.	a ☐ b ☐ c ☐	88.	a ☐ b ☐ c ☐	110.	a ☐ b ☐ c ☐	132.	a ☐ b ☐ c ☐		

	Ad	Am	Bo	Co	En	Ga	Gp	Im	In	Ld	Ma	Mh	Mo	Sc	Se	Sh	Ss	Su	Sw	Tn	Vi
Rs																					
Ss																					

CHAPTER 18

MYERS-BRIGGS Personality Type, MBTI, and FIRO-B

LEARNING OBJECTIVES

- To discuss MYERS-BRIGGS Personality Type.
- To understand working out your own preference.

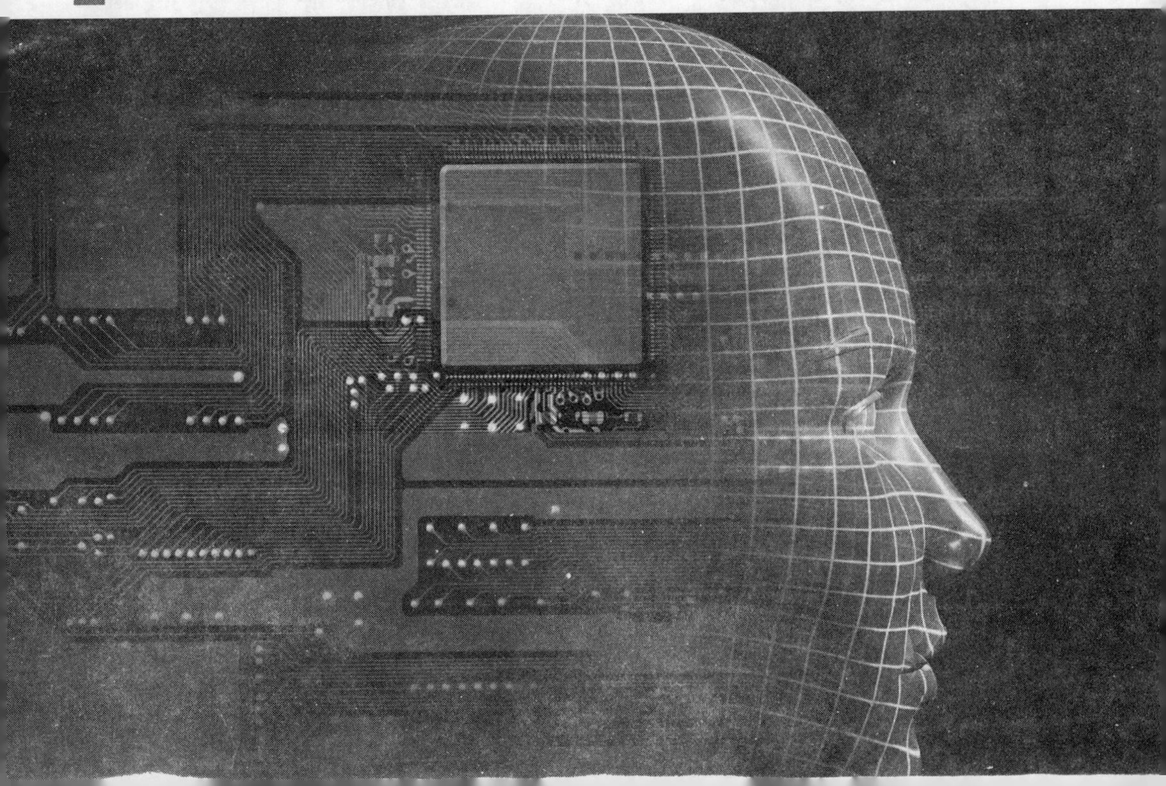

INTRODUCTION

Personality Type or Psychological Type are terms most commonly associated with the model of personality development created by Isabel Briggs Myers, the author of the world's most widely used personality inventory – the MBTI or Myers-Briggs type indicator – is built in relation to the ideas and theories of psychologist Carl Jung, a contemporary of Sigmund Freud and a leading exponent of Gestalt Personality Theory.

Beginning in the early 1940's, Briggs & Myers extended jung's model with the initial development of the MBTI. They put Jung's concepts into language that could be understood and used by the average person. Isabel Myers' book "*Gifts Differing*", published posthumously in 1980, provided a comprehensive introduction to the Jung/Myers theory. Myers' book and her philosophy of celebrating human diversity anticipated the workplace diversity movement.

The MBTI is now a registered trademark of Consulting Psychologist Press, Inc. (CPP) who also publishes and distributes the inventory. The MBTI is available from CPP and its licenses in approximately 20 foreign languages. In addition, alternate versions of the inventory have been scientifically customised and validated for other languages and cultures for which a straight translation of English languages terms would yield inaccurate results.

The Centre for Applications of Psychological Type (CAPT) is a non-profit educational organization founded by Myers and psychologist Mary McCaulley to promote continued research into psychological type and application of psychological type to foster enhanced personal development, increased human understanding, and improved management of human conflict. Another non-profit organization, the Association for Psychological Type (APT) is an international member education and certifying organization for professionals who use type in their occupations and professionals practices. Membership is also open to lay persons who want to enrich their understanding and applications of type.

THE BASIC MODEL

In her studies of people and extensive reading of Jung's theories, Myers concluded there were four primary ways in which people were different from one another. She labelled these differences "preferences", drawing a similarity to "hand preferences" to illustrate that although we all use both of our hands, most of us have a preference for one over the other and 'it' takes the lead in many of the activities in which we use our hands. The first set of mental preferences relates to how people 'perceive' or take in information. Those who prefer 'sensing' perception favour clear, tangible data and information that goes well with their direct here-and-now experience.

In contrast, those who prefer 'intuition' perception are drawn to information that is more abstract, conceptual, big picture and represents imaginative possibilities for the future. The second set of mental preferences identifies how people form "judgments" or make decisions. Those who prefer 'thinking' judgment have a natural preferences for making decisions in an objective, logical, and analytical manner with an emphasis on tasks and results to be accomplished.

Those whose preferences is for 'feeling' judgment make their decisions in a somewhat global, visceral, harmony and value-oriented way, paying particular attention to the impact of decisions and actions on other people. One of the practical applications of the MBTI and understanding these preferences is in supporting better teamwork. Differences in these mental preferences lead to quite different value structures and communications styles, which can hamper mutual understanding and cooperation.

For example, people who share 'sensing' and 'thinking' preferences find they are naturally on the same wavelength; they easily understand one another, making good teammates and partners. Likewise, people who share intuition and feeling have a similar kinship among them. However, in the 'real' world, it is more likely that you'll find a mixed bag of people, a variety of types, in the same work group. While this diversity can be a useful strength, contributing to greater depth and breadth of team competence, there will be natural communication barriers within the team due to their natural mental language differences.

Such differences can be overcome, and the communication gap bridged, with mutual respect and practice learning to 'talk' and 'think' in a second or third language. A MBTI workshop can be seen as an introduction to learning the language, habits and culture of other types. There are two other mental preferences that are part of the Myers-Briggs model. One pertains to energy consciousness (extraversion versus introversion). The other is life management orientation (judging versus perceiving).

The permutations of these four preferences result in the 16 personality types that form the basis of Myers' model and the MBTI inventory.

MYERS BRIGGS — WORKING OUT YOUR TYPE

Where, Primarily, do you direct your Energy?

To the outer world of activity, and spoken words or to the inner world of thoughts and emotions.

If it is toward the outer world of activity or words, it is called extroversion, denoted by the letter *e*. If it is toward the inner world of ideas, information, or thoughts, it is called introversion, denoted by the letter *i*. 'Extro' is a prefix meaning 'without' and 'intro' is a prefix meaning 'within'. During each day you will undoubtedly spend time spontaneously doing or saying things, as well as retreating into the inner world of contemplation and thought. If your working day has involved much interaction with the world, even the clearest extrovert may feel at the end of the day that he wants to be left alone with his thoughts. Conversely, if an introvert has been working in isolation all day, she may feel that she needs to 'party' in the evening to restore some balance.

You, like every other individual, need a particular balance of both introversion and extroversion. However, laying aside special circumstances like those in the previous paragraph, one of extroversion or introversion will normally increase your level of energy, whilst the other will decrease it. The following table (Table 18.1) lists words and expressions that are often associated with extroversion and introversion.

TABLE 18.1: WORDS AND EXPRESSIONS ASSOCIATED WITH EXTROVERSION AND INTROVERSION

Extroversion	Introversion
Social	Private
Expressive	Quiet
Many	Few
Broad	Deep
Interaction	Concentration
Outward	Inward
Action before thought	Thought before action

Which is your preference (i.e., what is your personality type)? How are you actually behaving most of the time (i.e., what is your MTR-I team role)? Sometimes, it can be difficult to tell. Every individual exhibits all of the above characteristics at some time or other, and one source of difficulty can be in distinguishing which behaviours are 'learnt', or a response to current demands, and which reflect true preference. Distinguishing between the two is where comparing your MBTI questionnaire and MTR-I questionnaire results can help. Preference, role, or learnt behaviour one feature differentiating Es from's is whether action or thought comes first. In situations that demand action, such as the sounding of a fire alarm, both types will act. Most people are trained to vacate the building immediately in an emergency, or to take other appropriate action. So the fire alarm results in most people doing something, and very few people decide to sit and think. They will adopt a team role that is extraverted. But their underlying preference is still the same. In situations that demand thought, such as solving a crossword puzzle, both types will think. Most crossword puzzles cannot be solved by taking action or by talking. Both extroverts and introverts need to spend time in thought first, to make some progress towards a solution. Their team roles are introverted, but their underlying preference remains the same. Team roles therefore, reflect how we respond to particular circumstances. Finding your true, inner preferences is therefore more difficult, because everyone adapts to some degree to each situation. However, the difference between people who have a preference for extroversion and introversion becomes more apparent when there is a free choice. In these situations, the extrovert will tend to act, and the introvert will tend to think. However, very few situations involve a truly free choice, as your behaviour (at work, or example) may be influenced by factors such as: the culture of the organization (some employers expect action-oriented behaviour, others expect considered responses) your training or upbringing a range of environmental factors, such as whether the situation is a new or familiar one, whether recognition or reward is given, and the effects of stress or illness. The need to restore balance may also be a factor (e.g.: an extrovert may need some time alone after a busy week). Nevertheless, your innate preferences will still influence, the way that you behave, as well a those factors listed above. In a situation demanding action, an introvert may nevertheless bring a more thoughtful approach, or delay the taking of action. In a situation demanding thought, the extrovert may tend to talk the problem through, or move to action more quickly. The mtr-I tm team role you perform depends on a combination of the demands being placed on you. Isabel Briggs-Myers believed your type is innate and stays the same throughout life. Another indicator or your true preferences coincide with the demands of the situation, you may find It quite enjoyable. An extrovert may find it frustrating when required to work in an introvert style, but enjoyable or energizing if required to work in an extrovert style, and vice versa for an introvert.

How Do You Prefer to Process Information?

In the form of known facts and familiar terms, or in the form of possibilities or new potential. If it is in the form of facts or familiar terms, it is called sensing, denoted by the letter *s*. If it is in the form of possibilities or new potential, it is called intuition, denoted by the letter *n* (*n* is used rather than I, to avoid confusion with introversion). The term sensing is used because information is taken in primarily by way of the senses. The term intuition is used because information is perceived primarily in an intuitive fashion. Sensing tends to be interested in tangible reality, focusing on the present, and seeing what is, rather than what might be. At an extreme, sensing can have its feet so well and truly on the ground that it misses out on possibilities for the future. The preference for intuition lays a greater emphasis on insight and the future. Focusing on what might be, rather than what is. At an extreme, intuition can focus so much on possibilities that it loses touch with current realities. Sensing tends to communicate in direct ways, whilst intuition prefers to communicates in creative ways.

The following table shows words that are normally associated with each of these two preferences.

TABLE 18.2: WORDS NORMALLY ASSOCIATED WITH SENSING AND INTUITION

Sensing	Intuition
Facts	Possibilities
Experience	Novelty
Present	Future
Practicality	Aspiration
Enjoyment	Development
Realism	Idealism
Using	Changing

How do you prefer to make Decisions?

On the basis of logic and objective considerations, or on the basis of personal values. If it is on the basis of logic and objective considerations, It is called thinking, denoted by the letter *t*. If it is on the basis of personal values, it is called feeling, denoted by the letter *f*. The following table lists words often associated with each of the two preferences.

TABLE 18.3: WORDS ASSOCIATED WITH THINKING AND FEELING

Thinking	Feeling
Analyzing	Sympathizing
Objective	Subjective
Logical	Personal
Criticism	Appreciation
Onlooker	Participant
Decides on principle	Decides using values
Long-term view	Immediate view

How do you Prefer to Organize Life?

In a structured way, making decisions and knowing where you stand, or in a flexible way, discovering life as you go along. If it is in a structured way, making decisions and knowing where you stand, then it is called judgement. If it is in a flexible way, discovering life as you go along – this is called perception. Someone whose preference is judgement prefers, in their lifestyle, to make decisions. This means that they prefer to make decisions about what to do, where to go, what to say, and so on. As a result of these decisions, their lifestyle appears organized. Someone whose preference is perception prefers, in their lifestyle, to learn or experience new things. This means that they prefer to find out more, rather than making decisions, and are more comfortable when they keep their options open. As a result of this openness, they can appear flexible. That is, someone whose preference is perception, prefers to perceive new things in the world of actions and spoken words, and therefore appears flexible. Some words often associated with judgement and perception are given in the table below:

TABLE 18.4: WORDS ASSOCIATED WITH JUDGEMENT AND PERCEPTION

Judgement	Perception
Close	Open
Decide	Explore
Structure	Meander
Organize	Inquire
Firmness	Flexibility
Control	Spontaneity

WORKING OUT YOUR OWN PREFERENCE

Everyone's personality reflects all aspects of the Myers Briggs model. You use extroversion as well as introversion, sensing as well as intuition, thinking as well as feeling and judgement as well as perception. You can perform any of the MTR-I team roles.

However, your type is a permanent influence in your personality, that influences your choice, where the opportunity allows, of which preference or team role to perform.

The letters that represent your preferences are combined to produce your Myers Briggs type, such as ENTJ. An ENTJ prefers extroversion, intuition, thinking and judgement. The ENTJ is likely to feel energized by having lots of things going on (e). He will tend to interpret events by seeing patterns or overviews (n). He will tend to make decisions on the basis of logic (t). And he organizes life on a logical basis (j). Look at the lists of words for each preference above, and think about your preference (not just the way you behave in, say, your work or social roles).

WHAT IS YOUR MYERS BRIGGS TYPE? – THE SIXTEEN TYPES

You have probably narrowed down your choice to a few types, but perhaps have not yet settled on one. Read the ones that you think may apply to you, and see if can yet narrow your choice down further. This section contains a brief overview of the sixteen types that result from the Myers Briggs model. Everyone is an individual, but Myers Briggs highlights general themes or similarities between people. Reading this section may help you to consolidate your understanding of the preferences, and help identify your own personality type.

❖ ESTJ

The ESTJ takes his/her energy from the outside world of actions and spoken words. He/she prefers dealing with facts and the present, and makes decisions using logic. His/her life is organized on a logical basis. He/she is therefore practical, and likely to implement tried and trusted solutions to practical problems in a businesslike and impersonal manner. He/she prefers to ensure that the details have been taken care of rather than spend time considering concepts and strategies.

❖ INFP

The INFP takes his/her energy from the inner world of thoughts and emotions. He/she prefers dealing with patterns and possibilities, especially for people, and prefers to make decisions on the basis of personal values. His/her life is flexible, following new insights and possibilities as they arise. He/she is quiet and adaptable (up to a point – when his/her stance). He/she will seem to be very interested in ideas, and he/she may sometimes make very creative contributions. He/she has a hidden warmth for people and a desire to see self and others grow and develop. He/she prefers to undertake work that has a meaningful purpose.

❖ ESFP

The ESFP takes his/her energy from the outside world of actions and spoken words. He/she prefers dealing with facts, which he/she usually takes at face value. He/she also prefers dealing with the present and with people, and probably derivers much enjoyment out of friendships. His/her life is flexible, living it very much in the present, and responding to things as they arise. He/she is impulsive and friendly, seeing enjoyment out of life, and makes new friends easily. He/she likes taking part in solving urgent problems, such as fire-fighting or trouble shooting. He/she operates best in practical situations involving people.

❖ INTJ

The INTJ takes his/her energy from the outside world of thoughts (and, maybe, emotions). He/she prefers dealing with patterns and possibilities for the future, and making decisions using impersonal analysis. His/her life is organized on a logical basis. He/she tends to be skeptical and critical, both of self and others, with a keen sense of deficiencies in quality and competence. He/she often has a strong intellect, yet is able to attend to details that are relevant to the strategy.

❖ ESFJ

The ESFJ takes his/her energy from the outer world of actions and spoken words. He/she prefers dealing with facts, and making decisions on the basis of personal values. He/she likes dealing with people, and organizes life on a personal basis. He/she is a very warm person, seeing to maintain harmonious relationships with colleagues and friends, who are a very important part of his/her life. He/she can find conflict and criticism very difficult to handle. He/she has a strong sense of duty and loyalty, and is driven by a need to belong and be of service people.

❖ INTP

The INTP takes his/her energy from the outer world of thoughts (and, maybe, emotions). He/she prefers dealing with patterns and possibilities, and making decision on a logical basis. His/her life is flexible, following new insights and possibilities as they arise. He/she is quiet and detached, and adaptable (up to a point – sometimes he/she may stop adapting, insisting that there is a clear principle at stake). He/she is not interested in routine, and will often experiment or change things to see if they can be improved. He/she operates at best when solving complex problems that require the application of intellect.

❖ ENFP

The ENFP takes his/her energy from the outer world of actions and spoken words.

He/she prefers dealing with patterns and possibilities, particularly for people, and makes decisions on the basis of personal values. His/her life is flexible, following new insights and possibilities as they arise. He/she is creative and insightful, often seeking to try new ideas that can be of benefit to people. He/she may sometimes neglect details and planning, but he/she enjoys work that involves experimentation and variety, working towards a general goal.

❖ ISTJ

The ISTJ takes his/her energy from the inner world of thoughts (and, maybe, emotions). He/she prefers dealing with facts, and making decisions after considering the various options. He/she organizes his/her life on a logical basis. He/she is quiet, serious and well prepared for most eventualities. He/she is a keen observer. He/she has a strong sense of practical objectives and works efficiently to meet them.

❖ ESTP

The ESTP takes his/her energy from the outer world of actions and spoken words. He/she prefers dealing with facts, which he/she usually views objectively, and he/she makes decisions on a logical basis. His/her life is flexible, consisting of a series of activities that interest his/her is an action-oriented problem-solver, and prefers to work with practical organizational issues. He/he can be impulsive, and likes taking part in trouble-shooting type work. He/she can sometimes neglect follow-through, but will work best when there is a lot going on that needs organizing and solving.

❖ INFJ

The INFJ takes his/her energy from the inner world of thoughts and emotions. He/she prefers dealing with patterns and possibilities, particularly for people, and makes decisions using personal values. His/her life is organized on a personal basis. He/she often has a private sense of purpose in life, and works steadily to fulfil that goal. He/she demonstrates a quiet concern for people, being interested in helping them to develop and grow. He/she is good at developing insights into people, though it can often remain unexpressed.

❖ ENFJ

The ENFJ takes his/her energy from the outer world of actions and spoken words. He/she prefers dealing with patterns and possibilities, particularly for people, and makes decisions using personal values. His/her life is organized on a personal basis, seeing to develop and maintain stable relationship with those people he/she likes. He/she is actively concerned with promoting personal growth in others. He/she is also highly sociable, and expressive of feelings towards others, but can find conflict and criticism difficult, particularly if it might damage long term relationships. He/she works best in situations involving people.

❖ ISTP

The ISTP takes his/her energy from the inner world of thoughts (and, maybe, emotions). He/she prefers dealing with facts and making decisions on a logical basis. His/her life is flexible, demonstrating a interest in acquiring new information that leads to a practical understanding of the way the world works. He/she is quiet and detached, and adaptable (up to a point). He/she is often good at solving organizational problems that need to be thought through. He/she is curious about how and why things work, and can seem impulsive, sometimes producing surprising ideas or doing something unpredictable.

❖ ENTJ

The ENTJ takes his/her energy from the outer world of actions and spoken words. He/she prefers dealing with patterns and possibilities, and making decisions after considering the consequences of the various courses of action. His/her life is organized on a logical basis. He/she tends to control life, organizing systems and people to meet task-oriented goals. He/she often takes the role of executive or director, using a business-like and impersonal approach. He/she may appear intolerant of people who do not set high standards for themselves or don't seem to be good at what they do.

❖ ISPF

The ISPF takes his/her energy from the inner world of thoughts and emotions. He/she prefers dealing with facts and people and making decisions on the basis of personal values. He/she is adaptable (up to a point), quiet and friendly. He/she is interested in people, enjoying their company preferably on an individual basis or in small numbers. He/she takes a caring and sensitive approach to helping others. He/she enjoys the present and tends to dislike confrontation and conflict. He/she usually acts as a very supportive member of a team.

❖ ENTP

The ENTP takes his/her energy from the outer world of actions and spoken words. He/she prefers dealing with patterns and possibilities, and making decisions on a logical basis. He/she is adaptable, tending to focus on new ideas and interests as and when they arise, particularly if they involve increasing his/her competence or skills. He/she is an ingenious problem-solver, constantly trying new ideas out, and can seem to enjoy a good argument. He/she is interested in instigating change and operates best in overcoming new difficulties where the solutions requires the application of creative effort.

❖ ISFJ

The ISFJ takes his/her energy from the inner world of thoughts and emotions. He/she prefers dealing with facts and people, and making decisions on the basis of personal values. His/her life is organized on a personal basis, seeking to enjoy relationships with people he/she likes, he/she is a quiet, serious observer of people, and is both conscientious and loyal. He/she prefers work that involves being of practical service to people, feels and dislikes confrontation and conflict.

THE MYERS-BRIGGS – TYPE INDICATOR

Another way of getting useful and objective feedback is to complete a personality questionnaire that has been specially designed for developmental purposes. A good example is the Myers-Briggs Type Indicator (MBTI), a questionnaire based on the work of the swiss psychologist Carl Jung, which identifies your preferences on four independent dimensions. The first, extroverted – introverted, should come as no surprise, but you may be less familiar with the other three.

❖ Extroverted (E) – Introverted (I)

Extroverted people have a preference for dealing with the outer world of people, activities and things. In a work context, they like dealing with other people and seek variety and action. The introvert, in contrast is concerned with the inner world of ideas and information. He or she likes quiet, tends to concentrate on one thing at a time, and prefers to work alone.

❖ Sensing (S) – Intuitive (N)

The sensing person focuses on the here-and-now and on information from the senses. He or she uses experience to solve problems and likes to undertake practical tasks. There is also a concern with detail and a preference for a step-by-step approach. Those who are intuitive are concerned with the future, strategy and possibilities. They like to consider the overview and new ways of doing things.

❖ Thinking (T) – Feeling (F)

Thinkers base their decisions on the logical analysis of situations. They tend to be firm minded, critical, no-nonsense sort of people. At times, decisions can appear to tack a personal element. In contrast, feeling people use values, and subjective and inclusive form of working.

❖ Judging (J) – Perceiving (P)

The judging person likes a planned, organized approach to life. He prefers to have things settle and actively seeks structure and schedule. In meetings, there may be much talk of purpose and direction, and a laser-like focus on the task in hand. Alternatively, the perceiving individual likes flexibility and spontaneity. The concern is with leaving options open and delaying decisions to allow for last-minute changes.

The result of the questionnaire are used to work out your position on each of the four scales. Your 'type' is then represented by a four-letter code, which is associated with a unique set of behavioural attributes and characteristics. For example, the description for an 'ENTJ' is given below.

These can be understood as follows:

Extroverts often:

1. Have high energy;
2. Talk a lot;
3. Think out loud;
4. Like to be around people a lot;
5. Are easily distracted.

Introverts often:

1. Have quiet energy;
2. Talk less;
3. Think before they act;
4. Are comfortable spending time alone;
5. Have good concentration.

Sensors often:

1. Admire practically;
2. Focus on the facts and specifies;
3. Are straightforward;
4. Are more realistic – see everything as it is;
5. Are more present-oriented.

Thinkers often:

1. Are cool and reserved;
2. Are objective;
3. Are honest and direct;
4. Are naturally critical;
5. Are motivated by achievement.

Feelers often:

1. Are warm and friendly;
2. Get their feelings hurt easily;
3. Are sensitive and diplomatic;
4. Are hard to please others;
5. Are motivated by being appreciated.

This test help the individual to find out their own combination of personality types and, therefore, those aspects of their personality which they could capitalize on and those which needed to be improved.

Example – MBTI Development Narrative

ENTJ – Extraverted Intuition with Thinking

People with ENTJ preferences use their thinking preference to run as much of the world as may be theirs to run. They enjoy executive action and long range planning. Reliance on thinking makes them logical, analytical, objectively critical, and not likely to be convinced by anything but reasoning. They tend to focus on ideas, not the people behind the ideas.

They like to think ahead, organize plans, situations and operations related to a project, and make a systematic effort to reach objectives on schedule. They have little patience with confusion or inefficiency, and can be tough when the situation calls for toughness.

They think conduct should be ruled by logic, and govern their behaviour accordingly. They live by a definite set of rules that embody their basic judgments about the world. Any change in their ways requires a deliberate change in their rules.

They are mainly interested in seeing the possibilities beyond the present, obvious, or known. Intuition heightens their intellectual interest, curiosity for new ideas, tolerance for theory, and taste for complex problems.

ENTJs are seldom content in jobs that make no demand upon their intuition. They are stimulated by problems and are often found in executive jobs where they can find and implement new solutions. Because their interest is in the big picture, they may overlook the importance of certain details. Since ENTJs tend to team up with like-minded people, who may also underestimate the realities of a situation, they usually need a person around with good common sense to bring up overlooked facts and take care of important details.

Like other decisive types, ENTJs run the risk of deciding too quickly, before they have fully examined the situation. They need to stop and listen to the other person's viewpoint, especially with people who are not in a position to talk back. This is seldom easy for them, but if they do not take time to understand, they may judge too quickly, without enough facts or enough regard for what other people think or feel.

ENTJs may need to work at taking feeling values into account. Relying so much on their logical approach, they may overlook feeling values – what they care about and what other people care about. If feeling values are ignored too much, they may build up pressure and find expression in inappropriate ways. Although ENTJs are naturally good at seeing what is illogical and inconsistent, they may need to develop the art of appreciation. One positive way to exercise their feeling preference is through appreciation of other people's merits and ideas. ENTJs who learn to make it a rule to mention what they like, not merely what needs correcting, find the results worthwhile both in their work and in their private lives.

A full report would also include individual comments on potential pitfalls and suggestions for development. For an ENTJ, these might be that you overlook other people's needs, appear impatient, and that you may suppress your own feelings. The associated suggestions for development would then be that you should make a point of considering how other people think and feel, check what is practical before leaping in, reflect on things before making decisions, and take time to learn how to identify and value your own feelings.

The insights you can gain from the MBTI are extremely powerful and can act as an important catalyst to change. In particular, it gives a focus to the sort of behaviour you need to practice, and where to practice it.

INTRODUCTION TO FIRO-B

The basic style of our behaviour through which we establish relations with others can be studied by FIRO-B (Fundamental Interpersonal Relationship Orientation Behaviour).

In FIRO-B, 54 questions are to be answered. Schultz's FIRO-B is a self-report group administered questionnaire reflecting a person's fundamental interpersonal relations orientation and behaviour. The following three fundamental needs enter into any permanent or temporary relationship.

1. Need for Inclusion;
2. Need for Affection; and
3. Need for Control.

Each of these three needs, which are the cause of interpersonal relationships, again has two dimensions: Expressed (e) and Wanted (w).

Please select the answer that best applies to you and put a tick in the respective place to show your response.

Please be as honest as you can.

1. I try to be with people.

   1. usually 2. often 3. sometimes 4. occasionally 5. rarely 6. never

2. I let other people decide what to do.

   1. usually 2. often 3. sometimes 4. occasionally 5. rarely 6. never

3. I join social groups.

   1. usually 2. often 3. sometimes 4. occasionally 5. rarely 6. never

4. I try to have close relationship with people.

   1. usually 2. often 3. sometimes 4. occasionally 5. rarely 6.never

5. I tend to join social organizations when I have an opportunity.

   1. usually 2. often 3. sometimes 4. occasionally 5. rarely 6. never

6. I let other people strongly influence my action.

   1. usually 2. often 3. sometimes 4. occasionally 5. rarely 6. never

7. I try to be included in informal social activities.

   1. usually 2. often 3. sometimes 4. occasionally 5. rarely 6. never

8. I try to have close, personal relationship with people.

   1. usually 2. often 3. sometimes 4. occasionally 5. rarely 6. never

9. I try to include other people in my plans.

   1. usually 2. often 3. sometimes 4. occasionally 5. rarely 6. never

10. I let other people control my actions.

   1. usually 2. often 3. sometimes 4. occasionally 5. rarely 6. never

11. I try to have people around me.

   1. usually 2. often 3. sometimes 4. occasionally 5. rarely 6. never

12. I try to get close and personal with people.

   1. usually 2. often 3. sometimes 4. occasionally 5. rarely 6. never

13. When people are doing things together I tend to join them.

   1. usually 2. often 3. sometimes 4. occasionally 5. rarely 6. never

14. I am easily led by people.

   1. usually 2. often 3. sometimes 4. occasionally 5. rarely 6. never

15. I try to avoid being alone.

   1. usually 2. often 3. sometimes 4. occasionally 5. rarely 6. never

16. I try to participate in group activities.

   1. usually 2. often 3. sometimes 4. occasionally 5. rarely 6. never

For the each of the next group of statements, choose one of the following answers.

17. I try to be friendly to people.

   1. most people 2. many people 3. some people

   4. a few people 5. one or two people 6. nobody

18. I let other people decide what to do

   1. most people 2. many people 3. some people

   4. a few people 5. one or two people 6. nobody

19. My personal relations with people are cool and distant.

1. most people 2. many people 3. some people
4. a few people 5. one or two people 6. nobody

20. I let other people take charge of things.

1. most people 2. many people 3. some people
4. a few people 5. one or two people 6. nobody

21. I try to have close relationship with people.

1. most people 2. many people 3. some people
4. a few people 5. one or two people 6. nobody

22. I let other people strongly influence my action.

1. most people 2. many people 3. some people
4. a few people 5. one or two people 6. nobody

23. I try to get close and personal with people.

1. most people 2. many people 3. some people
4. a few people 5. one or two people 6. nobody

24. I let other people control my actions.

1. most people 2. many people 3. some people
4. a few people 5. one or two people 6. nobody

25. I act cool and distant with people.

1. most people 2. many people 3. some people
4. a few people 5. one or two people 6. nobody

26. I am easily led by people.

1. most people 2. many people 3. some people
4. a few people 5. one or two people 6. nobody

27. I try to have close, personal relationship with people.

1. most people 2. many people 3. some people
4. a few people 5. one or two people 6. nobody

For the each of the next group of statements, choose one of the answers.

28. I like people to invite me to things.

1. most people 2. many people 3. some people
4. a few people 5. one or two people 6. nobody

29. I like people to act close and personal with me.

1. most people 2. many people 3. some people
4. a few people 5. one or two people 6. nobody

30. I try to influence strongly other people's action.

1. most people 2. many people 3. some people
4. a few people 5. one or two people 6. nobody

31. I like people to invite me to join in their activities.

1. most people 2. many people 3. some people
4. a few people 5. one or two people 6. nobody

32. I like people to act close toward me.

1. most people 2. many people 3. some people
4. a few people 5. one or two people 6. nobody

33. I try to take charge to things when I am with people.

1. most people 2. many people 3. some people
4. a few people 5. one or two people 6. nobody

34. I like people to include me in their activities.

1. most people 2. many people 3. some people
4. a few people 5. one or two people 6. nobody

35. I like people to act cool and distant toward me.

1. most people 2. many people 3. some people
4. a few people 5. one or two people 6. nobody

36. I try to have other people do things the way I want them done.

1. most people 2. many people 3. some people
4. a few people 5. one or two people 6. nobody

37. I like people to ask me to participate in their discussions.

1. most people 2. many people 3. some people

4. a few people 5. one or two people 6. nobody

38. I like people to act friendly toward me.

1. most people 2. many people 3. some people

4. a few people 5. one or two people 6. nobody

39. I like people to invite me to participate in their activities.

1. most people 2. many people 3. some people

4. a few people 5. one or two people 6. nobody

40. I like people to act distant toward me.

1. most people 2.many people 3. some people

4. a few people 5. one or two people 6. nobody

For each of the next group of statements, choose one of the following answers.

41. I try to be the dominant person when I am with you.

1. usually 2. often 3. sometimes 4. occasionally 5. rarely 6. never

42. I like people to invite me to things.

1. usually 2. often 3. sometimes 4. occasionally 5. rarely 6. never

43. I like people to act close toward me.

1. usually 2. often 3. sometimes 4. occasionally 5. rarely 6. never

44. I try to have other people do things I want done.

1. usually 2. often 3. sometimes 4. occasionally 5. rarely 6. never

45. I like people to invite me to join their activities.

1. usually 2. often 3. sometimes 4. occasionally 5. rarely 6. never

46. I like people to act cool and distant toward me.

1. usually 2. often 3. sometimes 4. occasionally 5. rarely 6. never

47. I try to influence strongly other people's action.

1. usually 2. often 3. sometimes 4. occasionally 5. rarely 6. never

48. I like people to include me in their activities.

1. usually 2. often 3. sometimes 4. occasionally 5. rarely 6. never

49. I like people to act close and personal with me.

1. usually 2. often 3. sometimes 4. occasionally 5. rarely 6. never

50. I try to take charge of things of thing when I'm with people.

1. usually 2. often 3. sometimes 4. occasionally 5. rarely 6. never

51. I like people to invite me to participate in their activities.

1. usually 2. often 3. sometimes 4. occasionally 5. rarely 6. never

52. I like people to act distant toward me.

1. usually 2. often 3. sometimes 4. occasionally 5. rarely 6. never

53. I try to have other people do things the way I want them done.

1. usually 2. often 3. sometimes 4. occasionally 5. rarely 6. never

54. I take charge of things when I'm with people.

1. usually 2. often 3. sometimes 4. occasionally 5. rarely 6. never

If your answer tallies with any one of the responses given alongside, tick the relevant response and make 1 as score.

Statement No.	Score	Response	Statement No.	Score	Response No.
I (e)			I.(w)		
1		1 2 3	28		1 2
3		1 2 3 4	31		1 2
5		1 2 3 4	34		1 2
7		1 2 3	37		1
9		1 2	39		1
11		1 2	42		1 2
13		1 2	45		1 2
15		1	48		1 2
16		1	51		1 2
Total score			Total score		

Statement No.	Score	Response No.	Statement No.	Score	Response No.
C (e)			C (w)		
30		1 2 3	2		1 2 3 4
33		1 2 3	6		1 2 3 4
36		1 2	10		1 2 3
41		1 2 3 4	14		1 2 3
44		1 2 3	18		1 2 3 4
47		1 2 3	20		1 2 3 4
50		1 2	22		1 2 3 4
53		1 2	24		1 2 3
54		1 2	26		1 2 3
Total score			Total score		

Statement No.	Score	Response No.	Statement No.	Score	Response No.
A. (e)			A. (w)		
4		1 2	29		1 2
8		1 2	32		1 2
12		1	35		5 6
17		1 2	38		1 2
19		4 5 6	40		5 6
21		1 2	43		1
23		1 2	46		5 6
25		4 5 6	49		1 2
27		1 2	52		5 6
Total score			Total score		

CHAPTER 19

Applications of Psychometric Testing in Corporates: Case and Experiences

LEARNING OBJECTIVE

- To explain applications of psychometric.
- To testing through case and operations.

PSYCHOMETRIC TESTING ALONG WITH OTHER ASSESSMENT TOOLS: A CASE OF SHL (INDIA) LTD.

SHL (India) Pvt. Ltd. part of SHL Group, a British Multinational, and a world leader in providing objective assessment solutions conducted a survey across HR professionals in India over a period of three months that provided insights into the market for assessment tools in India. The research aimed to gain a better understanding of the Indian market for occupational assessment tools and understand existing and potential customers in terms of challenges faced, recruitment trends and usage pattern of assessment tools, etc. With the above objective in mind, a preliminary list of 250 organizations was prepared to whom the questionnaire could be addressed. The list of these top organizations in India was developed by identifying different parameters like best employers, revenue, market capitalization, etc. Finally, to undertake this research, an online survey was designed to collect data by sending the email to HR professionals working for the organizations in the list. Apart from this, the survey was also posted on popular Indian HR discussion boards/ e-groups and the results were monitored over a period of two months and the responses were collected before the responses were collated and analyzed.

The survey generated over 250 responses form HR professionals and 111 organizations. However, for a useful analysis incomplete entries and multiple entries from the same organization were excluded wherever required. A few questions were optional. Hence the number of responses to each question varies. The figures in this survey analysis included the total number of respondents considered for the specific analysis. Where possible, survey findings were supplemented with facts and figures from authentic sources. Almost all major sectors of Indian economy were represented. The largest representation (23%) was from the technology sector.

Usage of Assessment Tools

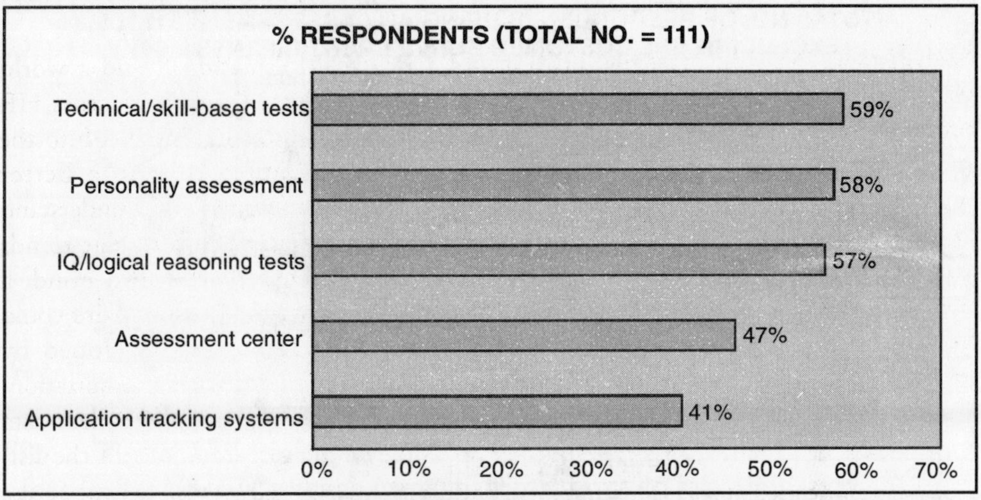

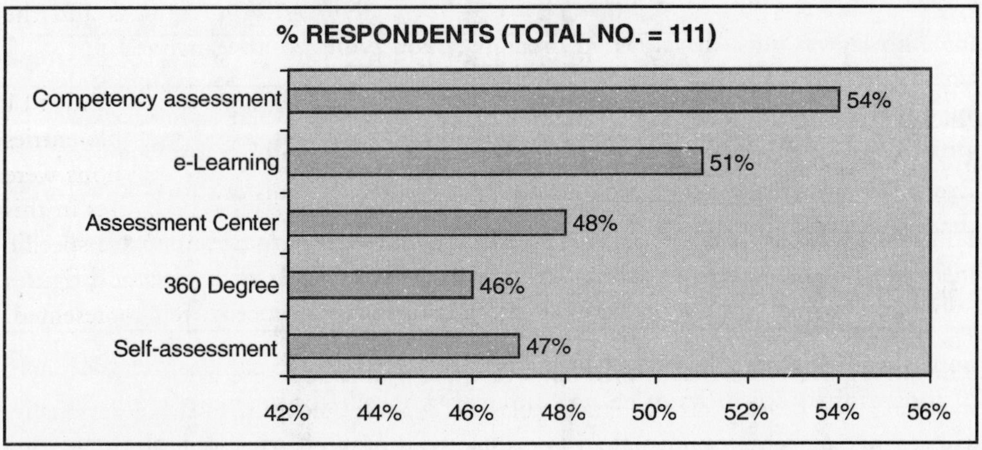

❖ Key Finding

Nearly 60% of the respondents using tools for assessment (internally developed, external/vendor provided or both).

Tools for Recruitment

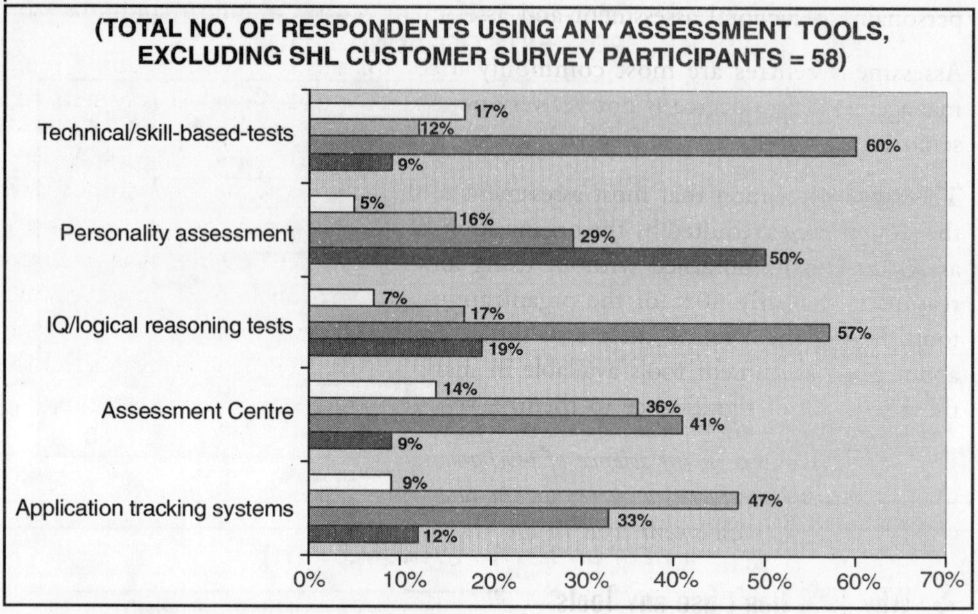

❖ Key Finding

Except for personality assessment, internally developed tools are used more often than external/vendor tools.

Usage Pattern of Assessment Tools

The survey indicated that nearly 60% of the organizations use assessment tools – including tools developed by internal managers. Typically, technical tests and personality assessments are more popular than assessment centres while the application tracking tools are least used.

Among the tools used for employee development (including internally developed tools), competency assessment is the most common tool, 360 degree the least. Internally developed (assessments developed by internal experts) tools are more commonly used than externally provided tools except in case of personality assessment (psychometric tests). However, most preferred to use internally developed technical or skill based tools.

The survey also attempted to find out another aspect of assessment tools' use pattern – which tools are used for which groups of applicants/employees by the respondents. IQ/logical reasoning tests and technical tests are most common tools for assessing engineering graduate applicants. In the case of management graduates they are IQ, logical reasoning and personality assessment. For senior management recruitment personality/behavioral assessment and assessment centres are most common.

Assessment centres are most commonly used for selecting or developing senior management. 360 degree is not yet very popular in India. If used, it is generally for senior management to get feedback.

There is a perception that most assessment tools available in the market don't assess the competencies required by the organization, tools are expensive and are not essential as results can be obtained without using any tools. These are the most common reasons why nearly 40% of the organizations surveyed do not use any assessment tools. Few of them found these tests difficult to answer, while many were not aware about good assessment tools available in market. While most of them did feel that these tests are of significance to them, a very few felt this wasn't their priority.

SHL, pioneers in the science of psychometric testing and objective assessment recently conducted a survey on the latest trends, challenges and usage of assessment tools in the market. A report...........

❖ Why 40% Don't use any Tools

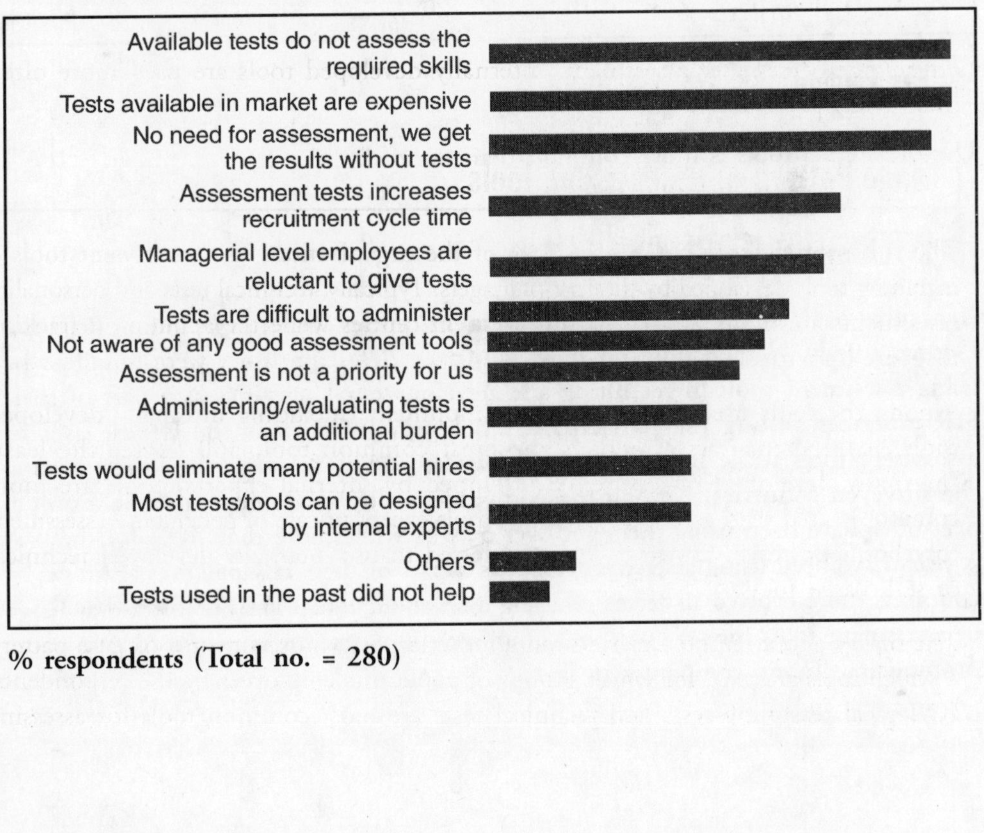

% respondents (Total no. = 280)

Tools for Employee Development

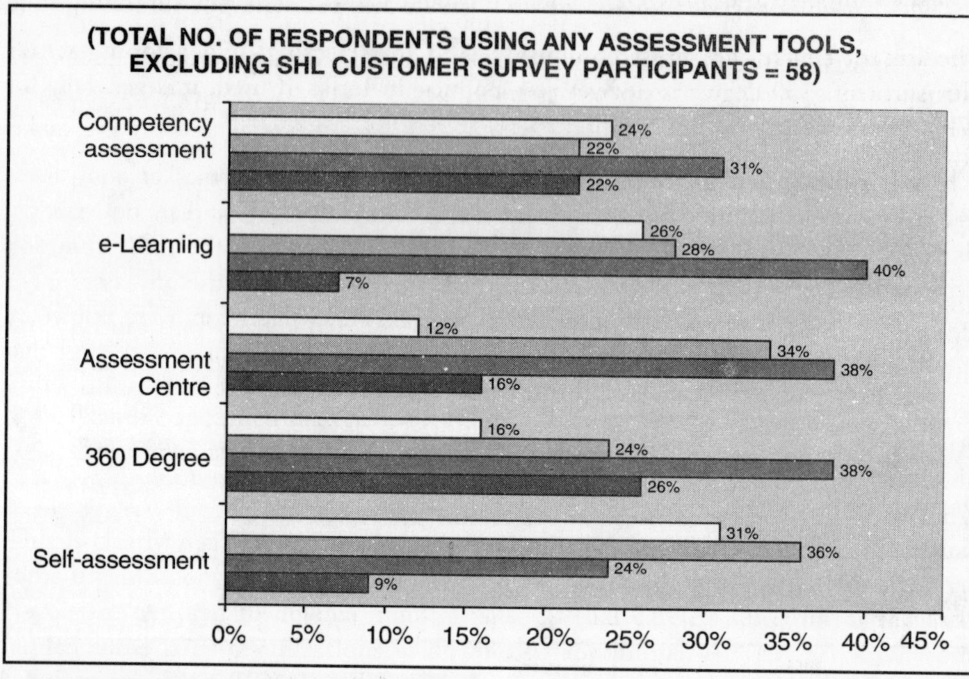

❖ Key Finding

Use of internal tools is more common than external.

INTERNATIONAL TRENDS

In another SHL survey undertaken in several European countries including Belgium, Germany, Italy, Netherlands and Italy, etc., over 70% companies were found to be using assessment tools in recruiting and developmental activities as a part of their HR practices among the participants. Belgium (85%) was the largest user of assessment tools while Italy (65%) and Sweden (65%) stood at the lowest among the surveyed countries. Among the companies using assessment tools in Europe, over 60% have been using them for over 3 years while more than 40% for the past 5 years have been using assessment tools as a part of their HR practices. Europe, of course, is more evolved in terms of using assessment tools. SHL predicts that usage of assessment tools for selection and employee development is poised to gain more prominence among companies in India.

VIEWS AND REVIEWS OF HR AND TOP MANAGEMENT PROFESSIONALS ON APPLICATIONS OF PSYCHOMETRIC TESTING

The link between hiring disasters and personality fit is becoming common knowledge. Not surprising, a range of psychometric assessment tools are flooding the market. What are the pitfalls to avoid while selecting and using a tool? How can you make psychometric profiling to deliver best results for you?

❖ Talent Discovery — The Psychic Way

Research indicates that candidates with top scores in departments like skills, experience and academics may not always make the perfect choice. The link between hiring disasters and personality fit is evident. But getting to know the real person behind the mask can take a complete lifetime. What's thirty minutes of Q&A in a situation that literally demands artificiality. (The job interview)? Subjectively labelling someone as 'outgoing' or 'ambitious' or 'self starter' is ridden with risks. What recruiting managers can bank upon are precisely and scientifically designed assessment tools. Enter psychometric profiling!

❖ A Variety of Wares

Peaking the popularity charts are proven products like 16 PF, FIRO, MBTI, OPQ, DISC and Thomas Profiling. Technical skills, cognitive ability, analytical reasoning, or personality traits — there are dozens of instruments up for grabs, each with a unique application, used either singly, or in combination with others for greater impact. One can buy tests off-the-shelf from licensed international service providers, some of them who have representatives in India too. Unfortunately, the hunt is tiring, since it is rare to find all goods under the same roof. Some would prefer customized tests but the costs involved are fairly high.

Companies need to invest in some basic homework before rushing off to shop around and a discerning eye would be more than helpful. Opines Sundara Rajan, managing partner, Thomas International India, "The key drivers for success of any such system are accuracy, speed, ease of application and cost. The longer any such test takes, higher is the probability of its failure since Indians inherently try to read and look for patterns in such exercises." At the same time, experts also caution against the tendency to blindly follow fads or choose instruments simply on grounds of convenience of usage.

A more sound approach could be to start with identifying the competencies to be assessed, suggests Dr. Abhijit Gangopadhyay, professor and head, department of

PM&IR, Tata Institute of Social Sciences, Mumbai. "A competency and skill dictionary could be helpful in providing guidelines for the selection of psychometric tests to be used in the organization."

A common thumb rule is to ensure features of validity and reliability. To be valid, a test must demonstrate consistency over a time and with different employees. To be reliable, it should be able to measure what it says it can measure. Another criterion is whether the test has been adapted to the different cultural contexts. In other words, the relevance of statements may differ from country to country. Therefore, a local version of the test would be the most beneficial. But as Dr. R. K. Premarajan, professor of HR, XLRI Jamshedpur advises, "A claim that the test has been validated using an Indian sample should not be the sole criterion for choosing the test. What is important is the similarity with the target group and the validation group. It is crucial to compare nature of competencies measured by the test with those of the target group."

Latest Global Trends

1. Automation of psychometric tests adds to convenience, reliability and credibility.
2. There is emerging of more and more tests to measure competencies.
3. Trend towards use of multiple methods, like behavioural combined with ability testing.
4. Use of lateral thinking tests to eliminate 'frivolous' candidates.

❖ Get Geared up to Use Them

Not mystical, not magical, mental measurement is serious business. International agencies have stringent rules and certification procedures for procurement, administration and use of psychometric tests. But, this need not prevent the HR specialist from becoming familiar with the legal implications prevalent in other countries.

Professionally developed tests come with manuals for scoring and analysis. But test interpretation is a science more than an art, calling for specific training and basic cognitive understandings of psychometry. Premarajan believes that a basic degree in psychology is ideal, but for an HR specialist with an MBA degree, specific courses in the field of testing would also suffice. Gangopadhyay adds that in the absence of full-time qualified and certified psychometricians, it is advisable to get the expert help from the outside agency, with follow-up and facilitation by internal HR. Arbitrary selection and improper use of psychometric tests could lead to selection errors, he avers.

Service providers, on the other hand, feel that a good understanding of business and special training from the system providers are good enough. Says Abhimanyu Acharya, vice president, corporate philosophy and chief knowledge officer, C&K Management Ltd., "Users need to be aware of the exact requirements in terms of profile and attitude for the jobs for which they are testing. This supersedes job descriptions and key result areas. Often recruiters reverse the order and manage to hire people with the right qualifications but the wrong attitude, discovering later, at great cost, the unsuitability of the candidate. The best would be for organizations to approach experienced recruiters who have developed tests under several categories and post > 94% success rate."

❖ Look out for the Pitfalls

Many recruiting managers are clueless about what to expect from psychometric testing, including the facts that tests do not provide black and white answers, there are no passing scores. Rather, they are indicative of a person's ability or personality at a particular point of time, and under a particular set of circumstances. For example, if the person taking the test is under stress, or is experiencing a personal crisis, then the results would be different from when that person is in a relaxed state. As Premarajan explains, no test can measure personality with perfect accuracy for every single person or accurately predict performance.

Another issue to remember is that there is no such thing as a one-size-fits-all test. Says Acharya, "The recruiter must be willing to commission a slew of tests that would validate or invalidate one or more of the others." And then there is the danger of addiction and over-dependence. "Test results should never override the individual judgement and decision. It is a tool at the hands of a surgeon. Use it with knowledge and use it where it is needed," advises Sundara Rajan.

❖ Popular Myths to Break

1. All kinds of tests require specific training in psychometry.
2. Procurement costs are too prohibitive to justify usage.
3. Senior people resist being subjected to psychometric tests.
4. Faking responses to questions in psychometric tests is easy.

Industry Speak

According to the British Psychological Society, 80 percent of companies in the UK use personality profiling for all levels of recruitment. The trend is just as popular in the US. Back home too, there is more than just a random sprinkling of interest in the area. While many have systematically refined their selection systems over the years to incorporate a variety of tools specific to functions, levels and roles, others are cautiously experimenting without venturing too deep.

The hiring process at LG Electronics is incomplete without psychometric assessment. The combo of MBTI, Belbin, Social Style Inventory, FIRO-B helps identify traits like responsiveness, assertiveness and target orientation at executive level and above. For workers, Rorschach Ink Blot and hand exercises are used. According to Dr. Y.V. Verma, Vice President, Human Resources, "The key to accurate interpretation lies in cross-testing and cross validating scores across tests. A high score on one test does not always mean a high score on another test. For instance, a person who is target-driven may not be judgment oriented. Chances of bluffing can be also be minimized by cross-testing."

All entry level applicants for the post-graduate programme in hotel management run by Oberoi Centre of Learning and Development go through the 16 PF and FIRO-B. The difference is that the test is given after the interview. Going a step further, the assessment garnered from the tests is taken as a basis to guide the candidate in understanding his strengths and potential. Says Sarat Chandran, General Manager, Human Resources, Oberoi Group of Hotels, "We view tests as complementing, rather than conclusive selection tools. In the hotel business, the qualities we look for are intangible, you can't expect to find a perfect profile. There's only so much a test can predict. Skill upgradation completes the process."

Instead of training the HR team, the organization prefers to utilize the technical skills of a certified psychologist, working as a retainer. "Certification is an expensive process", explains Chandran, "and secondly, external experts come without the extra baggage of industry... objectivity is a important consideration."

Another believer in the power of 16PF is insurance major, Max New York Life. The company needed a test that checked on personality factors like ability to handle risk, face failures and accept rejections for insurance agents and 16PF fitted the bill. For Max, the assessment process itself is a non-core activity because of the sheer volumes involved. Shares M.S. Venkatesh, Assistant Vice President, Human Resources, "On an average, 150 new agents come aboard every month. Scoring templates are standard and preferred profiles are fixed, so outsourcing of test administration and analysis is the ideal option."

Unlike Oberois, here the first level screening is through the psychometric assessment. "Candidates who do not comply with our preferred standards are rejected, irrespective of the relevance of their experience or work profile," says Venkatesh. "At the same time, one should be sensitive to the fact that psychometric assessment pinpoints preferred behaviors as opposed to ability. Its success lies in using it as a validation technique," he adds.

When it comes to IT giant Wipro Ltd., its the PAPI (PA Preference Inventory) Job Profiler that delivers. At leadership roles, the company banks on PAPI for understanding the person's strengths and provide feedback for coaching and counseling. Wipro chose to invest in comprehensive training for the entire HR team by sponsoring them to a five-day technical programme run by the PAPI licensee firm. As Joydeep Bose, general manager, corporate human resources, puts it, "We see the tool as a source of information which the interviewing panel may not otherwise have had, instead of a sole predictor of future performance."

The consensus seems to be that selection is only one part of the story. There's a whole world to be explored with psychometric assessment. And so the smarter organizations are going full steam ahead by exploiting the power of psychometric tools like MBTI and PAPI to enrich the futures of their employees' work lives and careers.

WHICH IS THE RIGHT ONE FOR YOU?

❖ 16 PF (16 Personality Factor)

Measures 16 temperament traits: warmth, reasoning, emotional stability, dominance, liveliness, rule – consciousness, social boldness, sensitivity, vigilance, abstractness, privateness, apprehension, openness to change, self-reliance, perfectionism and tension.

❖ DISC

Groups people under four distinctive personality styles: drive, influence, steadiness and compliance.

❖ MBTI (Myers Briggs Type Indicator)

Measures a person's preferences, using four basic scales with opposite poles: extraversion/introversion, sensate/intuitive, thinking/feeling, and judging/perceiving. The various combinations of these preferences result in 16 personality types. Recommended more for developmental purposes.

❖ Thomas Profiling

Utilizes predictive ability and aims to match the behaviour to jobs. It can also be used to map the existing work behaviour of an individual so as to assess the individual's behavioural aptitude. The gap between behaviour and the company's requirements can be bridged through retraining and redefining the individual's skill sets and processes.

❖ FIRO-B

Defines leadership style in relation to interpersonal relationships by measuring:

1. *Inclusion:* How much you generally include other people in your life and how much attention, contact, and recognition you want from others.
2. *Control:* How much influence and responsibility you need, and how much you want others to lead and establish procedures and policies.
3. *Affection:* How close and warm you are with others and to what extent you want others to show warmth and support to you. FIRO is not a theory of inherent, immutable personality traits. Rather, it provides material for development efforts.

❖ Belbin Team Role Profiling

Assesses nine team roles: action-oriented roles (shaper, implementer, and completer finisher); people-oriented roles (coordinator, teamworker and resource investigator); cerebral roles — (plant, monitor evaluator and specialist). Belbin team roles describe a pattern of behaviour that characterises one person's behaviour in relationship to another in facilitating the progress of a team.

❖ PAPI (PA Preference Inventory) Job Profiler

A personality assessment tool used both at the beginning of the recruitment process when devising a job profile, and then later on at the interview stage when assessing a candidate's personality. It gives companies an objective way of measuring how closely the interviewee's personality matches the personality required by the job profile. Job profiles are created by asking people with particular insight into a role (job experts) to complete a short questionnaire. This identifies the characteristics seen as important to that role such as, for example, a person's motivation to control and influence others. Job experts are then asked to decide whether a high, low or mid-scorer on a particular characteristic is required. This job profile can be overlaid on an individual's profile in the PAPI Electronic software allowing the user to view the extent of the 'match' or 'fit' between the respondent and the job, and lead to discussion around this.

Addresses of Major Test Publishers

American Publishers

AAMR
American Association on Mental Retardation
444 North Capitol Street, N. W., Suite 846
Washington, DC 2000 1-15 12

ABPP
American Board of Professional Psychology
Z 1 OQ East Broadway, Suite 313
Columbia, MO 65201-6082

ACA
American Counseling Association
5999 Stevenson Avenue
Alexandria, VA 22304-3300

ACT
American College Testing Program
ACT National Office
2201 North Dodge Street
P.O. Box 168
Iowa City, IA 52243-0168

AERA
American Educational Research Association
1230 Seventeenth Street, N.W.
Washington, DC 20036.

AGS
American Guidance Services, Inc.
4201 Woodland Road
Circle Pines, MN 55014.1796

APA
American Psychological Association
750 First Street. N.E.
Washington. DC 20002.4242

ASC
Assessment Systems Corporation
2233 University Avenue, Suite 200
St. Paul. MN 5S 114

ATP
Association of Test Publishers
655 Fifteenth Street, N.W. Suite 320
Washington, DC 20005

BoTA
Board on Testing and Assessment
National Research Council
2101 Constitution Avenue, N.W.
Washington, DC 20418

Buros
Buros Institute of Mental Measurements
P.O. Box 880348
135 Bancroft Hall
Lincoln. NE 68588-0348

CEEB
College Entrance Examination Board
45 Columbus Avenue
New York, NY 10023.6992

CPP
Consulting Psychologists Press. Inc.
3803 East Bayshore Road
P.O. Box 10096
Pain Alto. CA 94303

CPS
C.P.S., Inc.
P.O. Box 83
Larchmont. NY 10538

CTB
CTB/McGraw-Hill
20 Ryan Ranch Road
Monterey. CA 93940

EdITS
Educational and Industrial Testing Service
P.O. Box 7234
San Diego. CA 92167

EEOC
Equal Employment Opportunity Commission
1801 L Street
Washington DC 20507

Erlbaum
Lawrence Erlbaum Associates, Inc.
10 Industrial Avenue
Mahwah, NJ 07430-2262

ETS
Educational Testing Service
Publications Order Services
P.O. Box 6736
Princeton, NJ 08541-6736
ETS Test Collection
Mailstop 30- B
Rosedale Road
Princeton, NJ 08541-0001

For Thought
For Thought, Ltd.
Nine Trafalgar Square
Nashua, NH 0.3063

GRE
Graduate Record Examinations
Educational Testing Service
P.O.Box 6000
Princeton, NJ 08541-6000

Harcourt Brace
Harcourt Brace Educational Measurement
Educational Testing Division of TPC
555 Academic Court
San Antonio, TX 78204-2498

Harvard
Harvard University Press
79 Garden Street
Cambridge, MA 02138

HAS
Hogan Assessment Systems, Inc.
P.O. Box 521176
Tulsa, OK 74152

H&H
Hogrefe & Huber Publishers
United States Office
P.O. Box 2487
Kirkland, WA 98083
Swiss Office:
Verlag Hans Huber
U1ng8ns-Strac 76
CH.3000 Bern 9
Switzerland

IBM
IBM K-12 Education
4111 North side Parkway
Atlanta, GA 30327

Infantest
Infantest Corporation
P.O. Box 18765
Cleveland Heights, OH 44118-0765

IPAT
Institute for Personality and Ability Testing, Inc.
P.O. Box 1188
Champaign, IL 61824.1188

MRI
Management Research Institute, Inc.
6701 Democracy Blvd., Suite 300
Bethesda, MD 20817

NCME
National Council on Measurement in Education
1230 Seventeenth Street, N.W.
Washington, DC 20036

NCS
National Computer Systems Inc.
P.O. Box 1416
Minneapolis, MN 55440

NFER-Nelson
NFER-Nelson Publishing Company, Ltd.
Darville House
2 Oxford Road East
Windsor-Berkshire, SL4 IDF
United Kingdom

Oxford
Oxford Psychologists Press, Ltd. I
Lambourne House 311
321 Banbury Road
Oxford OX2 7J1-I
England

PAR
Psychological Assessment Resources, Inc.
P.O. Box 998
Odessa, FL 33556-0998

PDI
Personnel Decisions International
2000 Plaza VII
4S South Seventh Street
Minneapolis, MN 55402-1608

PRO-ED
PRO-ED
8700 Shoal Creek Boulevard
Austin, TX 78757.6897

Riverside
The Riverside Publishing Company
425 Spring Lake Drive
ltasca, lL60143

RNL
Reitan Neuropsychological Laboratory
2920 South Fourth Avenue
Tucson, AZ 85713-4819

The Score
Newsletter for Division 5 of the American Psychological Association
4201 Woodland Road
Circle Pines, MN 55014

Sigma
Sigma Assessment Systems, Inc.
United States Office:
lUO, Military Street
P.O. Box 610984
Port Huron, MI48061.0984
Canadian Office:
Research Psychologists Press, Inc.
650 Waterloo Street, Suite 100 P.O. Box 3292
Station B London, ON N6A 4K3

Silver Platter
Silver Platter Information
100 River Ridge Drive
Norwood, MA 02062-5043

SlOP
Society for Industrial and Organizational Psychology, Inc.
P.O. Box 87
Bowling Green, OH 43402

SPA
Society for Personality Assessment
750 First Street, N.E.
Washington, DC 20002-4242

SRA
McGraw Hill/London House
SRA Business and Industry Assessments
9701 West Higgins Road
Rosemont, IL 60018-4720

Stoelting
Stoelting Company
620 Wheat Lane
Wood Dale, lL 60191

Swets
Swets Test Services
Heereweg 347b
2161 CA Lisse
Nederland

Thomas
Charles C Thomas Publisher
2600 South First Street
Springfield, IL 62794.9265

TPC
The Psychological Corporation
555 Academic Court
San Antonio, TX 78204.2498

UAD
Universal Attention Disorders, Inc.
4281 Katella #215
Los Alamitos, CA 90720

UIP
University of Illinois Press
1325 South Oak Street
Champaign. IL 61820

UMP
University of Minnesota Press
Test Division
111 Third Avenue South, Suite 290
Minneapolis. MN 55401

USES
United States Employment Service
Western Assessment Research and Development Centre
140 East 300 South
Salt Lake City, UT 84111

U.S. Military
United States Military Entrance Processing Command
Attn.: Technical Directorate 'J
2500 Green Bay Road
North Chicago, IL 60064.3094

Wonderlic
Wonderlic Personnel Test, Inc.
1509 North Milwaukee Avenue
Libertyville, IL 60048-1380

WPS
Western Psychological Services
12031 Wilshire Boulevard
Los Angeles, CA 90025-1251

UK Publishers

Assessment for Selection and Employment Hanover House
2-4 Sheet Street Windsor
Berkshire SL4 1 BG
Telephone: 01753 850333
Web site: www.ase-solutions.co.uk

Tests:
Business Personality Indicator (BPI)
Global Gordon's Personal Profile Inventory (Global GPP-I) Neo Five Factor Inventory (NEO-FFI)
Sixteen Personality Factory Questionnaire (16PF)

CIM Publications
23 Dunkeld Road
Ecclesall Sheffield S 11 9 IN
Telephone: 01142363811

Test:
Manchester Personality Questionnaire (MPQ)

The Morrisby Organization
83 High Street
Hemel Hempstead Hertfordshire
HPI 3AH
Telephone: 01442 215521
Web site: www.morrisby.co.uk

Tests:
Objective Personality Tests (OPT) Personality Research Form (PRF)

Oxford Psychologists Press
Lambourne House
311-321 Banbury Road Oxford
OX2 7JH
Telephone: 01865 510203

Tests:
California Psychological Inventory (CPI)
Elements of Awareness - Behaviour, Element B (EAOB)*
Fundamental Interpersonal Relations Orientation -Behaviour (FIRO-B)*
Myers-Briggs Type Indicator@ (MBTI@)*
Note: The MBTI is the most popular questionnaire for staff development.

Psychological Consultancy Ltd
4 Mount Ephraim Road
Tunbridge Wells
Kent
TNl lEE
Telephone: 01892 547500
Website: www.psyconltd.com

Tests:
Hogan Development Survey (HDS) Hogan Personality Inventory (HPI)
Motives, Values, Preferences Inventory (MVPI)

The Psychological Corporation
24-28 Oval Road
London
NWl 7DX
Telephone: 020 7424 4200
Website: www.psychcorp.com

Tests:
Orpheus Giotto

Psytech International Ltd
The Grange
Church Road
Pullox Hill
Bedfordshire
MK45 5HE
Telephone: 01525 720003
Website: www.psytech.co.uk

Tests:
Fifteen Factor Questionnaire (15FQ)
Jung Type Indicator (JTI)*
Occupational Personality Profile (OPP)

Saville & Holdsworth Ltd
The Pavilion
1 Atwell Place
Thames Ditton
Surrey
KT70NE
Telephone: 0870 070 8000
Website: www.shlgroup.com

Tests:
Occupational Personality Questionnaire Concept® (OPQ® -c)
Occupational Personality Questionnaire – Factor® (OPQ®-F)
Occupational Personality Questionnaire – IMAGES®

The Test Agency
Cournswood House
North Dean
High Wycombe Buckinghamshire HP144NW
Telephone: 01494 563384

Test:
Rapid Personality Questionnaire (RPQ)

Thomas International Systems Ltd
Harris House
17 West Street
Marlow
Buckinghamshire
SL7 2LS
Telephone: 01628 475366

Test:
Personal Profile Analysis (PPA)

Bibliography

Abrahamson, D., *The Psychology of crime*, New York: John Wiley & Sons Inc., 1960.

Arlyne, Lazerson., *Psychology Today: An Introduction*, CRM: Random House, (U.S.A), 1975, 210-213.

Allport, G.W., Odbert, H.S., Trait names, a psycho-lexical study, *Psychological Monographs*, 1936, 47.

Anastasi, A., *Psychological Testing*, New York: MacMillan and Co., 1961.

Anne Anastasi & Susana Urbina, *Psychological Testing*, Prentice Hall.

Arvinder Singh, Personality of juvenile delinquents: A comparison of NSQ and EPI scores, Indian *Journal of Clinical Psychology*, 1981, 8(2), 177-181.

Barrat, E.S., Factor analysis of some psychometric measures of impulsiveness and anxiety, *Psychological Reports*, 1965, 16, 547-554.

Bhatia, H.R, *Abnormal Psychology*, Oxford and IBH Publishing Co., New Delhi, 1969.

Biswas, P.K., & Rai, R.N., A cross-cultural study of personality of tribal and non-tribal adolescent girls, *Indian Journal of Clinical Psychology*, 1991, 18, 59-61.

Bonney, E.E., Interrelationships between content analysis and personality self-ratings in studying high and low normality in a college population, *Journal of Social Psychology*, 1967, 71, 277-285.

Bull, RH., & Strongman, K. T., Anxiety, neuroticism and extraversion, Psychological Reports, 1971, 29(3), 1101-1102.

Cattell, RB., Psychological measurement of anxiety and depression: a quantitative approach, *Canadian Psychiatric Association Journal*, 1962, 7, 11-23.

Cattell, R.B., *Personality and Mood by Questionnaire*, San Francisco: Jossey-Bass, 1973.

Cattell, R.B., & Cattell, Marry D.L., *Handbook for the Jr. -Sr. High School Personality Questionnaire*, Campaign, lllinois: Institute for Personality and Ability Testing, 1969.

Cattell, R.B., Eber, H.W., & Tatsuoka, M.M., *Handbook for the Sixteen Personality Factor Questionnaire* (I6PF), Champaign, lllinois: Institute for Personality and Ability Testing, 1970.

Chakrabarti, P.K., & Kundu, R., Personality profile of the management personnel, *Psychological Studies*, 1984, 29, 143-146.

Chakrabarti, P.K., Kundu, R. & Roy, J., Prediction of leadership traits of teachers from certain other personality variables, *Personality Study and Group Behaviour*, 1983, 3, 74-78.

Chitra, C., & Asha, C.B., Creativity, intelligence and vocational maturity among secondary school children, *Indian Journal of Applied Psychology*, 1991, 28 (1), 1-4.

Cloward, Richard, A., & Ohline, Lloyd, E., *Delinquency and Opportunity*, The Press: New York, 1960.

Coleman James C., *Abnormal Psychology and Modern Life*, D.B. Taraporevala Sons and Co. Pvt. Ltd., Indian Reprint, 1970.

Cyril, Burt, *The Young Delinquent*, University of London Press Ltd., 1927.

Davison, G.C., & Neale, J.M., *Abnormal Psychology*, John Wiley and Sons, Inc., 1978.

Denney, D.R., Active, passive and vicarious desensitization, *Journal of Counselling Psychology*, 1974, 21, 369-375.

Digman, J.M., Personality structure: Emergence of the five factor model, In M.R. Rosenzwig and L.M. Porter, (Edn.) *Annual Review of Psychology*, Paolo Alto, San Francisco: Annual Reviews Inc. 1990, 41, 417-440.

Freeman, F.S., *Theory and Practice of Psychological Testing*, Calcutta: Oxford and IBH Publishing Co., 1965.

Garrett, H.E., *Statistics in Psychology and Education*, Bombay: Allied Pacific Pvt. Ltd., 1962.

Gibbens, T.C.N., *Trends in Juvenile Delinquency*, W.H.O. Public Health Paper, 1961, 5, 56.

Good enough, F.I., *Mental Testing: Its History, Principles and Application*, New York: Rinehart & Co, 1949.

Hall, C.S., & Lindzey. G., *Theories of Personality*, New York: Wiley, 1978.

Guilford, J.P., *Fundamental Statistics in Psychology and Education*, New York: McGraw Hill Book Co., 1956.

Gulati, A.I.A., Study in motivation towards unionization, *Indian Journal of Industrial Relations*, 1969, 5(1), 68.

Gupta, M., & Gupta, P., Adolescence: A calm or stressful phase of development in India, *Indian Educational Review*, 1979, 14(2), 128-132.

Hilgard, E.R, Atkinson, RC., & Atkinson, RL., *Introduction to Psychology*, Calcutta: Oxford and IBH Publishing Co., 1975.

Horne, A.M., Effect of personality type in reducing specific anxiety with behavioural and psychodynamic therapy, *Journal of Counselling Psychology*, 1974, 21(4), 340-341.

Hundal, P.S., Sundhakar, Y.P., & Sidhu, K., Factor analytical study of measures of anxiety, intelligence and academic achievement, *Journal of Psychological Researches*, 1972, 16(1), 28-34.

Hurlock, E., *Adolescent Development, International Students Edn.*, McGraw Hill Book Co. Inc., 1955.

Husain, A., Cognitive personality factors and pattern of marital interaction, *Journal of Personality and Clinical Studies*, 1990, 6 (1), 91-95.

Jawa, S., Birth order and age related changes in anxiety among adolescents, *Indian Journal of Applied Psychology*, 1973, 10 (1), 6-11.

Jersild, A.J., *Child Psychology*, Englewood Cliff, New Jersey: Prentice Hall Inc., 1966.

Jiloha, R.C., & Vij, J.C., Personality profile of patients suffering from peptic ulcer, *Journal of Personality and Clinical Studies,* 1989, 5(1), 85-86.

Jim Barrett, *Test Yourself*, Kogan Page, 2004.

Jim Barrett, *Aptitude, Personality & Motivation Tests*, Kogan Page, 2004.

Johnson, J.H., Upper left hand placement of human figure drawings as an indicator of anxiety, Journal of Personality Assessment, 1971, 35 (4), 336-337.

Kakkar, A., A study of relationship among certain adolescent areas of adjustment, *Journal of Psychological Researches*, 1967, 11, 93-97.

Kannappan, R, & Cherian, RR, Personality factors and alcoholism, *Journal of Personality and Clinical Studies*, 1989, (1), 43-46.

Kisker, G.W., *The Disorganized Personality*, New York: McGraw Hill, 1985.

Kline, P., *Personality: Measurement and Theory*, London: Hutchinson, 1983.

Kothari, S., & Joshi, K., A comparative study of delinquents and non-delinquents with regard to some personality characteristics, *Indian Journal of Psychology*, 1992, 67(3-4), 87-94.

Krug, S.E., & Cattell, R.B., A test of the trait view theory of distortion in measurement of personality by questionnaire, *Educational & Psychological Measurement*, 1971, 31, 721-734.

Kuhlen, RG., *The Psychology of Adolescence Development*, N.Y. Harper, 1952.

Kulkarni, S.S., & Puhan, B.N., Psychological assessment: Its present and future trends, In L. Pandey (Ed.), *Psychology in India: The state of art*, New Delhi: Sage Publication, 1988.

Kundu, R, Development of personality inventory, *Indian Journal of Psychology*, 1962, 37, 171-174.

Kundu, R., Bhattacharaya, A.K., & Biswas, B., *An investigation into the relationship between personality types and interest patterns*, Research Bulletin (Department of Psychology, Osmania University) 1980, 9, 50-59.

Kundu, R., & Bhowmick, G., Introversion-Extraversion and Neuroticism: Two outstanding personality correlates of juvenile delinquent boys, *Indian Journal of Criminology*, 1982, 10, 37-41.

Kundu, R., & Chakrabarti, P.K., Impression management in personality tests, *Indian Psychological Review*, 1976, 12, 25-29.

Kundu, R., & Mitra, I., Personality, adjustment pattern of post-graduate male students, *Psychological Studies*, 1969, 14, 94-99.

Levitt., E.E., Brady, J.P., & Lubin, B., Correlates of hypnotizability in young women: Anxiety and Dependency, *Journal of Personality*, 1963, 31 (1), 52-57.

Levy, L.H., Concept of Personality: Theories and Research, New York: Random House, 1970.

Ley, P., Speelman, M.S., Davies, A.D.M., & Riley, S., The relationships between intelligence, anxiety, neuroticism and extraversion, *British Journal of Educational Psychology*, 1966, 36, 185-191.

Mark Parkinson, *How to Master Personality Questionnaires,* Kogan Page, 2005.

Mehta, P., & Kumar, D., Relationship of academic achievement with intelligence, personality, adjustment, study habits and academic motivation, *Journal of Personality and Clinical Studies*, 1985, 1 (2), 57-68.

Meredith, G.M., Personality correlates to religious belief systems, *Psychological Reports*, 1968, 23, 1039-1042.

Mike Bryon, *Graduate Psychometric Tests*, Kogan Page, 2004.

Mischel, W., *Personality and Assessment*, New York: Wiley, 1968.

Mischel, W., *Introduction of Personality: A New Look*, New York: CBS Publication, 1986.

Mohan, J., & Avtar, R., A study of personality and adjustment of adolescent, *Journal of Personality and Clinical Studies,* 1986, 2(1), 41-47.

Mohan, V., & Kaur, S.J., A study of personality as related to conservatism and radicalism, *Indian Journal of Psychology*, 1991, 66(1-4), 43-50.

Morgan, C.T., *Introduction to Psychology*, New Delhi: Tata McGraw Hill Publishing Co., 1979.

Nandi, A., & Kakar, S., Culture and personality, In U. Pareek (Edn.), *Survey of Research in Psychology*: 1971-1976 (Part II), Bombay: Popular Prakashan, 1981.

Pareek D., & Rao, T.V., *Handbook of Psychological and Social Instruments*, Baroda: Samasthi, 1974.

Philip Carter, *IQ and Psychometric Tests*, Kogan Page, 2004.

Rao, V.N., & Prasadarao, P.S.D.V., Personality and family interaction among neurotics, *Journal of Personality and Clinical Studies*, 1988, 4(1), 35-38.

Sam AL-Jajjoka, *How to Pass-Professional Level Psychometric Tests*, Kogan Page, 2003.

Shanmugam, T.E., *Abnormal psychology*, New Delhi: Tata McGraw Hill, 1981.

Sharma, T., & Husain, A., Relationship between marital adjustment and interaction dimensions of personality, *Journal of Personality and Clinical Studies*, 1992, 8(1), 87-90.

Singh, A.J., Incidence of anxiety among teachers under training and teachers in service, *Journal of the Indian Academy of Applied Psychology*, 1972, 9(2), 61-64.

Singh, A.J.& Kang, S.A., Study of adjustment of college students in relation to anxiety, *Indian Educational Review*, 1977, 12 (3), 109-111.

Sinha, D., & Singh, J.R., Anxiety and academic performance, *Psychologia*, 1961, 4, 119-122.

Sinha, D.A., Psychological analysis of some factors associated with success and failure in university education -intelligence, anxiety and adjustment of achievers and non-achievers, *Psychological Studies*, 1966, 11(2), 69-88.

Singh, S.B., Nigam, A., Gahlaut, D.S., & Sinha, G.c., Attempted suicide: A personality study, *Journal of Personality and Clinical Studies*, 1987, 3 (2), 117-121.

Spielberger, C.D., & Katzenmeyer, W.G., Manifest anxiety, intelligence and college grades, *Journal of Consulting Psychology*, 1959, 23, 278.

Srivastava, S., & Broota, K.D., Personality factors in cancer, *Journal of Personality and Clinical Studies*, 1990, 6(1), 63-67.

Stagner, R., *Psychology of Personality*, McGraw Hill Book Co. Inc., 1961.

Strassberg, D.S., Relationship among locus of control, anxiety, and valued-goal expectations, *Journal of Consulting and Clinical Psychology*, 1973, 41 (2), 319.

Tabassum, W., & Hamayun, S., Intelligence and personality differences among children from orphanages and intact families, *Journal of Indian Academy of Applied Psychology*, 1993, 19(1-2), 13-20.

Ta tsuoka, M.M., *Selected Topics in Advanced Statistics—An Elementary Approach*, No.2., Campaign, Illinois: Institute of Personality and Ability Testing, 1969.

Taylor, J.A., A personality scale of manifest anxiety, *Journal of Abnormal and Social Psychology*, 1953, 48, 285-290.

Thankachan, M. V., & Kodandaram, P., A study of life events and personality among alcohol dependent individuals, *Journal of Personality and Clinical Studies*, 1992, 8 (1), 27-34.

Theresa J.B. Kline, *Psychological Testing*, Vistaar Publications, 2005 .

Tomasine, J. Effect of peer-induced anxiety on a problem-solving task, *Psychological Reports*, 1973, 33 (2), 355-358.

Vohra, S., & Ahmed, H., Personality and value patterns of delinquents and non-delinquents: A comparative study, *Journal of Personality and Clinical Studies*, 1993, 9, 31-37.

Vohni, S., & Kapoor, M., Psychological trait analysis of delinquents and non-delinquents, *Psycholingua*, 1990, 20(2), 79-86.

Watson, R.I., Historical review of objective personality testing: The search for objectivity, In B.M. Brass and LA. Berg (Edn.), *Objective Approach to Personality Assessment*, Princeton: Van Nostrand, 1959.

West, S.G., Methodological developments in personality research: An Introduction, *Journal of Personality*, 54, 1-17, 1986.

Wolman, B.B., *Handbook of General Psychology*, New Jersey, Prentice-Hall, Inc., Englewood Cliffs., 1973.

Wolman, B.B., *Dictionary of Behavioural Sciences*, Van Nostrand Co., 1973, 6.

Index